ATLANTIC OCEAN

PACIFIC OCEAN

Rio de Janeiro

São Paulo

Curitiba

Florianópolis

PARAGUAY

Asunción

Cascavel

Foz do Iguaçu

Passo Fundo

Santa Maria

Porto Alegre

Uruguaiana

Salto

Rivera

URUGUAY
page 324

Punta del Este

Montevideo

Mar del Plata

CHILE

Antofagasta

Copiapó

La Serena

Valparaíso

Santiago
page 320

Talca

Concepción

Temuco

Osorno

Puerto Montt

Isla Grande
de Chiloé

ATACAMA

Salta

Tucumán

Santiago
del Estero

La Rioja

San Juan

Mendoza

Aconcagua
6962

Córdoba

Río Cuarto

San Luis

San
Rafael

ANDES

San Carlos
de Bariloche

page 292

Esquel

ARGENTINA

Santa Fe

Rosario

Resistencia

Goya

Río Bermejo

Río Pilcomayo

Río Paraná

Buenos
Aires

Santa
Rosa

Tandil

PAMPAS

Bahía
Blanca

Península
Valdés

Trelew

PATAGONIA

Puerto Deseado

Puerto
Moreno

Lago
Viedma

El Calafate

Lago
Campo

Lago
Argentino

Wellington Island

Puerto
Natales

Península
de Taitao

Cabo de Hornos

Ushuaia

Río
Gallegos

Punta
Arenas

Isla Grande de
Tierra del Fuego

Falkland Islands (UK)

South Georgia (UK)
Island

INSIGHT GUIDES

SOUTH AMERICA

CHANNEL

APA PUBLICATIONS

Part of the Langenscheidt Publishing Group

ABOUT THIS BOOK

INSIGHT GUIDE
SOUTH AMERICA

Editorial
Project Editor
Natalie Minnis
Managing Editor
Huw Hennessy
Editorial Director
Brian Bell

Distribution

United States
Langenscheidt Publishers, Inc.
36–36 33rd Street 4th Floor
Long Island City, NY 11106
Fax: 1 (718) 784 0640

UK & Ireland
GeoCenter International Ltd
Meridian House, Churchill Way West
Basingstoke, Hampshire RG21 6YR
Fax: (44) 1256 817988

Australia
Universal Publishers
1 Waterloo Road
Macquarie Park, NSW 2113
Fax: (61) 2 9888 9074

New Zealand
Hema Maps New Zealand Ltd (HNZ)
Unit 2, 10 Cryers Road
East Tamaki, Auckland 2013
Fax: (64) 9 273 6479

Worldwide
**Apa Publications GmbH & Co.
Verlag KG (Singapore branch)**
38 Joo Koon Road, Singapore 628990
Tel: (65) 6865 1600. Fax: (65) 6861 6438

Printing

Insight Print Services (Pte) Ltd
38 Joo Koon Road, Singapore 628990
Tel: (65) 6865 1600. Fax: (65) 6861 6438

©2009 Apa Publications GmbH & Co.
Verlag KG (Singapore branch)
All Rights Reserved
First Edition 1990
Fourth Edition (updated) 2007
Reprinted 2009

CONTACTING THE EDITORS
We would appreciate it if readers
would alert us to errors or out-
dated information by writing to:
**Insight Guides, P.O. Box 7910,
London SE1 1WE, England.
Fax: (44) 20 7403 0290.
insight@apaguide.co.uk**

www.insightguides.com

The first Insight Guide pioneered the use of creative full-color photography in travel guides in 1970. Since then, we have expanded our range to cater for our readers' need not only for reliable and practical information about their chosen destination, but also for a real understanding of the history, people, culture and workings of that destination. Now, when the internet can supply inexhaustible (but not always reliable) facts, our books marry text and pictures to provide those much more elusive qualities: knowledge and discernment. To achieve this, they rely heavily on the combined authority of locally based writers and photographers.

How to use this book

This book has been carefully structured both to convey an under-standing of the subcontinent, its diverse peoples and cultures, and to guide readers through its major sights and activities.

♦ To understand contemporary South America, you need to know something about its past. From the Inca Empire to the Spanish Conquest and from some chilling military dictatorships through to reforming modern democracies, South America has had a dramatic and eventful history.

The **Features** section covers the history and culture of the whole region in a series of lively and informative essays.

♦ The main **Places** section provides a complete country-by-country guide to all the major sights and areas worth seeing, including opening times of museums, archeological sites, and art galleries.

Places of special interest are coordinated by number with specially drawn full-color maps.

♦ The **Travel Tips** section provides a convenient reference for information on transport, accommodations, restaurants, useful addresses, outdoor activities, language, etc.

Information may be located quickly by using the index printed on the back cover flap.

♦ The **Photographs** have been carefully chosen not only to convey the beauty of the countries, the landscape, the flora and the fauna, but also to give an accurate impression of the people of South America and their everyday lives.

The contributors

This edition was coordinated in Insight Guides' London office by **Alyse Dar**, **Rachel Fox**, and **Rachel Lawrence**. It builds on previous editions produced by **Tony Perrottet** and **Natalie Minnis**. The editors used writers who combined affection for and detachment from their specialist subjects.

The chapters on South American history were contributed by **Nick Caistor**, who also updated the chapter on Peru. Nick is a specialist Latin America analyst. Natalie Minnis wrote about the people of South America, and the music and dance chapter was written by **Shannon Shiell**, a Glasgow-based Latin dance expert who has lived in South America.

The arts and architecture chapters were contributed by **Mike Gonzalez**, a senior lecturer in the Department of Hispanic Studies at Glasgow University. The outdoor sports chapter and new writing on Ecuador were written by **Jane Letham** and **Mark Thurber**, based in Quito, who run their own trekking and mountaineering tours around Peru and Ecuador.

Chapters in the Places section have been thoroughly updated by an experienced team of local experts: **Claire Antell** (The Guianas), **Ruth Bradley** (Chile), **Nick Caistor** (Paraguay, Uruguay, Argentina, and Falkland Islands), **Dominic Hamilton** (Venezuela), **Gabi Mocatta** (Peru), **Christopher Pickard** (Brazil), **Janet Santamaria-Fox** (Ecuador), **Liz Tremlett** (Bolivia), **Luisa Urueña** and **Susan Wunderli** (Colombia).

The chief photographers were **Mireille Vautier** and **Eduardo Gil**. Many photographs of Brazil were supplied by **H. John Maier**. The book was proofread by **Sylvia Suddes**.

Map Legend

▬ ▪ ▪	International Boundary
▬ ▬ ▬	State Boundary
⊖	Border Crossing
▬ ▪ ▬ ▪	National Park/Reserve
▬ ▬ ▬ ▬	Ferry Route
Ⓜ	Metro
✈ ✦	Airport: International/ Regional
🚌	Bus Station
🅿	Parking
❶	Tourist Information
✉	Post Office
⌂ † ⸙	Church / Ruins
†	Monastery
☾	Mosque
✡	Synagogue
🏰 🏚	Castle / Ruins
∴	Archeological Site
∩	Cave
⚱	Statue/Monument
★	Place of Interest

The main places of interest in the Places section are coordinated by number with a full-color map (e.g. ❶), and a symbol at the top of every right-hand page tells you where to find the map.

INSIGHT GUIDE
SOUTH AMERICA

CONTENTS

Girl from the Bolivian Altiplano

Insight on ...

Information panels

Travel Tips

THE UNDISCOVERED CONTINENT

From the Andes to the Amazon, from dense forests to alluring beaches, South America's diversity is extraordinary

According to the Colombian novelist Gabriel García Márquez, foreigners see South America as "a man with a mustache, a guitar, and a revolver." More perhaps than any other continent, South America has been the victim of stereotypes and misconceptions. Most people see it as one huge, mysterious jungle, a mountainous wasteland or a backward rural world languidly lost in an eternal *siesta*.

But from the moment you step out of an aircraft anywhere in South America, it's obvious that the images fail to capture even a fraction of the reality. There are mighty rivers, wilderness areas and final frontiers, but also ancient civilizations and vibrant new cultures. The Amazon Basin and its remote outposts grab the imagination of novelists, screenwriters and adventure seekers, while the elegant salons of Buenos Aires and the stylish resorts along the Caribbean attract a less vocal following. Like the Amazon rainforest, the Andes are home to communities that have barely changed for centuries, unlike the enormous metropolises of Brazil and Argentina, where life is so modern and energetic it will leave you breathless.

The countries in South America share a common history – thousands of years of indigenous cultures broken by European intrusion over 500 years ago; colonial rule followed by bitter wars of independence; then an unsteady progress at the fringe of world events. Despite these shared experiences, each country retains its own character.

On the north coast *(see page 85)* are Colombia and Venezuela, Guyana, Suriname and French Guiana, racially mixed and geographically divided between rugged mountains, hot equatorial coastline and dense Amazon rainforest. Peru, Bolivia, and Ecuador form the Andean heartland of South America *(see page 139)*. They have the highest Amerindian populations on the continent, clustered around the barren highlands where the mighty Inca Empire once reigned, and are now the continent's least developed countries.

The east *(see page 223)* is dominated by the giant Brazil, in a world of its own, separated from its Spanish-speaking neighbors by a Portuguese heritage – despite bordering on every single country in the continent except Ecuador and Chile. In the cooler southern zones *(see page 259)* are Paraguay, Chile, Uruguay, and Argentina, the most European-influenced and prosperous of South American republics, with vast empty spaces that stretch along the spine of the Andes to the last stop before Antarctica: Tierra del Fuego. ❑

PRECEDING PAGES: Grey Glacier, Torres del Paine National Park, Chile; the "Devil's Throat", Iguaçu Falls, Brazil; reed boat on Lake Titicaca, Bolivia; beach in Rio, Brazil.
LEFT: "El Tren a las Nubes" ("The Train to the Clouds"), northern Argentina.
FOLLOWING PAGES: Machu Picchu, the Inca sacrificial city on a mountain top.

20,000–4500 BC

PRE-COLUMBIAN TIMELINE

Human settlement in South America began with nomadic hunter-gatherers traveling southward, and reached its peak with the Inca Empire at the time of the Conquest

EARLIEST ORIGINS

The first humans arrived in South America in around 20,000 BC, and were related to hunter-gatherers who crossed the Bering Straits "ice-bridge" between Asia and the Americas, following herds in search of food.

◁ *Ceramic vessel in a feline form, Chavín culture, Peru, c.900 BC.*

3000–400 BC

POTTERY AND METAL

The first production of ceramics in South America began around 3000 BC, according to carbon-dated remains found in Colombia and Ecuador. These earliest ceramics were fashioned by hand, and were mostly utensils, but highly sophisticated ornamental and ceremonial items were soon being produced, from the Andes to the mouth of the Amazon.

Gold was the first metal known to be worked in the Andes, with remnants found in central Peru dating from around 2000 BC. The practice soon spread to Bolivia and later to Ecuador and Colombia. Gold and silver items of incredible beauty and technical quality were produced in huge quantities, as symbolic decorations of the ruling classes of the emerging state societies.

▷ *Silver breastplate, Chibcha culture, Colombia, c.1200 BC.*

---

400 BC–1100 AD

MASTER WEAVERS

The earliest textiles, found in central Peru, have been dated from as early as 8600 BC. Around 400 BC, the Nazca and Paracas cultures rose to prominence along the coastal desert of southern Peru. These people were technical masters at weaving and pottery, much of which has survived in funeral chambers, preserved by the dry air. Some of the textiles found have more than 200 threads to the square inch –

finer than most modern materials. The Nazca culture also produced the famous lines on the desert floor, which still mystify visitors and archeologists alike – with interpretations ranging from a giant astronomical calendar to a landing strip for extraterrestrials.

◁ *Woven cotton cloth decorated with feathers, Paracas culture, Peru c.1000 BC.*

1100–1569 AD

BIRTH OF THE INCAS

c.1100 AD, Manco Capac, rising out of Lake Titcaca, was hailed to be the Sun god and divine leader of the chosen Inca race. The city of Cusco was founded by Manco Capac. The Inca state was called *Tawantin-suyu*, the "Land of the Four Quarters," with Cusco at

its center, as the "Umbilicus of the Universe."

c.1430 AD, the Incas defeated Chancas and extended their empire across a huge area of South America, based on military efficiency, road networks, terracing, irrigation, and stone architecture.

◁ *Quipu knotted cords, used by Inca officials to keep an inventory of goods and produce.*

SETTLING DOWN

Cave remains and shell mounds *(sambaquis)* in Brazil and stone tools in Peru suggest that the earliest humans lived here from c.17,000–5000 BC. But the most reliable evidence of the first human settlement is at Monte Verde in Chile, where remains have been dated at 12,500 BC.

◁ *Pottery figure of religious leader, Chavín culture, Peru, c.1200 BC*

FISHING AND FARMING

Between 7500 BC and 4500 BC Andean peoples began the seasonal cultivation of crops, including potato, maize, manioc, and sweet potato; and the domestication of dogs, llamas, alpacas, and guinea pigs. Coastal tribes from present-day Ecuador to northern Chile harvested the rich marine life of the Pacific, enriched by the Humboldt Current. The fishermen made hooks from shell, bone, and cactus spines.

SOCIAL SKILLS

From about 2800 BC, societies began to form in the central and northern Andes. The earliest of these were the Chavín in northern Peru, the Tiahuanaco to the south of Lake Titicaca, and the San Agustín culture in southern Colombia. They built massive ceremonial urban centers in stone, and produced highly sophisticated ceramics, textiles, and religious artifacts in gold and other precious metals and stones. They formed large populations of up to hundreds of thousands, organized in complex social hierarchies and covering large administrative regions. Amazonian societies also flourished at about this time, if not earlier. Aruak-speaking people inhabited a region near to present-day Manaus from as early as 3000 BC.

◁ *Gold "Darien pectoral" from Colombia, 900–1200 AD. The figure has an alligator-like head, thought to represent a supernatural being, a priest, or a shaman.*

IMPERIAL EXPANSION

Based in the deserts of northern Peru, the Moche culture built up an empire from about 100–800 AD, that covered much of the north of the country. Their military and commercial influence was aided by their roadbuilding and irrigation works, skills later picked up by the Incas. Above all, the Moche were superb artisans, producing ceramics and fine metal and precious stone ornaments to a standard never seen before in the Americas. The Moche Empire disappeared dramatically and mysteriously, around 700 AD. From about 600–1000 AD the religious Tiahuanaco culture combined with the militaristic Huari of the central Andean highlands to form an empire that at its peak spread into present-day Bolivia.

◁ *Gold burial mask, Lambayeque culture, Peru, 1100–1400 AD.*

PEAK AND FALL

Around the mid 1400s, the Inca Empire expanded rapidly, firstly under Pachacutec and later under his son, Topa Inca. The Chimu Empire, based in northern Peru, was defeated by the Incas c.1466 AD. **1532 AD**, the Spanish conquistadors arrived in Peru; Inca Atahuallpa was executed a year later. In 1572, Tupac Amaru, the Last Inca, was killed by the Spanish and the Conquest is complete.

◁ *Gold ornament, Sinu culture, Colombia, 1100–1600 AD.*

◁ *European missionaries bring the Gospel to Amazon peoples.*

THE FIRST PEOPLES

Pre-Columbian South America was a place of cultural diversity where enduring traditions and unique lifestyles were forged and great empires were built

The first colonization of South America is shrouded in mystery. Knowledge of those early times has had to be pieced together from archeological finds and linguistic evidence. Experts now believe that the first Americans arrived from the Asian continent, crossing the Bering Straits when they were solid with

ice during the last Ice Age, some 40,000 years ago. These bands of hunter-gatherers gradually spread down America; some sites in Patagonia show the far south was inhabited by around 9,000 BC. Remains of mastodon, sloth, and other animals that have since disappeared, found together with arrowheads, demonstrate that these people were hunter-gatherers, but little else is known of their way of life or social organization.

Over several thousand years, these small groups turned from hunting to a more settled farming existence. According to archeological evidence, some lived close to the seashore and subsisted on a diet of fish and shellfish; some settled in the Andean highlands, and others adapted to the tropical lowlands of the Amazon. These early settlers appear to have grown beans and peppers, and to have used domesticated dogs to help them hunt small game. Maize is thought to have been cultivated from Peru down to Argentina by 3,000 BC, and some of the highland groups also began to herd llama and other camelids. The first pottery remains found date from about 3,000 years ago.

First societies

As these groups became based around seasonal agriculture, population gradually increased, and more complex societies emerged, with officials, including chieftains and priests or shamans. Some of the earliest remains discovered are from **La Tolita** in Ecuador, which date from around 2,000 years ago, but the **San Agustín** culture in southern Colombia appears to have been one of the outstanding early sites. Here, burial mounds and intricate sculptures speak of a high degree of social organization, with religious ceremonies and complex burial rites.

Over the centuries, these small population centers grew into larger regional units, with ceremonial sites that have yielded a great deal of information. In some cases, such as the **Taironas** of the northeastern highlands of Colombia, it is thought that up to 250,000

THE MYTH OF EL DORADO

One of the early Colombian cultures, the Chibcha, gave rise to perhaps the most enduring South American legend, that of El Dorado. The Chibchas were divided into two kingdoms who worshiped the sun as their chief deity, and practiced human sacrifice. The ceremony for appointing a new Chibcha ruler apparently involved throwing gold statues into a lake, covering the new leader in gold dust and immersing him in the water until it had washed off. This made him "El Dorado" – the Golden One, giving rise to the legend.

people lived on one site; by now, the main buildings were made of stone, and gold, emeralds, and other precious stones were used both for ornament and for trade.

The great edifices

In Peru and in the Andean highlands of Bolivia, there is evidence that settled occupation began as early as 5,000 BC. By 2,000 BC large monumental structures were being built, by population groups estimated at around 1,000 or 1,500 people. One of the most significant of these early centers grew up around 1,000 BC in the **Moche Valley** near the northern Peruvian coast-

ture, which flourished from AD 200–700. The Moche are known for their prolific production of beautiful stirrup-spouted pottery, which depicted every aspect of their life, from violence and erotica to medical treatments. They also produced fine gold, silver, and copperwork. Their imposing capital at **Moche** is dominated by two large structures – the **Huaca del Sol** and the **Huaca de la Luna** – temples of the sun and moon, built around a large plaza or central square. In around AD 500 natural disasters probably forced them to move from Moche; their later center at **Pampa Grande** shows that the culture continued to thrive until the 8th cen-

line. It is known as the **Chavín** culture, after the archeological site at **Chavín de Huántar**, about 3,000 meters (10,000 ft) up in the Andean mountains. The most impressive structure here is a platform of earth and rock with a hollow interior, known as **El Castillo** or The Castle, probably used for religious ceremonies.

The Chavín culture, which also produced fine pottery and intricate stone stelae, is believed to have gone into a decline around 200 BC. It was superseded in northern Peru by the **Moche** cul-

tury. Later, the **Chimu** culture, based at **Chan Chan** *(see page 165)*, showed a continuity of development in these coastal sites.

At the same period in the south of Peru, the **Nazca** culture came to the fore *(see page 150)*. The Nazca people are best known for the extraordinary lines they drew in the desert, which from the air can be seen to represent figures such as hummingbirds, monkeys, or fish, but which do not make sense from ground level. The size and complexity of the lines gave rise to the theory that extraterrestrials must have visited South America in ancient times: although this idea is now dismissed, as yet there is no convincing explanation as to why a farming

LEFT: pre-Columbian artifact from the Gold Museum, Bogotá, Colombia. **ABOVE:** the Gateway of the Sun, Tiahuanaco, Bolivia.

community should have spent so much time making such an immense display.

Further inland, near Lake Titicaca in northern Bolivia, the **Wankarani** people who lived by fishing, herding llama, and growing potatoes, gave rise to the fascinating society known as the **Tiahuanaco** culture *(see page 181)*. Their main center, **Pukara**, was 3,600 meters (12,000 ft) up on the Altiplano of the Andes. Some 40,000 people are thought to have lived in this city, with an impressive ceremonial complex at its heart. The people of Tiahuanaco are

ENORMOUS EMPIRE

The Inca Empire is believed to have encompassed around a third of South America's population.

succeeded in taking over the most important Andean centers. The Incas continued to extend their rule – south into Chile and north into what is now Ecuador, where Huayna Capac set up a second imperial center in Quito. By 1525, the Inca Empire extended 4,000 km (2,500 miles) from northern Ecuador to central Chile. Between six and 12 million people are estimated to have lived in the empire known as **Tawantinsuyu** or "Land of the Four Quarters".

At the top of the Inca hierarchy was the emperor, or Sapa Inca, thought to be a descen-

among the first in South America to have used stone to create large permanent buildings; about 1,200 years ago their power reached down as far as the Atacama Desert in Chile.

The Incas

The last and most impressive of these Andean highland cultures was the **Inca** Empire. This was based in the valley of Cusco, in what is now Peru, and only emerged around AD 1400, during the rule of the semi-mythical leader Viracocha. In 1438 his son Yupanqui defeated the Tiahuanaco people around Lake Titicaca, and Yupanqui's son Topa defeated the Chimu to the north, so that in two generations the Incas

dant of the sun god Inti. The emperor was married to his sister, but had many other wives as well. Beneath him was a complicated priestly and administrative system, designed to control the extensive empire. Communications were based on a 30,000-km (18,640-mile) network of paved roads, many of which still exist, along which relays of runners carried messages.

The imperial language, *Quechua,* was imposed throughout: the sons of royalty among the conquered peoples were taken to Cusco to learn it along with other important elements of Inca culture. The Incas had no writing as we know it, but used knotted pieces of string to record important dates and numbers, which were memorized by a special group of officials. The Inca ceremonial centers at Machu Picchu, Cusco, and elsewhere show their mastery of architecture, based on cutting and fitting large blocks of stone together without mortar.

First peoples

No-one knows how many people lived in South America before the arrival of the Europeans. Estimates vary between 5 and 50 million; in recent years discoveries in the Amazon region have led archeologists to think that there may have been several million inhabitants there.

Over the centuries these first peoples have

19th century. Other indigenous groups in Argentina were wiped out in the so-called "Wars of the Desert" in the 1870s. It was only on the remote coasts of Patagonia and Tierra del Fuego that small groups living lives similar to those of their ancestors thousands of years ago managed to survive well into the 20th century.

The European attitude toward these peoples is illustrated in an extract from Charles Darwin's journal when he sailed down these coasts on HMS *Beagle* in 1832: "I could not have believed how wide was the difference between savage and civilized man: it is greater than that between a wild and domesticated animal...'

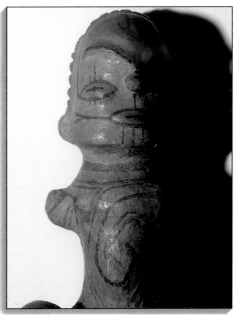

been absorbed into the dominant system, or persecuted and their way of life destroyed. This process began in the 1530s, when the Inca Empire was conquered by the Spaniard Francisco Pizarro with just 150 men *(see page 26)*. Since then, although the indigenous people have often rebelled and resisted rule by others, they have gradually been all but eliminated.

In the south of the continent, the Mapuche people of Chile and Argentina resisted the longest, living independently until the end of the

LEFT: gold treasure from Bogotá Gold Museum.
ABOVE: Inca "Mamacona" or "chosen woman" figure.
ABOVE RIGHT: Marajó figurine, Brazilian Amazon.

Such attitudes led to the extermination of indigenous groups as frontiers were opened up in the 20th century. Although there are some groups in the Amazon region who have had no contact with the outside world, their way of life is under threat, while peoples like the Yanomami in Brazil and the Ashaninka in Peru have had to organize to defend their rights.

Elsewhere, the descendants of the Inca and other highland groups, the Mapuche in Chile, the Tairona and other groups in Colombia and Ecuador live today as part of the mixed heritage of Latin American civilization. But they also stand apart, with many of their beliefs and traditions still powerful below the surface. ❑

LOST EMPIRES AND DISCOVERED TREASURE

What was life like in South America before the Europeans arrived? It's a mystery that continues to enthrall, and there are some intriguing clues

As no writing has been found from pre-Columbian South America, the artifacts left behind are likely to remain mere clues, giving us exciting glimpses into the lives of a host of very different communities that flourished and declined through various times and locations. The central Andes is by far the richest region for finding artifacts of the ancient past – partly because the dry desert conditions prevalent in the area are much more suitable for preserving ancient remains than the humid climate of the Amazon rainforest. But there is no doubt that the central Andes, especially the region that is now Peru, was a center for skilled activity of all kinds for centuries, producing numerous advanced communities long before the great Inca civilization arrived on the scene. Some ancient finds have echoes in the modern cultural practices of local communities, while others, like the mysterious people who built the megaliths of San Agustín, Colombia, seem to have disappeared without a trace.

MAKING SENSE OF THE PAST

Trying to remember all the names of the pre-Columbian groups can be a mind-boggling task. Most were named by archeologists after the locations where their remains were found, and grouped according to type, location, and dating. Their complexity can be confusing, but the visitor with enough time to go to the excellent museums and archeological sites from Colombia to Chile will gain a picture of a fascinating era when civilizations waxed and waned, fought and conquered one another, and exchanged goods, skills, and ideas.

▷ **GOLDEN YEARS**
Metallurgy flourished in South America long before the Incas, as this Chimu funerary mask shows (Lambayeque Valley, Peru).

△ **SAN AGUSTIN**
Little is known about the people who built 500 stone statues at this Colombian site *(see page 99).*

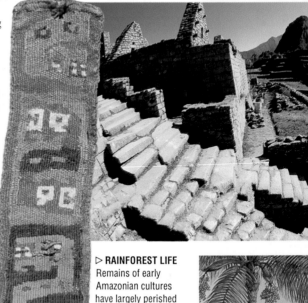

▷ **RAINFOREST LIFE**
Remains of early Amazonian cultures have largely perished in the humid climate.

◁ **MADE TO LAST**
This striking belt was woven by the Huari people of ancient Peru – 1,500 years ago.

LIFE AND TIMES OF THE MOCHE

If the Incas were master architects and empire builders, the much earlier Moche culture must be one of the most artistic and intriguing in South America. The Moche settled near the modern city of Trujillo in northern Peru, and flourished for a few centuries before and after the time of Christ. What sets the Moche apart is the high quality and quantity of the artifacts they left behind; from adobe pyramids to finely crafted gold jewelry. The recent discovery of the tomb of the "Lord of Sipán," pictured above, was one of the most important finds ever in the Andes *(see also page 166)*, displaying Moche mastery of metallurgy. The vast collection of Moche ceramics found provides a remarkably accurate and detailed record of life 2,000 years ago; some superb textiles have also been found.

◁ **MACHU PICCHU**
The most fabulous of all the Inca ceremonial centers, yet just one of many awe-inspiring Andean citadels in near-inaccessible locations.

▽ **GATEWAY OF THE SUN**
The pre-Inca site of Tiahuanaco, near Lake Titicaca *(see page 168)* in Bolivia, was built in beautiful and sophisticated masonry.

◁ **INCA HAT FROM CHILE**
In the late Inca period, vicuña wool was worn only by kings, as cloth was a symbol of wealth.

▷ **MAIZE WORSHIP**
This Moche maize effigy may have been a fertility charm, used to help ensure a good crop.

THE EUROPEAN CONQUEST

In the 16th century, most of South America quickly fell to Spain and Portugal, except for the far south, which would remain unconquered for three centuries

At the end of the 15th century, Christopher Columbus explored the shores of Central and South America. Soon afterwards another Italian sailor, Amerigo Vespucci, was to give the new continent its name. Both these Italian explorers were in the pay of the Spanish crown, and before long, numerous Spaniards

were arriving. From their bases on the islands of Hispaniola, Puerto Rico, and Cuba, they started to explore Central America and the South American mainland.

Gold was the lure that enticed most of them into the unknown territories of the continent. El Dorado was the legendary paradise where, Midas-like, everything was made of gold. In 1532 Francisco Pizarro set out to find these fabled riches in the Inca Empire, which then stretched from Quito (in present-day Ecuador) in the north down through the areas now known as Peru, Bolivia, and northern Chile. With only 150 followers, Pizarro managed to take control of the entire Inca Empire in just two years. This

was achieved with ruthless determination aided by the fear that the Spaniards, mounted on horseback and using firearms, struck into the indigenous armies. Also, after years of refined centralization and uniformity, the Inca Empire was severely weakened at the very moment that Francisco Pizarro began his conquest.

Downfall of the Incas

Before the Spaniards arrived, the Incas had expanded their empire from Cusco, Peru, to Quito, Ecuador. The Inca Tupac-Yupanqui had founded the magnificent city of Tomebamba (now Cuenca) after subduing the southern Cañari people. His son, Huayna-Capac, married the daughter of the local king to consolidate their kingdoms.

Their son Atahuallpa was to become Huayna-Capac's favorite, but Atahuallpa's half-brother Huascar, descended from Inca lineage on both sides, was the legitimate heir. In 1527, Huascar ascended the Cusco throne, dividing the empire for the first time between Quito and Cusco. Atahuallpa won the ensuing five-year civil war, killing his brother and establishing the new capital of Cajamarca in northern Peru. But the war had severely weakened both the infrastructure and the will of the Incas.

The Spanish arrived in Cajamarca in 1532. At a pre-arranged meeting, Atahuallpa and several thousand followers – many unarmed – entered the great square, where a Spanish priest called on them to embrace Christianity and accept the sovereignty of the Spanish king, Charles V. When Atahuallpa refused, Pizarro and his men ambushed the Incas. Pizarro was the only Spaniard wounded, when he seized Atahuallpa, while hundreds of Incas were killed.

Pizarro took Atahuallpa prisoner, demanding a room full of gold to pay his ransom. This was done, but the Inca was not freed. During his captivity, Atahuallpa learned to speak and write Spanish and to play chess. After nine months, the Spaniards accused him of treason, and garrotted him. The Spaniards then marched on the Inca capital, Cusco, and immediately used the Inca bureaucracy and administrative divisions for their own ends. By 1533 they were in command of the entire Inca empire.

The Spaniards founded the city of Lima in 1535. Lima grew and prospered, as did its religious zeal, prompting some to dub it the "Rome of South America." Churches and monasteries sprang up, each more ostentatious than the next. Nuns, bishops, priests, and monks flocked to Lima, and with them, eventually, came the terror of the Holy Inquisition, which meted out its frightful tortures in Peru from 1570 to 1761.

Lima was the seat of the Spanish Empire in South America for several centuries. The city of Orinoco and Amazon river systems. This brought the Spanish and Portuguese crowns into conflict over who should be allowed ownership of the new territories. The dispute was settled at the Treaty of Tordesillas in 1494, which established that Portugal should have the right to all lands east of the mouth of the Amazon – which meant the whole of the Brazilian coastline. Pedro Alvares Cabral claimed Brazil for Portugal in 1500. For many years, its most important export was dyewood or Brazil wood, but European settlement was slow, as the Portuguese preferred to trade with their new colony rather than to settle it. Eventually, a system of

Cusco was the last redoubt of Inca rule, which ended completely in 1572, when Tupac Amaru was defeated and killed.

Further north, Gonzalo Jiménez de Quesada set out to explore New Granada (Colombia). He quickly subdued the Chibcha kingdoms, and in 1538 Santa Fé de Bogotá was founded.

The birth of Brazil

Europeans were soon busy exploring down the Atlantic seaboard of South America and the

LEFT: Amerindians buckling under the weight of colonial demands. **ABOVE:** the meeting of Pizarro and Atahuallpa at Cajamarca.

"captaincies" was set up, in which ownership of the land was granted by the Portuguese crown to individuals. Many of these people, such as Martim Afonso, brought in cattle and began to cultivate sugar, using enslaved Amerindians initially, and then people shipped from Africa.

The new settlements of the south

In the far south, explorers were still seeking a sea route from Europe to Asia. Between 1519 and 1522, Fernando Magellan's fleet rounded Cape Horn and sailed out into the Pacific Ocean, making them the first Europeans to land in Patagonia and Chile. Sailors like Antonio Pigafetta enhanced the mystery of the new lands to wide-eyed Europeans, with lurid descriptions of the strange beings encountered there: giants, men with heads under their arms, or with tails like pigs.

Another wave of Spaniards set out to explore the Rio de la Plata (River Plate) network. Pedro de Mendoza founded Buenos Aires in 1536, and Asunción de Paraguay the following year. But the settlers were soon driven out of Buenos Aires by the indigenous people. It was only in 1580 that colonists sailed down from Asunción and set up the fort on the south bank of the River Plate again, this time successfully.

On the Pacific Ocean side, Pedro de Valdivia

cannon. The Spanish had to make do with maintaining garrison towns on the coast, and making marauding slave runs into indigenous territory.

In Argentina, the "frontier" was no more than 200 km (350 miles) south of Buenos Aires until well into the 19th century.

A Spanish treasure trove

This first wave of conquest of South America lasted for two generations. From then until the beginning of the 19th century, the Spanish and Portuguese crowns sought to administer their vast empires. Economic activity was based on mining – first for gold, then silver, which by

pushed south from Inca territory into Chile, and established the capital city of Santiago in 1541. The Incas had only exacted tribute as far south as the Bíobío River, and Valdivia fared little better when he marched south of the river, meeting his match in the Araucanian warriors, for whom death in battle constituted a supreme honor. In 1554, they captured Valdivia, bound him to a tree, and beheaded him. Legend has it that the executioner ate Valdivia's heart.

The south (now Patagonia) "belonged" to the Araucanian (or Mapuche as they are known today), and other Amerindians well into the 19th century. They organized a cavalry force of 10,000 men and learned to use firearms and

THE HORRORS OF DISEASE

Diseases carried by the European conquerors wrought more devastation on the native peoples of South America than the weapons they brought. Indigenous populations, who had evolved over centuries without developing immunity to infectious diseases such as smallpox, cholera, measles, and even malaria, fell by 95 percent in some regions. Further waves of disease followed the arrival of African slaves, and the ensuing reduction in the native population led to the importation of more African slaves.

the middle of the 16th century became South America's most valuable export.

Agriculture was developed, with Spaniards being awarded large tracts of land and "given" large numbers of local indigenous people to work it, in what was known as the *encomienda* system. This was a feudalistic method of securing plantation labor in exchange for a subsistence living. Taxation in the form of animals and vegetables was exacted from the Amerindians, and labor was unrewarded.

But the power in South America was firmly located in the growing towns and cities. It was here that Spanish authority was rooted, and here too that the Catholic church followed in the wake of the conquerors. Most of South America became a viceroyalty based in Lima and its port at Callao. From here, Spain attempted to impose a commercial monopoly on all its South American colonies. The inhabitants of the colonies were only permitted to sell their products to Spain, and could only purchase products from the mother country. A Council of the Indies was set up in Seville in southern Spain to administer the territories. The riches of South America were dispatched back to Europe in yearly fleets, which soon attracted the interest of English, Dutch, and French pirates.

A new society

Through the 16th and 17th centuries, the Spaniards consolidated their rule. In each country there were a small number of Spanish-born administrators and clergy. Below them in rank were the criollos, people born in South America but claiming both parents as having Spanish blood. But the fastest-growing sector of the colonial population were the mestizos, mixed-race people, most of whom were born of a Spanish father and an indigenous mother due to the preponderance of male immigrants. One of the conquerors of Chile, Francisco de Aguirre, admitted to having at least 50 such children, and proudly affirmed that "the service rendered to God in engendering mestizos is greater than the sin incurred in so doing."

Many indigenous groups remained outside Spanish society, or were forced to work in slave-like conditions on the big estates. As

more labor was needed, so the trade in slaves from Africa grew; they were brought mostly to the Caribbean coast of Venezuela and Colombia, and to the coast of Peru. But it was Brazil where African slaves made most impact on the rest of society. As the Brazilian sugar plantations grew in importance, so did the numbers of slaves shipped in from west Africa and Angola, rising to a million by the 18th century.

When the demand for sugar fell, the discovery of gold and diamonds in Minas Gerais led to a further boom in Brazil, and Rio de Janeiro became increasingly important as a port. In 1763 it was made the capital, and it had

expanded further by the end of the century, with the growth of Brazil's new treasure crop, coffee.

As Brazil's economic strength grew, so relations with Portugal became more difficult. Brazilian merchants wanted to be free to trade with other countries, and local politicians wanted more control over their own affairs.

A similar situation arose in the Spanish colonies. Most of the treasures shipped back to Spain had been used to finance its wars in Europe, but by the end of the 18th century, Spain had fallen behind both France and Great Britain as an industrial and colonial power. By the 19th century, European wars were to lead to the loss of its South American empire. ❑

LEFT: Pukara (fortress), the last Inca stronghold in Chile. **RIGHT:** Pedro de Valdivia, who was put to death by the Mapuche after invading their territory.

INDEPENDENCE

Spain's defeats on the battlefields of Europe led to the loss of all its South American territories, but independence for the criollos brought neither peace nor democracy

When the Emporer Napoleon invaded Spain in 1808, the consequences were felt all over "Spanish America", as criollos took advantage of Spain's weakness to free themselves from the demands of the Spanish Empire. In previous decades, republican ideas from the revolutions in North America commanding a British naval squadron on the way home from South Africa, decided to capture Buenos Aires and open it up to British trade. He occupied the city for several months until the *porteños* (inhabitants of Buenos Aires) rose in rebellion and captured the whole enemy force. Reinforcements from Britain were

and in France had been taken up enthusiastically by many South Americans, who wanted to be able to trade freely with countries other than Spain, and to elect their own leaders.

Rebellions in the south

In the 18th century, Buenos Aires (the modern-day capital of **Argentina**) was a thriving smuggling center, allowing trade to enter South America without having to pass through Lima or Panama, as the Spanish Crown had decreed. The city grew in importance with the creation in 1776 of the viceroyalty of La Plata along with the relaxation of trade restrictions.

In 1806 an Englishman, Sir Home Popham,

defeated by a popular militia. The victory gave *porteños* extra confidence in their ability to govern themselves.

The fortunes of Asunción, which is now the capital of **Paraguay**, were tied by the Río de la Plata (River Plate) to those of Buenos Aires. When the Spanish colonial seat in Lima closed the port of Buenos Aires to ensure that trade (and taxation) would pass through Lima, Paraguay suffered as well. As the power of Buenos Aires grew, the leaders of Asunción began to resent their own growing insignificance, refusing to go along with the Argentine declaration of independence in 1810. A military junta led by Fulgencio Yegros declared the state of Paraguay independent on May 14, 1811.

Montevideo, the modern capital of **Uruguay**, had also been in British hands for a brief period, in 1807. Later, dictates from Spain and Buenos Aires aimed at limiting contraband and expelling small land-holders from the great estancias caused growing resentment in the region. In 1811, revolutionary forces representing the interior and led by José Gervasio Artigas, a criollo army commander, rebelled against the Spanish authorities in Montevideo. One of the aims of the revolution was to redistribute wealth to the poor, including Amerindians and freed slaves.

With the assistance of Buenos Aires, the revolutionary forces managed to eject the Spanish authorities, but Artigas and a growing number of *orientales* (people from the eastern shore) did not want to substitute the old colonial power with the newer power of Buenos Aires. In 1815 he succeeded in ejecting the *porteños* and establishing his authority throughout the new country.

In 1816 the Portuguese invaded, fearing the spread of revolutionary ideas to Brazil. They defeated Artigas in 1820, with support from sections of the upper class who resented his confiscation of their lands. The country remained in Brazilian hands after Brazil's independence, in 1822. However, many *orientales* were becoming disillusioned with the Brazilian influence, and in 1825 a revolt, led by the legendary "Thirty-three Orientales" began against Brazil. Independence was finally declared on August 25, 1825.

Britain played a part in Uruguay's independence and in mediating a peace settlement. The River Plate was one of the most important trading channels to South America, and British trade interests did not want it to be controlled by Argentina alone, or disrupted by Brazil.

The wars of independence

The collapse of the Spanish monarchy when Napoleon's troops entered Madrid had dramatically shown criollos not just in Argentina but throughout South America that Spanish rule could be defeated.

By 1810, these political leaders had declared autonomous governments or juntas in many parts of Spanish South America. When Spain

LEFT: early painting of Punta Arenas, Chile.
RIGHT: General Simón Bolívar, *El Libertador.*

tried to repress these movements, the real wars of independence broke out. In the south these were led by the Spanish-born general José de San Martín. He defeated Spanish forces in Argentina, and in 1817 led his army across the Andes – a tremendous feat of organization – to help the Chileans in their struggle. In 1811, **Chile** had opened its ports to neutral countries, in defiance of Spain's monopoly on trade. But forces loyal to Spain had regained control, and the Chilean insurgents had been forced into exile in neighboring Argentina. Many of them returned to Chile with General San Martín, and this time managed to overthrow Spanish rule.

In the northern part of South America, the independence struggle was led by *El Libertador* – "The Liberator" – Simón Bolívar. The struggle began in his native Venezuela, where he successfully fought off the Spanish loyalists to become dictator. He was very successful at first, winning six battles against royalists in 1813, but with the defeat of Napoleon in 1815 and the restoration of the Spanish monarchy in Europe, the fight to recover the colonies began in earnest. Bolívar was forced to retreat to Haiti and Jamaica: letters he wrote from exile were to become the fundamental ideology behind the independence struggle. Three years later, he was back on the mainland, leading a force of

Venezuelans and British veterans from the Napoleonic Wars. The Battle of Boyacá in northern Colombia on August 17, 1819, marked the end of royalist resistance there, and not long afterwards, Bolívar entered Santa Fé de Bogotá in triumph.

Peru had been the center of the Spanish Empire in South America, and it proved the hardest country of all to liberate. Gradually San Martín's forces advanced from the south and Bolívar's from the north, and independence was declared in Lima in

decade, **Ecuador**, **Venezuela**, and **Colombia** had seceded and gone their separate ways.

Disillusioned and dying, Bolívar spent his last days at Santa Marta in Colombia. His verdict on his life's dream was harsh: "America is ungovernable. He who serves the revolution plows the sea." San Martín had a similar experience in Argentina, discovering that the new generation of politicians had no place for a troublesome general. Eventually he left his home in South America and lived out his last years in France.

VENEZUELAN HERO

Simón Bolívar was an inspiration to many foreign romantics. The English poet Byron named a boat after him and planned to sail it to Venezuela.

1821, although most of the rest of the country remained under Spanish control until 1826.

When General Antonio José de Sucre's victories in Peru helped Bolívar put an end to Spanish rule there, the provinces of "Upper Peru" were declared a new republic named in honor of the Liberator: **Bolivia**. With nothing in common, these disorganized territories, stretching from the Amazon to the icy sierra, were now forced to fuse and develop as a nation.

The immediate years following independence were in many ways more difficult than the battles themselves. In the north, Bolívar dreamt that the newly emerging countries could stay united as La Gran Colombia, but within a

It was only years later that these heroes of independence were honored: every country in South America now has statues, street names, and even currencies named after them.

Rise of the dictators

For several decades after Independence, there was virtual civil war in most of the emerging republics. The fight for control was usually between two groups: those from the interior who wanted some kind of loose federal political arrangement, and those from the cities who traded more with the outside world and wanted strong central control of the new nation. Those groups were usually identified with conservatives and liberals, allegiances which survive to this day. Often the struggle for power between these two factions was only settled by the emergence of a strong autocratic leader, which hindered the growth of democratic rule. By the mid-19th century, many South Americans found they had thrown off the tyranny of rule from Spain for a more brutal local variety.

Brazil: independence without war

Portugal, Brazil's imperial power, was also invaded by Napoleon's troops. The Portuguese Emperor Dom João fled and moved his entire court to Brazil in 1808. Brazil then became a

pean ancestry, the local indigenous groups, and some 2 million black slaves. In 1847, Dom Pedro's son took over the Brazilian throne, and in 1850 outlawed the importation of slaves, but the practice continued. Brazil was dominated by the large estate owners of the north, who used huge numbers of slaves to grow sugar and other crops with little concern for efficiency or social progress. Dom Pedro II set out to encourage European immigrants to settle in the south of Brazil. This new population settled in Rio Grande do Sul and made São Paulo a new pole for development. There were increasing tensions between these two power groups, with

dominion in its own right, until the emperor returned to Portugal in 1821, leaving his son Dom Pedro I in charge. When Pedro was recalled to Portugal in 1822, he rebelled, replacing the Portuguese insignia with the new national colors of yellow and green, and shouting "independence or death!" This, in effect, was Brazil's declaration of independence, celebrated each year on September 7.

In the early 19th century, Brazilian society was made up of about a million people of Euro-

slavery at the center of the debate over what kind of country Brazil should be. In 1888 the Brazilian Parliament abolished slavery, making Brazil the last country in the western hemisphere to do so. This move exposed the conflict in Brazilian society, and the following year Pedro II was deposed and a constitutional republic created. As in other countries of South America, the new parliamentary regime was weak compared to the real power held by the military, which was often used to impose their own solution to political problems.

The battles of independence were over, but the struggle for power in South America's new republics had only just begun. ❑

LEFT: the Llanero Lancers in Venezuela's wars of independence. **ABOVE:** many blacks freed from slavery were press-ganged into the Brazilian Army.

INTO THE 21ST CENTURY

The republics of South America have trodden a rocky road to stability,

and many have failed to prosper, despite being rich in natural assets

By the late 19th century, South America was completely free of Spanish rule, but power and influence were still in the hands of a privileged minority. The land was largely under control of the owners of huge estates, who were usually resistant to any change. The economies were dominated by and Chile eventually occupied the whole of the territory of Patagonia, finally subduing and largely destroying the indigenous cultures in the process. In Argentina, General Julio Roca's "Conquest of the Wilderness" in the 1870s opened up the pampas and Patagonia. Any native standing in his path was killed, the rest

exports, whether of products like coffee in the case of Brazil and Colombia, wheat and beef from Argentina, or minerals such as copper from Chile and later, oil from Venezuela. Governments found it easier to tax these exports and buy imported goods than to encourage local industry. Britain took the lead in selling products to South America.

Despite this new kind of dependency, the independent South American countries quickly forged a strong sense of their own identity. Wars consolidated national boundaries, but could be extremely destructive to populations as well as burgeoning economies.

In the south, the governments of Argentina

BUYING BRITISH

Britain did brisk trade with South America in the 19th century. In the 1850s the British Consul in Argentina wrote the following about the gauchos, wild horsemen of the Argentinian pampas:

"Take his whole equipment, examine everything about him – and what is there not of hide that is not British? If his wife has a gown, ten to one it is from Manchester. The camp kettle in which he cooks his food, the common earthenware he eats from, his knife, spoon, bits and the poncho which covers him – are all imported from England".

herded into reservations. The land was used to raise cattle for European markets, taking advantage of new methods of freezing meat.

By the end of the 19th century, the ten republics of South America were firmly established. They all had elected parliaments, but the struggle for power had only just begun. The fight between democratic forces and those resisting change dominated political life for much of the 20th century.

South America was lucky not to be involved in the great wars of the 20th century. The consequences of these conflicts were seen mainly in the influx of people from many European coun-

An urban society

These political developments were responses to the challenges and tensions within South American society. The population has grown rapidly: in 1900 there were around 40 million South Americans. In the 21st century it is nearly ten times that figure. In a relatively short time, South America has evolved into a continent where more than two-thirds of the population live in towns or cities.

The haves and have-nots

A huge growth of both the middle and working classes took place in the 20th century in these

tries, who were fleeing persecution or hardship to seek a new life in the new continent.

At the same time, the ideological battles that divided Europe and other regions for many years were reflected in South America. Military rulers often brought in fascist ideas formulated in Spain or Italy, while workers began to organize thanks to communism, and guerrilla groups based on Marxist ideologies sought to end the huge disparities of wealth and power through revolutionary change.

LEFT: mine workers in Chile's northern desert.
ABOVE: the Peróns on the balcony of the Casa Rosada, Buenos Aires.

urban centers. **Argentina**'s booming beef industry and conquest of more territory in Patagonia meant that more labor was required, and in the 1880s thousands of European immigrants flocked to the country, mainly poor peasants from Italy and Spain. It was the greatest influx of immigrants in relation to population patterns in world history. But the immigrants usually arrived penniless, and did not get to share in the country's wealth, as the great landowning families refused to break up their massive holdings. The immigrants were given small plots, but only to work for three to five years before moving on. Unlike North America, which was settled by millions of small landowners, Argentina remained the property of around 200 close-knit families referred to simply as "the oligarchy". The new immigrants remained in the urban areas, and the population of Buenos Aires grew from 750,000 in the early 1900s to more than two million in 1930.

In Argentina, as elsewhere in South America, a growing population and its desire for political representation led to bloody confrontation. Attempts at reform were often brought to an abrupt end by military intervention. This created further polarization in society, so that by the end of the 1960s, there were left-wing guerrilla movements throughout the continent. This

in power, Vargas built up a strong state and promoted Brazilian industry, in ways reminiscent of Mussolini in Italy.

After Vargas' fall, a long period of constitutional rule followed. Brazil's economy and population grew rapidly, a growth symbolized by the construction of Brasília as the country's new capital in the late 1950s *(see page 240)*. But as in the rest of South America, the growing numbers of landless people in the rural areas, added to increasingly militant political groups in towns and cities, began to pose a threat to stability – or so it appeared to the armed forces, who took over Brazil's government once more in 1964.

in turn led to further military repression, and the breakdown of law and respect for human rights.

In **Brazil** the pattern was also one of economic instability leading to periods of military dictatorship. In the early part of the 20th century, most of the country's wealth came from the export of rubber and coffee. But Malaysia began to grow rubber too, and in 1930 the world price of coffee fell dramatically. With military backing, Getulio Vargas seized power from a weak civilian government. The so-called "father of the people" used a populist rhetoric to win the support of poor workers and peasants, and brought in legislation that encouraged trade unions and organized labor. During his 15 years

Foreign ownership

Many South American countries saw the wealth generated within their own borders trickle away overseas. **Bolivia** is arguably the worst example, with most of its silver going to Spain where it was used to finance European wars *(see page 173)*, and the profits from its massive tin wealth staying in the hands of a few entrepreneurs and mostly being squandered abroad, leaving it today one of the world's poorest countries.

Another country which is still extremely poor, **Ecuador**, did brisk international trade in bananas, coffee, cocoa pods, and Panama hats. The sole beneficiaries, however, were a few hundred criollo families and the foreign companies who controlled the industries. For decades Ecuador has been the world's largest exporter of bananas, but until the 1960s the entire industry was owned by the Boston-based United Fruit Company. Until the recent growth of the oil industry, bananas accounted for most of Ecuador's export earnings – and the fact that all the profits left the country is one reason why Ecuador has remained so poor for so long.

Colombia's wealth was also traditionally based on the export of bananas and coffee. But these industries were either owned by foreign companies like the United Fruit Company, or by a small number of national landowners who

siphoning off a large part of this new wealth, nor about rewarding his family and cronies with lavish gifts (including the archbishop who gave him special dispensation to eat meat on Good Friday). Little of the profits from the "black gold" found their way to the vast majority of Venezuelans, who moved in increasing numbers from the poor, backward countryside to the attractions of the capital city, Caracas.

The death of Gómez in 1935 led to riots and strikes until the typical combination of military officers and conservative landowners took power. Eventually one strong man emerged – Colonel Pérez Jiménez, who brought in a series

had control of vast plantations. As the population grew, poverty increased, as did social tensions, exploding in 1948. Years of violence and civil war followed *(see page 91)*.

Neighboring **Venezuela** suffered political turmoil in spite of the discovery of huge oil deposits, which did bring great wealth to the country – but not without a struggle. In 1917, oil was found in Lake Maracaibo. At that time, Venezuela was ruled by the dictator Juan Vincente Gómez, who had no scruples about

LEFT: Brazil's president, Juscelino Kubitschek, at the 1960 inauguration of Brasília. **ABOVE:** the bombing of La Moneda, Santiago, Chile, during the 1973 coup.

of populist measures, allowing labor organization and investing some of the oil profits into public works and low-cost housing. Once again though, this autocratic rule led to instability.

In 1958, after riots which caused the death of 600, Jiménez was overthrown. Elections heralded an unbroken period of parliamentary rule.

Territorial conflict

North America had one major civil war, but many of the republics of South America have been severely weakened by repeated territorial disputes. Some benefited – in the 19th century, Chilean dictator Diego Portales won a war with a Peru/Bolivia Confederation (1836–39), taking Antofagasta, later claiming Patagonia, Tierra del Fuego, and Magallanes, and founding Punta Arenas in 1847.

In the 1879 War of the Pacific, Peru and Bolivia declared war on Chile, resulting in a Chilean takeover of southern Peru, along with its valuable nitrate and mineral mines, and Bolivia losing its only access to the sea. And in 1903, Brazil annexed a vast stretch of Bolivia's Amazon basin, known to be rich in rubber trees.

Wars could be costly for the winners too. Paraguay won much of the southern Chaco from Bolivia in the 1932 Chaco War. While Bolivia held on to its Chaco oilfields, no oil has

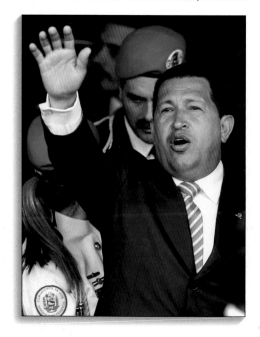

ever been found in the Paraguayan Chaco lands. The desperately fought war bled both countries dry economically and in manpower.

Historic territorial disputes rumbled on into the 21st century. Bolivia is still trying to regain access to the Pacific, while Peru and Chile squabble over their borders. Peru also fought a recent war over disputed territory in the south of Ecuador, and although a peace treaty was signed in 1998, neither side was entirely happy with the compromise. Venezuela lays claim to a large part of the territory of Guyana, while at the other end of the continent, Argentina resolutely refuses to accept that the Falkland Islands (known there as Las Malvinas) belong

to the United Kingdom, despite a 1982 war in which more than 1,000 Argentines died.

A turbulent decade

Ironically, it was the countries with the most stable political traditions and the biggest economic growth which suffered the most brutal military dictatorships in the 1970s. Uruguay had the longest democratic tradition and one of the world's first welfare states, but the 1950s and 1960s saw economic downturn, social disruption and the rise of guerrillas. A military takeover in 1973 led to 12 years of dictatorship with widespread repression and torture *(see page 313).*

The situation in Argentina was even worse. After political turmoil following Perón's death in 1974, the armed forces took power in 1976, and fought a "dirty war" resulting in at least 10,000 "disappearances" – people captured by state security forces and then tortured and killed without any legal process.

In the 19th century, Chile was the most stable nation in the region. In 1970 the Socialist Party President Salvador Allende came to power, but in 1973 the military wrested control under General Pinochet, once again with the backing of conservative forces *(see page 280).* Pinochet remained in power for 17 years, bringing in the free-market economic model that has since been adopted by most other countries in South America. In many ways, this has meant their economies have come full circle: earnings once again mainly come from exports. Local markets have been opened up to all kinds of foreign goods, with a parallel decline in domestic production. This has led to a new economic stability, but with high levels of unemployment.

The new challenges

The early years of the 21st century promise a bright future, if South America learns to integrate as a region, realizing Bolívar's dream of unity. Sadly, chronic poverty and unemployment are causing massive unrest in some countries, and governments need to do much more to narrow the huge gap between the rich and poor, to harmonize life in the cities and the countryside, and to offer the continent's young population – almost 40 percent of the total – the chance to realize their full potential. ❏

LEFT: in 2006, Venezuelan president, Hugo Chávez, won a third term in office.

The Drugs Trade

A common sight in Bolivian street markets is huge sacks of coca leaves for sale. The local people buy them to make tea or to chew in order to stave off the effects of altitude, cold, or lack of nourishment *(see page 188)*. In many highland and jungle areas of South America, indigenous groups use their knowledge of plants and essences to concoct drugs for use in ceremonies.

But in the past 40 years, with the spectacular growth of the export of refined drugs to the United States and Europe, drugs and drug-trafficking have become a huge problem for the region. Coca leaves are converted into the basic paste for cocaine in distant hide-outs (chewing coca leaves does not have the same effect as taking the powdered drug, as massive amounts are needed to make cocaine).

In the 1980s, the fight for control of the production and distribution of cocaine for foreign markets led to increased violence. Hoodlums from Colombian cities such as Medellín and Cali made vast profits out of the shipments, and showed little mercy for rivals or anyone trying to maintain the rule of law. They formed cartels to keep prices up and competitors out, and soon drugs became Colombia's most valuable export. Colombia produces 80 percent of the world's supply of cocaine and over a third of the heroin.

Successive United States governments, aware that the problem was manifesting itself on the streets of their own cities, tried to harness attempts to control the trade. They insisted that South American governments carry out programs to "eradicate" the plantation of crops like coca; that police and armed forces co-operate with the Drug Enforcement Administration in tracking down the traffickers; and that governments be willing to extradite those convicted of trading in illegal drugs.

This led to a virtual civil war in Colombia at the end of the 1980s, as traffickers like Pablo Escobar took on the state in their efforts to avoid arrest. Escobar and his followers are believed to have blown up a passenger aeroplane with 200 people on board, and several hundred policemen among others were killed in their war against the state. Escobar was finally killed after escaping from jail, and the power of the Medellín and Cali drugs cartels was tamed. This did not mean the problem

RIGHT: coca leaves from the Andes, which can be used to produce cocaine.

went away – new people took over, and the trafficking moved to other countries – Brazil, Ecuador, and Mexico, which shares a long border with the principal client, the United States.

Throughout South America today, the drugs trade is still a huge if largely invisible presence. Drugs money has financed new banks, hotels, and buildings from expensive beach resorts in Chile or Uruguay to high-rise blocks in downtown Bogotá and Caracas.

It is one of the chief reasons for the high levels of corruption in government and other offices – in Colombia for example, President Ernesto Samper, who was in power from 1994 to 1998, was never

able to shake off allegations that his successful election campaign benefited from several million dollars' worth of contributions from the drugs bosses *(see page 92)*. From poorly paid border guards and customs officials, to equally badly paid police and army recruits, to politicans and high-ranking officers, money from the illegal trade perverts the system.

In countries such as Bolivia, there has been a strong reaction against the "eradication" programs called for by the US government. The election of Evo Morales as president in 2005 owed much to the support of peasant coca growers, who insisted they be allowed to grow coca for traditional purposes. ❏

A LAND OF MANY FACES

The people of South America are as diverse as the countries they came from, yet they also share a distinctive Latin American heritage

Ever since Colombus landed in what is now the Bahamas and thought he had arrived in the East Indies, the indigenous peoples of the Americas have been lumped together and collectively termed Indians. The number of terms used to describe ethnicity in South America today may daunt the visitor – it's an indication of not just the continent's racial diversity, but also of the importance of ancestry here.

In Brazil, mestizo or *mameluco* describes someone who is part indigenous, part European. Mulatto describes someone whose origins are African and European, while *cafuso* describes someone who is of Amerindian and African heritage.

All this complex ethnic terminology probably grew out of people's attempts to define their identity in a continent that has seen so much immigration in the past 500 years, and where national boundaries have only been defined in the past few centuries and are often in dispute. This is a continent where people from the world's most diverse nations and cultures meet, mix, and intermarry. Nationalities to make the continent their home include the Welsh in Patagonia, Slovenians in southern Chile, Koreans in Paraguay, and Japanese in Peru and Brazil. Yet the surface multiculturalism of South America hides a complex mesh of social and racial hierarchies.

In addition, national characteristics and patriotic pride are very strong, although outsiders tend to group South Americans together as "Latins". Inhabitants of neighboring countries such as Venezuela and Colombia are very different from each other, while Brazil offers a very special world of its own. One of the pleasures of traveling through the continent is to discover how much variety and individuality each country has to offer, expressed in everything from food and dress to music and the versions of Spanish that are spoken.

PRECEDING PAGES: Quechua people at a wedding near Cusco, Peru; Carajás boy, Amazon. **LEFT:** Quechua woman. **RIGHT:** teenage girls in Rio, Brazil.

The new arrivals

South America's ethnic make-up changed dramatically after the arrival of Europeans in the 16th century, who were predominately Spanish and, in Brazil, Portuguese. They initially arrived as single men, intermarried with the indigenous women, and brought in slaves from

Africa. By 1888, when slavery was finally abolished in Brazil, immigration from Europe was being actively encouraged, particularly to Brazil and Argentina. Most of the immigrants initially came from Spain and Italy, but there were also Germans, eastern Europeans, Syrians, Lebanese, Japanese, and Chinese.

The people of the Andean countries – Peru, Colombia, Ecuador, Bolivia, and Chile – are predominately mestizo. These countries also have the highest pure Amerindian populations, partly because there were a lot of indigenous people living in this region at the time of the Conquest, and partly because of the large-scale destruction of the indigenous societies in the south.

People of African descent are concentrated in northern Brazil and the coastal regions of Colombia, Venezuela, Ecuador, Peru, and the Guianas, places where their ancestors were taken as slaves. Argentina and Southern Brazil are predominately caucasian, and Chile is roughly 20 percent European.

Guyana, Suriname, and French Guiana, on the north Caribbean coast, have a particularly interesting ethnic make-up, due to their histories as crop-producing outposts of three world empires – Dutch (Suriname), British (Guyana) and French

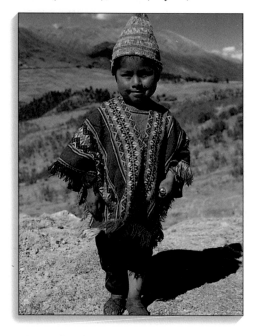

(French Guiana). African slaves were brought in to work the sugar, coffee, and cotton plantations, and many then fled into the rainforest to form "Bush Negro" communities, retaining many of their African traditions.

After the abolition of slavery, indentured labor was imported from other parts of the empires, leaving all of these countries with highly mixed populations composed of Asians, Amerindians, Africans, Portuguese *mulattos* and Europeans.

New communities

The Bush Negroes are not the only group to have taken advantage of South America's for-

midable territory in order to pursue their chosen lifestyle. This continent has a number of discrete independent communities which often transcend national boundaries, such as the gauchos of Argentina *(see page 338)*, and the fundamental religious Mennonite groups *(see page 274)*. Don't be surprised if you come across lederhosen on the Caribbean coast, or Welsh hats in Patagonia – these are the legacy of groups of immigrants who might have felt their way of life restricted in their country of origin, or who just wanted to build a new life in a new country.

The continent's racial diversity is reflected in its languages. Although Spanish is by far the dominant language in South America today, and Portuguese is the official language of Brazil, many other languages are spoken.

Native American languages are frequently spoken in the Andean regions, and in Bolivia, Spanish, Quechua (or Quichua), and Aymara are all official languages. In Peru, Spanish and, since 1975, Quechua, are both official languages. In Paraguay, Spanish is the official language, but most people speak Guaraní. The Guianas follow a colonial pattern, with English the main language of Guyana, Dutch the main language of Suriname, and French the language of French Guiana.

The racial hierarchy

In many areas the melting pot has been blended so completely that local people are unexpectedly homogeneous. In the cities of northern Chile, Bolivia, and Peru, for example, pale European tourists are distinctive enough to turn heads, as do people with darker skin coloring, who will frequently hear themselves described as *moreno* or *negrita*.

In many South American countries, skin color and racial origins have a distinct bearing on status. The palest people are frequently concentrated in the professional establishments, behind the counters of smart department stores or in front of television cameras. In bars, restaurants and on long-distance buses you can often detect a striking color difference between the faces that appear on the television screen and the faces watching it, with the few dark or black faces on screen usually relegated to servile roles.

Off the screen, indigenous people – particularly in the Andes region – are usually seen laboring in the fields or behind market stalls. Many have steadfastly continued to practice their ancient customs and traditions, often in the face of strenuous opposition. The distinctive dress of Bolivian *campesina* women is believed to have developed as a response to the conquistadors' prohibition of tradtional dress. The death penalty was imposed in many cases for Amerindians who resisted conversion to Christianity, so it's not surprising that the countries of South America are overwhelmingly Catholic (except for Guyana, formerly a British

seen as a stigma in most South American countries, to the extent that most people prefer to describe themselves as white rather than mestizo, particularly in urban areas. However, in recent years, several of the Andean countries have elected presidents of indigenous origin, and there is a new pride in being able to relate to the traditional societies, but it is still the more "European" groups who wield the power and dominate the economy almost everywhere.

Lifestyles under threat

People who live in South America's urban regions may feel economically and socially

colony). Yet many communities have incorporated their religious traditions into Catholicism, producing hybrid religions in some areas, like *Macumba* in Brazil *(see page 246)*.

In the years following the Conquest many indigenous societies were forced to either adapt or be obliterated. The tribal societies in the lowlying Amazon regions were devastated by European disease and violence. Some of the numerical reduction may be explained by the fact that Amerindian heritage persists in being

LEFT: Peruvian boy in the Sierra.
ABOVE LEFT: Venezuelan farmer.
ABOVE RIGHT: Guajira woman, Venezuela.

BRAZILIAN HOLOCAUST

In 1639 the Spanish Jesuit Cristóbal de Acuña wrote that "Amazon Indian settlements are so close together that one is scarcely lost sight of before another comes into view." But this state of affairs was not to last – 17th-century officials in Brazil boasted that they killed 2 million Amerindians in the lower Amazon. Brazil's indigenous population was estimated at 2½–6 million at the time of the Conquest. Although numbers fell by around a third in the 20th century, tribal groups have grown in recent years and now account for about 350,000 people.

under pressure to deny their Amerindian ancestry, but for many tribal peoples of the Amazon, their heritage and distinctive traditions are among the few resources they have left in their struggle for the survival of their communities. Many of these lifestyles are constantly evolving and adapting in response to their changing environment, which is particularly vulnerable to the encroachments of the technological age.

In some areas, tribal groups are benefitting from an increased tourist interest, which brings in some income while encouraging the continuity and development of their way of life.

Some such schemes are criticized as creating tribal theme parks, but there is reason to believe the alternatives for the tribes concerned could indeed be oblivion.

Some indigenous groups, like the Mapuche of Chile, have found it necessary to take political action to ensure their survival. Increasingly, since the commemoration of the fifth centenary of European arrival in 1992, indigenous groups have organized themselves politically to have their voice heard. This has led to upheavals in Ecuador and Bolivia, where these groups are in a majority, but almost everywhere the pressure has produced a new awareness of this distinct element within South American society.

Social hierarchies

The middle classes are becoming more influential, but in many South American countries, old social hierarchies refuse to shift. Numerous revolutions and government coups have failed to dislodge the influence of the handful of old family names that still wield formidable power.

These social hierarchies often originally derived their power from the old feudalistic *encomienda* system, whereby families of Spanish conquistador origin would control huge estates, worked by indigenous serfs who would provide labor in return for being allowed to work small plots of land for their own use. This system was still officially condoned in Peru until the mid 1960s, and in Ecuador until 1971.

Women's changing role

In recent years, South American women have been playing an ever more prominent role in political and professional life. In 2006, Chile elected its first woman president, Michelle Bachelet, while many other countries have women ministers. As doctors, lawyers, and in civil society pressure groups, women are to the fore. Young women are often the best and most enthusiastic students in many academic disciplines.

Yet in this mainly Catholic continent, there is still a general assumption that a woman should above all be a good wife and mother. The word machismo was, after all, coined to describe the Latin male; and there are frequently activities and attitudes that reject women. Often they are expected to combine motherhood with a full day's work, although they are rarely paid as much as their menfolk.

THE YANOMAMI

The Yanomami people of northern Brazil and Venezuela were undiscovered by the rest of the world until the 1970s, when "civilization" began to encroach on their Roraima rainforest home. Latter-day gold miners moved in and, in 1993, 20 Yanomami were massacred by them. The Yanomami have managed to publicize their plight, but attempts by the rest of the world to do something about it have not been so successful, notably since the disastrous Amazon rainforest fires that broke out during the drought of early 1998, destroying an area the size of Belgium.

Young people

At all levels of society, it seems, children are the focus of South American life. Families are large, contraception is often frowned upon, and women tend to start producing children at a lower age than in Europe and North America.

Some visitors might be alarmed at the incessant noise of children's exuberant shouts, which will often continue late into the evening – these playful noises are not tolerated or endured but indulged and encouraged, with the adults often joining in. The best thing to do for everyone's peace of mind is to shrug your shoulders, join in, and put off any quiet-time activities you may

publicize and alleviate the situation, but for many children of poor families in South America, life can be a very hard slog indeed.

Music and dance is an outlet for all levels of society in exuberant South America. Youth is celebrated and indulged, not by prolonging it with plastic surgery, but more through the feelings of youth, recaptured throughout life at fiestas and in the dance clubs, where anyone can dress up in tight Lycra and get away with it. Youth brings romance, often rapidly followed by procreation and more children. But there is nothing perfunctory about this eternal cycle. Try to count the number of times you hear the

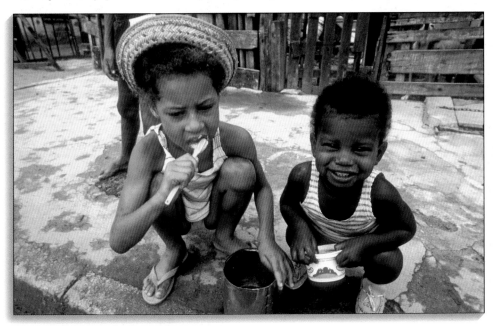

have planned until the next day's siesta. Or invest in a good pair of earplugs.

The importance of children in South America makes the plight of the street children, orphaned and abandoned to scavenger lifestyles on the streets of big cities like Rio de Janeiro, seem all the more shocking. This is another case of social status coming into play, with the children forced to carry the burden of their parents' social disgrace. People from inside and outside South America have worked hard to

words "*mi corazón*" ("my heart") in popular songs. South American men may have a reputation for machismo, but it's probably just a front to disguise the very obvious passion for romance that pervades this emotionally charged part of the world.

Fun, pleasure, and romance are of the highest priority in South America, and can transcend the boundaries of religion, race, politics, and social standing. Everyone, whatever their background, is expected to indulge in the lighter side of life at least occasionally. Music, dance, a determination to enjoy life whatever the burden – the diverse people of South America are clearly linked with a common bond.   ❏

LEFT: chieftain and his wife, western lowlands, Ecuador. **ABOVE:** young children on the street in the slum area, *favela*, of Rio, Brazil.

THE IRRESISTIBLE LURE OF THE UNKNOWN

From gold-crazy conquistadors to modern eco-adventurers, South America has attracted a long line of explorers in pursuit of elusive dreams

The earliest Spanish and Portuguese explorers were primarily concerned with charting the length and breadth of the newly discovered continent. In 1520, the great ocean navigator Fernando Magellan rounded the globe, giving his name to the stormy straits he passed at the southern tip of present-day Chile. In the same era, conquistadors Gonzalo Pizarro and Francisco de Orellana led arduous expeditions into the Amazon jungle in search of the mythical city of gold, El Dorado. They never found much gold but, in 1541, Orellana's expedition sailed down the Amazon to the sea, becoming the first Europeans to cross South America.

△ **SURVIVAL RATIONS**
Humboldt and Bonpland were reduced to a diet of ground cacao beans and Amazon River water when damp and insects destroyed their supplies.

SCIENTIFIC EXPLORATION

In the 18th century, the Age of Enlightenment in Europe sparked off a new, scientific interest in the little-known South American wildlife.

One of the foremost European explorers was Alexander von Humboldt, a Berlin-born student of botany, chemistry, astronomy, and mineralogy. With his companion, French botanist Aimé Bonpland, Humboldt set off on an expedition from Venezuela to Ecuador in 1799, charting the link between the Orinoco and Amazon rivers. He assembled meticulous lists of plants and animals, which led to the publication of *Essays on the Geography of Plants*, pioneering studies into the relationship between a region's geography and its flora and fauna.

▷ **MARINE IGUANAS**
Whilst on the Galápagos Islands, Charles Darwin observed these unique reptiles, which have a breathing system that has adapted to life in the ocean.

△ **CHARLES DARWIN**
The originator of the theory of evolution was inspired by studies made during an expedition to the Galápagos Islands in 1835.

THE ORIGINAL INDIANA JONES

In 1906, a British army officer, Colonel Percy H. Fawcett, went to South America, contracted by the Bolivian and Brazilian governments to help demarcate their jungle borders.

Fawcett had his own plan, however, which was to locate the fabled continent of Atlantis. He arrived armed with an 18th-century Portuguese document, and a stone idol thought to be of Brazilian origin and identified by psychics as having come from Atlantis.

On Fawcett's second expedition in 1925, he was accompanied by his son Jack and a man called Raleigh Rimell. The three men all vanished without trace in the Matto Grosso area of the Amazon – the predators swallowed up by their prey. (The dog that had accompanied them returned unharmed.)

But the story did not end there. Tales of Fawcett's quest attracted more explorers over the years, several of whom sent back reports of white men living with jungle Amerindians; none, however, succeeded in finding him.

Fawcett's mystery and fame still live on today, and he is credited with being the inspiration behind the Hollywood hero, Indiana Jones.

▷ **FALKLANDS FOUNDER**
As well as having the bougainvillaea plant named after him, the 18th-century French navigator, mathematician, and soldier Comte Louis Antoine de Bougainville also first colonized the Falkland Islands for France. He then made his name by becoming the first Frenchman to successfully circumnavigate the globe.

△ **AMAZON CRUISE**
Despite the harsh realities met on arrival, expeditions were often well-funded and publicized, to considerable popular enthusiasm.

▽ **GREEN HELL**
Early explorers endured long, mosquito-ridden journeys, with little food, and fear of attack by fierce beasts, and even cannibals.

MUSIC AND DANCE

South America pulsates to the beat of many rhythms as, through music and dance,

people express their joys, their struggles, and often their longing for home

A bus journey in South America can be a whole new experience; a bumpy ride from somewhere you can't remember to somewhere you can't pronounce. Your driver will probably make numerous unscheduled stops to pick up passengers, call over a friend or jump out on an errand, and may also want to demonstrate his DJ skills to his captive audience. As your bus pitches and thunders down perilous mountain trails or bleak, dusty stretches, local musical delights blare at deafening volume from crackling speakers. For the driver, savoring the delights of his playlist, staying on the road is not always top priority.

Music is considered a staple in the South American diet, being as important as food itself, feeding and replenishing the soul. Popular Latin music is laden not just with passion, sentiment, happiness, and anguish, but with history and nostalgia. Just as early musical expression symbolized resistance for slaves and fueled struggles for independence in the 17th and 18th centuries, music and dance is revered by the underdogs of modern South American society. It is a tonic to counteract the harsh realities of everyday life.

Dancing for everyone

Dancing serves as a pressure valve, a reprieve from life's chaos or a celebration that tomorrow it's Friday and you feel lucky. Throughout South America dance is viewed as a fundamental right that may be expressed freely and openly at any hour or occasion of the day. It offers a refreshing change from attitudes in many northern hemisphere countries, where dance seems so often to belong exclusively to youth and beauty, and has subsequently been exiled to nightclubs.

To understand the evolution of musical and dance forms on the subcontinent is to attempt to fathom the tremendous demographic upheaval that took place over 500 years. The

richness and diversity of Latin music is a reflection of of the many colonizing and colonized forces present over the centuries. Along with native South America, Africa, Europe, and the United States all had a hand in the shaping of this magical music.

Music grew from a brutal and loveless rela-

tionship, out of enslaved Amerindians and Africans, European settlers, and colonial powerbrokers. Often oceans away from their homelands, these early inhabitants all had their music and dances. They were a way of remembering home and who you were in an uncertain landscape. Thrown together in an ethnic melting pot, many traditions were either discarded or bonded together.

Out of this struggle was born regional and national musical traditions which, in a sense, represent different colonial experiences and development. So there are historical reasons for the tango belonging to Argentina, the samba to Brazil and the *cumbia* to Colombia.

LEFT: the colorful display that is *Carnaval*, Brazil.
RIGHT: dancers perform in Bogotá, Colombia.

A spicy mix

Arguably the most international of all Latin American rhythms is what we now call **salsa**. The term itself is really nothing more than a marketing ploy adopted by the United States music industry in the late 1960s, which assumed that people could not cope with the many different types of music Latin America had to offer. *Son*, mambo, *guaracha*, and many other styles were lumped together so that they could be easily packaged for consumption. Salsa means "sauce" and the name was inspired by many musicians who would scream "Salsa!" at a pulsating audience to excite them even fur-

offbeat (piano, bass, and brass). This is all useful to know if you want to blame your dance partner for messing up when they are clearly the better dancer.

If salsa means sauce then the musical ingredients in these complex arrangements need a master chef to work. As music is food for the soul to Latin Americans, culinary references in the lyrics are compulsory.

Modern *son* and salsa, predominant in Colombia, Venezuela, and throughout Central America, have been enhanced by the addition of the piano, bass, and heavy brass sections. Cuban **charanga** replaces the brass instruments

ther. This artificial grouping of many different styles means that most discussions about the origin of salsa become as hot and spicy as the dancing that the music inspires. Most unbiased opinion, however, follows the view that today's salsa is really a jazzed-up version of **son**, whose origins date back to eastern Cuba in the 1880s.

Son intermingled African rhythms with Spanish verse forms, and its early means of expression were drums, maracas, Cuban tres guitar, and claves or sticks tapping out the beat. The beat is syncopated and loaded with polyrhythms of regular pulses provided by the clave (two sticks that beat at a 2–3 or 3–2 tempo), the *campana* (cowbell), and accents that are

with violins and flutes, but the structure is similar. In Cuba the accent remains heavily on improvization, and the force of this and fluctuations in the salsa rhythm has caught out even the most expert musicians. Whilst jamming with some Cubans even the great Dizzy Gillespie couldn't keep up, famously crying out in bafflement "Where's the beat?"

The accompanying dance may look easy but it is as intricate and erratic as the music, fluctuating between regular and countermovements. Salsa is electrifying, sensual, and dynamic, yet it can be cheeky and passionate at the same time. Don't be discouraged by the stylish, fast footwork, for much of the rhythm is contained within set steps. You will get as much of a kick out of observing the rhythmic exchange between the couples spinning and strutting their stuff or caught in a swaying embrace as from actually taking part.

A crisp, frothy beat

Merengue came to South America via the Dominican Republic in the Caribbean. It comes, as you might expect, from the French "meringue", meaning "whipped egg whites and sugar". Both the dessert and the dance have a frothy, exciting mix. From its origins in the formalized 18th-century dances of the French

and at times chaotic, with one beat suddenly dropped and another picked up. Merengue is less intense than salsa and it starts with a bang and adrenaline rush, making you feel instantly giddy and producing a strong urge to jump about in a silly fashion or run around the room. The lyrics adopt a tongue-in-cheek tone, heavy with double meaning and conveying either a social critique or commentary on everyday life. Native Dominican superstars Juan Luis Guerra and Wilfredo Vargas command great respect among their audience for their musical creativity and brazen addressing of the country's social and political problems in their lyrics.

court, merengue acquired African influences as it settled in the Dominican Republic. It provided the beat for many protest marches against foreign intervention in the 20th century as well as being a vehicle to address social problems.

Its infectious rhythm adheres to a frenetic, repetitive "thump, thump, thump" beat present in disco and rock music. An ensemble of guitar, *guira* (scraper), tambour and marimba (African piano) or accordion traditionally plays the merengue. The beat is crisp, accelerated,

The dance that compliments merengue is easily picked up compared to salsa. The basic version consists of bending one knee then the other forward and then back in clockwork alternate movements whilst not lifting your heels off the ground. Couples mirror each other, as in salsa, and when dancing close together, the woman places her right foot in between the man's feet. The couples resemble palm trees swaying in the breeze as they move to the beat.

Recent adaptations have seen merengue embracing North American crazes such as rap, hip-hop and techno music. This has proven highly popular among the youth in Dominican and Caribbean barrios in the United States, who

LEFT: belting out the beat in a Caracas nightspot, Venezuela. **ABOVE:** the unforgettable rhythm of a merengue band.

see hip-hop merengue as a Latin expression of the "brotherhood" practiced by their African-American counterparts. The new sound was first introduced by a group of young people of Dominican descent calling themselves *Proyecto Uno*. The adaptability of the rhythm and the facility of the dance has given it the upper hand over salsa in many Latin communities in the US and in Andean South America.

A dance for lovelorn men

The **tango** is closely associated with Argentina *(see page 330)*. To many the most sensual and erotic of all South American dances, its origins lie in the Buenos Aires slums of over a century ago. There, lovelorn male migrants, bereft of female company, would re-enact the intimacy of man and woman. Hence, the tango was a dance of men. One male would play the part of the female coquette whilst the other represented the rough wooer. The upper classes looked with initial disdain on the immodest hips and swift foot movements of a dance whose sexual connotations could only arouse dismay and moral approbation. In fact, it wasn't until tango caused a sensation in the dancehalls of pre-First World War France that it gained acceptance internationally and among Argentine high society.

NEW LATIN RYTHYMS

South American music has adopted styles from many different countries to produce a hybrid of dance rhythms. Traditional *cumbia* sounds have been enhanced with synthesizers and drum n' bass to produce *techno-cumbia*, popular in Peru and Bolivia. Hip-hop and rap from the US have been taken up by urban groups from Colombia, Venezuela, and Brazil. *Reggaeton*, a fusion of hip-hop and reggae, is now danced to all over the continent. Similarly, garage music has influenced tango experiments in Argentina, while *bailanta*, based on traditional folk rhythms, can be found in many nightclubs.

Today, tango is enjoying an extraordinary resurgence. Following on from the dance form's global appeal, a whole new generation of young Argentines are ensuring the survival of tango in the steaming cafés and clubs of Argentina.

Samba-mania

If the tango is Argentinian, the samba belongs to Brazil. **Samba** comes from an African word, *semba*, meaning "a type of belly dance". It originated in Africa as a reel dance and is first recorded in the 1875 festivals in Bahia in northeast Brazil. Samba today takes many forms. Ballroom, *carnaval*, and *pagode* (a slower São Paulo version) are just a few. It is universally popular and has influenced the **bossa nova** musical form, the first recording of which was made by Elizabeth Cardosa in the 1950s.

The samba danced at *Carnaval* differs from one city to the next. Its proper name is *samba enredo*. First introduced in the 1930s, this is the form of samba most of us would associate with phenomenal footwork and bottom-shaking. Samba dancers are reminiscent of leaves quivering violently in the wind as they are driven along by the feverish beat of the *bateria* (rhythm section) of drums and percussion.

Brazil's biggest show

It was the Portuguese who brought the practice of *Carnaval* to Brazil at the end of the 17th century as a festivity celebrated by pelting each other with flour and water bombs *(see page 236)*. The music and dance is essentially African in origin. *Carnaval* is undoubtedly one of the biggest displays of modern Brazilian popular culture, blending festivity with show, and art with folklore, as everyone takes to the streets in extravagant and colorful costume.

The excitement escalates from the Christmas period and New Year celebrations. In the run-up to Lent, an eerie hysteria hangs heavily in the air like the tension before a monsoon. The observer is washed along by a wave of infectious anticipation and then buffeted by relentless musical elements for four days and nights as this tropical storm sweeps over the country. It is a test of stamina that leaves you feeling numb, exhausted, and giddy whether you participate or are kept awake by it.

Carnival in Rio is distinct from the rest of the country with its purpose-built Sambadrome stadium and world-famous samba schools of up to 4,000 participants each, who jealously compete for the title of champion. The din filling the Sambadrome comes from the samba percussion *baterias* and sounds like torrential rain beating down on a tin roof. Scantily clad women shake violently as if possessed, and a chorus of several hundred voices chant responses to the samba caller.

In recent years the Bahia carnival, which is held in the colorful northeastern city of Salvador, has grown in popularity. Held as a massive street party, *trios eléctricos* – floats which

transport deafening speakers pumping out 100,000 watts of **samba**, **axé** and **frevo** music – lead the processions through the winding cobbled streets. The air dances and heads undulate. The smell of *vatapá* – a maize and shrimp dumpling dish – forms a haze, served by mountainous Baiana women swathed in traditional white dresses.

Home to Brazil's acclaimed writer Jorge Amado, who died in 2001, and international musical exports Olodum, with their army of drummers who have played with Michael Jackson and Latin music superstars Daniela Mercury and Caetano Veloso, Bahia is the bastion

of Africanism in Brazil. It is also home to the Santería religion known as *candomblé* and the African martial-arts dance **capoeira**. Bahia is considered the center of musical innovation in Brazil, and draws heavily on its African roots. Many dance crazes originate in the northeast before being eagerly snapped up by the rest of the country.

The plaintive panpipes

A world away from the samba drums and salsa tambours is the haunting, plaintive sound of Andean panpipe music – **peña**, played in such countries as Ecuador, Bolivia, and Peru. Drums, rattles, flutes, panpipes, and the famous

LEFT: carnival, the biggest party in town.
RIGHT: tango, the passionate dance for two.

charango (a miniature guitar made from an armadillo shell) characterize it. *Peña* is a mixture of pre-Columbian and Spanish instrumentation, which traditionally involves no lyrical accompaniment – but this has changed recently. The music is now accompanied by ballads sung most often in Quechua, Aymara, and Spanish. These plaintive yet raucous songs record the daily lives, romances, and ribald interludes of rural Amerindian communities.

It is music to dance to. Andean music is a foot-stomping version of a barn dance. It is very moving. It shakes the soul and makes the air jump. The sound can be frenetic, accelerating from a ballad to a musical duo reminiscent of that classic country piece *Duelling Banjos*. The pitch becomes feverish and your feet seem to move of their own accord. This kind of indigenous folk music attests to the survival of the ordinary, complex history of local populations. Music is, in a sense, the last place to hide what is left of yourself.

Songs of struggle

Used by dictatorial powers as a propaganda tool, traditional music has, nevertheless, also been a useful source of social revolution and protest. The **Nueva Canción** (New Song)

PANPIPES OF THE ANDES

The panpipe dates back at least 2,000 years. Ecuadorian panpipes were named *rondador* after the nightwatchmen in colonial Ecuador who played the instrument on their rounds. A typical *rondador* is made of varying lengths and widths of cane or bamboo tied together in one long row; the different lengths and diameters produce unique and distinct tones. The *zampoña* is the panpipe typical of Peru and Bolivia; it is tuned quite differently from the *rondador* and usually has two rows of pipes that are lashed together, to produce a deeper and more breathy sound.

movement that emerged in Chile in the 1960s and 1970s put music at the forefront of the struggle in South America. One of the leading lights of *Nueva Canción* was the musician and poet Violeta Parra, who received little recognition in her own country, Chile, until after her death by suicide in 1967. *Nueva Canción* was to voice the struggle and suffering of those Chileans who were persecuted during the dictatorship of the 1970s and 1980s. Cuba's equivalent, *Nueva Trova*, produced Silvio Rodríguez and Pablo Milanes, two of Latin America's most respected musicians.

General Pinochet was aware of the danger that *Nueva Canción* posed to his regime, and had its leading exponent Victor Jara incarcerated in the notorious football stadium in Santiago. The inspirational Jara sang to his fellow prisoners, for which Pinochet had his hands smashed, his tongue cut out, and then had him murdered.

Another important Chilean dance style is **la cueca**. It began as a pantomime; a game of coy evasion and rebuttal by women and playful conquest by men. The woman holds a white handkerchief. It was at one time a dance of remarkable restraint. There was no physical contact between the pair until the point of the *vacunao* when the man claims the woman with a pelvic movement, gentle kick or swat.

What is more moving about *la cueca*, however, is that it was employed by women to protest against the mass disappearances of their sons and husbands under Pinochet's regime during the 1970s and 1980s. *La cueca* became a dance of anger and grief. The women danced alone, their partners lost, disappeared. Their plight was brought to world attention when the British artist Sting paid tribute to them in his song *They Dance Alone*.

Dances of the countryside

On a more cheerful note, the giddy **cumbia** is a popular coastal dance from Colombia. It consists of a rousing, regular beat with a steady "molasses" bass line and brassy horns.

Urban myth has it that the movements to the *cumbia* reflect gender-based rural activities. The man makes a sweeping movement with his hand that mimics the machete cutting a path through the bush. The woman, with one hand, raises her petticoats, and with the other hand, holds a candle. This purportedly alludes to her guiding the man through the wilderness.

There is a close relationship between the *cumbia* and *vallenato* *(see page 103)*; both come from the coastal regions of Colombia. Traveling *vallenato* musicians would move from one small town to another. They were gossips who shamelessly grafted local scandal and intrigue into their songs. The lyrics were built piece by piece from the feckless lives of isolated communities. Crowds would gather and eagerly devour the news brought by these musicians. This was before the advent of telephones, and the gossip was juicier.

In recent years *vallenato* has enjoyed a surge in popularity. Carlos Vives spirited this revival with his modern sound. He appeared in a Colombian television soap opera as a wide-eyed *campesino* called upon to defeat Lucifer in a singing contest. The fate of a village lies in his hands. At first things don't look good for Vives. You worry about the village and his dubious wardrobe. Still, Vives and his accordion manage to deal a fatal blow to Lucifer by striking an original chord, securing the future of the village and the *vallenato*. As is so often the case in South America, music conquers all. ❑

VIOLETA PARRA (CHILE)

LEFT: traditional Peruvian band. RIGHT: singer Violeta Parra, often described as the "mother" of Chile's *Nueva Canción* movement.

FURTHER STEPS

Major music retailers stock Latin music. The Tumi Latin American Music Sampler (Tumi music label) is a good introduction, featuring panpipes, *vallenato, cumbia, forro*, salsa, merengue, and *son*. The more adventurous may wish to attend dance classes specializing in salsa, samba or merengue. Informal classes offering tuition for beginners are best. They are great fun but, being little advertised, may be hard to locate. Your best bet is to inquire at a Latin American restaurant or bar, contact University Hispanic departments, or check out the Internet for Latin American dance websites. Don't confuse Latin ballroom with any of these options.

ARTS AND CRAFTS

Visitors to South America will find art all around them – indigenous crafts,
pre-Columbian treasures, colonial baroque art, and powerful modern paintings

For over five centuries, South Americans saw themselves through the eyes of others. In 1492 Spain conquered a continent it had not known existed; within a few short years it had overwhelmed the population who already lived there – the 30 million or so indigenous peoples of South America – and made them "disappear". Those 20 percent or so who were not killed or assimilated were pushed into the background, perceived as barbarians and savages.

The native population of South America and the black African communities imported as slaves were rarely painted after the Flemish artist Theodore de Bry produced his famous engravings of the Conquest. When they did appear it was usually as curiosities, exotic figures in the landscapes of European travelers documenting this New World after Spain finally lost its South American empire in the early 19th century – artists like Jean-Baptiste Debret in Brazil, or Camilo Fernández in Colombia (his watercolors can be seen in Bogotá at the Biblioteca Nacional).

Occasionally you can catch glimpses of the work of anonymous indigenous artists – in the paintings of the Cusco School in Peru, for example, with its black Madonnas and curious Amerindian faces painted in the background or carved into the frames. Yet the arts of the native and the black population did survive, in what we now call craftwork or folk arts – papiermâché figures, painted gourds, fine weaving, and so on. In a way, contemporary crafts represent a continuous line from that past, although at the same time they have changed beyond recognition from their original models.

A new consciousness

It was not until the mid-19th century that South American painters began to see their own world as worthy of attention. José Correia de Lima painted Brazil's black people for the first time

(Museu de Belas Artas, São Paulo), while in Peru, Pancho Fierro recorded the Amerindian and mestizo people on Lima's streets (Museo de Arte de Lima). In the Museo Nacional de Artes Plasticas in Montevideo, Uruguay, the paintings of Juan Manuel Blanes record the inhabitants of the pampas, the open grasslands

ECHOES OF THE PAST

Many of the contemporary crafts and traditions of the Andes have clearly evolved from pre-Columbian times. By studying local culture, art, architecture, and artisans, modern archeologists have been able to advance their understanding of ancient artifacts. The people of northern Peru still regularly use ceramic pots surprisingly similar to their ancient Moche precursors. Similarly, the backstrap loom, which is attached to the weaver's back so that she can adjust the tension by moving her body, is still used in modern Peru, yet very similar models are depicted in 2,000-year-old ceramics.

LEFT: modern art captures an age-old scene, Peru.
RIGHT: making *shigras* (sacks), Ecuador.

where the gauchos lived. Pedro Figari, painting much later, created delicate and evocative images of a life of poverty in a similar world.

Change was coming – and it exploded upon South America at the beginning of the 20th century. After a century of political independence, the ties of external domination were still strong. Any bid to find real freedom meant turning the artistic gaze inward and rediscovering both the reality and the traditions that were authentically South America's own.

Ironically, the new cultural nationalists were often artists who, as their contemporaries so often did, first traveled to Europe in search of

the Mexican Revolution reverberated around the whole continent, influencing university students, who began to demand an art and an education that reflected their own reality.

The *Semana de Arte Moderna*, a famous exhibition that took place in São Paulo in 1922, announced the new movement in music, literature, and all the arts. Most representative of its extraordinary innovations was the work of painter Tarsila do Amaral. Her famous painting *Central Railway of Brazil*, like much of her work, marries bright colors and geometric forms set in a primitive landscape; it is on display in the Museu de Arte Contemporânea of

culture. Many became involved in the new modernist movements there and brought the avant garde back to South America, where it came face to face with a different and dramatic reality. South America's modern art movements were born out of that encounter.

The past rediscovered

The 1910–1920 period was a time of political and social upheaval – and of nationalism above all. Every country of Latin America began to rediscover – unearth almost – its past; Hiram Bingham's "rediscovery" of Machu Picchu in Peru in 1911 was a signpost to the *Indigenismo* movement of the 1920s *(see below)*. In 1910

the University of São Paulo. Amaral, with contemporaries such as Anita Malfatti, represented one face of the new movement; beside them Emílio de Cavalcanti and Cándido Portinari used the mediums of etching, woodcutting, and engraving to portray the experience of the ordinary people of Brazil.

European influences

Joaquín Torres-García, like his contemporary Barradas, returned from Europe and the United States to his native Uruguay in 1932, and began to generate his own version of the geometric three-dimensional designs learned from the Constructivists. The exciting and inventive

MADI group, founded in Buenos Aires in 1945, developed that work in entirely new directions.

The extraordinary purity of Armando Reverón clearly owes its origins to Manet and the post-Impressionists, searching as it does for the perfect expression of light and color that led him finally to the blinding whites of his last canvases. Reverón's claim was to have captured the essential atmosphere of his own coastal town in Venezuela – an achievement far removed from the innovative and daring new directions for which his country earned an international reputation. For in the capital, Caracas, the architect Carlos Raúl Villanueva

dimensions in the museums and streets of Rio, where much of their work may still be found. In Chile, Roberto Matta drew on European surrealism to create a universe of mysterious gardens and landscapes full of color and menace.

The *Indigenismo* movement

Yet even the most non-representational kind of painting in Latin America has wrestled with the past, the "invisible" South America. The powerful *Indigenismo* movement that began in the late 1920s in Peru, Ecuador, and Bolivia sought out the indigenous communities in all its artistic expressions – in music, literature, and in

was building a new university and inviting a younger generation of exciting new artists to participate in the design of new and very modern spaces *(see page 69)*. This invitation was eagerly accepted by artists like Alejandro Otero, Jesús Rafael Soto, and Carlos Cruz Díez, whose disturbing optical games with light, movement, and geometric form can be seen in their settings in Caracas Central University.

The "neo-concrete" artists of Brazil – Lygia Pape, Lygia Clark, and Helio Oiticica among others – explored space and color in several

LEFT: masks from Terra Nova, along the Amazon near Manaus, Brazil. **ABOVE:** woodcarving in action, Peru.

painting. José Sabogal was the doyen of *Indigenismo* in the visual arts, influencing a whole generation in Bolivia and Ecuador. But for some he was too close to an exaggerated socialist realism that owed much to the Mexican muralists.

A newer generation of artists took that brute realism in new directions – particularly the controversial artist Oswaldo Guayasamín, who moved toward a kind of primitive abstraction, his paint piled on the canvas as if the physical gesture of painting itself conveyed the emotions it contained. His enormous popularity and commercial success invited the accusation that he painted to pander to the metropolitan world's vision of the south.

Satires on complacency

Colombian artist Fernando Botero's satirical portraits of a plump and complacent South American bourgeoisie have brought him both success and the enmity of some of his subjects.

This variety of individual expression has its counterpoint in movements whose object is to create art that is collective in its nature. The radicalization of Chilean political life between 1968 and 1973 produced a mural art reflecting a movement in the streets. This movement was founded by the group Brigada Ramona Parra, named after a young art student who was killed in a demonstration. Else-where, that impulse took art into the realms of sculpture and performance – art as a kind of public statement, ranging from Chilean Eugenio Dittborn's poignant "airmail paintings", mailed to exhibitions around the world, to Argentine Antonio Berni's provocative and highly political collages.

A meeting of art and crafts

In another direction, art left the studio to reconnect with a completely different, popular tradition – colorful, naïve, passionate. It had its representatives in Brazil, and in Chile in the work of Luis Herrera Guevara.

It was here that art met "craft". In the aftermath of the Chilean military coup of 1973, for example, groups of women began to make *arpillerías* – patchworks – that employed traditional skills to make powerful symbolic statements about freedom, pain, and the search for the "disappeared". Of course, these crafts had evolved and changed from their origins in pre-Columbian America or in Africa, yet they remained the property of the poorest sections of South American society.

Craftsmen and women often produced useful items – beautifully woven *ruanas* (capes) in Ecuador, sweaters of llama or alpaca wool in Peru, woolen ponchos, hats, and gloves in the Andes – all are functional as well as beautiful. The growth of tourism has often contributed to the resurgence of some of these traditional domestic crafts – in the Ecuadorean community of Otavalo, for example *(see page 202).* But it has almost certainly changed them too.

Hand-made clay sculptures with enormous hands and feet can be bought everywhere in Peru – their faces are those of the highland peoples. The beautifully painted scenes inside bamboo stalks or hollowed-out nuts are survivals of authentic skills as well as attractive mementos for sale to tourists.

In markets across the continent, plastic items and tacky electronic goods cohabit on blankets on the street with delicate paper-lace cutouts or fine ceramics. This coexistence of dramatically different ways of life and methods of production is part of the contradictory reality of South America. ❑

LEFT: *Maternity*, woodcarving by R.P. Athyde, Ceará Museum, Fortaleza, Brazil. **RIGHT:** tapestries in an Otavalo market, Ecuador.

ARCHITECTURE

South American cities have been at the forefront of modern architectural movements, and there are also much older architectural wonders to be seen

We do not know the names of those who built the extraordinary Inca cities – Cusco and Machu Picchu – or the magnificent ceremonial structure of Sacsahuayman in Peru. Pablo Neruda, the great Chilean poet, called them only "John Stonesplitter and John Woodheaver". But whoever they were, their

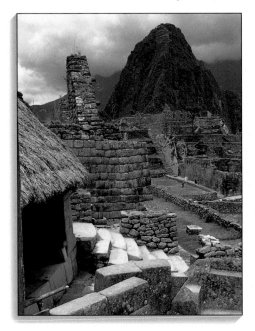

Stone was considered sacred, or *huaca*, to the Incas. Hundreds of sites display the outstanding masonry skills of the Incas, such as the famous 12-angled stone at Cusco, or *Inti-huatana* at Machu Picchu, the "hitching post of the sun". The Incas were also expert at earthquake-proofing their buildings. The colonial church of Santo Domingo was built on top of Qorincancha, the Inca Temple of the Sun, in Cusco. Over the centuries Inca foundations have proved much more resistant to earthquakes than later Spanish constructions.

constructions were built to last forever. In Cusco, the Spanish colonialists built their houses on the walls of the Inca city, for example.

There are still remains of older ancient cities like Chan Chan on the coastal plain of Peru. Elsewhere, the ancient indigenous peoples of what are now Argentina, Chile, and Brazil, did not leave monumental signs of their passing. Mostly they were hunters, gatherers, or fishermen without imperial ambitions. But Cusco was built at what the Incas saw as the center of the world, and to symbolize this, it is divided into four districts representing each corner of the empire, surrounding a central square.

The Spanish influence

When the Spanish conquered Latin America, they brought their own values, their own religion, and their own forms of artistic expression. Where they could, as in Mexico, they destroyed the buildings they found and used the stones to make their Christian cathedrals. Where they could not move the stones, as in Cusco, they built their own cities on Inca foundations. But they were able to preserve the structure of the cities, since Spain built its cities on a grid system around a central square. For in a real sense, Spain's was an urban culture and, apart from the great plantation houses, rural building was left to the communities who lived there, relying on their skill in using local materials.

For more than 300 years, Latin America's building styles originated in Spain – at first, the highly decorative *plateresque* style; later there were echoes of European baroque, where elaborate decorated surfaces and cascades of gold reflected the confidence of a colonial order. Compared with the first imperial buildings in Mexico, Quito's churches were austere in their facades; yet inside, they could be exuberant – sometimes blue and red washes were added to the endless swirling gold; sometimes they were influenced by *Mudéjar* (Moorish) styles, and incorporated wooden beams, carved closed balconies, and geometrical patterns.

Despite the codes of austerity that were

imposed by the Spanish imperial center in Madrid, Latin America did adapt these received styles, particularly in the late 17th- and 18th-century baroque edifices.

The Amerindian influence

Indigenous craftsmen in Bolivia left their mark on Sucre Cathedral and the churches of San Lorenzo in Potosí or San Francisco in La Paz, and in Peru in the carved soft lava stone used in Arequipa. Bright colors, animals and plants, and occasional dark-skinned faces carved into the stone are testimony to their presence, for example in the facade of the old Jesuit University in the statues of the Prophets at Congonhas do Campo *(see page 243)*.

Looking to Europe

Landscape and geography affected construction too. New Granada (as the Andean republics were called under Spanish rule) lay across an earthquake zone, to which many of Lima's buildings have fallen victim. The Torre Tagle Palace (now Peru's Ministry of Foreign Affairs) is one of the few colonial buildings to have survived in the city.

Once freed from Spain, the leaders of a newly independent subcontinent turned their

Cusco's central square. And in Brazil, where the imported Portuguese style encountered no local architecture to stand in its way, the reality of the tropics found its way into the baroque facades of Pernambuco or the extraordinary San Francisco da Penitencia churches of Recife and Bahia.

The most outstanding expression of this "tropicalized" baroque is the work of the crippled sculptor-architect Aleijadinho on churches and other buildings throughout Ouro Preto. His most enduring and idiosyncratic expression are

---

LEFT: Machu Picchu, Peru: a miracle of architectural achievement on an Andean mountain top.
ABOVE: twelve-angled Inca stone in Cusco.

attention to other parts of Europe. The 19th century produced an imitative grandeur, mimicking the wide boulevards and grand palaces of France and London and their new enthusiasm for neoclassical styles. La Moneda, the famous presidential palace in Santiago, Chile, now restored after being destroyed by bombing during the 1973 military coup against Salvador Allende, was a typical example of this trend.

In Buenos Aires, growing to dominance in the latter half of the 19th century, the newly wealthy bourgeoisie used architecture to emphasize their European roots, producing their own versions of the grand boulevards of the Champs Elysées. In Lima this change was exemplified by the demolition of the old city walls to make way for the new avenues.

Outside the planned, structured heart of Latin American cities, buildings tend to be somewhat improvized and transient. By the late 19th century the spaces between the grand houses and tenements had themselves become living places for a poor immigrant population. In the 20th century these areas swelled, spreading like mushrooms (*callampa*, the name for a shanty town in Chile, means mushroom) around and through the burgeoning metropolises. The hillside *favelas* of Rio *(see page 237)* are extreme examples of this phenomenon.

planners, and Brazil's 1930 revolution, which was led by young military officers promising to modernize and industrialize at every level, provided the opportunity. The architect Gregorio Warchavchik set out the new ideas: architecture would be functional and geometric, celebrating the materials and structures of a new urban and industrial world.

The Ministry of Education and Health in Rio was the landmark of the new movement. Completed in 1937 by a team that included Lucio Costa and Oscar Niemeyer, it was the center of a completely urban utopia. Not just buildings, but whole cities would be built like efficient

Beacons of the technological age

The past 70 years have brought South America – and in particular Brazil and Venezuela – to the very center of innovation in architecture. The architects responsible for the modernist revolution in Brazil traveled to Europe and brought back new and experimental ideas. They seized on the ideas of the great Swiss architect Le Corbusier and the Dutch architect Mies van der Rohe as they imagined great modern cities. They hoped the subcontinent would be catapulted into the 21st century by gilding its new urban spaces with the most daring "machines for living". Le Corbusier's lecture tour of Argentina and Brazil galvanized local urban

machines with clean lines, open and flexible spaces set in planned landscapes like those designed by the Brazilian architect and landscape gardener Roberto Burle Marx. The high blocks along Rio's Copacabana beach are one such example; the recreational complex at the suburb of Pampulha another. The church of São Francisco de Assis at Pampulha, decorated by Portinari, symbolized the marriage of painting, sculpture, and the constructive arts.

The triumph of the idea was Brasília *(see page 240)*, the most ambitious of several new cities purpose-built in the late 1950s that illustrate the meeting of architecture and sculpture. Oscar Niemeyer, the principal architect, imagined a city that would in turn create a way of living. In just ten years the Brazilian movement transformed architecture everywhere, as the 1943 "Brazil Builds" exhibition at New York's Museum of Modern Art testified.

Modern icons

Less well known abroad, but equally dramatic in its significance, was the movement led by Carlos Raúl Villanueva in Venezuela, and in particular, Caracas. Villanueva's first major projects – the El Silencio (Silence) and El Paraíso (Paradise) workers' housing complexes built in the 1940s – symbolized a utopian and optimistic

buildings – this was a landscape where natural lines and plants and trees were symbolically represented in concrete and metal.

In Argentina, where the neoclassical forms persisted longer than elsewhere, the Teatro Colón *(see page 328)* expressed both the high point and the ending of the movement. The next generation of architects were as responsive as their colleagues elsewhere to the modern movement as the country began its process of industrialization. Clean sharp lines and open space characterized the work of new architects like Amancio Williams, whose house in Mar del Plata for his brother, the composer Alberto, was

modernism. As in Brazil, the mass housing projects represented the promise of an organized and smooth transition to urban growth; the concrete and glass that were its chief materials were not indigenous but they were cheap and readily available. Like the Brazilians, Villanueva saw architecture as a meeting point between spatial and visual arts. The Central University, the construction of which began in the early 1950s, expressed the confidence of a newly oil-rich country. In a sense, Villanueva created more than

LEFT: colonial buildings, Quito, Ecuador.
ABOVE: the unmistakable style of Oscar Niemeyer is seen in the Museu de Arte Contemporânea, Rio, Brazil.

entirely functional and without artistic pretensions. In Chile the long, low buildings of Emilio Duhart and Alberto Piwonka reflected an adaptation of the same ideas to the earthquake-prone Santiago valley.

In the 1980s and 1990s, architectural innovation took place largely in the commercial sphere. However, Niemeyer – who planned Brasília – continues to design in his unique style. In 1996, he completed the Museum of Contemporary Art in Niterói, a city next to Rio de Janeiro. It resembles an enormous, sculptural flying saucer more stunning than the works of art it contains, perched on a cliff edge overlooking the sea. ❑

THE GREAT OUTDOORS

Not all outdoor activities in South America center on the rainforest – increasingly sophisticated leisure facilities are available, from sand-boarding to paragliding

South America is a paradise for outdoor enthusiasts. Down the spine of the continent is the Andes, the longest continuous range of mountains in the world. This lofty landscape has snow-capped peaks for mountaineers, trekking, horseback riding, mountain biking on remote trails through isolated villages, and world-class kayaking and river rafting.

Within the Amazon basin to the east lie thousands of miles of virgin rainforest best explored by dugout canoe. Beaches offer excellent surf and the northern Pacific and Caribbean reefs are great for scuba diving. Adrenaline sports such as snowboarding, paragliding, and bungee jumping are on the increase. But there is little regulation of the adventure travel business, so care needs to be taken in finding a reputable company.

National parks

Nahuel Huapi, the first national park in South America, was created in Argentina in 1903. Since then hundreds of parks have been established throughout the continent, protecting beautiful wilderness. Access to parks is becoming easier with improved transportation and infrastructure. In the more developed countries, notably Chile and Argentina, the parks have established trail systems with visitor centers.

Cusco in Peru is the Mecca for outdoor adventure, the most popular excursion being the Inca trail trek to Machu Picchu *(see page 158)*. Cusco's surrounding mountains are also perfect for mountain biking. There is a popular ride to the Inca terracing and salt ponds at Moray. Instead of a bus tour, the Sacred Valley can now be experienced by rafting the Urubamba River, on horseback, or paragliding from the cliffs.

Further south, the spectacular alpine and coastal wilderness of southern Chile brings in visitors from October through April. The town of Pucón is a good base for hikes, climbs, river rafting, mountain biking, and horseback riding

LEFT: Argentina: a climber contemplates Mt Fitzroy.
RIGHT: tackling the Urubamba River, Peru.

into the nearby national parks of Huerquehue and Villarrica. Even further south is spectacular Torres del Paine National Park *(see page 298)*.

Mountaineering

The high peaks of the Andes attract high-caliber international climbers every year. Acclimatiza-

tion, proper equipment, and preparation are paramount. The highest of these peaks is Aconcagua (6,962 meters/22,841 ft) in Argentina. In northern Peru, from June through September, the small town of Huaraz is filled with climbers organizing expeditions to the many glaciated peaks in the Cordillera Blanca, the highest being Huascarán at 6,768 meters (22,200 ft). Snowboarders sometimes precariously descend its slopes. Ecuador's volcanoes can offer the novice a taste of high-altitude mountaineering.

Skiing

The world's highest ski run is at 5,420 meters (17,782 ft) in La Paz, Bolivia, on the slopes of

Chacaltaya *(see page 180)*. It was developed in the 1930s and is still accessed by the oldest ski lift in South America – horror stories abound regarding its safety. More sophisticated ski areas have been developed in Chile and Argentina, with the huge ski area of Las Leñas in Argentina considered the most prestigious. The resorts near Santiago such as Valle Nevado and Portillo also have many challenging slopes. The best time to go is June through October.

Cycling

Every year a few serious cyclists pedal the length of the Andes to the southern tip of the

canyons" in southern Peru, said to be twice as deep as the Grand Canyon. Condors soar above, a volcano smokes in the distance, and sheer cliffs tower hundreds of meters on either side. The Bío Bío River in central Chile has a temperate climate, excellent white water, spectacular gorges and waterfalls, and Mapuche settlements, making it one of the most exciting rivers in the Andes to run.

Paragliding

In Rio de Janeiro, Brazil, you can paraglide tandem over Atlantic rainforest, soaring above the skyscrapers and landing at Pepino beach, São

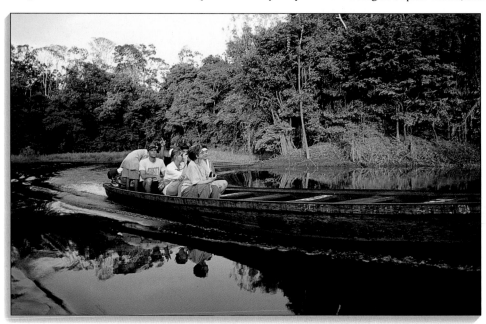

continent, Argentinian Tierra del Fuego. Most recommend taking detours off the Pan-American Highway, for example up into Cajamarca or the Cordillera Blanca in northern Peru, for the best views and to avoid traffic. For the less serious cyclist there are one-day cycle tours coasting down the flanks of the active Cotpaxi volcano or pedaling from the mountains of Baños to the jungle town of Puyo in Ecuador.

Rafting and kayaking

Beginners can descend the fun and safe class III rapids of the Upper Napo River, near Tena, Ecuador. More experienced rafters can run the Colca River rapids down the "Everest of river

Conrado. Paragliders are often seen flying off the coastal cliffs of Miraflores in Lima, Peru. The craze has also hit Mérida in Venezuela and Tucumán in Argentina. You can also have a go at ballooning in Rio from the Autodromo de Jacarepaguá, a half-hour ride ascending to 1,500 meters (4,921 ft).

Beach and watersports

Crazy *buggeiros* (buggy drivers) will take you out on their buggies along the beaches and sand dunes of Brazil. The noise may disturb people trying to relax on the beach, but others love the wild spins in the dunes and dodging incoming tides. Some of the most popular areas are the

Natal beaches of Río Grande do Norte. The massive sand dunes in the desert of Huacachina near Ica in southern Peru offer a different kind of dune fun. All you need is a board (cheap to rent) for sliding down the sand and to be prepared to walk to the top of the dunes.

Surfing

The Humboldt Current brings constant surf to the west coast of South America. Various towns along the Pacific coast such as Montañita, Ecuador and Huanchaco, northern Peru, have become hip places for foreign surfers to hang out. Puerto Chicama, set in the arid marine life. Morrocoy National Park is also a popular center for snorkeling and scuba diving off Venezuela's coastline.

Jungle trips

Dugout canoe trips along small tributary rivers in the Amazon basin are far more exciting than floats along the wide Amazon River where the banks are too far off to see any wildlife. Adventure trips into the Cuyabeno Nature Reserve in Ecuador, Manu National Park in southern Peru, and from Rurrenabaque, Bolivia offer real jungle experiences, with piranha fishing and hiking through swampy forests. ❑

coastal desert of northern Peru, has become famous for its long left point break.

Snorkeling and diving

You can snorkel with hammerhead sharks, rays, starfish, seals, and penguins off the Galápagos Islands, Ecuador; scuba diving is also possible. Along the Caribbean coast, palm-fringed beaches offer the perfect start for snorkeling and scuba diving. The small coral islands of Los Roques, off the coast of Venezuela, are teeming with

LEFT: bird-watching along the Ariau River, Amazonas state, Brazil. **ABOVE:** a party of trekkers pitch camp in an Andean valley.

SOUTH AMERICAN EXPLORERS CLUB

The South American Explorers Club is an invaluable resource for anyone planning adventure excursions and expeditions. This is a non-profit organization with clubhouses in Lima, Cusco, Quito, and Buenos Aires, offering travelers advice and various useful services. The clubhouses share information on members' experiences, and they are also a good place to meet people and compare notes with other travelers.

There is a yearly membership fee of US$50 ($80 for couples.) The SAEC can be contacted in the US at 126 Indian Creek Road, Ithaca, NY 14850; tel 607-277-0488; fax 607-277-6122; www.saexplorer.org

80

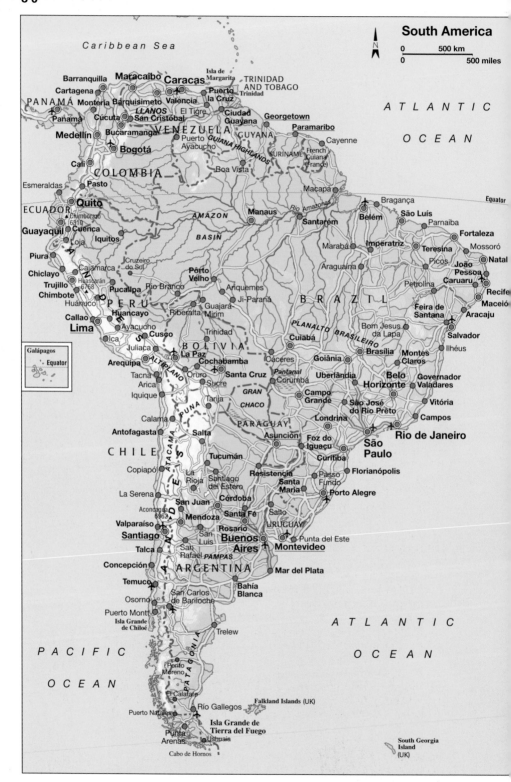

PLACES

*A detailed guide to the whole of South America, with major
sites cross-referenced by numbers to the maps*

First-time visitors may be daunted at the range of sights and new
experiences on offer in this diverse region. On a short visit it's
best to confine yourself to a limited geographical area, or to
certain types of experience, and there are many to choose from: rainforest expeditions, archeological tours, adventure sports, tropical
beach life, subantarctic forays, music and nightlife, and much more.

To help you plan your South American itinerary, we have divided
the subcontinent into four sections, devoting a chapter to each country.
We start at the north coast: Colombia, Venezuela, Guyana, Suriname,
and French Guiana, countries which run from west to east. Colombia
and Venezuela have an abundance of tropical white-sand beaches as
well as large modern cities. All of these countries have densely
forested interiors which harbor a plethora of exotic species and are
home to some of the world's most traditional communities.

Next, we come to the countries of the Andean Highlands, Peru
and Bolivia, linked by enormous Lake Titicaca, and Ecuador. In this
region – also in Colombia – are found the treasures of fascinating
ancient civilizations, as well as the distinctive living cultures of the
Andean people. These countries are also known for their natural
diversity, with mountains, tropical lowlands, and desert. Ecuador in
particular is a Mecca for wildlife enthusiasts, who flock to the famous
Galápagos Islands, 970 km (600 miles) off its coast.

From the Andes we move east to Brazil, which sprawls over an
area nearly half the size of all South America. Everything in Brazil
seems to be on a large scale: its massive Amazon rainforest in the
north, the huge and vibrant cities of the east coast, its passion for
football, sensual music and dance culture, and of course its world-
famous carnival.

Finally we head south, to the Southern Cone, where long, thin
Chile lines the west coast from tropical to subantarctic latitudes. The
Atlantic coast is covered by small Uruguay and huge Argentina,
which shares the Lake District, Patagonia, and the island of Tierra del
Fuego with Chile. Landlocked Paraguay, directly north of Argentina,
is also bordered by Bolivia and Brazil. The Southern Cone countries are characterized by large urban centers, wide open spaces,
sheep and cattle ranching, and a pioneering tradition.

The tiny Chilean islands of Juan Fernández lie 670 km (415 miles)
west of Valparaíso, and 3,790 km (2,355 miles) west of the Chilean
coast lies Easter Island, one of the most isolated inhabited islands
in the world, and a colony of Chile since 1888. Some 500 km (300
miles) east of Argentinian Patagonia lie the chilly Falkland Islands
(Islas Malvinas), Great Britain's most far-flung colony.   ❏

PRECEDING PAGES: Moreno Glacier, Los Glaciares National Park, Argentina; the
Amazon rainforest; the colonial city of Potosí, Bolivia.

THE NORTH COAST

*Great adventures start here – on the balmy Caribbean coast,
or in the remotest reaches of the rainforest*

Hot palm-fringed beaches, languid lifestyles, and fast nightlife characterize South America's northern Caribbean coast, but just inside the coastal belt are miles of tropical rainforest, and mountain ranges high enough to provide some cool respite in these equatorial zones. Both Colombia and Venezuela attracted gold-seekers in colonial times, and later fortunes were made from Venezuela's oil, or "black gold", while in Colombia it was drugs that made fortunes – and unfortunate headlines. Today, gold and diamond hunters are causing controversy in Venezuela's rainforest.

The people who live in the highland regions are mostly mestizos – mixed European and Amerindians – while on the coast, African heritage bears testimony to the slavery of colonial times. In Guyana, Suriname, and French Guiana, fascinating communities of African descent have settled in the interior, living in the traditional manner of their ancestors. There are also Amerindian communities in these regions and in Venezuela also, some of whom were unknown to the rest of the world until the 1960s.

Colombia, in the northwest, is notorious for its guerrilla networks and urban violence, but most of the country is safe for visitors, and it is becoming an increasingly popular destination among tourists for its friendly people, breathtaking scenery, and exciting dance culture. Colombia has some remarkable historical sites, including the ancient ruins of San Agustín *(see page 99)*, the Spanish fortress city of Cartagena *(see page 103)*, and the finest gold museum on the continent *(see page 94)*, which is in the capital city, Bogotá.

Venezuela is an oil-rich country with beautiful beach resorts, many of which surround the paradise island of Margarita *(see page 120)*. Venezuela is also a naturalist's dream, with some magnificent wildlife and dramatic scenery. The landscape of the central regions around Mérida and Trujillo *(see page 116)* is alpine and picturesque, with many outdoor sports on offer in the hills. The remote Guayana region *(see page 121)*, where the world's highest waterfall, Angel Falls *(see page 122)* cascades, is characterized by enormous sheer rock formations, golden savannah, and dense jungle.

East of Venezuela lie three smaller and less well-known countries – Guyana *(see page 127)*, Suriname *(see page 130)*, and French Guiana *(see page 132)*. These sparsely populated lands mainly attract visitors who want to explore their extensive rainforest hinterlands, inhabited by people who lead very distinctive and traditional lives. All five continents are represented in the populations of these countries, due to their histories as plantation outposts for three different world empires. ❑

PRECEDING PAGES: young boy in a colorful Caribbean restaurant.
LEFT: a perfect morning on a perfect Venezuelan beach.

COLOMBIA

Despite its initial notoriety as the land of El Dorado and latterly the drugs capital of the world, this is still a beautiful, friendly country of enormous natural diversity and historical treasures

Map on page 90

olombia has gained a fearsome reputation as the world's foremost producer of cocaine and for relentless violence and civil unrest. This, however, tells only part of the story of a country, where myth and modernity mingle to produce a diversity of culture which can be matched by few other countries. This is where the myth of El Dorado and the lure of untold riches caught the imagination of the Spanish conquistadors. Miners still pursue this dream, in search of emeralds as well as gold. Modern and outward-looking on the surface, the architectural and social legacy of Spanish colonial rule is here for all to see, as well as the remains of some of the great pre-Columbian civilizations.

Geographically, Colombia is the fourth-largest country in South America and is unique in having both a Pacific and Atlantic coast. In the south lies the forbidding Amazon jungle. Three *cordilleras* (mountain ranges) stretch north from the southern border with Ecuador to meet the lowland plains of the Caribbean. Most of the country's 44 million inhabitants live in the central region, which incorporates the capital, Santa Fé de Bogotá, set high amid the mist and rain of the eastern *cordillera*, and the two modern cities of Medellín and Cali. In between the *cordilleras* lie the valleys of the Cauca and Magdalena rivers, the most fertile agricultural areas. Eastern Colombia is made up of vast, largely uninhabited grasslands known as *Los Llanos*, stretching down to the Orinoco basin. The northern Sierra Nevada of Santa Marta is the highest coastal mountain range in the world. On a clear day you can stand on a Caribbean beach and see snow-capped mountains.

PRECEDING PAGES:
Bogotá by night.
LEFT: Bogotá
Cathedral, Plaza
Bolívar. **BELOW:**
Puerta del Reloj,
Cartagena.

While Bogotá is undoubtedly the cultural center of the country, each region has developed a distinct identity that is reflected in almost every strand of life. Musical styles range from the traditional string-based forms of the Andes to the accordion-led *vallenato* and *cumbia* of the Caribbean coast. One of the country's most popular figures is the Nobel Prize-winning writer Gabriel García Márquez with his particular brand of "magical realism". Other writers such as Alvaro Mutis are less well known but have helped place Colombian literature firmly on the map.

Soccer is by far the most popular sport; the country has also produced several world-class cyclists.

Colombia's exports include coffee, oil, emeralds, cut flowers, bananas, coal, and small quantities of gold. The population is predominantly mestizo, although there are sizable Afro-Caribbean populations on the Caribbean and Pacific coasts and around Cali, and more than 50 indigenous groups.

The turbulent past

Colombia has a turbulent political history. The 19th century was marked by 50 insurrections, eight civil

Colombia

0   100 km
0   100 miles

N

Caribbean   Sea

PANAMA
Istmo
del
Darién

Golfo
de
Panamá

PACIFIC

OCEAN

COLOMBIA

VENEZUELA

LLANOS

ECUADOR

BRAZIL

wars and several constitutions. The most violent civil war, the War of the Thousand Days, began in 1899, but the ensuing bloodshed and loss of 130,000 lives wrought few changes. The government remained in the hands of a criollo (European) minority who paid scant attention to the mestizos, mulattos, blacks, and Amerindians who formed the bulk of the population.

Meanwhile, the United States took advantage of Colombia's chaos to foment a secessionist movement in Panama, then a Colombian state. Soon afterwards, work began on the Panama Canal. Before receiving the Nobel Peace Prize, President Theodore Roosevelt boasted: "I took the Canal Zone and let Congress debate." The Colombian Government grudgingly accepted the loss in 1921.

The United Fruit Company of the United States created huge banana plantations along the coast, paying starvation wages and, in 1928, ending a long- running strike by using the Colombian Army to machine-gun unionists. As the banana boom died, coffee became the new hope for the economy, but the pattern of large plantations repeated itself. Small fluctuations in the world price would devastate whole areas of the countryside.

Map on page 90

By the end of the 1980s, Medellín drugs cartel boss Pablo Escobar had an estimated wealth of US$3 billion, making him the 14th richest man in the world, according to Forbes magazine.

Unprecedented brutality

In 1948, Jorge Eliécer Gaitán, a popular Liberal politician pushing for real political change, was gunned down in the streets of Bogotá. A spontaneous explosion of frustrations known as *La Violencia* (the violence) ensued, bringing angry crowds to the streets of the capital (the *Bogotazo*). Civil war in the countryside followed, with fighting between peasants, police, and soldiers reaching unprecedented levels of brutality. At least 300,000 people lost their lives. By 1953, armed peasant groups were beginning to develop a clear revolutionary philosophy. The Liberals and Conservatives quickly united in fear of a communist advance. In 1957, they agreed to share power for the next 16 years. Once again, the same politicians were back in power, ensuring that nothing would really change. Meanwhile, the various peasant armies in the countryside dragged on their battle with the armed forces, a fight that continues to this day, giving Colombia the dubious honor of having the oldest guerrilla forces in the continent.

Sporadic efforts to bring peace and greater democracy failed in the early 1980s, when the M-19 guerrilla group took over the Palace of Justice, central Bogotá. In the ensuing battle, more than 100 people lost their lives, including 11 judges of the Supreme Court.

BELOW: the *Bogotazo*, 1948.

Drug economy

The presidency of Virgilio Barco (1986–1990) opened the way for full competition in democratic elections but the government now had a battle against a new force – the Medellín drug cartel headed by Pablo Escobar that controlled 80 percent of the world traffic in cocaine; this illegal trade undoubtedly helped the economy.

Escobar died in a hail of bullets in 1993, putting more business in the hands of the Cali barons. Over the next two years the authorities had a number of successes, not least when the treasurer of the Cali cartel gave himself up to the US Drug Enforcement Adminstration. Among the damaging claims he made was that President Samper's 1994 election campaign was funded by US$6 million of drugs money. Samper's term of office was dogged by these accusations, but he managed to survive an investigation relatively unscathed. The country suffered a recession and unemployment rose, while left-wing guerrillas, right-wing paramilitaries, and the security forces fought on, and ordinary Colombians suffered.

Andres Pastrana won the presidency in 1998, promising economic regeneration and peace. To fight drug problems, Pastrana's government introduced the "Plan Colombia", costing US$7.5 billion – partly financed by the US and the European Union – but with little success. In 2002, right-wing lawyer Alvaro Uribe, whose campaign was supported by the Bush administration, won a landslide victory, and vowed to get tough on FARC (the Marxist rebels). In 2005 reduced jail terms were offered to paramilitaries who turned in their arms. Uribe was re-elected in 2006 following an amendment to the Constitution allowing presidents to serve up to two consecutive four-year terms. Although the peace talks have made progress, violence and kidnapping are still rife; visitors should avoid public transport at night and seek official advice before visiting what is otherwise a beautiful and fascinating country.

Bogotá, capital and intellectual hub

Shrouded by clouds in the midst of the northern Andes (and beset by air pollution), the city of **Bogotá ❶** grew 20-fold in the second half of the 20th century. Layers of history peel away like the rings of an onion: outlying slums give way to towering skyscrapers of polished steel and glass; grand government palaces tower over quaint English mansions. The center is colonial Spanish with flower-covered courtyards and regal monuments of stone and weathered brass.

BELOW: modern sculpture in Bogotá.

This highland city, 2,642 meters (8,670 ft) above sea level, is often viewed with incomprehension by people of the Colombian coast, who see its inhabitants as cold and aloof. Reflecting a popular view, Gabriel García Márquez once described Bogotá as "a gloomy city where on ghostly nights the coaches of the viceroys still rattled through the cobbled streets."

The image has never worried *bogotanos*, who see themselves as intellectual, cultured, and cosmopolitan. Anything and everything can be found in Bogotá's chaotic avenues: opulent restaurants, homeless children, vendors selling emeralds, peasants in ponchos, endless traffic jams, and walls covered with graffiti. Above all, it is the intellectual hub of Colombia, a place where the Iberoamerican Theater Festival, the largest of its kind in South America, is held every two years. You will find dozens of theaters, vibrant university life, classic museums, bookshops, and avant-garde art galleries, all joined in a creative tumult.

Orientation

Bogotá's El Dorado airport is impressively efficient, with the world's third-largest landing field. Miles of glasshouses surround the airport, growing some of Colombia's lesser-known exports – flowers.

The best view of the city is from the top of **Cerro de Montserrate**, which can be reached by funicular railway and cable car. On weekends, *bogotanos* stroll to the summit to enjoy the view, join the Holy Mass, and pray to the statue of *El Señor Caído* (the Fallen Christ). Below, the city is arranged in a grid pattern, with numbered *calles* running east–west and *carreras* running north–south. On the way down, call in at the **Quinta de Bolívar** (open Tues–Sun), a magnificent colonial mansion with expansive gardens, once the home of Simón Bolívar. It is full of paintings depicting Bolívar's life as well as many of his personal effects.

To the west of the city, the **Jardín Botánico Jose Celestino Mutis** are the nation's botanic gardens (open daily). The extensive grounds have an impressive collection of Colombian flora.

The city center

In 1538, three conquistadors met at what is now the heart of the old city, the **Plaza de Bolívar**, to found a town in the fertile lands of the native Muisca people. Despite killing off the locals and later each other with surprising rapidity, their outpost grew, and became capital of Gran Colombia. The plaza has a statue of Bolívar, the Liberator, at its center. To the south, the **Capitolio Nacional**, where Congress sits, looks like a classic Greek temple. Beyond is the **Casa de Nariño** (president's residence), sacked in 1948 during the *Bogotazo* uprising. Try to catch the changing of the guards (Mon, Wed, Fri, & Sun 5pm), whose uniforms were modeled on pre-World War I Prussian outfits, complete with shiny silver spikes on their helmets.

On the western side of the plaza is the **Catedral**, which was begun in 1565, destroyed by an earthquake two centuries later and only completed after Colombia's independence. Alongside are the **Capillo del Sagrario** and the sumptuous

Map on page 90

Painted interior, Puracé National Park, near Popayán (see page 99).

BELOW: hotel interior, Villa de Avila, near Bogotá.

A Golden Heritage

Protected like Fort Knox, the **Museo del Oro** (Gold Museum; Calle 16, 5–41, tel: 01-343 2221, www.banrep.org/museo; open Tues–Sun) in the heart of Bogotá is unsurpassed. Its collection of bracelets, earrings, masks, statues, and rings runs to more than 36,000 pieces from a dozen pre-Columbian cultures, all revealing a mastery of technique that leaves modern jewelers astounded.

Even before many of its pieces were revealed to be false, the Gold Museum in Lima was a pale collection in comparison to this one. This is largely due to the impatience of the gold-crazed Spanish conquistadors, who were too busy plundering the Inca Empire to the south to search deep below the surface of the earth for the occasional piece of jewelry from long-forgotten cultures. Thus the great art of the Incas and other Peruvian cultures, easily robbed by the Spaniards, was melted down into gold bars to be shipped back to the royal coffers, while the jewelry of the Colombian cul-

tures was left to be discovered by the archeologists of later years and also, sadly, by the ever-present *guaqueros* or grave robbers who have scoured the countryside for generations.

The metalworking tradition of the Americas developed from the middle of the 2nd millennium BC up to the 16th century. The gold technology of ancient Colombia is remarkable, embracing all the known gold-working techniques then available in the New World. Its diversity is extraordinary: each of the cultures, isolated by the country's wild and inhospitable geography, developed its own peculiar style.

Hammering was the most primitive technique for making gold objects, although great skill is required to manage the metal. Some cultures in Colombia developed smelting, using combinations of alloys to strengthen the gold. Joining techniques were perfected to connect sheets of gold into more complex figures, and it is probable that the technique of lost-wax casting – using molds of wax models which dissolve on contact with the alloy – was first developed in Colombia.

Pre-Columbian people used gold for decoration and religious rites, recognizing the value of a metal that did not tarnish. Clear guidelines were laid down as to who could and could not wear the metal, while in some areas it was also used as an item for trading.

Run by the government-owned Banco de la República, the Museo del Oro is in the Parque de Santander. On the first level there is an excellent model of La Ciudad Perdida, the lost city of the Taironas *(see page 102)*.

One of the museum's prize possessions is a tiny boat created by the Muisca people, showing the ritual of throwing gold into Lake Guatavita as an offering to the gods, while the chief gilded himself with gold, giving rise to the first myth of "El Dorado."

The climax of any visit is the huge strong-room on the top floor. Only 20 people at a time are allowed to enter the room, which is in complete darkness, until lights are turned up to reveal more than 12,000 pieces, almost blinding in their brilliance. Atmospheric piped music transports visitors to the mysterious golden world, the reality of which can now only be imagined. ❏

LEFT: native Muisca turn their king into "El Dorado", the Gilded One.

Teatro Colón, the city's principal theater, which can only be visited by guided tour (Tues–Sat on the hour, except during performances).

Map on page 90

The colonial quarter

A short stroll from the Plaza de Bolívar takes you to Bogotá's colonial quarter, **La Candelaria**. Single-story whitewashed buildings seem to creep up a hillside, their red tile roofs and decaying cupolas stretching out to the city center.

Like all of South America's colonial cities, Bogotá has a wealth of religious art. **Iglesia de Santa Clara** (Calle 9/Carrera 8), built during the 17th century, has a sumptuous interior with works by the most famous of Bogotá's painters at the time, Gregorio Vásquez de Arce y Ceballos. On a less sublime note, history records that the church became notorious for the kidnapping of several novices – on one occasion Vásquez himself was implicated and imprisoned.

The **Museo de Botero** (Calle 12 No. 4-41; open Mon–Sat 9am–7pm, Sun 10am–5pm), right next to the **Luís Angel Arango Library**, offers a large collection of Fernando Botero's masterpieces as well as works by Monet, Renoir, Dalí, Matisse, and others. Nearby, on Carrera 1A No. 18A-10, is the campus of the **University of the Andes**.

To get a taste of the flourishing emerald business, head for the corner of Avenida Jiménez and Carrera 7. Colombia controls 60 percent of the world's production of these precious gems, and fortified shops sell them to travelers with a few thousand dollars to spare. Emeralds are graded by their brilliance, color, and purity, but beware of fakes.

Bogotá's most famous and unmissable museum is the **Museo del Oro** *(see opposite)*. The **Museo Nacional** (open Tues–Sun) is housed in the Panopticon building, which was designed as a prison by Englishman Thomas Reed in the early 19th century, and built so that the 200 cells could be observed from a single vantage point. It was used as a prison until 1946, and has been meticulously restored. Each corridor displays a different episode from Colombian history. The lower level is devoted to art.

Cathedral of salt

Traveling from Bogotá along the North Highway through 48 km (30 miles) of lush countryside, an excursion can be made to the **Cathedral of Zipaquira** (open Tues–Sun), carved out of salt. The salt mines had been worked for centuries by the local people when the Spanish took them over. By the 1920s, such a large cavern had been dug that the Banco de la República decided to build a cathedral inside. Cut from a mountainside above the small town of Zipaquira, a tunnel leads into a sulfur-laden darkness. Finally an altar appears silhouetted in the distance: the cathedral is 25 meters (78 ft) high and has held more than 10,000 people at one time, but the walls are black, giving the unsettling sensation of walking through space. Despite the color, they are 75 percent pure salt – as can be affirmed by a quick taste – and mining is still going on elsewhere in the mountain. Colombians will proudly tell you that the mountain could keep the world supplied with salt for more than 100 years.

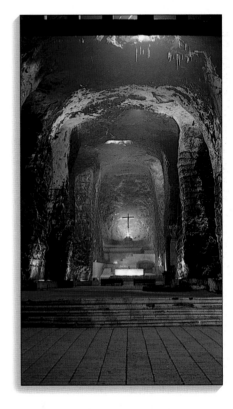

BELOW: altar of the Salt Cathedral, Zipaquira.

Medellín's annual
flower festival in
mid-August is one of
the most colorful
events in Colombia.

The other side of Medellín

Four hundred kilometers (250 miles) northwest of Bogotá is **Medellín** ❷, Colombia's second-largest city and the capital of Antioquia province. The city has done its best to shed its infamous image as murder and kidnap capital of the world and the home of the country's main drug cartel. Violence is less common than it was, but it is still a place where foreign visitors should be careful. Medellín is sometimes known as the "city of eternal spring" due to its pleasant climate. Residents have a reputation for being passionate about most things, including business, food, and enjoyment. One of the best ways to see the city is on the metro, much of which runs above street level. Don't expect too much in the way of colonial architecture – Medellín is above all a modern city – but the red-brick cathedral on **Parque Bolívar** is interesting. There is a permanent exhibition of the work of Colombia's best-known sculptor and artist, Fernando Botero, in the **Parque San Antonio** (Calle 46/Carrera 46).

Bananas and coffee

For a more relaxed pace, head northwest on the road toward Turbo to **Santa Fé de Antioquia**. Set among rolling hills, Santa Fé is a beautifully preserved colonial town. Two-story houses with brightly painted balconies line the streets. At weekends people travel in from the countryside, often on *chivas* – open-sided buses covered in gaudy paintings. From Santa Fé the road continues northward to the port of **Turbo** ❸ in the banana-growing region of **Urabá**. Unless you are going to the World Heritage Site of **Parque National Los Katíos** this area is best avoided. A few travelers pass through heading overland to Panama but this is not recommended as armed groups operate in this region.

BELOW: coming
home from market,
San Agustín.

South of Medellín lies the main coffee-growing region, the *zona cafetera*. Coffee remains Colombia's biggest export and almost all the hillsides around here are dotted with small coffee farms. **Manizales ❹**, some 270 km (168 miles) south of Medellín, is regarded as the capital of the coffee-growing zone. It is a modern city, founded in the mid-19th century when Antioquian farmers migrated south in search of new agricultural land. The city suffered several fires and earthquakes in the early 20th century, but its huge cathedral survived. Its streets are built on steep hills – strolling can be tiring. From Manizales you can gain access to **Parque National Los Nevados** via the village of **La Enea**. This is a trekker's paradise, but take local advice about routes. The park's highest peak is the **Volcán Nevado del Ruíz**, which erupted in 1985, wiping out the town of Armero on the other side of the cordillera.

Map on page 90

From Manizales the road to Bogotá passes through **Honda ❺**, a picturesque colonial town and weekend resort on the Río Magdalena. Directly south of Honda is **Ibagué ❻**, a rapidly expanding, but still pleasant, industrial city.

Salsa city

Going west from Ibagué the main road ascends steeply to cross the central cordillera. The pass can be freezing cold and for much of the year it is shrouded in mist. The Pan-American Highway then heads south and descends into the fertile valley of the Río Cauca where sugar, rice, and cotton are grown, providing important sources of income for **Cali ❼**, Colombia's third-largest city.

Cali was founded in 1536 but remained relatively small until the early 20th century when, with the arrival of the railway and the growth of the sugar industry, the city expanded at an unprecedented rate. Today it is the most important

Cali is famous for its nightlife, in particular its salsa scene. The city's annual festival is held between Christmas and New Year, with bullfighting, beauty contests, and impromptu salsa parties.

LEFT: mysterious statue in the Magdalena Valley. **RIGHT:** the muddy streets of San Agustín.

Fruit and vegetable market, Popayán.

BELOW: Cali: drug money is often laundered through construction projects.

commercial center in southeast Colombia, and this is reflected in the modern architecture and high-rise office buildings around the city center. When the drug cartels of Cali were partly broken up during the mid 1990s, the city declined somewhat, as unemployment and crime soared. There are several interesting colonial churches such as **San Francisco** (Carrera 6/Calle 10) and **La Merced** (Carrera 4/Calle 7), as well as **La Ermita**, in Gothic-style but built in the 1930s, the star of numerous postcards of the city. A short walk north from the center is the church of **San Antonio**, built in the mid-18th century on a hill, the **Colina de San Antonio**, with good city views. In the main square, **Parque Caicedo**, tall, arching palm trees can provide shade from the heat and humidity that smothers the city during the day. At night, fanned by cooling winds, the city comes alive and its numerous dance clubs can be heard from miles away.

For a more relaxing pace, visit one of several haciendas (farm estates) north of the city. One of the most interesting is **El Paraíso**, a beautifully preserved colonial mansion where the writer Jorge Isaccs wrote *María*, a highly regarded work of romantic realism. The house and its garden have been turned into a museum (open daily except Mon). Nearby is the hacienda of **Piedechinche** with a sugar refinery and sugar museum (open daily except Mon). The haciendas can be visited on a tour with a Cali travel agent, or take a bus to Amaime on the road between Buga and Palmira and walk from there (but don't travel alone).

Traveling northwest from Cali for 120 km (75 miles) takes you to the Pacific coast port of **Buenaventura ❽**. The town looks fairly ramshackle, but some of the country's best salsa musicians were born here, so there is usually something going on at night. From here, launches run up the coast to the fishing villages of **Juanchaco** and **Ladrilleros**, which have dark sandy beaches.

A few hours south of Cali by road is the city of **Popayán ❾**, founded in 1536 following a brutal campaign to exterminate the indigenous Pubenza. The town prospered in colonial times due to its location on the road between Lima, Quito, and Cartagena. In 1983 its Holy Week processions ground to a halt when a massive earthquake struck the region, reducing most of the city's oldest buildings to rubble. Almost all have been painstakingly restored. One of the most successful restorations is the white cathedral on the main square, the **Parque Caldas**. Behind the altar there is an impressive statue of the Madonna. Other churches worth visiting include **La Encarnación** (Calle 5/Carrera 5), **San Agustín** (Calle 7/Carrera 6), and **Santo Domingo** (Carrera 5/Calle 4). Popayán's Holy Week processions are famous throughout the Catholic world.

Silvia, a small village in the hills north of Popayán, is home to the culturally distinctive Guambiano, who come to sell their goods at the market on Tuesdays. Just northeast of Popayán, near **San Andrés de Pisimbalá**, is the National Archeological Park of **Tierradentro**. This World Heritage Site is made up of a number of pre-Hispanic burial chambers, some of which have motifs and figures carved onto the walls, and stone statues. Little is known about the culture that built the tombs, but the statues are believed to have been carved at a later date, probably around the same time as those further east at San Agustín.

Map on page 90

Some of Colombia's richest and most aristocratic families lived in Popoyán, and the city proudly proclaims to have produced 11 Colombian presidents.

Natural beauty and ancient wonders

From Popayán a poor road goes east to **Parque Nacional Puracé**, an outstandingly beautiful spot with volcanoes, lakes, waterfalls, thermal springs, and many species of wildlife, including bears, condors, and tapirs. The park's altitude, from 2,500 to 4,800 meters (8,200 to 15,750 ft), accounts for the natural diversity. There are tourist facilities at **Pilimbalá**, at the northern end of the park.

Southeast of Popayán, is **San Agustín ❿**, a village famous for its ancient stone statues, mysterious remnants of a lost culture from one of the most important archeological sites in South America. Layers of red-tiled roofs lead past a church tower to the surrounding hills, covered with banana trees. The mountains beyond are a rich green because it rains every day for nine months of the year in a light, erratic drizzle. The village, with its laid-back atmosphere and beautiful surroundings, has long attracted tourists. Transport is mostly by horse: on every corner, cowboys in ponchos and wide-brimmed hats stand by their trusty steeds.

Baffling figures

The statues of San Agustín have continued to baffle archeologists. Around 500 figures have been found in the surrounding Magdalena Valley: some resemble masked monsters, others eagles, jaguars, or frogs. Nobody knows who carved the statues or for what reason. Even today, investigators can only date the civilization from between the 6th and 12th centuries. Some experts argue that it was earlier, others that it grew later and was suppressed by the Incas, since this was the northernmost point of their empire.

Some of the statues are arranged neatly in archeological parks near the village. Within walking distance

BELOW: selling lottery tickets, Cali.

are the **Bosque de los Estatuas**, with more than 35 figures, and the **Alto de los Idolos**, where the largest statue is 7 meters (23 ft) high. Nearby are four *mesitas*, ancient burial sites with mounds, statues, and funeral temples. Most exciting to visit are the statues deeper in the countryside. Many can be reached only on horseback as the paths are difficult and often knee-deep in mud, though the landscape is spectacular.

Cradle of liberty

North from Bogotá the rugged eastern cordillera runs for just under 1,000 km (620 miles) to the modern industrial city of **Bucaramanga** , known for a local delicacy – the *hormiga culona*, an edible species of ant. Before the Spanish arrived much of this area was populated by the native Muisca. There is little evidence left of their culture but the wild, mountainous landscape is arguably the most dramatic in Colombia.

North of Bogotá, the first major city you encounter is **Tunja** . The Spanish founded the city in 1539, but there was a settlement here long before that. A monument and bridge commemorate the Battle of Boyacá, the decisive battle in the independence struggle, which was fought just south of the city. For a short time after independence, Tunja was the capital of Nuevo Granada. Simón Bolívar referred to it as his "cradle and workshop of liberty." The capital shifted south when a number of important families moved to Bogotá. A measure of Tunja's importance during colonial times lies in the number of churches that were built – anyone interested in religious art should visit Tunja. The cathedral contains several paintings by Gregorio Vásquez and Ricardo Acevedo. Also worth visiting are, between calles 19 and 20, the churches of

BELOW: villages in the Nariño region, southwestern Colombia.

Santo Domingo (Carrera 11), with its ornate wooden interior, and **Santa Clara** (Carrera 7), with a 16th-century convent.

Tunja is a good base to explore the small villages and towns scattered around the Boyacá highlands. One of the most popular is **Villa de Leyva** which, with cobbled streets lined by low, whitewashed, tile-roofed houses, has become a national monument. The main focus of the town is the wide central square with a museum dedicated to the work of well-known painter and sculptor Luis Alberto Acuña (open daily). The town is deeply rooted in national history. Antonio Nariño, an intellectual and statesman who led the call for independence at the end of the 18th century, lived and translated Thomas Jefferson's *Declaration of the Rights of Man* at No. 19-58, Carrera 9.

There are several other buildings worthy of note, including the **Carmelite monastery** and its church opposite in the Plazuela del Carmen. But what makes this town special is its unhurried atmosphere, particularly during the week. From Villa de Leyva buses and *colectivos* leave for nearby towns like **Ráquira**, known for its pottery; and **Chiquinquirá**, where pilgrims from all over Colombia converge to visit a painting of the Virgin, supposedly Colombia's oldest painting, by Alonso de Narváez. From Chiquinquirá, the lawless emerald mining towns of **Muzo** and **Coscues** can be reached, although the journey, on an unpaved road, can be arduous in the rainy season.

From Tunja a twisting road goes northeast for 460 km (286 miles) to the Venezuelan border at **Cúcuta ⓭**. The scenery along the route is spectacular and passes through several whitewashed towns such as **Málaga ⓮** before arriving at **Pamplona**, which has one of the oldest universities in South America. The main road from Tunja goes north to **Santander**, a province filled with old

Map on page 90

Floral cowboy, Medellín flower festival.

BELOW: pueblo Paisa, near Medellín.

colonial towns, most notable of which are **San Gil**, **Baríchara**, and **Socorro**, from where the *comuneros* led the first revolt against the Spanish in 1781. This event is remembered in the town's **Casa de Cultura** (open daily), housed in a colonial mansion on Calle Real beside the brick cathedral.

The Caribbean coast

Arriving from Bogotá to Colombia's Caribbean coast is like stepping into a completely different world. It is as if they are two separate countries: one cool and remote, the other tropical and sensual.

A gateway to the coast and many attractions of the north is **Santa Marta ⓯**, capital of Magdalena province. One of the most pleasant cities in Colombia, it was founded by the Spaniards in 1525, but there are few colonial relics in the popular modern resort town. Visitors come here to loll in the sun along **El Rodadero beach**, considered one of the best in Colombia; to stroll up and down the tourist promenade while being bombarded with salsa; or simply sit in a pavement bar and enjoy the view across the bay to the rocky island of **El Morro**.

Santa Marta is a good jumping-off point to **Parque Nacional Tairona**, with its string of pristine and often deserted white-sand beaches. This stretch of jungle, once the territory of the native Tairona population, is at the foot of the **Sierra Nevada de Santa Marta**, a pyramid-shaped mountain that drops into the Caribbean Sea. Further east is the **Santuario de Flora y Fauna Los Flamencos**, a nature reserve which, as the name suggests, is full of pink flamingos.

Santa Marta is also the place to reach **La Ciudad Perdida**, the Lost City of the Tairona that was only found in 1975. Larger than Machu Picchu in Peru, the discovery is considered one of the most important of the 20th century in South

BELOW: classic Caribbean sunset.

America, confirming that the Tairona were not just accomplished craftsmen but built one of the largest cities on the subcontinent, with wide boulevards and road links. The city was discovered by *guaqueros* (grave robbers) in the tropical jungle of the Sierra Nevada. Calling it *El Infierno Verde* (Green Hell), they fought over the finds until the government intervened. In the absence of any written records, archeologists can only guess when the city was built – probably the 13th century – and what disaster led the inhabitants to disappear without trace. Today this legendary city can only be reached by a six-day trek.

Map on page 90

García Márquez country

The first image many foreigners have of South America comes from the Caribbean coast of Colombia, thanks to the works of author Gabriel García Márquez. His writings have preserved the life and history of the region, and today the small town of **Aracataca** where he was born and raised – and which he fictionalized as the town Macondo in his 1967 novel *One Hundred Years of Solitude* – can be visited for a glimpse of coastal life. Buses leave several times an hour from the Santa Marta terminal. Aracataca has a plaza with a statue of Bolívar, an old church tower, several shabby billiard halls and a couple of empty restaurants. Tucked away in a back street is a modest building with the sign "GGM Museum". In a garden full of chickens is the house where Márquez was born in 1928 – wooden, whitewashed, and without a stick of furniture.

A few hours south of Aracataca is the city of **Valledupar ⓰**. Founded in the mid-16th century, there is little evidence of its colonial past apart from the main square, where people sit around a giant mango tree to shelter from the searing midday heat. Every year this space becomes the focus of the country's attention during the festival of the Legend of the Vallenato. For five days at the end of April Colombia's top accordion players battle it out in Valledupar to be crowned King of the Vallenato, a popular style of music which originated here. The festivities are fueled by rum and large quantities of *aguardiente* ("fire water").

Cartagena, Spain's New World fortress

Of the many colonial jewels in South America, **Cartagena de Indias ⓱** is perhaps both the most romantic and the least known. Placed on the tropical Caribbean coast, saturated by heat, music, and feverish dreams, this fortress city of the Spaniards is a living museum. It is recognized internationally as a World Heritage Site. Just walking its streets recalls the days of bloodthirsty pirates, galleons full of bullion, and swordfights beneath the palm trees. Founded in 1533 by the first of Spain's scurvy-ridden conquistadors, the town quickly blossomed to become the main colonial port on the Caribbean and the gateway to the whole South American empire. But as the wealth plundered from the local populations piled up in galleons to be taken to Cádiz, the city became a target of every pirate and desperado cruising the Caribbean seas.

During the 16th century, Cartagena was besieged five times by buccaneers and cut-throats. The Spanish decided to create fortifications so powerful that the port would be impregnable. Stone ramparts and

Sir Francis Drake sacked Cartagena in 1586 and extorted a 10-million peso ransom from the inhabitants. This was shipped back to England for Queen Elizabeth, along with the bodies of several crocodiles, blasted from nearby swamps with cannons and stuffed with straw.

BELOW: taking a break on the Caribbean coast.

battlements were constructed over many decades, the like of which had never been seen in the Americas. The pirate attacks continued, but never with the same success – Cartagena was even able to survive several sieges by the English and the French.

Exploring the old city of Cartagena

Arriving from the airport, a highway passes along Marbella beach toward **Las Murallas**, the stone ramparts that still surround the old city. Many small forts, where cannons and other defensive weapons were placed to ward off sea attacks, remain intact. The colonial section of Cartagena is only a small part of the metropolis, but it contains enough relics to warrant several days' exploration.

Farmer stitching a saddle blanket, Antioquia province.

BELOW: fortress at San Fernando, Cartagena.

Facing the **Plaza de Bolívar** is the **Palacio de la Inquisición**, one of Cartagena's finest buildings. Its museum recalls the fearful proceedings of the Holy Inquisition, during which 12 people suffered a public auto-da-fé in the plaza. When Cartagena declared its independence, this palace was one of the first places that the angry crowd came to sack.

Adjoining the Plaza Bolívar is the fort-like cathedral. Three blocks south is the **Plaza de la Aduana**, once used as a parade ground for troops, and now based around a statue of Christopher Columbus (Cristobal Colón in Spanish). Call in at the **Museo de Arte Moderno** in the former Royal Customs House, then take a stroll under the **Puerta del Reloj**, which once linked the inner walled town to the poorer Getsemaní district by a drawbridge over a moat. Following the city wall closely around to the south, you will run into the **Iglesia y Convento de San Pedro Claver**, named after a Spanish monk who spent his whole life looking after African slaves. Nicknamed the "Slave of the Slaves", St Peter Claver

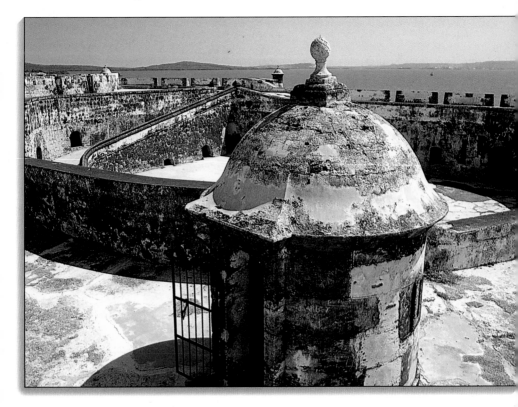

(1580–1654) was the first person to be canonized in the New World. Today the monastery is a haven of solitude and peace, with arched stone patios built around a garden of flowers and foundations.

Map on page 90

There are dozens of other colonial houses, churches, and monuments worth visiting in Cartagena. Drop in at the colonial **Casa de la Candelaria** – once a noble's mansion, now a restaurant but also open to non-diners – then stroll around the city walls to **Las Bovedas**, built two centuries ago as dungeons, with walls 15 meters (50 ft) thick. Today they are home to tourist shops and bars.

Barriers of stone

To keep their stolen gold extra secure, the Spanish built even more extraordinary fortifications in key points. Looming over the city from the San Lorenzo Hill is the impregnable **Castillo de San Felipe de Barajas**, a complicated system of batteries, tunnels, and hiding places engineered from massive chunks of stone. The tunnels, which can be visited, were constructed so that any sound would echo and warn guards of approaching soldiers. The view over the old city from the castle is one of the best in Cartagena.

At the entrance to Cartagena Bay is the **Fuerte de San Fernando**, a fort which can only be visited by water. A huge chain was hung between it and another outpost across the bay to prevent surprise attacks. Many films have been shot in its well-preserved interior. On top of a large hill behind the city is the **Convento de la Popa**. The Augustinians built a wooden chapel at the summit in 1607, soon replaced by a monastery with an image of the patron of Cartagena, La Virgen de la Candelaria.

Near the Puerta del Reloj is the city's dock area, **El Muelle de los Pegasos**, where you can sit at a juice stall and watch the port life go by. El Muelle is the departure point for tourist boats to the idyllic **Islas del Rosario** ⑱, just 45 minutes away. For a cheap seafood dinner, stroll up **Avenida Venezuela** and call in at the *ostrerias*, small booths selling delicious shrimp and oyster cocktails. For more sophisticated nightlife, head for **Bocagrande**, a resort suburb several minutes out of town by taxi, or the Old Town and Calle Arsenal.

Around Cartagena

Heading northeast along the coast is the large port city of **Barranquilla** ⑲, famous for its magnificent carnival held in February. **Mompóx**, 240 km (150 miles) south of Cartagena on an island in the Río Magdalena, is a UNESCO World Heritage Site. In the 18th century the Río Magdalena changed course, isolating Mompóx, which had flourished in the Spanish era as the river provided the most important line of communication between the interior and the north coast. The city now has some of the finest examples of colonial architecture in Colombia.

Of particular note is the yellow church of **Santa Barbara**, with a Moorish octagonal tower. The **Casa de Cultura** (open daily) stands beside the church of **San Agustín**, where crowds gather during the town's Easter processions. Buses and launches depart from here for the hot, dusty, and decaying town of **El Banco** ⑳. ❑

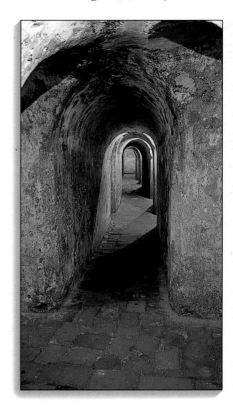

BELOW: Spanish tunnel inside the San Fernando Fortress, Cartagena.

VENEZUELA

*This young, vibrant, and varied country, at once Caribbean,
Andean, and Amazonian, has a wealth of fabulous natural treasures
for beachcombers and adventurers alike*

Map
on pages
110–11

Venezuela, led by its controversial president, Hugo Chávez Frías, has of late gained a reputation as a thorn in the side of the United States Government. Chávez's anti-globalization stance, his alternative vision for Latin America, and his ability to spend his oil revenue freely, have made headlines around the world. However, it would be a shame if the country only gained international attention for its politics. With its diverse geography, ranging from the snow-capped Andes to vast plains with sprawling cattle ranches, from quaint villages to modern metropolitan areas with non-stop nightlife, it offers a huge variety of destinations and experiences. Venezuela has immense natural beauty, with virgin tropical rainforests inhabited by indigenous tribes, the Guayana Region straddling ancient rock formations from which gush the world's highest waterfalls, and more Caribbean coastline than any other nation.

As one of the world's largest oil-producing countries, petroleum has been a key element in Venezuela's recent history. During six decades of boom, beginning in the 1920s, money flowed freely. With the seemingly bottomless pot of "black gold", agriculture was virtually abandoned as people left farms to get a piece of the pie in the principal cities. National industry atrophied as imports soared, and no one took note of corruption and neglect of the country's basic structure. But oil prices began to tumble in the early 1980s and, with the infamous "Black Friday", February 18, 1983, hard reality hit. The value of the national currency was slashed and exchange controls were imposed. The party was over, with the good times only returning in the early 2000s, albeit to a country radically changed.

The real crisis was not felt until Carlos Andrés Pérez returned for a second presidential term in 1989, riding on the popularity from his first time in office in 1974–79. His tough economic measures led to two bloody military coup attempts that year. Pérez survived, but on May 20, 1993, he was indicted on charges of corruption and was convicted in 1996.

Rafael Caldera, president 1969–74, was re-elected in 1994. Faced with mounting foreign debt, the failure of 17 financial institutions representing nearly half the total of the nation's deposits, massive capital flight, and the public's lack of confidence, the value of the bolívar was slashed and exchange controls imposed from June 1994 to April 1996. The devaluation of the currency hit Venezuelans hard.

Talk rather than action followed promised spending cuts, and the country's public debt increased. Plummeting real earnings and high unemployment have since placed the majority of Venezuelans below the poverty line. Robberies directed against the "haves" have turned them into prisoners of their privilege, living behind

PRECEDING PAGES:
Isla Margarita.
LEFT: Avenida
Bolívar, Caracas.
BELOW: taking it
easy in Ciudad
Bolívar.

Venezuela

e a
Grenada
St George's
anquilla

0   50 km
0   50 miles

Tobago

Isla de Margarita
Playa
Medina
Porlamar
Parque Nacional
Península de Paria
Carúpano
Cueva de
Guácharo
Cumaná
Caripe
**TRINIDAD
AND TOBAGO**
Port of Spain
Güiria
Golfo de Paria
Trinidad
San Fernando

N

Maturín
Pedernales
Santa
Bárbara
ntaura
Temblador
Los Güires
Tucupita
El Tigrito
**Delta del
Orinoco**

Boca
Grande

Puerto Ordáz
Ciudad
Bolívar
taco
Guri Dam
Los Castillos de
Guayana La Vieja
Ciudad Guayana
Upata
El Palmar
Bochinche
Matthews
Ridge
Port
Kaituma

Embalse
de Guri
La Paragua
Tumeremo
Cuyuni

El Dorado
G U Y A N A
km 88
Canaima
Salto
Angel
(Angel Falls)
Auyan
Tepui
Kavanayén
**Parque Nacional
Canaima**
Chinak
Merú
Kama
Merú
Pakaraima
Mountains

Río Paragua
Río Caroní

**L A G R A N
S A B A N A**
Roraima
2810
Quebrada
de Jaspe
Santa Elena
de Uairén
ama
La Línea

Río Surumu

SIERRRA DE PACARAIMA

Río Uraricoera

B R A Z I L
Boa Vista

Mazaruni

Orinoco
có
Caracaraí

Río Catrimani

Río Demini
Río Branco

Manaus

---

guarded doors. Meanwhile, violence among the poor in the barrios of Caracas is rife.

Since 1997, Venezuela has been on the difficult road to recovery: rebuilding national industry, trying to stimulate agriculture, reducing inflation, and moving to a free market economy. In 1998, Colonel Hugo Chávez Frías won the presidential election and overhauled Venezuela's political system. He was re-elected in July 2000 with 60 percent of the seats in a new unicameral parliament, amid claims of vote rigging. Despite enormous windfalls from the quadrupling in price of Venezuela's oil, falling inflation, and increased public spending, the president has only just begun to bridge the gap between rich and poor. In 2001, civil protests culminated in a nationwide strike. In 2002 the bolívar was devalued; a huge decrease in foreign investment, mounting military discontent, and a strike by medium- and large-scale businesses led to the president's forced resignation on April 12, although he was reinstated two days later.

After winning a mid-term referendum on his presidency in 2004, Chávez has promoted a wide range of controversial policies at home, including land reform, contracting thousands of Cuban doctors, and imposing reforms on the media. Internationally, he has been at the forefront of OPEC's pricing policies, has steered Venezuela into Mercosur, and has been a vociferous critic of George W. Bush's foreign policy. Seeking to counter the influence of the US in the hemisphere, he has signed trade deals (mainly for oil and gas) with neighboring nations and intervened in politics up and down the continent. In 2006 Chávez won a third term in office.

Caracas: city of fortune

The first view of the country for most visitors is El Litoral – the central coast location of Simón Bolívar International Airport and adjacent National Airport. This area was struck by disaster in 1999, when torrential rain turned gentle mountain streams into swollen rivers surging down ravines, picking up ancient trees, giant boulders, and tons of earth as they rushed to the sea. The idyllic landscape was all but ruined.

Inhabitants of Caracas are known as Caraqueños.

Venezuela's capital, **Caracas** ❶, is 27 km (43 miles) away across the coasta mountain range. **Macuto** and **Caraballeda**, some 40 minutes to the east, were obliterated, although both are now recovering.

The mountains of **Parque Nacional El Avila** form a dramatic backdrop fo Caracas, called home by some five million inhabitants. The hillsides surrounding the airport road and slopes ringing the metropolis are blanketed with haphazardly constructed *ranchos* (shanty towns), inhabited largely by illegal immigrants and poor rural folk who came to seek their fortune. The central valley and upscale res idential areas of the east and south show a modern, dynamic, and affluent side.

El Centro is the traditional heart of the city and **Plaza Bolívar** is the core o its historic zone, with treasures including the 19th-century **Capitolio**, the 17th century **Catedral** and adjacent **Museo Sacro** (open Tues–Sun). **Casa Nata** was the birthplace of South America's liberator, Simón Bolívar. Next door, there is military memorabilia in the **Museo Bolivariano** (both open Tues–Sun). **Con cejo Municipal** was the birthplace of Venezuela's call for independence. Visi the **Museo de Caracas** (open daily) inside, which has a display of miniature created by Raúl Santana depicting every aspect of criollo life at the end of the 19th century, along with paintings by the impressionist Emilio Boggio.

Casa Amarilla, formerly a jail and presidential residence, now houses the For eign Ministry. Facing the northwest corner of the plaza is the **Gobernación**, sea of government of the Distrito Federal. The **Iglesia de San Francisco**, dating from 1575, has walls lined with gorgeous gilded altars and is connected to the **Palaci de las Letras**, the academies of history, language, and science. Several block north of the cathedral is the striking pink and gray **Panteón Nacional** (ope Tues–Sun), resting place for over 130 of the nation's greatest heroes.

BELOW: hats and hammocks, Ciudad Bolívar.

The excellent colonial art museum, **Quinta de Anauco** (open Tues–Sun), in San Bernardino, is well worth a visit. Surrounded by lush gardens, this elegant building has been restored with outstanding art and furnishings.

Financial hub

Interspersed with colonial gems in the Centro are sleek glass-faced skyscrapers, harboring many of the nation's financial, business, and political movers and shakers. Shoppers here can delight in the nine-story gold center, **La Francia**, facing Plaza Bolívar, and small shops selling shoes, clothing, and jewelry stretching east from the plaza to the **La Hoyada** metro station.

Chuao has one of the city's largest shopping centers, housed in an attractive mall, **Centro Ciudad Comercial Tamanaco (CCCT)**, filled with top-of-the-range shops, restaurants, nightclubs, travel agencies, a supermarket, and a four-star hotel. Facing it is the distinctive **Cubo Negro** (black cube) office building, one of the many examples of attention-grabbing contemporary architecture in the city, with a dramatic hanging kinetic sculpture by Venezuelan artist Jesús Soto.

Traffic and parking are perennial headaches in Caracas but the fast, clean, economical subway system, the Metro de Caracas, takes you across the city in minutes. Though a slower option, there is also a non-stop flow of dirt-cheap buses that go everywhere. Taxis are numerous and inexpensive, but few drivers speak English, so have your destination written in Spanish if you can.

A few minutes east from the Centro is **Parque Central**. This massive urban renewal project has 53-story twin towers, seven 44-story apartments, and the outstanding **Museo de Arte Contemporáneo de Caracas Sofía Imber**, with sculp-

TIP

The best way to get around Caracas is by the metro (subway). To save money, buy *ida y vuelta* (round-trip tickets for one destination), *multi abono* (10 rides of any distance for a discounted rate), or *integrado* (metro plus metrobus).

LEFT: old and new in Caracas.
RIGHT: Los Caobos Park, Caracas.

Colonial facade,
Coro.

ture garden and restaurant. Visitors can go up to the 52nd floor of the East Tower for 360-degree views of the city. There is also a fabulous hands-on museum for children, **Museo de los Niños**, and the **Museo del Teclado**, a keyboard museum with weekly concerts. Nearby is the spectacular **Teatro Teresa Carreño** and the **Teatro Rajatabla**, home of a popular alternative theater group. Other attractions are three great museums (all open Tues–Sun): the **Museo de Ciencias Naturales**; the **Museo de Bellas Artes**, with international contemporary art; and the **Galería de Arte Nacional**, showing Venezuelan artists. Behind them is the sprawling **Los Caobos Park** and in the background the **Ibrahim bin Abdulazis al Ibrahim Mosque**, the largest in South America.

Continue on the metro to **Plaza Venezuela**, then walk east to **Chacaíto** along the kilometer-plus *gran avenida* of **Sábana Grande**. This wide pedestrian boulevard is lined with shops, cafés, street vendors, and chess tables, where office workers often spend their lunch hour. It is fun by day, but at night hookers and transvestites take over and the adjacent hotels are primarily rented by the hour.

A little further east, exit the metro at **Parque del Este** to explore the 80-hectare (200-acre) park by Brazilian landscape architect Roberto Burle Marx, with planetarium, mini-zoo, and artificial lake. The **Museo de Transporte** (open Wed–Sun) facing its east side is connected by walkway over the busy freeway.

Among the city's other parks, two blocks south of **Plaza Venezuela**, with a giant central fountain, is the **Jardín Botánico** (open daily), which has extensive gardens, an arboretum of some 100,000 trees, and sculptures by national artists. Or take the No. 2 spur of the metro from Capitolio to the **Zoológico** stop to visit the 486-hectare (1,200-acre) "no cages" **Parque Zoológico Caricuao.**

BELOW: Bahia Cata,
Henri Pittier
National Park.

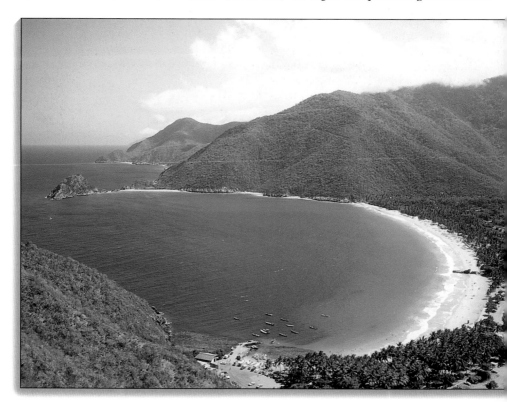

The greatest concentrations of upscale restaurants are found in the commercial zone of **Las Mercedes** and the shopping center of the same name, as well as at the flashy Centro San Ignacio mall. **La Candelaria**, east of the Centro, is a Spanish sector with many traditional restaurants and *tascas*, bars serving tapas.

Map on pages 110–11

West of Caracas

Colonia Tovar, about an hour away by car, is a village high in the mountains that was founded in 1843 by Germans from the Black Forest, who transplanted their architecture, language, cultural practices, farming tradition, and cuisine. On weekends, *caraqueños* jam the narrow streets lined with produce and crafts stands. It has numerous cozy hotels and a yearly international chamber music festival in March or April. **Maracay** ❷, 90 minutes west of Caracas via freeway, is the entry point for **Parque Nacional Henri Pittier**, Venezuela's oldest protected environmental zone (since 1937), renowned among bird-watchers for over 550 species seen here, and by non-birders for its winding scenic routes surrounded by bamboo groves, cloud forests, and mammoth vine-draped trees.

Entry via **El Limón** leads to the beautiful palm-lined arc of **Bahía de Cata**. A short distance before the park is **Ocumare de la Costa**, with various lodging options. Continuing past **Cata**, the beach of **Cuyagua** is a favorite for surfers. Follow the route via Las Delicias to reach the picturesque colonial village of **Choroní** and the coast at the fishing village of **Puerto Colombia**, with many *posadas* (guest houses), a few kilometers on. The broad, palm-shaded swimming beach is about 1 km (⅔ mile) to the east. Local fishermen offer boat transfers to the popular beaches of **Chuao** and **Cepe** from Puerto Colombia.

From **Valencia** ❸, Venezuela's manufacturing capital, take the road north for a 20-minute mountain drive to the coast, passing the hot springs of **Centro Termas Las Trincheras**. From here, turning east takes you to **Puerto Cabello**, one of Venezuela's most important ports. Here, a beautiful waterfront colonial zone faces **Castillo Libertador**, an impressive fort built in 1732. **Fortín Solano**, the last colonial fortification erected in Venezuela, completed in 1770, stands on a hill in the background.

Turning west at the coast brings you in 40 minutes to **Tucacas**, the first entrance to **Parque Nacional Morrocoy**. Alternatively, continue to another entrance via **Chichiriviche**, with the bonus of a drive through **Cuare Wildlife Refuge** where the flashiest inhabitants are scarlet ibis and a flock of some 20,000 flamingos. The park is also popular for its white sand, palm-fringed islands and keys. Boat shuttles are available from Tucacas and Chichiriviche.

The westbound coastal highway traverses desert plains to reach **Coro** ❹, which was declared a World Heritage City by UNESCO for its concentration of outstanding colonial structures, including an exceptional **Diocesan Museum**. A side trip north to the windswept **Paraguaná Peninsula** takes you past the towering sand dunes of **Parque Nacional Los Médanos de Coro** to **Adícora**, a windsurfer's paradise. Fans of colonial architecture can admire houses that demonstrate the Dutch influence of the nearby islands of **Curaçao** and **Aruba**.

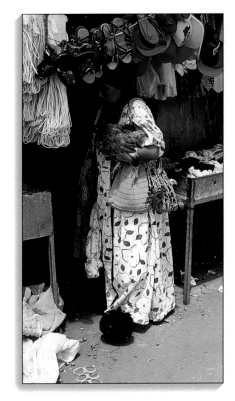

BELOW: Guajiro woman at a market north of Maracaibo.

TIP

For a fast route to
Táchira, take Highway
6 along the west side
of Lake Maracaibo,
following signs out
of town indicating
Machiques.

Source of the black gold

Arriving at the country's westernmost state, Zulia, one encounters **Lago Maracaibo**, the largest lake in South America (and one of the world's most valuable containing enormous oil reserves and some 40 percent of the country's gas reserves). Cross the **Rafael Urdaneta Bridge**, the longest pre-stressed concrete span in the world at the time of its construction, to reach the state capital **Maracaibo ❺**, Venezuela's second-largest city. Maracaibo is the center for the nation's oil industry, and is also populated by thousands of native Guajiro and Paraujano, the women proudly wearing traditional long flowing dresses.

Near the seven-block long **Paseo Ciencias** park is the colonial **Catedral** and the **Casa de Capitulación**. The **Basílica de Nuestra Señora de la Chiquinquirá** honors Zulia's beloved patron saint, nicknamed "La Chinita." **Calle Carabobo** (or Calle 94) is a street of colorful "Maracaibo-style" houses, now mainly shops and restaurants, and a huge municipal market restored and converted into the **Centro de Arte de Maracaibo Lia Bermúdez** (open daily). In the Santa Lucía district, along with good shops and popular restaurants, is the **Museo de Arte Contemporáneo del Zulia** (MACZUL; open Tues–Sun), the second-largest contemporary art museum in Latin America.

A cheap shuttle boat runs from El Moján to the colonial fort and extensive beach of **Isla San Carlos**. At nearby **Laguna de Sinamaica** boat excursions visit communities of Paraujano who live in houses built on stilts in the lagoon.

Where the Andes begin

The Andean states of **Táchira** and in particular **Mérida** and **Trujillo**, are the most picturesque in the country. Though accessible by air, this area should be

BELOW: drilling on
Lake Maracaibo.

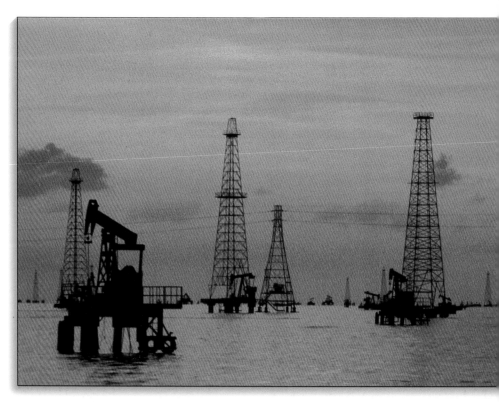

visited by car to appreciate the stunning landscapes of glacier-fed lakes bordered by colorful flowers. There are quaint villages with traditional architecture, and wayside restaurants where you can savor trout or smoked cheese on a wheat-flour *arepa* washed down with warm, spiked *ponche andino* or *calentado*.

Taking the Transandean Highway from the coast through **Barquisimeto** ❻, with side trips to the weavers' colony in **Tintorero** and to **Quibor**, known for its ceramics and ancient indigenous heritage, you will enter the area from **Guanare** ❼, in the heart of the central farmlands. Here, you can visit the impressive **Templo Votivo Nacional de la Virgen de Coromoto**, inaugurated in 1996 by Pope John Paul II and dedicated to Venezuela's patron saint.

Alternatively, go via **Boconó**, driving through coffee plantations, or approach from **Barinas** via **Santo Domingo**. Because of their isolation (roads here were not surfaced until the mid-1950s), the Church became the center of social as well as religious life for the *andinos*, and this is still evident. Visitors are likely to encounter some sort of religious or folkloric celebration during their stay.

Paso El Águila crowns the highest paved road in the country at 4,007 meters (13,146 ft). The surrounding *páramo* (high moorland) is dominated by the tall *frailejón*, with fuzzy silver-green leaves and bright yellow flowers (best in October). Near **Apartaderos** ❽ is the **Observatorio Astronómico Nacional del Llano del Hato**, with four giant telescopes and public viewing.

East of the highway from **Santo Domingo** lies **Parque Nacional Sierra Nevada**. Principal entrances to its many hiking trails are at **Laguna Mucubají**, the largest of Mérida's 200 glacial lakes, most full of trout, and **Mucuy Alto**.

A rather touristy but nonetheless interesting stop, about 20 minutes north of Mérida city, is **Los Aleros**, the reproduction of an entire Andean village as it

Map on pages 110–11

BELOW: the village of Jají.

would have looked before the highway came through. Along with traditional construction and period artifacts, participants carry out daily chores, and music of the era and even a wedding are performed daily. Park creator Alexi Montilla followed up with the all-encompassing **Alexi's Venezuela de Antier**, between Mérida and the restored colonial village of **Jají**.

Views of Venezuela's snow-capped peaks, the highest of which is Bolívar, at 5,007 meters (16,427 ft), can be enjoyed in the year-round spring-like weather of the city of **Mérida** . *Posadas* around **Plaza Las Heroinas** (by the cable-car station) are the gathering places for those in search of mountain activities such as trekking, climbing, and paragliding, with equipment rental, guides, and *toyoteros* – drivers of four-wheel-drive vehicles who take visitors to the remote mountain villages of Los Pueblos del Sur, or to entry points for excursions.

Mérida has the world's highest and longest cable car, along with 43 parks and plazas, including **Parque Zoológico Chorros de Milla**, with a mini zoo and pretty gardens; and **El Acuario**, which has an aquarium and vignettes with life-size figures showing life in the Andes of the past. The **Museo de Ciencia y Tecnología** is also well worth a visit, as is the **Museo de Arte Moderno** (daily; free) and the massive **Catedral Metropolitana** on **Plaza Bolívar**.

No state more fully epitomizes the unique character of Venezuela's vast *llanos* (central plains) than **Apure**. Huge *hatos* (cattle ranches) covering thousands of hectares, the *llaneros* who work them, *moriche* palms, the traditional *joropo* music and dance, and an incredible abundance of wildlife are its trademarks. Some *hatos* can be reached by road, via the state capital of **San Fernando de Apure** ❿ from the east, or **Ciudad Nutrias** from the west; others are accessible only by private plane, boat, or four-wheel drive.

Roadside basket shop in the Andes

BELOW: Plaza Bolívar, Mérida.

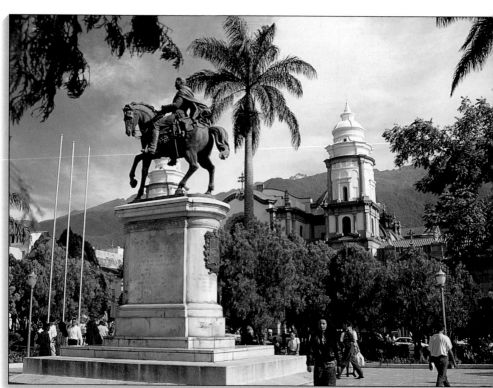

The Eastern Gold Coast

The marine paradise of **Parque Nacional Los Roques Archipelago** is only 35 minutes away by air, though both day trips and overnight stays are expensive. Along with excellent diving and beautiful (but shadeless) beaches, Los Roques offers unparalleled game fishing. From Caracas you can reach the 'Route of the Sun", between Puerto La Cruz and Cumaná, on the eastern coastal highway (avoiding public holidays, when traffic comes to a standstill for hours). While most people head directly to Barcelona and Puerto La Cruz, other great beaches en route include the outer banks of the **Laguna de Unare** (enter via Boca de Uchire) and **Puerto Píritu**.

Barcelona, Anzoátegui state's capital, has a well-preserved historic zone with such attractions as the **Museo de Tradiciones**, along narrow streets bordered by vintage architecture. At the other extreme, beaches along a narrow neck of land lead to the mammoth **El Morro Tourist Complex**. Some 12 km (7½ miles) east along the coast lies **Puerto La Cruz ⑪** – action never stops along its beachfront boulevard, **Paseo Colón** (but leave swimming to island beaches, since the water here is contaminated). **Pozuelos Bay**, dotted with luxury yachts and traditional fishing boats, and the dramatic rocky islands of **Parque Nacional Mochima**, forms the seaward backdrop for the boulevard. A shuttle service is offered by a boatmen's union from the eastern end of the beach to the island beaches, with the best snorkeling and diving spots.

Continuing eastward along the coastal highway, you can stop off at beaches like **Playa Colorada** and **Arapito** on the way to **Cumaná ⑫**, Venezuela's oldest continental city (founded in 1521). A ferry crosses from Cumaná to the **Araya peninsula ⑬**, landing near ruins of a colonial fort and pretty beach.

Map
on pages
110–11

TIP

The dry season (mid-November to the end of April) is the time to visit Los Llanos, when wildlife is concentrated around shrinking watering holes – the rest of the year, rain is incessant and many places are inundated (or closed), with fauna widely dispersed.

BELOW: Caribbean islands of Los Roques Archipelago National Park.

Further east still, you could spend a day relaxing on the fabulous beach of **Playa Medina** near the attractive town of Río Caribe.

To the south, near **Caripe** , is the **Cueva del Guácharo** (officially Monumento Natural Alejandro Humboldt), the country's largest cave, named for the thousands of *guácharos* (night-flying oil birds) that call it home.

La Asunción church, Isla Margarita.

Margarita and the Pearl Islands

Isla Margarita, less than an hour by air from Maiquetía or two to four hours by ferry from Puerto La Cruz, is the main attraction of the three-island Pearl group which constitutes Nueva Esparta state. Water temperature varies from 23–30°C (73°F–86°F) around the island's numerous white sand beaches. Activities include water sports, fishing, and horseback riding. The island is beginning to rival Hawaii as a windsurfing hotspot – **El Yaque Beach** is considered one of the world's top beaches for the sport. With numerous historical sites, a rich tradition of crafts, shopping (the island has more than 2,000 duty-free shops), lodging ranging from intimate *posadas* to luxury resorts, a multitude of restaurants, and a lively nightlife, it is little wonder that Isla Margarita has become a prime tourist destination.

Spanish settlement of the **Pearl Islands** in 1500 was the first in all South America. The colonizers were attracted by the discovery of the first pearls found in the New World in the rich oyster beds surrounding the island of **Cubagua**. However, greed leading to over-harvesting, a devastating storm leveling the stone buildings, and pirates who took whatever the storm had not destroyed, brought an end to the settlement barely four decades later. Pearl fishing continued, but is now permitted only in season (Jan–Apr) every other year.

BELOW: Playa El Agua, Margarita.

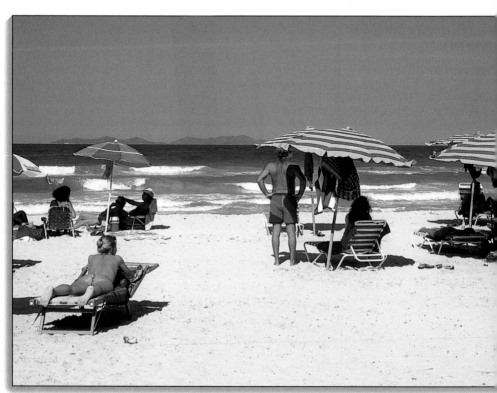

Ruins of the site (along with pristine beaches) on this nearly uninhabited island can be visited on day tours from **Porlamar ⓰**, Margarita's largest city. Most of the island's hotels and shops, plus numerous restaurants, nightclubs, and casinos are concentrated in downtown Porlamar. The city also has a ferry service to **Coche Island**, which is just beginning to develop its great tourism potential, with excellent windsurfing and several small resort hotels.

The majority of accommodation on Margarita is near the most popular beaches. North of Porlamar, **Playa Guacuco ⓱** has some tourist facilities. Further up the coast, **Playa El Agua ⓲** is the most popular (a beautiful beach, but with a treacherous undertow). The beaches continue to **Manzanillo ⓳**, the islands's most northerly point, and down to the west.

The capital city **La Asunción ⓴** is smaller and more peaceful than Porlamar. Sights in this historical town include the 16th-century colonial cathedral (one of the oldest churches in Venezuela); the **Museo de Nueva Cádiz** (open Tues–Sun), which depicts the history of the town of the same name, destroyed by an earthquake in 1541; and the colonial **Castillo de Santa Rosa** fort (open Mon–Sat) some 10 km (6 miles) northeast, **Pampatar ㉑** also has some interesting colonial buildings including a pretty church and fortress.

The town of **Juangriego ㉒**, famed for its sunsets, offers a tranquil beach and nearby communities known for handicrafts. Pottery is made at **La Vecinidad** and **El Cercado**; basketry is the craft at **Pedrogonzález**; hammocks can be purchased at **Tacarigua**; and straw hats at **San Juan**. Within the town of **Tacuantar** is the Taller de Arte Así con las Manos – Tierra, Agua y Fuego artisan village. Contrasting with the bustling eastern half is the island's rugged, scarcely populated **Macanao peninsula** to the west. **Parque Nacional Laguna La Restinga** lies along the narrow link between the two sections. Boatmen can take you through channels among mangrove swamps en route to the spectacular beach along the outer banks of the lagoon.

The Guayana region: the last frontier

Venezuela's vast southern sector (covering Delta Amacuro, Bolívar, and Amazonas states) is known as the Guayana region, named for the Guayana Shield, composed of pre-Cambrian rock, among the oldest on the continent at 1.2 to 2.5 billion years. The unique features in Bolívar and Amazonas are *tepuyes*, towering mesas of ancient rock. The most famous are **Roraima**, subject of Sir Arthur Conan Doyle's *Lost World* and **Auyantepui**, from which Angel Falls drops.

Except for a few roads near the state capitals of **Delta Amacuro** (Tucupita) and **Puerto Ayacucho** (Amazonas), travel is by boat or by air. Difficult access has been the greatest factor in maintaining the mystery, natural state, and allure of the region. The tourism potential in the huge delta of the **Orinoco River**, making up most of Delta Amacuro state, has only recently been exploited. Now some half a dozen rustic tourist camps operate here, with an emphasis on the observation of fauna and visits to the indigenous Warao, principal inhabitants of this unique ecosystem. Warao means "the boat people", and their crafts, particularly basketry, are highly prized.

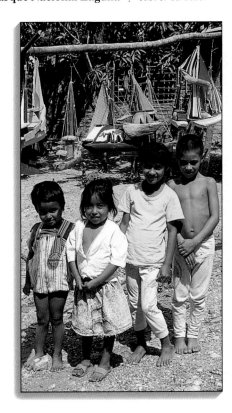

BELOW: young salespeople on the "Route of the Sun", east of Caracas.

Map on pages 110–11

Obelisk marking the meeting place of three countries: Venezuela, Guyana, and Brazil, on top of Roraima Tepuy.

BELOW: water-logged plant life on Roraima Tepuy.

Bolívar, Venezuela's largest, and one of the most richly endowed states, has huge reserves of gold, diamonds, iron, bauxite, hardwoods, and water power from its great rivers. **Ciudad Guayana ㉓**, on the northern border, was created in 1961, as headquarters for development of Venezuela's heavy industry. Mammoth steel, iron, and aluminum plants use electricity generated at **Guri Dam**, one of the most powerful hydroelectric plants in the world, an hour to the southwest, with a visitor center and interesting tours. Tourist attractions include the waterfalls in **Parque Cachamay** and **Parque Llovizna** and ruins of the colonial **Caroní Mission Church**. About an hour away are the 17th- and 18th-century forts, **Los Castillos de Guayana La Vieja**, overlooking the Orinoco.

An hour west of Ciudad Guayana by freeway is **Ciudad Bolívar ㉔**, the state's capital. Founded in 1764 on the banks of the Orinoco, it became a patriot stronghold, Simón Bolívar's base of operations, and capital of the Third Republic, 1817–21. It was also a gold center, and a thriving river transport hub.

The opening of the highway joining San Fernando de Apure with the central coast spelled the demise of the river trade and its commercial importance. But evidence of the city's prosperous past can be seen in the impressive architecture, including the colonial **Catedral**, the **Museo Etnográfico de Guayana**, the **Casa del Congreso de Angostura**, and the **Museo Manuel Piar**. Other worthwhile stops are the **Museo de Arte Moderno Jesús Soto** (honoring the city's most famous modern artist) and the **Quinta de San Isidro** (where Bolívar often stayed and now the **Museo Casa San Isidro**). The **Angostura Bridge** can be seen from the river banks, the only span so far across the 2,140-km (1,330-mile) length of the Orinoco (other crossings are by ferry). The rest of the state is mostly accessible only by small plane, with vast unexplored areas and a population of scattered indigenous groups and miners.

The paved road, completed in 1991, linking Ciudad Guayana with **Santa Elena de Uairén**, by the frontier with Brazil, permits even city cars to traverse the length of **Parque Nacional Canaima** and **La Gran Sabana**. Along the highway, observe gently rolling hills of this vast savannah dotted with *moriche* palms; settlements of native Pemón with thatch-roofed, mud-walled dwellings; and stately *tepuyes* in the distance (among them **Roraima**, the highest in the Guayana Region). There are numerous impressive falls along the roadside, including **Kama Merú** and **Quebrada de Jaspe**. The mission of **Kavanayén** and the spectacular falls of **Chinak-Merú** can be visited by four-wheel-drive vehicles.

Canaima ㉕, one of the first areas in Venezuela to be developed for adventure travel, and a major tourist destination, is in the northwest corner of the 30,000-sq. km (11,500-sq. mile) Canaima National Park. This sector of the park is only accessible by air, and visitors can take day tours from Maiquetía, Porlamar, or Ciudad Bolívar, or stay overnight. Canaima's principal draw is its proximity to **Angel Falls**, named after the American bush pilot Jimmie Angel, who "discovered" them in 1935. The falls are the world's longest, at 979 meters (3,212 ft), of which 807 meters (2,648 ft) are free fall, and cascade over the edge of **Auyantepui**, the park's largest *tepuy*, which covers 700 sq. km (270 sq. miles).

Weather permitting, visitors may get a look at the falls from the air. Excursions leave from Canaima in the rainy season, May to November.

Despite fierce opposition, in 2000, Venezuela built electricity pylons and transmission lines through Canaima National Park and La Gran Sabana to transport hydroelectric power to Brazil. As well as the irreparable impact on the delicate ecosystems and beautiful scenery of the region, the power lines have encouraged large-scale mining on all the reserve's borders.

A fragile wilderness

Flying over Amazonas, with a vista of virgin tropical forest, interrupted only by the snaking black lines of rivers, engraves a lasting impression of the vastness of the state and the magnificence of nature it embraces. Though it covers an area larger than Portugal, Holland, and Denmark put together, Amazonas only has about 45,000, mostly indigenous, inhabitants. Paved roads extend only 100 km (60 miles) from the capital, **Puerto Ayacucho** ㉖, in its northwestern extreme. The rapids of the Orinoco long prevented extensive penetration. The construction of tourist camps has allowed visitors to savor this extraordinary territory. Independent travelers can reach Puerto Ayacucho by car (or bus) from Caracas via Caicara del Orinoco in about 10 hours, passing through landscapes dominated by enormous sandstone formations called *laja*, and the Panare and Guahibo communities. Do not miss Puerto Ayacucho's outstanding **Ethnological Museum**. Near the capital are the giant petroglyphs of **Tobogán de la Selva**, and the indigenous Piaroa and Guahibo settlements. More distant (and costly) excursions by boat or charter plane include trips to **Autana**, the sacred mountain of the Piaroa, and to the native Yanomami *(see page 48)*. ❏

Outline formed by Caroní River, near Angel Falls.

BELOW: awesome Angel Falls.

GUYANA

*This lush, exotic, and richly forested former British
colony is geographically larger than Britain,
but has a mere fraction of its population*

Map
on page
128

Guyana means "Land of Many Waters" in a local Amerindian language. Life in this country on the northeast shoulder of South America is indeed dominated by its mighty rivers – the Essequibo, Demerara, and Berbice. They act as highways into the rainforests, mountains, and savannahs of the interior, regions which are, in turn, dissected by a network of lesser tributaries and creeks. Initially colonized by the Dutch in the 17th century, the territories which make up present-day Guyana came under British rule in 1814, and remained so until independence in 1966. It is populated mainly by the descendants of African slaves and indentured workers from India, together with smaller numbers of Chinese and Portuguese, brought to work the sugar, coffee, and cotton plantations of the coast. Amerindians, the original inhabitants, number just 5 percent.

Because of her colonial history, modern Guyana is South America's only English-speaking country, and is Caribbean in culture and outlook. However, unlike her Caribbean neighbors, Guyana has no palm-fringed powdery sand or limpid waters. Instead, the narrow coastal belt consists mainly of reclaimed swamps, marshland, and deltas of the great rivers, rich in alluvial soil and intensively cultivated. These areas, and small towns such as **New Amsterdam ❶** and **Charity ❷**, are protected from the sea by a system of dams and dikes (a practice initiated by the Dutch). Ninety percent of a total population of 768,000 in a country larger than Britain, live on this coastal belt.

Georgetown ❸, the capital, lies below sea level on the east bank of the Demerara River. The city is laid out in a grid with wide streets lined with colonial buildings constructed of tropical hardwoods. The skyline is dominated by **St George's Anglican Cathedral**, said to be the world's tallest wooden church; and the tower crowning the immense, covered Stabroek Market where the full pageant of Guyana's ethnic mix barters goods of every conceivable desciption, from manioc flour to gold. **Georgetown Cricket Club** – the oldest cricket club in the West Indies – and the pan yards where steel bands prepare for the annual carnival, speak loudest of Guyana's Caribbean identity. Georgetown also has comfortable modern hotels and a lively nightlife. However, it is to explore the interior that the great majority of visitors travel to Guyana.

Towering forest and fabulous falls

Kaieteur Falls, the world's highest single-drop waterfall, is at the top of most visitors' lists. It is feasible to journey overland to the falls by driving to **Linden ❹**, the bauxite mining town, then continuing along a track through the rainforest to join the Potaro River for two days' struggle by boat against the current. It is also just possible, at certain times of the year, to journey to

PRECEDING PAGES:
Rupununi River,
Guyana.
LEFT: close to the
edge, Kaieteur
Falls, Guyana.
BELOW: Bartica,
Guyana.

Turtle petroglyph.

Kangaruma ⑤, near Kaieteur. The easier option is to fly by light aircraft from Georgetown. For about an hour and a half passengers gaze down at a disk filled to the horizon in every direction with forest, interrupted by glinting hairs of water. Occasionally they might identify tiny riverside settlements where solitary gold panners and diamond prospectors sieve for their fortunes.

Abruptly, the forest rises about 300 meters (1,000 ft) at the point where two folds of the earth's crust overlap. The Potaro River flows calmly through the forest, spills over and plunges down, uninterrupted for 226 meters (741 ft) of its 250-meter (820-ft) fall. Airborne tourists are usually treated to a full-frontal vista of the entire falls, before sweeping low over the foaming white cauldron and dropping down on a strip of jungle cleared for a runway. A forest trail leads to the falls, as the gathering roar seems to come from every direction, including below ground. The viewing promontory is just meters from the falls. A huge volume of black water flows over the lip every second, seemingly in slow motion, turning copper, yellow, and finally a foaming white frenzy.

If this doesn't give you your fill of falls, you can fly for 30 minutes on to **Orinduik Falls**. Here the Ireng River thunders over a series of steps and terraces on a fold of rock which marks Guyana's border with Brazil. Although Orinduik does not offer the full, elemental drama of Kaieteur, the location is stunningly beautiful with views over the rolling, grass-covered Pakaraimae Hills.

Rainforest idyll

A stay at a rainforest lodge is another feature of Guyana's fledgling tourist industry. Close to Georgetown, **Timberhead** is reached by whooshing up the wide, aptly brown sugar-colored Demerara River, then chugging up the oozing

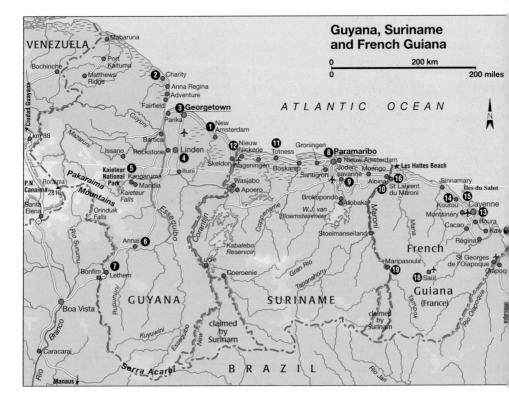

Kamuni Creek, its waters blackened by decomposing vegetation. The banks are overhung with undergrowth supported by aerial roots. Enormous blue morpho butterflies flitter about in abundance and troupes of monkeys can be heard crashing through the branches overhead. There are jaguars, pumas, tiger cats, and bush pigs in the forest, though sightings are more likely further south in Iwokrama Rainforest Reserve in the heart of Guyana. Stay at Rock View Lodge *(see Travel Tips page 387)* at **Annai ❻**, where the savannah meets the Pakaraima mountains. Here you can take boat trips at dawn and dusk to see myriad birds, butterflies, black caiman, and the Victoria Amazonica waterlilies.

Along the upper reaches of the Rupununi River, the landscape changes dramatically into savannah grassland bordered by a ridge of mountains pricking the horizon. Here *vaqueros* (cowboys) ride across the plains, barefoot in the stirrup, rounding up their cattle.

A flight over the rainforest to the airstrip at **Lethem ❼** near the Brazilian border takes you to the heart of this region. A trip across the savannahs by open-backed jeep reaches Dadanawa Ranch. From here, visitors ride horses into the mountain foothills and nights can be spent under the stars, after a supper of beef roasted on an open fire. The area is a bird-watchers' and naturalists' dream and the rare red siskin has recently been discovered here.

As you fly over Guyana's endless rainforest, it's easy to believe that there are forest-dwellers who have never had contact with the outside world. In fact, in the 1960s, contact was made for the first time with the Wai-Wai, a tribe living as hunter-gatherers between the Essequibo and Amazon watersheds. To minimize the impact on their culture, very few expeditions into their territory are permitted, and every potential participant is interviewed. □

Jungle lodges are rustic but with basic comforts.

BELOW: a giant anteater hunts in the grass.

Map
on page
128

SURINAME

*This little-known former Dutch colony has a fascinating
cultural mix in its sleepy coastal towns and vast
swathes of rainforest*

T he 1667 Peace of Breda treaty granted New York to Britain and Suriname
to The Netherlands. In the intervening centuries the two places have
become, respectively, perhaps the most renowned city on Earth, and one of
the world's most obscure countries. The irony is not lost among Surinamese, for
many of whom it is self-evident that the Dutch got the better deal.

Suriname is the former Dutch Guiana, sandwiched between Guyana (formerly
British Guiana) and Guyane, or French Guiana, which remains officially a
département of France. The Suriname coast was first settled by English and
Dutch merchants in 1613, followed by Jews from the Netherlands, Italy, and
Brazil. Slaves were shipped from West Africa to work the plantations, mainly of
sugar and cotton. Imports of slaves were banned in 1818, and slavery itself abolished in 1863. During this period, East Indians, Pakistanis, Chinese, and Javanese
from Dutch Indonesia arrived as indentured laborers. Add to these the indigenous
Amerindians, and the result is an extraordinary ethnic cocktail.

Suriname gained independence from the Netherlands in 1975. Since then,
relations between the two countries have rollercoastered, reaching a low point
in 1982 when military dictator Colonel Desi Bouterse had 15 opposition leaders executed. Diplomatic relations were severed for five years, until democratic elections were held. Huge numbers of Surinamese
emigrated to the Netherlands, leaving a depleted population which today numbers just under 480,000. The
official language is Dutch, while Sranan Tongo, an Eng-
lish-based creole, is widely used as a lingua franca.
Runaldo Ronald Venetiaan of the New Front has been
president since 2000. Under his leadership the economy has improved and international loans have helped
finance health and education, although the country
faces several problems including gold smuggling and a
long-standing border dispute with Guyana over oil.

BELOW: mosque,
central Paramaribo.

Suriname's sleepy capital

As in the other Guyanas, roughly 90 percent of the
people live in towns strung along the loamy mud flats
of the coast. The capital, **Paramaribo ❽**, is a small,
quiet city of faded and peeling colonial wooden
buildings arranged in a grid pattern, on the west bank
of the Suriname River. It is hard to comprehend the
violence and upheavals of the 1980s as you wander
the sleepy squares graced by statues of Simón Bolívar and Mahatma Gandhi. (Home-grown Surinamese
heroes and potentates are thin on the ground.)

Suriname is remarkably free of racial tension. The
synagogue stands fraternally next to the mosque.
Down the road, restoration of the wooden **Saint Peter
and Paul Cathedral** is due for completion. The
museum, in the old Dutch **Fort Zeelandia** is a

modest affair. The **central market** is more lively; the aroma of spices brought from India mingles with the smell of fresh shrimps sold by fishermen.

A popular day trip from Paramaribo is to cross the Suriname River by ferry to the Dutch fort of **Nieuw Amsterdam** and drive eastward along the coast, north of the old Jewish settlement of **Jodensavanne ❾** and through the bauxite-mining town of **Moengo**. The road ends at **Albina ❿**, a thriving little frontier town on the Marowijne, the river border with French Guiana. Another road, westwards, passes through the village of **Totness ⓫**, curious only for its name, which dates back to a Scottish settlement that has long since dispersed. The only other town on the road is **Wageningen**, the rice-growing center, before **Nieuw Nickerie ⓬**, the border town with Guyana at the mouth of the Corantijn River.

Into the forest

Like its neighbors, the majority of Suriname's territory is covered by dense, virgin rainforest, cut through by great, black rivers. In "Operation Grasshopper", a government-sponsored scheme in the 1950s, a few short airstrips deep in the darkest interior have been hacked out of the forest. Near three of these, the Movement for Eco-Tourism in Suriname (METS – owned by Suriname Airways), have built simple lodges where visitors can experience life in the rainforest.

Central market, Paramaribo.

One of them is on an island in the **Gran Rio**, in the heart of Saramaccan country. The Saramaccan are a tribe of so-called "Bush Negroes", the descendants of African slaves who escaped to the forests of the interior as rebellions swept through the plantations on Suriname's coast. They speak a hybrid language of West African dialects, smattered with English, Dutch, and Portuguese words. Many of their practices – drum-playing, dancing, and animist religious beliefs – can be traced directly to West Africa. Other means of forest survival were learnt from indigenous Amerindians. For example, they cultivate manioc on small slash-and-burn clearings, and build houses roofed with plaited palm.

BELOW: Suriname River.

A typical visit to this area begins with a light aircraft flight to **Kajana Airstrip**, and transfer in a motorized dugout canoe up to **Awarradam Lodge** at some impassable rapids. Here, the air is heavy and moist. The double wolf whistles of screaming piha and a cacophony of croaks, caws, and the occasional growl of a howler monkey, float over the canopy. Sightings of larger creatures are rare – unless you count the peccary (bush pig), shot or trapped in the forest, which the lodge's Bush Negro staff roast on open fires. However, the black caiman, an Amazonian crocodile up to 2 meters (6 ft) long, is common. They are often seen lazing by the bank during the all-day canoe trip to **Grandam rapids**. Outsiders are usually welcomed by the village chief or "Kapiteni" and introduced to villagers who sing as they spin cotton or grate manioc, while mischievous naked children follow.

Palumeu, the second lodge, is next to an Amerindian village deeper into the interior on the Tapanahony River, a tributary of the Marowijne. Palumeu is the most stunningly located of the lodges, on a broad hillside clearing with sweeping river views, but the people are shyer and interaction can be awkward. ❏

Map
on page
128

FRENCH GUIANA

*Formerly home to a notorious penal colony, this heavily
forested and naturally diverse* département *of France
is today the launch site for Europe's Ariane rockets*

To the east of Suriname lies the small French colony of French Guiana
(Guyane), almost a fifth of the size of France with more than 350 km (220
miles) of coastline. Eighty percent of the 199,000 inhabitants live in the
coastal regions, as beyond the coast lies a dense carpet of Amazon rainforest.

Ancient petroglyphs near the village of Kaw bear testimony to thousands of
years of human habitation in the area, but as in neighboring countries, European
colonization, from the early 17th century, dramatically changed the ethnographic make-up of the region.

The territory was tenuously held by the French in the face of short-lived
appropriations by the British, Dutch, and Brazilian-Portuguese. African slaves
were brought in to work the plantations, to be replaced when slavery was abolished by indentured laborers from other parts of the French Empire, notably
Indo-China. After a minor gold rush in the 1850s the territory became best
known as a brutal penal colony, immortalized in the novel *Papillon* by Henri
Charrière, and in the famous movie of the same name. The Jewish army officer
Alfred Dreyfus, whose imprisonment for treason in the 1890s caused a political storm, was held at the notorious Devil's Island.

French Guiana became an overseas *département* of France in 1946. In the

BELOW: Devil's
Island.

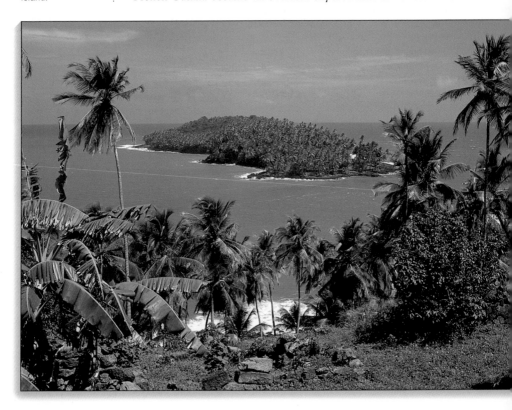

1960s a satellite and space exploration center was established at Kourou, which brought jobs and urban development, but the rest of the country has suffered unemployment and economic stagnation. The population is highly racially mixed, with input from Africa, Europe, native South America, China, and Vietnam. There are many Amerindian groups living in the rainforest areas, and also communities of "Noir Marrons", or Bush Negroes, descendants of African slaves, who live along the banks of the River Maroni in a traditional African manner with Amerindian influences.

Cayenne ⓭, the capital, has some interesting colonial buildings, but is a relatively expensive town. The **Musée Départemental** has a mix of historical and archeological artifacts including exhibits on the penal colonies. There is a vegetable and flower market, and a fish market on Wednesday, Friday, and Saturday.

The town of **Kourou** ⓮, 55 km (34 miles) northwest of Cayenne, revolves around the **French Guiana Space Center**. There is a **Space Museum** (open Mon–Fri and Sat pm), from where rocket launches can be witnessed. Europe's largest and most expensive satellite was launched from the center in March 2002. The modern part of town, known locally as the "white city" due to the preponderance of families from mainland France, is very different from the more traditional old village at the mouth of the Kourou River. Boats are available from here to the three Îles du Salut ⓯, which lie 15 km (9 miles) to the north. The famous **Île du Diable** (Devil's Island) is inaccessible due to hazardous landing conditions, but accommodation is available on the Île Royale.

Painted "maluana" disk of the Wayana people.

The Transportation Camp at **St Laurent du Maroni** ⓰, 250 km (150 miles) northwest of Cayenne, was the largest prison in the territory, and can be visited. Dugout canoes can be hired from the town for trips on the Maroni River. About 40 km (25 miles) north of St Laurent, at the mouth of the Maroni and Mana rivers, is **Les Hattes Beach**, which is a breeding site for leatherback turtles. The laying season is from April to July and hatching takes place from July to September. The turtles have no shell but a dark blue leathery skin, and measure up to 170 cm (67 inches) long when fully grown. Nearby is the Amerindian village of **Awala Yalimapo**.

The interior of French Guiana has much to interest naturalists and adventure seekers. Roughly 60 km (40 miles) southeast of Cayenne are the **Kaw Marshes**, an area of forest and mangrove swamps, rich in birdlife and inhabited by the rare black caiman. Houseboat accommodations are available in **Kaw** ⓱ village. At **Montsinéry**, 43 km (27 miles) southwest of Cayenne, a botanical hiking trail leads to the **Annamite Penal Colony**, where deported Indo-Chinese were detained. Other hiking trails lead to waterfalls and wildlife-infested creeks. The interior can also be explored by *pirogue*, or dugout canoe.

South of Cayenne, the village of **Cacao** is inhabited by a Hmong community of Laotian descent. Visitors can sample traditional Hmong cuisine, and Hmong handicrafts can be bought. There are inland jungle expeditions centered around the ancient gold-mining village of **Saül** ⓲; in the west, the town of **Maripaoula** ⓳, home to Bush Negro communities, is a popular expedition destination. ❏

BELOW: children in the Place Leopoldo, Cayenne.

ANDEAN HIGHLANDS

The ancient heart of the subcontinent, these high-altitude countries continue to fascinate, both for their imperial past and for the rich cultural heritage they proudly maintain

Clustered around some of the most inhospitable territory in South America are the countries of the Andean highlands: Peru, Bolivia, and Ecuador. The area was home to some of the world's most extraordinary civilizations for thousands of years before being finally united by the Inca Empire in the 14th century. Although the Incas were the most famous rulers of South America, they had a relatively brief moment of glory before the Spanish conquistadors crushed them into submission *(see page 26)*. The colonists subsequently kept themselves distant from their subjects and to this day the old Inca lands are dual societies: one Amerindian, impoverished and traditional; the other mestizo or white, looking to Europe or the United States for cultural inspiration.

Nowhere is this more so than in the Inca heartland of Peru. The capital, Lima *(see page 146)*, lies on the barren coast facing the sea, while the ancient capital of Cusco *(see page 151)*, regarded by the Incas as the navel of the world, sits in the mountains, nursing its shattered past. From these two cultural poles Peru's many wonders can be reached: the ancient Inca Trail leads from Cusco to Machu Picchu *(see page 158)*, arguably South America's most spectacular ancient city. In the south are the baffling Nazca lines *(see page 150)*; in the north the ancient adobe city of Chan Chan *(see page 165)*. The world's deepest canyons are near the colonial city of Arequipa *(see page 157)*. Peru's Amazon region *(see page 161)* is unforgettable, despite being opened up to settlement at breakneck speed.

Across from Lake Titicaca *(see pages 168–9)* is the landlocked mountain country of Bolivia. The most ethnically native American and the poorest of South America's republics, this is a land of ancient traditions and colonial relics. Carved from the bleak altiplano or "high plain," La Paz is the highest capital city in the world *(see page 177)*. In the shadow of spectacular peaks, the nearby Yungas *(see page 182)* is a subtropical region of banana, coffee, and coca leaf. Back in the windswept heights is the town of Potosí *(see page 189)*, once the Spanish Empire's main source of silver and still a mining town.

To the north of Peru is the Republic of Ecuador. This compact country can be explored in short trips from the mountain capital Quito *(see page 201)*, a colonial gem now placed on the World Heritage list. Nearby is the town of Otavalo *(see page 202)*, famous for a remarkable weaving tradition which is attracting new wealth, while around the capital are mountains and nature reserves *(see page 205)*. A short jump east lands you in the steamy Oriente jungle *(see page 209)*. In the west lie the Pacific beaches of Ecuador's coast *(see page 212)*, 965 km (600 miles) beyond which are the country's pride and joy: the wildlife-rich Galápagos islands *(page 214)*. ❏

PRECEDING PAGES: pre-Columbian gold mask; Peruvian llamas.
LEFT: traditional weaver, near Cusco.

PERU

The birthplace of ancient empires, Peru has towering mountains, steaming rainforests, and parched deserts. It's the ultimate destination for culture seekers, adventurers, and eco-tourists

N o other country in South America, possibly in the whole world, has such an astonishing archeological heritage as Peru. Most tourists come to see the monumental citadel of Machu Picchu; the other big archeological attraction is the mysterious desert lines of Nazca, which can only be viewed from the air. This is a country packed with archeological wonders – the fabulous remains of Inca and pre-Inca civilizations housed in numerous museums, as well as countless pyramids and ruined cities, many still unexcavated. Then there are the treasures of the colonial period which gild the magnificent cities of Cusco and Arequipa. Lima, the capital, once the center of the Spanish Empire in South America, is an exciting city that moves at a frenetic pace. Many of its colonial buildings fell victim to earthquakes and urban planning, but it still has some beautiful architecture and an enormous range of museums.

Peru is an exceptional country even for those who don't have an interest in history or archeology. Arid desert in the south and the splendid Pacific coastline with beaches that attract surfers from around the world give way abruptly to the snowy heights of the Andes mountain range that edges along the country's coastal belt. Beyond the Andes lies the Amazon basin, a rainforest area teeming with exotic plants, insects, birds, and animals.

Tourism is rapidly developing as this is a country that recognizes the importance of protecting its rich natural and historical heritage. But poverty is still widespread, from the poor indigenous communities eking out a living in the barren Andean plains to the people who inhabit Peru's volatile coastline, which is frequently hit by drought, earthquakes, and by the floods brought by the El Niño current. In August 2007, the Ica region was badly affected by an earthquake which killed over 500 people. Some tourist services have resumed, but visitors should check with tour operators before visiting the area.

Most areas of tourist interest are safe, although there have been reports of mugging in and around Cusco and Lima – personal effects should not be flaunted. Take care, but don't let such reports spoil your trip – most tourists enjoy the wonders of Peru without encountering any trouble at all.

Peru after independence

José de San Martín proclaimed Peru's independence in Lima on July 28, 1821, although most of the country was still held by the Spanish crown. Simón Bolívar finished the job of freeing the country and, in 1826, the last Spanish troops surrendered. The first years of independence saw few real changes in the way that Peruvians lived. But midway through the century, military leader Mariscal Ramón Castilla took over the

Maps on pages 144 & 146

PRECEDING PAGES: the Colca Canyon.
LEFT: portal of Lima Cathedral.
BELOW: Quechua girl.

Equator Otavalo Lago Agrio
Santo Domingo Tarapoa Güeppí
de los Colorados **Quito**
Bahía de Ohone Coca
Caráquez Latacunga Nuevo Rocafuerte
Manta Quevedo Cotopaxi **Parque Nacional**
5897 Napo **Yasuní**
Jipijapa Portoviejo 6310 Ambato Tena
Puerto Chimborazo Baños Puyo
López Guaranda **Riobamba**
Daule Babahoyo E C U A D O R
Salinas **Milagro**
La Libertad **Guayaquil** Santa Clotilde
Posorja Azogues
Golfo de **Cuenca** Andoas
Guayaquil
Machala Gualaquiza
Huaquillas Santa Rosa M a y n a s
Tumbes Zaruma Loja
Máncora Zamora Delfus Barranca Marañón
Talara Macará Orellana
Sullana Zumba Chiriacu Reserva
Paita Chulucanas Canuapanas **Nacional**
Sechura **Piura** Huancabamba Bagua Lagunas
Jaén Grande **Pacaya-Samiria**
Bayóbar Olmos Pucara Yurimaguas
Lambayeque Bambamarca Cutervo Moyobamba Santa Isabel
Chiclayo 19 S. Cirilo Balsea **Chachapoyas**
Guadalupe 4183 Beltavista **Tarapoto**
Pacasmayo Chilete **Cajamarca** Contamana
Paiján 18 Cajabamba Campanilla
Chan Chan Otuzco Aricapampa **P.N. Abiseo** Polvora
Trujillo Viru Pallasca Tiruntán
17 Sindas
Pomabamba Huacrachuco **Pucallpa 14**
Chimbote Nev. Aucayaco Masisea
6768 Huascarán Tingo Aguaytia
Casma **Huaraz** Huari María **Puerto**
P.N. Inca
Huascarán **Huánuco**
Huarmey Chiquian Pozuzo **Parque Nacional** Bolognesi
Chasquitambo Nev. Cerro de **Yanachaga-**
Yerupajá Pasco **Chemillén**
Barranca 6634 Oxapampa P E R U
Huayllay **P.N. Junín** Atalaya
Huacho Junín San Ramón
Punta Salinas Sayán **Tarma** Satipo
Chancay Canta **La Oroya** Monobamba
Callao Matucana Concepción Puerto
Lima 1 **Huancayo** Bermudez
Yauyos Surcubamba
Chilca Huancavelica Pampas **Parque**
San Vicente Go. Chocca Huanta **Nacional**
de Cañete 5231 Lircay **Manú 16** Manú
Chincha Alta **Ayacucho**
Bahía de Paracas Huancano Lucma **Machu**
Pisco Nev. Chicllaraza Andahuaylas **11 Picchu** Calca
Punta Paracas 5168 Chungui **4**
Reserva Nacional Chuquibambilla **Cusco**
de Paracas Ica Colcabamba
2 Chalhuanca Abancay Urcos
Palpa Antabamba
Nazca Puquio
Bahía San Nicolás Cotahuasi **Cordillera de Chila**
3 Pullo
San Juan Cahuacho Cañon Sibayo
Punta San Juan del Colca
Yauca Caravelí 6314 R.N. **Juliaca** **P.N.**
Nev. Ampato **Salinas y** Puno **Titicaca**
P A C I F I C Atico **Aguada**
Occoña **Arequipa 12 Blanca** Ilave
Camaná Omate **La P**
O C E A N Mollendo Moquegua
Ilo Tarata
Punta Coles Tacna
Peru Los Baños Putre
Arica
0 100 km
0 100 miles C H I L E

Map on page 144

residency, and under his rule modernization shook the country. Basic services such as water and street lights were installed in Lima and a rail track – the first in the subcontinent – linked the capital with the nearby port of Callao. Castilla abolished slavery and directed approval of the 1860 national Constitution. But setbacks were incurred in the bloody War of the Pacific against Chile, which lasted from 1879 to 1883. Despite these tumultuous changes, life in the 19th century continued much as in the 17th for the bulk of the population – the native peoples living in the highlands; the two worlds of Peru, the "Indian" and the "European", were drifting further apart.

A divided nation

Of all the nations of South America, Peru saw the most violent clash between native and European cultures. Until recently, this conflict provided fertile ground for terrorism. Today, it is more evident in the chaos of Lima, and the country's vibrant creativity. Peru has been run by a number of military strongmen. Most intriguing among them was the left-wing dictator General Juan Velasco Alvarado, who, in the 1970s, temporarily turned over the biggest newspaper – *El Comercio* – to a peasant group and renamed all of Lima's streets after national heroes.

Sprinkled amongst these dictators have been 30 elected presidents, all conservatives until left-of-center Alán García Pérez was elected in 1985. The charismatic García drew support from the poor and rural dwellers, who cheered his decision not to pay the foreign debt incurred by past governments. But the cutoff in development aid from the US, the unwillingness of businesses to invest in the country, and political maneuvering provoked an economic crisis in 1988 after two years of growth.

The political division and social upheaval accompanying García's presidency opened the way for an independent candidate, Alberto Fujimori, to take over as president. His government waged a savage campaign against the guerrilla group *Sendero Luminoso* (Shining Path), whose activities had severely affected tourism in the 1980s, and captured their leader, Abimael Guzmán, which led to the collapse of the group. In December 1996, the Movimiento Revolucionario Tupac Amaru took hostage nearly 500 guests during a siege of the Japanese ambassador's residence which lasted until April 1997. Fujimori won a controversial third term in 2000, but leaked videos implicating him in bribery forced him to flee to Japan. Alejandro Toledo, leader of the Perú Posible party and the first Peruvian president of Andean indigenous extraction, formed a government. Toledo's presidency was characterized by civil unrest, strikes by teachers and government workers, and public discontent at the perceived stagnation of the economy. In 2005, he was found guilty of electoral fraud, but Congress voted not to impeach him. Although Toledo began his term a popular leader, by the end of his presidency his popularity rating had fallen to just 8 percent In 2006 national elections returned Alán García Pérez to the presidency with 52 percent of the vote. Since then, economic growth and social stability have brought relative calm to this ancient country.

In 2003, the Peruvian Government earmarked US$800 million to compensate victims of the guerrilla war in the 1980s, during which, according to official estimates, over 69,000 people died, most of them innocent peasants.

BELOW: macaw, Peruvian Amazon.

Lima: capital of the New World

Spanish conquistador Francisco Pizarro considered the site where he founde
Lima ❶ on January 18, 1535, inhospitable: rain seldom fell, earthquakes wer
common and winter was a time of gray skies and dreary fog. But his soldiers sa▾
it as the best place for a quick sea escape in the event of a native uprising. Li▾
tle did they suspect this open plain would become the political and militar
capital of the New World, seeing the reign of 40 viceroys before the "City o
Kings" was declared capital of an independent Peru in 1821.

*Colonial door
knocker.*

The **Plaza Mayor** is where for centuries the power of the new colony wa
concentrated, and it remains one of the city's most active and attractive squares
At its center are rose gardens, a stone fountain and park benches that dra▾
young couples, shoeshine boys, and families in their Sunday best posing fo
photos. The foundations of the **Palacio de Gobierno** are from Pizarro's time, bu
its facade was changed in the early 1900s. Every day at noon there is a cere
monial changing of the guard, with a band playing, but visits to the palace hav
to be pre-arranged in the Oficina de Turismo of the Municipalidad. The best spo
for viewing the ceremony is the wide front balcony of the **Palacio Municipal**
The original structure used as a city hall burned down in 1923, but its neoclas
sical replacement is impressive, with marble stairways, gilt mirrors, and crys
tal chandeliers. The library, with massive leather chairs, huge wooden tables, an▾
the smell of old books offers a calming respite from the traffic outside. Its cir
cular stairway was hand-carved from a single piece of Nicaraguan cedar.

Across the square, the **Palacio del Arzobispo** has one of the most beautifu
wooden *Mudéjar*-style balconies in the city. Take a peek in the archbishop's pati▾
before heading next door to the **Catedral** (open Mon–Sat), which contain▾

Pizarro's remains. A block away is the **Museo Banco Central de Reserva**, with a small but impressive pre-Columbian collection (open Tues–Sun). Nearby is the splendid **Palacio de Torre Tagle**, constructed in 1735, now used as the Foreign Affairs Ministry. A few blocks to the northeast is the jewel of Lima's old churches, the **Monasterio de San Francisco** (open Mon–Sat). Lovingly repaired after every earthquake in the past four centuries, this cloister features fine mosaic tiles from Seville, frescoes discovered when an earthquake demolished part of an outer wall, and an impressive collection of religious art. Most fascinating are its catacombs, stacked with skulls and bones from the colonial period.

Saints and sinners

Behind the Palacio de Gobierno is **Estación Desamparados** (railway station), the city's first iron building. Brought in pieces by boat from England and rebuilt here in 1908, it was formerly the depot for all trains out of the capital, but is no longer in operation. Also behind the president's office is the bridge that leads to **Rimac** ⓐ, one of Lima's oldest neighborhoods, named after the river that flows along its edge. A working-class barrio, where women in doorways chat with their neighbors while children play soccer in the streets, it once was the city's top spot for promenading. Then, the stars were the *tapadas (see box, page 148)* – seductive women whose skirts shamelessly showed their tiny feet, whose necklines were scandalously low, and whose faces were covered by a veil that bared only one eye. In the afternoons, they were likely to be found on the **Alameda de los Descalzos**, courting and flirting but never lifting their veils to reveal their identities. This promenade, built in 1611, is lined with Italian marble statues representing the months of the year and bordered by lawns and flowers.

Maps
Area 144
City 146

BELOW: changing of the guard, Plaza Mayor, Lima.

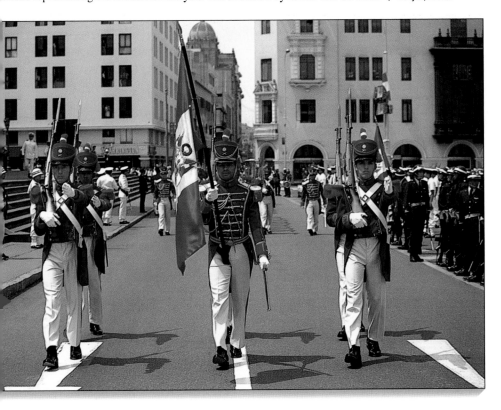

It leads to the **Monasterio de los Descalzos** (Monastery of the Barefoot Friars, open Tues–Sun), which is well worth the walk to get there.

Lima was home to two of South America's most famous saints: Rosa de Lima and Martín de Porres. Rosa, who died of tuberculosis at age 31, had a fervent following during her lifetime and was credited with curing thousands, performing innumerable miracles and even saving the city from pirate attacks. For Martín de Porres, fame came after his death. He lived in the **Santo Domingo** monastery in Jirón Camaná, but was barred from becoming a priest because he was black. His duties included working as the janitor, and statues and paintings of the saint usually show him with broom in hand. Both saints are buried in Santo Domingo, which is open to visitors.

Lima's religious devotion may have been proportional to the terror inflicted by the Holy Inquisition. Chills will run up your spine when you descend into the depths of the **Museo de la Inquisición** in Plaza Bolívar (open daily). Gruesome tortures were inflicted to obtain "confessions" of heresy, Judaism, and witchcraft. The "guilty" had their property confiscated and were marched off to the Plaza de Armas (now Plaza Mayor) to await their fate, which ranged from public flogging to burning at the stake.

Lima's most active square is **Plaza San Martín**, linked to Plaza Mayor by the pedestrian walkway **Jirón de la Unión**. Plaza San Martín is where most of the money-changing houses are located (alongside the Gran Bolívar Hotel). A few hundred meters south of the plaza, the **Museo de Arte ❺** (open daily except Wed) contains an extensive collection of Peruvian art from the Conquest to the present day. The Filmoteca here is a low-price movie club. It has two auditoriums for concerts, and is surrounded by a public park.

BELOW: the scandalous *tapadas*, or "covered ones."

THE SCANDALOUS *TAPADAS*

If the 17th century was Lima's religious period, the 18th century was its romantic era when poetry, promenading and pomp were the mainstay. It was during this time that the *tapadas* appeared, the shockingly sensual upper-class mestizo women. It wasn't long before a rivalry arose between these flirtatious *tapadas* and the more reserved Europeans. While the Spanish females cinched their skirts to show their tiny waistlines and fluttered fans before the eyes of admirers, the mestizos narrowed their skirts to emphasize their ample hips and bared their arms. But they always kept their faces veiled – with the exception of one eye. French feminist Flora Tristan, visiting her father's homeland, described the *tapadas'* Moorish costume as a "skirt... so tight that it allows just enough room to put one foot in front of the other and to take very little steps. This costume so alters a woman – even her voice since her mouth is covered – that unless she is very tall or very short, lame, hunchbacked or otherwise conspicuous, she is impossible to recognize. I am sure it needs little imagination to appreciate the consequences of this time honored practice which is sanctioned or at least tolerated by law." Those "consequences" ranged from men unknowingly flirting with their own wives, to infidelity.

Outside the city center

Some of the most interesting museums, shops, and beaches are in Lima's suburbs, accessible by bus or taxi from downtown. Just south of the city center, on Avenida Javier Prado Este, is the excellent **Museo de la Nación** Ⓖ (open Tues–Sun), with artifacts from prehistoric times to the present day (Spanish only). The once-popular **Museo de Oro** (Gold Museum; open daily) on Avenida Alonso de Molina in the Monterrico district fell from grace in 1998 with the startling revelation that a large proportion of its artifacts were fakes. After a brief enforced closure it re-opened, and claims to have removed all non-authentic items from display. The museum also has a collection of textiles, stone carvings, and ceramics on display.

Southwest of the center, in Pueblo Libre, the **Museo Arqueológico Rafael Larco Herrera** Ⓓ (open daily) has a fascinating display of pottery spanning 3,000 years, including a huge collection of pieces from the Moche, Sican, and Chimú cultures of northern Peru. There is also an exhibition dedicated to the gold and silver of ancient Peru. A blue line painted on the sidewalk leads to the **Museo Nacional de Arqueología, Antropología y Historia** Ⓔ (open Tues–Sun), with pre-Columbian displays and colonial paintings.

In the suburb of San Isidro, bougainvillea grows beside the pre-Inca burial site of **Huallamarca** (open daily), with a small museum of mummies and artifacts.

In **Miraflores** Ⓕ, stomping ground of the children of Peru's wealthy families, you can people-watch at outdoor cafés, shop, or enjoy good meals and music. The pretensions of the Miraflores youths – the *mirafloriños* – are vividly described in the novels of Mario Vargas Llosa. Miraflores is the best place for theaters, trendy boutiques, and nightclubs. Nearby is **Barranco** Ⓖ, the bohemian quarter made immortal in Peruvian waltz and home to the city's best artists, poets, and jazz bars. Here you'll find the lover's lane, **Puente de los Suspiros** (Bridge of Sighs), lined by fragrant jasmine and hyacinth bushes. It heads down to a lookout point over the Pacific Ocean, and to a steep stairway to the beach. Strolling here at sunset you may hear Peruvian flute music or Argentine tangos wafting from open windows.

The most important archeological site near Lima is **Pachacámac**, 31 km (19 miles) south of the city and accessible by bus or tour from the city center. Rising to prominence around AD 700, this pre-Inca shrine was later used as an Inca temple for adoration of the sun god, and there is also a reconstruction of the Templo de las Virgenes (House of the Chosen Women), who were also known as *mamaconas*.

Some 220 km (135 miles) south of Lima, and worth visiting if you are traveling by road to Nazca, is **Ica** ❷, famous for its vineyards and March wine festival, but especially for the **Museo Regional**, one of Peru's most interesting small regional museums. Exhibits include mummies, ceramics, and skulls from the Paracas, Nazca, and Inca cultures; an excellent collection of Paracas textiles and feather weavings; and a number of *quipus*, the knotted strings believed to have been used to keep calculations and records for the Incas.

Outside Ica, Hotel Las Dunas Sun Resort is a luxurious complex that pioneered the sand-surfing frenzy in this dune-covered area. Cerro Blanco, some 14 km

Craftsman with gold jewelry.

BELOW: elaborate colonial facade.

Maps: Area 144 City 146

TIP

Unless you fly from Lima, the only way to reach Nazca is by bus – a trip that can take up to eight hours from the Peruvian capital. Flights over the lines are often canceled because of poor visibility – early morning is the best time to see them.

BELOW: aerial view of hummingbird design, Nazca lines.

(8 miles) north of Nazca, is purportedly the world's biggest sand dune. Nearby is **Laguna de Huacachina**, a green lagoon of sulfur waters that Peruvians claim has medicinal value. The colonial-style Hotel Mossone is an idyllic place to stay. Next door, the slightly crumbling, but charming, Salvatierra is a cheaper alternative.

The mysterious Nazca lines

Until the 1930s, **Nazca ❸** was like any other small Peruvian town, with no claim to fame except that you had to cross one of the world's driest deserts to reach it from Lima. Since then, the pampa north of the city has become one of the greatest scientific mysteries in the Americas. The Nazca lines are a series of drawings of animals, geometric figures, and birds up to 300 meters (1,000 ft) in size, scratched on to the arid crust of the desert and preserved for 2,000 years owing to a complete lack of rain and unique winds that clean, but do not erase the pampa. The huge figures can only be properly appreciated from the air.

In 1939, North American scientist Paul Kosok, flying over the dry coast noticed the lines that were previously believed to be part of a pre-Inca irrigation system. A specialist in irrigation, he quickly concluded that this had nothing to do with water systems. By chance, the day of the flight coincided with the summer solstice and, on a second flight, Kosok discovered that the line of the sunset ran tandem to the direction of one of the bird drawings. He called the Nazca pampa "the biggest astronomy book in the world." However, it was a young German mathematician who became the expert on the lines and put Nazca on the map. Maria Reiche was 35 when she met Kosok, and he encouraged her to study the pampa. Reiche, who died in 1998, devoted her life to studying the lines, which she measured, cleaned, analyzed, and charted daily from the air and from a 15-meter (49-ft) high platform. She developed the most widely accepted theories on the hundreds of drawings that cover a 50-km (30-mile) belt between Nazca and Palpa, describing them as an "astronomical calendar". For example, she speculated that the drawing of the monkey was the Nazca symbol for the Big Dipper, the constellation representing rain. When rain was overdue – a common occurrence here – the monkey was sketched so that the gods would be reminded that the earth was parched. Because the drawings are only visible from the air there are those who do not accept Reiche's theories, denying that the Nazca people would have drawn something they could not see.

The most damaging theory about the Nazca lines came seven years earlier, when Erik Von Daniken published *Chariots of the Gods*, in which he proposed that the pampa was part of an extra-terrestrial landing strip – an idea that Reiche discarded impatiently. Von Daniken's book drew thousands of visitors, who set out across the pampa on motorcycles and four-wheel-drive vehicles, leaving unerasable marks. Now it is illegal to drive or even walk on the pampa: Reiche used the profits from her book, *Mystery on the Desert*, to pay four guards to keep a constant watch on the plain.

There is a metal ladder and viewing platform at the side of the highway, but the best way to capture the impact of the lines is to fly over them. AeroCondor do a day-long package from Lima that includes a flight over the lines, plus lunch and a visit to Ica's Museo Regional and the Laguna de Huacachina. Flights can also be booked at travel agencies and hotels (including the Hotel Alegría and Hotel Nazca Lines) in Nazca. They last from 30 to 45 minutes and can be bumpy. If you want to make the trip more economical, some of the pilots at the Nazca airstrip may be open to offers.

Pre-Columbian mummy, Chauchilla cemetery, Nazca.

BELOW: detail from an ancient Paracas textile.

Cusco: capital of the Inca Empire

The stallholders in Cusco's market speak Spanish with tourists and Quechua with one another. The buildings behind them are colonial, built on Inca foundations. The elaborately carved facades on the city's churches have detailed scenes of angels and saints – with Amerindian facial features. **Cusco ④** stands as a living testimony to the fact that the Inca civilization, one of the world's most sophisticated, could not be erased.

Of course, the Cusco of today is dramatically different from the awesome city that Francisco Pizarro and his conquistadors found when they reached the capital of the Inca Empire, home to that kingdom's noblemen, priests, and their servants. Five hundred years ago, an estimated 15,000 people lived in the city, which was linked to the rest of the empire by way of *chasquis* – long-distance runners who carried news and messages from the four corners of Tahuantinsuyo to its capital. It is now a fairly modern Andean community with a population of about 200,000 and daily plane and bus services to Lima.

When the Spanish headed here after executing Atahuallpa in Cajamarca, they entered the fertile valley where Cusco is located to find a lush, green countryside filled with fields of corn and golden and purple patches where *kiwicha* and quinoa – varieties of ama-

Ceramic bull on a rooftop for good luck, Cusco.

ranth, a high-protein grain – were planted. Corn was perhaps the most valuable crop in the kingdom. It was used for bartering and as a food staple that appeared in everything from main dishes to the alcoholic *chicha*, prepared by young women who chewed the corn, then spat it into jars where it fermented with their saliva. The amaranth, which grows well despite extremes in temperature and moisture, nearly fell victim to the Spaniards' attempt to "civilize" the local population. The conquistadors called it the "subversive grain", as it made the Amerindians healthy, and thus harder to enslave. Pressured by the Spanish the Vatican outlawed its cultivation and consumption. But now, four centuries later, *kiwicha* and quinoa once again flourish in the Sacred Valley, and are used in everything from soup to cookies.

In pre-Columbian times, anyone entering Cusco was greeted with the phrase *"Ama sua, ama quella, ama lulla"* – "Don't lie, don't steal, don't be lazy", summing up what was important in this cooperative society. Laziness was a capital offense punishable by death. Everyone in an Incan community – except for royalty and priests – was required to work on projects such as roads, irrigation ditches, and aqueducts owing to a philosophy that if all participated, all would take care of the finished product. When the Spanish took control of this country those cooperative projects – known as *mingas* – were replaced by forced labor. But they were not completely erased; today there are still *mingas* in the Peruvian highlands. Women begin preparing a community meal on *minga* day while the townspeople, regardless of age, set to work.

At its peak, Cusco was a city with sophisticated water systems, paved streets, and no poverty. But its leaders were not all wise and competent. One Inca chief, Urco, perpetrated such atrocities that his name was erased from Incan history

BELOW: hill-top view of Cusco.

and his mention forbidden. Another hung his enemies along the roadsides in the empire's cities. Yet another had the entire population of a nearby city executed for the rape of a virgin selected to dedicate her life to the sun cult. But these excesses fail to overshadow the magnificence of a civilization whose architecture could not be destroyed and whose feats could not be matched.

Walking into the past

The most startling and curious characteristic of Cusco at first glance is its architecture. Huge walls of intricately fit stone pay testimony to the civilization that over 500 years ago controlled much of the South American subcontinent. The Spaniards' attempts to destroy every trace of the "pagan" Inca civilization proved too ambitious a task, and the Europeans ended up erecting their own buildings on the indestructible Incan foundations, often using the same huge rocks that had been cut by the Incas. The cathedral in Cusco is made in part from stones hauled from Sacsayhuamán, the Inca fortress outside the city.

To explore this intriguing city, the **Cathedral** (open daily) is a perfect place to start. It is located on the north-east side of the **Plaza de Armas** which, in Incan times, was known as Huancaypata and in addition to being the exact center of the empire was the spot where the most important religious and military ceremonies were held. Although the most spectacular view of the cathedral comes after dark when its lights turn the plaza into a breathtaking sight, its interior can only be seen during the day – and you won't want to miss it. Built on what was once the palace of Inca Viracocha, the cathedral mixes Spanish Renaissance architecture with the stone-working skills of the Incas, and took a century to build. Its María Angola bell in the north tower can be heard up to 40 km (25 miles) away. Made of a ton of gold, silver, and bronze, the bell, which is more than 300 years old, is reportedly the largest on the continent.

El Triunfo (open Mon–Sat, at rather irregular hours), to the right of the cathedral, was built to commemorate a Spanish victory over the Amerindians, who unsuccessfully tried to burn the thatched roof chapel that originally stood on the site. On the other side of the cathedral is the church of **Jesús María** (irregular opening hours). At only 250 years old, it is one of Cusco's newer structures.

A mingling of cultures

Turn left from El Triunfo and walk one block up to the corner of Calle Hatunrumiyoc, literally "the Street of the Big Stones", and Calle Palacio, to the **Museo de Arte Religioso del Arzobispado** (open Mon–Sat). This Moorish building with complicated carvings on its doors and balconies was constructed on the site of the 15th-century palace of Inca Roca, under whose rule Cusco's schools were initiated. The museum displays a fine collection of paintings in the style known as the School of Cusco, which flourished from the 16th–18th centuries – a mingling of indigenous and Spanish cultures in which archangels are dressed as Spaniards carrying European guns, surrounded by cherubs with Amerindian features, and the Last Supper shows Christ and his Amerindian-looking apostles dining on roast guinea pig and Peruvian cheese. Outside is the **Twelve-Angled Stone**, a tribute

Map on page 144

TIP

An excellent value US$20 ticket allows entry to many highlights of Cusco and the Sacred Valley, including the Regional History Museum, Qenko, Sacsayhuamán, and Pisac.

BELOW: colorful Andean market.

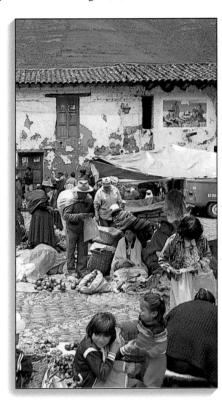

to the skill of Inca masons, proving that no piece of granite was too irregular to be fitted without mortar and every piece slotting together like a jigsaw puzzle.

In a city with so many churches, it is an honor to be dubbed the "most beautiful" but that is the title given to **La Compañía de Jesús** (open Mon–Fri), sitting on what was once the palace of Inca Huayna Capac on the southeast corner of the Plaza de Armas. Construction of the church, with its intricate interior, finely carved balconies, and altars covered in gold leaf, took nearly 100 years and is a fine example of Andean baroque.

The street to the side of the church leads to what was the most important place of worship in the Inca Empire. The **Iglesia Santo Domingo** (open daily) was once **El Templo del Coricancha** (or Q'urikancha, Quechua for "golden courtyard") – the Temple of the Sun – the most magnificent complex in Cusco. Its walls were covered in gold, and its windows were constructed so the sun would cast a near-blinding reflection of golden light from the precious metals inside. Spanish chronicles describe the astonishment of the Europeans when they saw Coricancha's patio filled with life-sized gold and silver statues of llamas, trees, flowers, and delicate butterflies. Current excavations promise to reveal more of the temple's mysteries.

Coaxing a llama.

LEFT: Cusco's narrow, cobbled streets.
RIGHT: street vendors, Cusco.

Retrace your steps toward the Plaza de Armas, and on Calle Arequipa you will find another Christian enclave that was formerly an Inca holy place. This is the **Convento y Museo de Santa Catalina** (open daily). Now a colonial-style building occupied by Roman Catholic nuns, this was home to the Chosen Women, virgins who were trained to serve their heavenly husband, the sun, or attend to the pleasure of his earthly son, the Inca. The museum contains a fine collection of School of Cusco art.

The valley of ruins

The megalithic fortress of **Sacsayhuamán** ❺ is a bold example of Inca architectural skills. Constructed from massive stones, this military complex overlooking Cusco has a double wall in zigzag shape. It also marks the birthplace of the river that runs under Cusco, channeled through stone conduits honed by the ancient Incas, invisibly supplying the city with water. Archeologists estimate that tens of thousands of workers labored on this massive structure for more than seven decades, hauling the immense stone blocks that make up its double outside walls and erecting the near-indestructible buildings that made the complex one of the most wondrous in all the empire. Inti Raymi, the Inca feast of the winter solstice, is celebrated every year on June 24 at Sacsayhuamán, with a procession, ceremony, and much merrymaking.

Some 7 km (4 miles) from Sacsayhuamán, **Qenko** ❻ is an Inca shrine that has a 5-meter (18-ft) high stone block that *cusqueños* claim looks like a puma. Its name means labyrinth, and this ceremonial center, dedicated to Mother Earth, has water channels cut into solid rock and a subterranean room. Farther along the road to Pisac (or Pisaq) is a smaller fortress, **Puca Pucara** ❼, believed to have guarded the road and the Sacred Valley of the Incas. It has hillside terraces, stairways, tunnels, and towers. To the north, **Tambo Machay** ❽ is the sacred bathing place of the Inca rulers and their royal women. A hydraulic engineering marvel, its aqueduct system still feeds water into a series of showers.

From there head down 400 meters (1,500 ft) into the valley on the curvy road leading to **Pisac** ❾, a friendly village known for its fishing, Sunday market, and the ruins above the town. To reach the ruins, climb past the mountainside terraces (local children will serve as guides for a small fee). It's a high-altitude hike

TIP

Sacsayhuamán is a short hike uphill from the city. Alternatively, you can take a minibus tour, or hire a cab to take you up and wait for you. This is one of the area's most spectacular spots to take photos at dawn. Keep a close watch on your belongings.

that may leave your heart pounding. The stones in Pisac's buildings are smaller than those at Sacsayhuamán, but the precision with which they are cut and fitted will amaze you. If you plan to do a full circuit of the valley, continue to the great fortress of **Ollantaytambo** , 72 km (45 miles) from Cusco. This elegant and intricate granite complex has temples, baths, and impressive military installations. Both Ollantaytambo and Pisac can be seen on the Cusco Visitor Ticket.

The massive stone ramparts at Sacsayhuamán.

The Andes

At 7,200 km (4,500 miles), the Andes, the longest mountain chain in the world, forms the backbone of South America. The range stretches from Colombia down to southern Chile and Argentina, and is made up of dozens of parallel mountain ranges known as cordilleras. In Peru, these ranges cluster together providing trekkers with easy access to some of the world's highest peaks outside the Himalayas. Except for the most rugged and remote areas, the Peruvian Andes are not an untouched wilderness. Every single piece of arable land is farmed by local *campesinos* (peasants).

The formidable Peruvian sierra (mountainous region) was conquered by the Incas, whose terraced system of agriculture enabled large areas of steep yet fertile land to be cultivated. This ancient system is still employed in some areas, and countless remains of ancient terracing give an insight into the productivity achieved by this civilization. Passing through these remote, yet populated areas is a bit like stepping back into the past. One- or two-room huts constructed of crude adobe bricks and topped with *ichu* grass have changed little in design since Inca times. There is no electricity, and water is drawn from a nearby stream. Small courtyards house chickens and *cuy*, or guinea pig, considered a delicacy in the sierra. Corn and other grains can often be seen drying in the midday sun.

BELOW: the fortress of Sacsayhuamán, near Cusco.

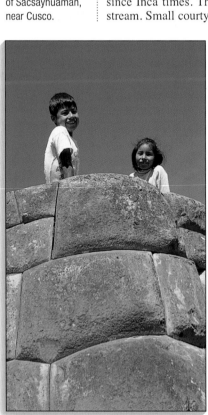

The Inca Trail

Of all the popular treks in South America, the three- to five-day hike along the Inca Trail (following the course of an old Inca roadway) to Machu Picchu is the best known. The adventure from Cusco begins with a four-hour overcrowded train ride along the Urubamba River, known by the Incas as the **Sacred Valley**. It is no longer possible to walk the Inca Trail independently; you must pre-arrange the trip either at home or in Cusco; this is best done well in advance. If you want to avoid the arduous trekking, the train also stops at Aguas Calientes, 8 km (5 miles) from the Lost City, and you can get off there, but you will miss out on some stunning scenery.

The first 12 km (7 miles) of the trail meander through easy terrain of dusty scrub, low-lying hills and hut dwellings. Then comes the **Huarmihuañusqa Pass**, beyond which lies a wealth of Inca ruins. Struggling to the top of this 4,000-meter (13,000-ft) pass is no small challenge. The hiker soon identifies with its name, which translates as "Dead Woman's Pass". The small guard post of **Runkuraqay**, often shrouded in mist, is the first reward of the Inca Trail. Further along, the more elaborately constructed ruins of **Sayajmarka** ("Dominant Town") perch on top of a narrow

Map on page 144

cliff. The fine stonework for which the Incas are famous is apparent. An incredible paved highway snakes along the valley below, masterfully constructed by a people the Spaniards did not consider civilized. **Puyapatamarka** (Cloud-level Town) is fascinating for its circular walls and finely engineered aqueduct system, which still provides spring water to the ancient baths. Along the road to **Wiñay Wayna**, a long stone staircase leads down into dense jungle. Clinging to a steep hillside, the last set of ruins is the most stunning. That something so complex was constructed in a ravine so vertical is almost beyond comprehension.

An hour away lies the jewel in the crown – **Machu Picchu** ⓫. To see it at sunrise, most trekkers stay at the camp beyond Wiñay Wayna, where rainy nights are filled with the howls of campers trying to sleep in leaky tents. The high pass of **Intipunku**, the Sun Gate, provides the first glimpse of the fabled city. Arriving as the Incas did centuries ago, the trekker begins the final descent into Machu Picchu. However, the sheer number of visitors hiking up the trail (up to 1,000 per day) has caused the tourist board to contemplate controversial changes, such as constructing a cable car from Aguas Calientes to Machu Picchu.

Cusco means "navel" in Quechua, because the Incas considered the city the center or source of their universe.

Arequipa: the "white city"

Although **Arequipa** ⓬ was far from Lima and isolated between desert and mountains when the country was young, it was on the route linking the silver mines of Bolivia to the coast. For that reason, the oasis at the foot of the Misti volcano grew to be the Peruvian town with the largest Spanish population and the strongest European traditions. Today, with buildings of white volcanic stone lending it the name "white city", it remains Peru's second most important city.

Arequipa's **Plaza de Armas** is one of Peru's most beautiful. One full side is

BELOW: craft stall and assistant, Chinchero.

TREKKING IN THE ANDES

One of the best places for trekking information is the South American Explorer's Club in Lima (membership fee US$50). Their office in Lima (Calle Piura 135, Miraflores, tel: 01-445 3306; www.saexplorers.org), keeps reports on trails, maps, and books. Another good place for advice is the Casa de Guías in Huaraz (Parque Ginebra 28G, tel: 42-811, fax: 42-2306; www.casadeguias.com.pe). Bring a down jacket and plenty of warm clothes for very cold nights at 4,000 meters (13,100 ft) and above. A tent and a good sleeping bag are essential. Equipment can be hired in the major trekking centers, but check the quality, since items are often the worse for wear.

Before setting off, spend a couple of days getting used to the thin, high-altitude air around Cusco and Huaraz, or you will quickly become exhausted. If you are trekking independently (no longer possible on the Inca Trail), stock up on food – you won't be able to buy anything on the way. A stove for cooking is essential: there is no wood for fires at higher altitudes, and using up scarce reserves at lower levels only adds to the serious problem of soil erosion in the area. And of course no litter whatsoever should be left behind. A guide who knows the area well can be invaluable – ask around, as competence varies.

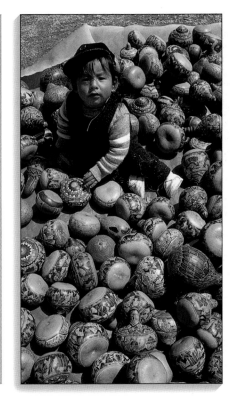

Machu Picchu

The mystery of Machu Picchu did not start in 1911 when archeologist, Hiram Bingham stumbled on the snake-infested mountain-top citadel hidden by a vast tangle of vines and trees. This site on the steep summit overlooking the raging Urubamba River was always a mystery – because only a chosen few in the Inca Empire were allowed to glimpse it. To call it a "lost city" is misleading; it was more like a sanctuary.

Machu Picchu means "Old Peak", and the higher Huayna Picchu (Young Peak), stands vigil over it. The site is accessible on the four-hour bus and train service from Cusco or by hiking the Inca Trail *(see page 156)*. The area is semitropical, and 900 meters (3,000 ft) lower than Cusco.

Machu Picchu was home to priests, high functionaries, craftsmen, and servants and, most importantly, the *mamaconas*, or virgins chosen to dedicate their lives to the sun god. It was a city of streets, aqueducts where

crystal clear waters still run, of liturgical fountains and walkways. Even after Bingham's discovery, the city remained inaccessible until the 1940s, when an archeological expedition working at the site discovered the Inca Trail cutting through the valley.

The fate of this city's inhabitants remains unknown. Spanish chronicles of the Cusco area make no mention of it. Theories of its demise range from epidemics to suggestions that the occupants were ostracized and forgotten in the bloody political disunity sweeping the empire before its fall.

Excavations have only added to the mystery. The skeletons of 173 people were found, 150 of whom were women. No gold objects were discovered. At the tomb of the high priestess, as Bingham called it, the remains of a woman and a small dog were found with some ceramic objects, two brooches, and woolen clothing. The woman had suffered from syphilis.

Today's visitors enter the ruins near the hotel, but the only entrance to the city in ancient times was the narrow doorway at the southwest section of the citadel. The city's cultivated land was farmed on narrow terraces on the steep slopes of the mountain-top, and the thousands of steps connecting them have survived for centuries.

The city is divided into sections: the cemetery, jails, small dwellings, and temples. The Temple of the Three Windows allows sunlight to pass through its windows to the Sacred Plaza. Climbing higher is the astronomical observatory and *Intiwatana*, the curiously shaped stone block believed to have been a solar clock or, as some claim, "the hitching post to the sun", where the sun's rays cast shadows used in planning seasonal activities and religious ceremonies.

Some of the buildings in Machu Picchu were two stories high, originally topped with sharply peaked straw roofs. What amazes architects today is the precision with which building stones were cut and assembled.

A steep and perilous path rises from the site to the top of Huayna Picchu. At the skirt of Huayna Picchu is the construction known as the Temple of the Moon, and from the summit there is an extraordinary view of the ruins and the Urubamba valley. ❑

LEFT: Machu Picchu.

Map on page 144

occupied by the massive **Cathedral** (open daily), rebuilt twice in the early 19th century after it was destroyed by fire and earthquake. Its clock is the city's unofficial timepiece. Make sure you see the cathedral's organ, brought from Belgium, and the elaborately carved wooden pulpit, the work of French artist Rigot in 1879. Two-story arcades grace the other three sides of the plaza, with palm trees, old gas lamps, and a fountain set in an English-style garden.

The city is full of patrician homes built in the 18th century which have withstood its frequent earth tremors. The one-story colonial structures are replete with massive carved wooden doors, grilled French windows, and high-ceilinged rooms around spacious patios. The best for visiting are **Casa Ricketts** (open daily), built as a seminary in 1738 and now used as a bank; the 200-year-old **Casa de la Monda** or former mint; and the **Casa Moral** (open Mon–Sat), named after the venerable mulberry tree on its patio, which has also become a bank.

La Compañía church (open daily) is well worth seeing. The sacristy's ceiling is covered with miniature paintings and carvings in crimson and gold. The view from the steeple is fabulous, especially at sunset when the fading light gives a rosy glow to the city's white rock buildings.

The most astonishing stop in Arequipa is the **Monasterio de Santa Catalina** (open daily), opened in 1970 after 400 years as a cloister for nuns. Although they lived behind closed doors, the nuns paid little heed to the traditional vows of poverty and silence. During its heyday, this convent's sleeping cells were furnished with English carpets, silk curtains, cambric and lace sheets, and tapestry-covered stools. Each nun had her own servant and dined off porcelain plates using silver cutlery. At its peak nearly 500 nuns were housed in the convent.

When the convent opened its doors again, its anecdotes and scandals were resurrected. But don't believe it when they tell you the story of Sister Dominga, the 16-year-old who entered the convent when her betrothed left her for a rich widow, then staged her own death to escape. This beautiful young woman really did place the body of a deceased Amerindian woman in her bed one night then set the room on fire, but it happened at the **Convento de Santa Rosa** (which is still cloistered).

Two other places worth visiting nearby are the **Museo Histórico Municipal** (open Mon–Fri), which is interesting for an overview of the city's history. From here it is only a few yards to the **Iglesia de San Francisco** (open daily), the focus of attention every December 8 during the Feast of the Immaculate Conception, when a coach topped with the image of the Virgin Mary is paraded through the streets in a colorful procession. The most interesting museum in the city, the **Monasterio de la Recoleta** (open Mon–Sat), lies across the Río Chili (use the Puente Grau or Puente Bolognesi). The monastery has a vast library of 20,000 books, many of them very old.

Independent spirits

Outside Arequipa, set in beautiful countryside, is **Sabandía** with its nearby flour mill that was restored, stone by stone, in 1973. Three hours away and drawing nearly as much tourist attention as the city itself is the **Colca Canyon**. From the Colca River at

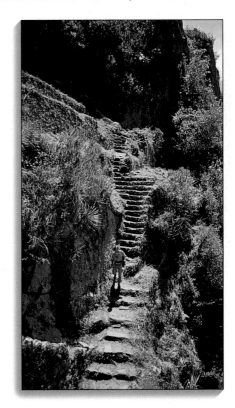

BELOW: walking the Inca Trail.

Convent of Santa Catalina, Arequipa.

its base to the mountains above, the chasm reaches depths of 3,400 meters (11,000 ft). Even more remote than Colca, the **Cotahuasi Canyon** is now believed to exceed Colca in depth (3,535 meters/11,600 ft), making it the world's deepest canyon. It is a pristine area of great natural beauty ideal for adventurers and nature lovers.

At the Cruz del Cóndor viewpoint you may see a condor, soaring on the warm thermal currents produced in the early morning or the early evening. The Cruz del Cóndor is included in a variety of one- and two-day trips, which can be organized in Arequipa. En route, many of the tours take in the **Reserva Nacional Salinas y Aguada Blanca** (at 3,900 meters/12,800 ft you'll notice how thin the air is), where groups of shy vicuñas can often be seen. The area is also accessible from Arequipa, first by bus, then switching to donkeys *(burros)*.

To unwind in Arequipa after a hard day's sightseeing, do what the locals do and head to a *picantería* for a cold *Arequipeña* beer and some spicy stuffed peppers, rabbit, or marinated pork.

Puno and Lake Titicaca

Lake Titicaca's great size and breathless altitude, its mysterious antiquity, and even its steamships constitute an exotic legend. At 174 km (108 miles) long and up to 64 km (40 miles) wide, Titicaca is South America's largest lake. The lake moderates the climate and facilitates cultivation around its shores, despite the frosty nights and short growing season. Peru and Bolivia share this lake peacefully, but in bygone times it was at the heart of warring tribalism and imperial ambition. About 1,500 years ago the powerful Tihuanaku civilization built a vast city on the Bolivian shore; its collapse led to centuries of sectarian

BELOW: Plaza de Armas, Arequipa.

Map on page 144

strife. At Sillustani, the towering tombs of the Colla kings, whose armies fought the Incas, can still be seen. Today, Quechua- and Aymara-speaking Amerindians occupy discrete stretches of Titicaca's shoreline.

You can visit two very different island communities that subsist on the lake. The Uros islanders, dwelling on spongy reed masses, live on the waters of **Puno** bay. This tourist hub is an old, cold town on the lake shore that has, thanks to the tourism industry, undergone something of a revival. Puno now offers a good selection of comfortable hotels, as well as lively bars and decent restaurants.

On solid **Taquile**, a traditional way of life manages to survive in spite of the steady flow of fascinated visitors. Taquile is a traditional Quechua-speaking community. The island is best known for its weaving, and two co-ops in the central square sell superb handicrafts. Overnighters should have sufficient time to climb to the highest point on the island. Follow a footpath that turns uphill off the street between the village and the main archway, allowing about 30 minutes to reach the top. Toward the summit there are some tombs dating from pre-Inca times. The summit views of Lake Titicaca, with Amantaní island to the north, are superb. In fine weather you can see a dazzling horizon of snowy peaks, the Cordillera Real, on the Bolivian shore.

Condor over Colca Canyon.

The lake's hinterland is a great plateau studded with isolated mountains known as the Altiplano, the high plain. **Juliaca** is its hustling commercial capital, known for its textile and leather goods, while the charming town of Lampa is becoming a center for tourism.

The Peruvian Amazon

Three-fifths of Peru is jungle – the Amazon. Despite the encroachment of modern life, this is where adventures can still occur and the exotic reigns. Here the roads are rivers and the vehicles are motorboats and canoes. It is the home of many natural healers, who say that its unique fauna might contain anything from new contraceptives to a cancer cure. The Amazon is the one place the Incas never managed to penetrate. When the Spanish conquistadors arrived, they heard wild tales of a golden city hidden in the heart of the jungle. In their search for El Dorado, they found nothing but disease and hostile tribes, although the legend lives on.

The Spanish explorer Francisco de Orellana is credited with discovering the Amazon River. He named it after the fierce female warriors of Greek legend when he mistook the long-haired Yagua men, who confronted him wearing fiber skirts, for women. A later Spanish expedition was fictionalized in the 1973 Werner Herzog film *Aguirre, the Wrath of God*, about the demonic conquistador Aguirre, who killed for pleasure during his 1560 trek along the Amazon. The search for gold was replaced by missionaries' quest to convert the indigenous population. From the late 1600s to the mid-1700s, thanks to an uprising led by Jesuit-educated Quechua Juan Santos, the jungle was kept free of Europeans, but the missionaries eventually returned, and the Catholic presence in the rainforest has received strong competition from Protestant evangelists.

BELOW: Colca Canyon.

The rubber barons

The colonization of the Amazon was consolidated at the end of the 1800s with the rubber boom. The period was one of overnight wealth for European and US rubber barons and overnight enslavement for the people of the rainforest. The best-known of the rubber barons was Carlos Fitzgerald, the son of an English immigrant and a Peruvian. Accused of spying for Chile during the 1879 war, "Fitzcarraldo" fled to the Amazon where he made a great fortune in rubber and became obsessed with a plan to travel from the Ucayali River (which flows into the Amazon) through the Madre de Dios River by steamship. Although Fitzcarraldo's quest failed, steamships later made the trip, effectively linking the Atlantic and Pacific oceans – with thousands of Amerindians hauling the ships across the isthmus. Fitzcarraldo and other rubber barons had no cause to miss Europe; they imported every luxury that struck their fancy, from Paris fashions to imported wines, and European theater and opera stars regularly performed in the midst of one of the world's densest jungles. But the opulence ended in 1920 when rubber grown in Asia and Africa began to compete on the world market.

Boom towns and exotic wildlife

Peru's most important rubber boom city – and the largest city in the Peruvian Amazon – is **Iquitos** ⓭. The old days of wealth are still evident in the houses covered with Portuguese tiles and, on the **Plaza de Armas**, in the ramshackle two-story metal house designed by Gustave Eiffel for the Paris Exhibition of 1889 and transported to Iquitos piece by piece by rubber magnate Jules Toth. On the waterfront is the colorful **Belén** port, where the houses float on rafts. From here, irregular riverboat services run to Leticia in Colombia and onward to

BELOW: local riverboats carry both passengers and cargo.

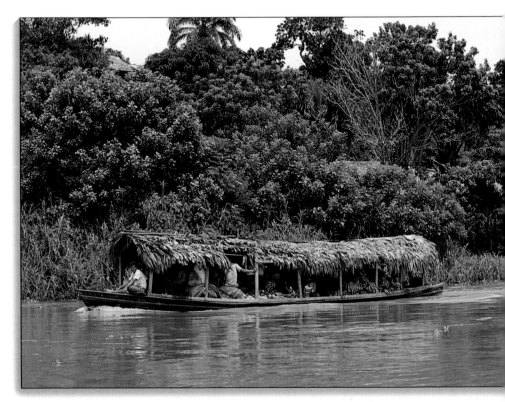

Manaus in Brazil, preserving a taste of the days when air travel was unknown and the only way to reach Iquitos was through weeks of journeying overland and upriver. Although Iquitos is a bustling city of 400,000 people, one only has to go a short distance on the Amazon, Yanamono or Manatí rivers to be in virgin jungle. On the way are the wood and palm houses on stilts inhabited by the *ribereños* – mestizos who speak a lilting Spanish reminiscent of Brazilian Portuguese. Exotic birds fly in and out of vine-covered trees, while brilliantly colored butterflies, tapirs, monkeys, peccaries, and pink river dolphins fascinate visitors. Only 100 km (62 miles) from Iquitos is the biggest national park in Peru, the 2-million hectare (5-million acre) **Reserva Nacional Pacaya-Samiria**, a wildlife-packed lowland jungle area that can only be reached by hiring a boat and a guide, in either Iquitos or the village of Lagunas.

Tourists generally stay in lodges in the jungle, the oldest and most recommended being the three Explorama complexes, ranging from the ultra-modern Explorama Inn with 24-hour electricity and private bathrooms in every cabin to the primitive Explornapo camp, where kerosene lamps, night walks, and mosquito netting tents add to the mystique *(see page 392)*.

The people in this part of the Amazon live isolated lives, except when they head off in their dugout canoes or hitch a ride on the "river buses" – boats that cruise up and down the river collecting passengers and their cargoes of bananas, yucca, corn, dried fish, and chickens headed for Iquitos.

Another important Amazon city is **Pucallpa ⓮**, a frontier lumber town and the furthest inland navigable port for ocean-going vessels on the Amazon. It is 9 km (6 miles) from **Lago Yarinacocha**, a 22-km (14-mile) body of water luring tourists fascinated by its spectacular sunrises and sunsets, its fishing, and the

Map on page 144

LEFT: Amazon Amerindians still use blow darts to shoot their prey. **RIGHT:** young puma, a rare sight.

San Pedro cactus, Chiclayo.

BELOW: window detail, Trujillo.

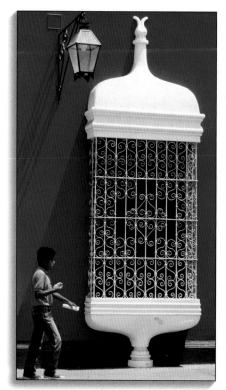

undisturbed native Shipibo villages along its banks. Its forests are full of cedar, pine, mahogany, and bamboo and serve as home to nearly 1,000 bird species, endless varieties of butterflies and exotic mammals – including sloths. Local boats called *pekepekes* are available for hire for day trips to some of the isolated villages or to visit the Shipibos and buy their hand-painted pottery and textiles. In nearby **Puerto Callao** you can visit the fascinating artisanal cooperative Maroti Shobo, where high-quality ceramics and weavings made by the Shipibo from the surrounding villages are displayed and sold, and sent to museums all over the world. Further south is **Puerto Maldonado** , just a few hours by river from one of the world's most important wildlife reserves and capital of the least-populated, least-developed and least-explored province in Peru.

At 1.8 million hectares (4½ million acres), the **Parque Nacional Manu** ⑯ is one of the largest conservation areas in the world. Founded in 1973, it was declared a Biosphere Reserve in 1977, and a World Natural Heritage Site 10 years later. Parts are accessible only to biologists and anthropologists with permits, one zone is set aside for two local native groups, and the reserve zone is aimed at eco-tourists. The excellent **Manu Wildlife Center** allows visitors to meet researchers and scientists on-site. Closer to Puerto Maldonado is another large reserve, the **Reserva Nacional Tambopata Candamo**. Created by the Peruvian Government in 1989, this 1.5-million hectare (3.8-million acre) zone has been set up both as an extractive reserve (for rubber, Brazil nuts, and other products) and for eco-tourism. The reserve encompasses the entire watershed of the **Río Tambopata**, one of the most beautiful and least-disturbed areas in Peru, and protects the largest macaw lick in South America, the **Colpa de Guacamayos**, where hundreds of parrots and macaws gather daily.

Peru's historical north

Trujillo ⑰, the "travelers' resting place" along the Spaniards' route between Lima and Quito, is a graceful coastal city. Founded in 1535 and named after Francisco Pizarro's birthplace in Spain, it soon became worthy of the title the "Lordliest City", and even today its well-preserved Andalusian-style wooden balconies pay testimony to the colonial days.

The city is famous for being the first in Peru to declare independence from Spain in 1820, and in the 1920s it was the birthplace of APRA (Alianza Popular Revolucionaria Americana) – Peru's longest-standing political party.

The best place to start exploring Trujillo is the **Plaza de Armas**, bounded by the city hall, the bishop's palace, and the cathedral with its marble pillars and gilt hand-carved wooden altars. The colonial building next to the cathedral is now the **Hotel Libertador Trujillo**. Off the main square, colonial mansions abound, although earthquakes have taken their toll. Most have been elegantly restored by national banks or other private enterprises (most open Mon–Fri and Sat am). **Casa de la Emancipación** is typical of the houses built in the 16th and 17th centuries and contains much of its original furniture. **Casa de Mayorazgo, Casa Urquiaga, Casa Bracamonte**, and **Casa de los Leones** (also known as the Casa Ganoza

Chopitea), now an art gallery, are all worth a look. The **Palacio Iturregui** houses the Club Central, with a permanent exhibition of ceramics. Trujillo's pre-Hispanic past is on display at the University of Trujillo's **Museo de Arqueología** (irregular hours, ask at tourist office). The **Museo Cassinelli** (open daily) in the basement of the Cassinelli gas station, holds a fascinating private collection of Moche and Chimu ceramics.

An ancient adobe city

On the northwest of Trujillo are the ruins of **Chan Chan**, which was one of the world's largest adobe cities at its discovery by the Spanish. Made up of seven citadels spread over 28 sq. km (11 sq. miles) and enclosed by a massive wall, Chan Chan was home to the Chimu people, who fished and farmed, worshiped the moon, and left no written records. On the city walls are carvings of fish, sea birds, fishing nets, and moons. The Chimus had such a sophisticated irrigation and aqueduct system that they were able to turn the arid wasteland around them into fertile fields of grains, fruits, and vegetables.

About 10 km (6 miles) southeast of Trujillo lie **Las Huacas del Sol y de la Luna** (the Tombs of the Sun and the Moon). You can get there by minibus or go on an organized tour. These pyramidal temples were built by the Moche people (100 BC–850 AD). The Huaca del Sol (arguably the largest pre-Columbian building in the Americas) is being excavated, but at the smaller Huaca de la Luna, 15 years of archeological work have unveiled a series of temples superimposed on one another to form a pyramid covered in beautiful, bright murals. Archeology enthusiasts should visit the **Huaca el Brujo**, a recently discovered site a few hours from Trujillo in the Chicama Valley. Ask at the tourist information office for details.

Map on page 144

BELOW: Plaza de Armas, Trujillo.

Where the last Inca leader met his fate

Historically, the most important northern city is **Cajamarca** . This is the city where the Incas and Spaniards had their final confrontation. According to Spanish chronicles, the Inca Atahuallpa *(see page 26)* was taken prisoner after offending the Europeans by accepting a proferred Bible then tossing it to the ground. To pay the ransom demanded by the conquistadors, people from all over the Inca empire brought gold and silver, filling **El Cuarto del Rescate** (the Ransom Room; open daily), a block from the Plaza de Armas. But the effort was futile and the Spaniards garrotted the last Inca king on the main square.

The **Plaza de Armas** is the hub of this slow-paced city of 120,000 and is ringed by colonial buildings and churches. Opened in 1776, the **Cathedral**'s carved wood altars are covered in gold leaf and its facade is of intricately sculpted volcanic rock. The **Iglesia San Francisco**, older and more ornate than the cathedral, is home to the **Museo de Arte Religioso** (open Mon–Fri) and some eerie catacombs. Also on the plaza is Restaurante Salas, the place to eat the city's best home cooking. Cajamarca is ideal for exploring the province of **Amazonas**, home of the Chachapoyan, who built several pre-Incan cities, including **Kuélap**, a great walled city perched high above the Río Utcubamba. Minibuses leave in the morning for the village of **Tingo**, from where a road goes to within 15 minutes' walk of the fascinating site.

Gold figure, Vicus culture, Brüning Museum.

BELOW: the ancient adobe citadel of Chan Chan.

Digging for the past

The Moche burial area at **Sipán** (open daily; guided tours available), about 30 km (18 miles) south of **Chiclayo** 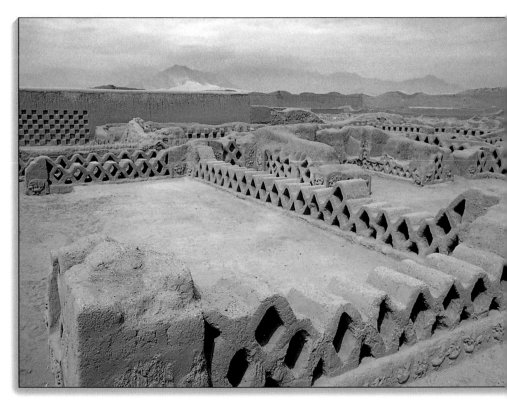, is the largest tomb excavated in the Americas. Known as the tomb of El Señor de Sipán, it was uncovered in the late

1980s, originally by *huaqueros* (grave robbers), before the excavation was taken over by the director of the Brüning Museum *(see below)*, Dr Walter Alva. He became aware of unusual objects on the black market and realised that a burial site was being ransacked. It is 15 meters (50 ft) deep and contained the remains of a high priest or prince wearing a spectacular gold mask with emerald eyes. In his tomb were numerous artifacts including gold and copper, and gilded cotton cloth. There were also the skeletons of 24 women. The whole burial complex comprises 14 tombs, one of which contained 50 kilos (110 lb) of gold. The continuing excavation at Sipán promises to provide crucial new evidence about the life of the Moche, a sophisticated pre-Columbian civilization that flourished from 100–700 AD.

The nearby **Sicán** site, the first to be excavated using radar, disclosed similar riches from the period betweeen the Moche and Chimu civilizations (9th–10th centuries). The artifacts and remains found are on the same scale as those unearthed in the tomb of Tutankhamun. The site is well worth visiting, but to see the stunning contents of the tomb of the Lord of Sipán, when they are not touring the world's museums, you should go to the tiny town of **Lambayeque** nearby to visit the remarkable **Museo Brüning** (open daily), which has Peru's finest publicly owned gold, silver, and ceramic collection, as well as the fabulous finds from the Sipán dig.

One of the most intriguing projects in the area was set up under the direction of the Norwegian explorer, Thor Heyerdahl. His archeological dig at **Túcume**, near Sipán, brought together a team of European and Peruvian archeologists. Túcume is a plain with 27 hills that are actually pyramids covered by centuries of dirt, and can be explored with the help of guided tours from Chiclayo. ❑

Map on page 144

Although Peru has strengthened its laws on the sale of archeological artifacts, large quantities are still smuggled out of the country. Ancient ruins are also plundered by squatters in search of materials to construct their own dwellings.

BELOW: totora reed boats, Huanchaco.

A REMARKABLE CRAFT

In 1948, a Norwegian expedition led by Thor Heyerdahl embarked on a voyage that would take it from Callao in Peru to French Polynesia in a balsa raft, the *Kon-Tiki*. Heyerdahl's intention was to prove that Amerindians could have colonized the Pacific Islands on balsa rafts, and his expedition launched a whole area of scientific investigation. His theory has since been discredited, but interest in the sea-going craft of the pre-Columbian South Americans and Pacific Islanders has increased. Many modern adventurers have their rafts built by Bolivians from the Lake Titicaca region, who are considered the best balsa-raft craftsmen in the world.

When the Spanish first reached the Americas they recorded these craft in detail, which ranged from the totora reed bundle rafts used today by the fishermen of Huanchaco, Peru, to huge cargo-carrying rafts. Chronicler Augustín de Zárate described rafts that could carry 50 men and three horses. In the 17th century, European navigators began to understand the "guara", or centerboard, a navigation instrument used by the Amerindians. Visitors to Peru today can witness the ancient craft in action around Lake Titicaca, or at Huanchaco, near Trujillo.

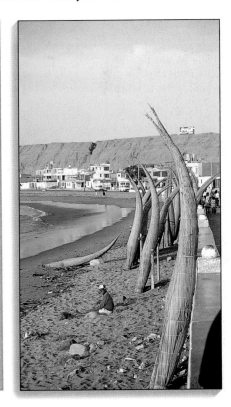

LAKE TITICACA: PERU'S LEGENDARY WATERWAY

Surrounded by snow-capped Andean peaks, this lofty expanse of clear, fresh water has fired the imagination for generations

▷ **REED BOATS**
People of the Lake Titicaca region have been building tortora reed boats since time immemorial to sail the vast expanses of the lake.

Linking Peru and Bolivia, the world's highest navigable lake is a large, remarkably clear blue body of water covering more than 8,000 sq. km (3,000 sq. miles) with more than 30 islands. The lake may look inviting, but bathers beware – at 4,000 meters (13,000 ft) above sea level, its waters are extremely cold all year round. Lake Titicaca is full of history, ancient legends, sacred sites, and living history, as age-old traditions are continued and developed on and around its waters.

△ **GATHERING REEDS**
Although the last full-blood Uros died in 1959, modern Uros islanders still use reeds to build homes, boats, islands, and even for food.

BIRTHPLACE OF THE INCAS

The Isla del Sol, in the middle of the lake, is at the center of the Inca creation myths as recorded by 16th-century Spanish chroniclers. One myth tells of the emergence of four sisters and four brothers from a stone door on the island, two of whom were the Incas Manco Capac and Mama Ocllo (or Huaca). Another legend relates that the sun was born on a sacred rock on the island. Ruined Inca temples and sacred sites can be visited on the Isla del Sol and the nearby Isla de Luna *(pictured above)*. Inca history holds that when the Spanish reached Cusco in Peru, the Incas took the 1,800-kg (2-ton) gold chain of Inca Huascar from Qoricancha, and hurled it into the lake. The late French oceanographer Jacques Cousteau spent two months exploring the lake with a mini submarine. He found no gold but he did discover a 60-cm (24-inch) tri-colored frog that apparently never surfaces. In 1996 the oldest known temple in South America was found near the lake, occupied between 1500 and 1000 BC, nearly 2,500 years before the Incas. Its discovery adds to the fascination of this remarkable region.

◁ **TAQUILE TRADITIONS**
The colorful te[...] designs of Is[...] Taquile are [...] just for decoration bu[...] can denote social [...] marital status. Some are [...] reserved for special tim[...] of the year.

THE WEAVERS OF ISLA TAQUILE

On the Peruvian side of the lake is Isla Taquile – the island of weavers. Under the Spanish it was a hacienda, and later it became a prison, but the Taquile people have managed to regain ownership. Since 1970 they have been running their own tourism operations to ensure their old traditions are not lost.

There are no hotels, but islanders open their homes to overnight guests, and there are small eating establishments specializing in lake trout.

Poverty has bred a cooperative lifestyle, which has won the islanders their reputation for hospitality. Textiles can be purchased from the weaving cooperatives, most knitted from finely spun sheep's wool dyed bright red and blue – the colors and weaves can reveal age, social position, and marital status. More textiles can be purchased at Amantaní, a peaceful island with temples and a carved stone throne on one shore.

◁ **FRESH FISH**
Lake Titicaca has waves, and can get very choppy! Trout from the lake can be tasted at restaurants in Copacabana and elsewhere.

▽ **UROS ISLANDERS**
The Uros Islands have become a popular tourist attraction. Islanders make small model boats out of reeds to sell to tourists.

◁ **FIESTA OF THE VIRGIN**
The quiet Bolivian town of Copacabana, beside the lake, bursts into life at fiesta time.

▷ **TIAHUANACO**
This mysterious pre-Inca site has advanced stonework that is over 2,000 years old.

BOLIVIA

Landlocked and isolated, Bolivia is one of South America's most unlikely treasures, attracting the most intrepid visitors for its rich cultural heritage and literally breathtaking mountain scenery

G eographically, Bolivia takes you from the heights of the Altiplano, the Andean plateau which elevates northeastern Bolivia, down to the balmy valleys of the Yungas and on to the fertile lowlands of the Oriente. Linking these physically dissimilar territories are hair-raising zigzag roads which [c]ling to near-vertical cliffs. Further south, the plateau shelves off a little more [g]ently, in the area known as the Valles.

Bolivia is also noted for its material highs and lows, particularly the vast gulf [b]etween rich and poor. The poverty is obvious – just look around on the streets [o]f La Paz, behind the cheerful smiles of the traders and colorfully dressed *[c]ampesinos* (farmers), or drive past families toiling in the fields early in the [m]orning. Bolivia's wealth is not so obvious, but is hinted at in certain genteel [c]afés in La Paz. Much of it, like the riches of the silver and tin mines, was con[c]entrated in the hands of a few, and spirited away to Europe. A good deal of the [c]ountry's physical wealth was taken by neighboring countries in a succession of [d]isastrous wars. Today, Bolivia is the subcontinent's poorest nation, with about [t]wo-thirds of its population, many of whom are subsistence farmers, living in [p]overty, and the highest infant mortality rate in South America.

A sizeable part of Bolivia's wealth is generated in the coca fields of the [O]riente and turned into cash on the streets of North [A]merican cities. In 2001, farmers rejected an offer [fr]om the government of US$900 each, annually, in [e]xchange for destroying coca crops.

The lust for silver

[I]n 1544 an Amerindian named Diego Huallpa dis[c]overed silver in the Cerro Rico of Potosí, and from [th]at moment, the country's fate was sealed. For the [n]ext two centuries, everything in Bolivia was geared [t]oward extracting this vein of precious metal, the [gr]eatest ever discovered. Towns were founded for the [so]le purpose of supplying Potosí with goods traded [fr]om other parts of the empire or to transfer silver [b]ack to Europe. Nothing mattered to the Spanish [e]xcept the ore and its transportation from the freezing [w]ilderness, least of all the fate of the local people: the [m]agnificent Inca systems of terracing and irrigation [fe]ll into disrepair and Christianity was imposed, al[th]ough the conversion was at best superficial. More [ob]vious was the imposition of a new form of dress [fo]r native women. Layered dresses, derbys (bowler [ha]ts), and plaited hair typify the most common tourist [vi]ew of the Bolivian people today – this appearance [ac]tually came about by Spanish decree in the 18th [ce]ntury. The local populations were theoretically free [su]bjects of the Spanish crown, but in reality they were [fo]rced to pay massive tributes, lived at the beck and

PRECEDING PAGES: musicians, La Paz. **LEFT:** La Paz seen from the rim of the Altiplano. **BELOW:** Aymara man playing the *zampoña*.

call of brutal overlords, and were regularly dragged from their farms to work in the mines of Potosí. Amerindians died by the thousands in the harsh conditions while colonial Potosí grew to match any city in the Old World.

The amount of silver that was taken from Potosí is staggering: 16 million kg (16,000 tons) arrived in Seville between 1545 and 1660, three and a half times the entire European reserves of the day. The wealth was squandered on Spain's futile religious wars, or wasted by the extravagance of its nobles and clergymen, almost all of it ending up in the coffers of Flemish, German, or English bankers.

The creation of Bolivia in 1825 *(see page 32)* launched the country into an apparently endless series of military governments, mostly bloodless reshufflings in the palaces of La Paz, with wealth and control being kept in the hands of a small number of families of Spanish descent. Meanwhile, the country proceeded to lose large chunks of its territory in wars with its neighbors. The only good news seemed to be the discovery of rich veins of tin, in Oruro and Potosí, by a prospector named Simón Patiño. But Patiño amassed a personal fortune from

Two-thirds of the Bolivian population are of native origin, the highest proportion of any country in South America.

is new boom, becoming one of the ten richest people on earth by the early 1900s. While Patiño lived in luxury, he kept miners on starvation wages and he quashed industrial disputes by organizing massacres as he vacationed in Europe.

Moves for change

A period of intense self-reflection followed the 1930s Chaco War, creating a movement for change, culminating in the Revolutionary Nationalist Movement (MNR) behind Victor Paz Estenssoro. Winning the elections of 1951, the party was blocked from office by a military coup and Paz Estenssoro was forced into exile in Buenos Aires. But the miners began an armed revolt and, after heavy fighting, defeated the military. Paz Estenssoro returned to La Paz and the MNR began to put its reforms into action. In the following years Bolivia saw the nationalization of tin mines, the granting of votes to Amerindians and extensive land reform. Unfortunately, the mines were still dependent on foreign capital, and land given to indigenous peoples was in plots too small to be productive. The economy began sliding and the MNR was ousted in another military coup.

Dictator followed dictator with monotonous regularity. The country's most infamous dictator came to power in 1980 in a coup that cost hundreds of lives: General Luis García Meza sent his tanks into La Paz, shot left-wing leaders, and bombed mining camps in Oruro. He ran an extraordinarily corrupt regime, inviting ex-Nazi Klaus Barbie to help organize his security forces and selling off national assets to line his own pockets. Finally García Meza was driven from power and in 1982 democracy was restored under Dr Hernán Siles Zuazo, who is unfortunately best remembered for leading Bolivia into one of the world's highest inflation rates, hitting a mind-boggling 35,000 percent a year.

Stone cross on Chacaltaya, with Huayna Potosí in the background.

BELOW: colorful cemetery near La Paz.

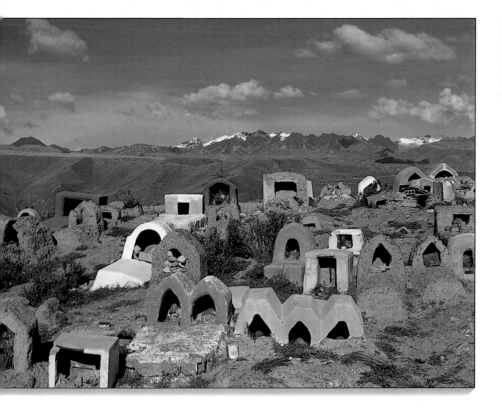

Tin price collapse

In 1985, with the economy on the verge of collapse, Paz Estenssoro returne
as president. He embraced conservative policies recommended by the IMI
and, with the collapse of tin prices, sacked 20,000 miners from the state-ru
COMIBOL, using the military to head off union protests. Inflation ground to
halt, at the price of massive unemployment.

Inconclusive results in the 1989 elections led to a congressional vote to elec
the president, and center-left Jaime Paz Zamora came to power under an allianc
with right-wing ex-dictator Hugo Banzer Suárez. Unemployment boosted cocain
manufacture as people looked for new sources of income, and in the early 1990
the US embarked on Operation Support Justice, an anti-narcotics program in Bc
livia, tied to US$78 million in aid. But high-profile raids on illegal laboratories le
to few arrests and the Americans were shortly asked to leave. Such programs hav
often provoked violent demonstrations by angry *cocaleros* (coca growers). Man
defend their traditional right to grow coca for uses other than drug productior
Others, desperately poor, defend the chance to grow a crop that is more durabl
than rice or potatoes and which can be many times more lucrative.

The 1993 elections brought to power the MNR, led by millionaire Gonzal
Sánchez de Lozada, but opposition to his program of aggressive economic an
social reform led to social unrest. In March 1997, Bolivia negotiated an agree
ment with Mercosur, the Southern Cone trade organization. Ex-dictator Hug
Banzer Suárez formed a coalition to take power. Banzer's government pledge
to end drug production and trafficking and succeeded in eliminating about 2
percent of the coca crop. In June 2002 Gonzalo Sánchez de Lozada was returne
to power. In February the following year, Bolivia's most violent protests in decade

BELOW: woodcut of
Potosí from 1555,
the earliest known
drawing of a New
World mining
enterprise.

vere sparked when Sánchez de Lozada's government tried to introduce income ax. Among others, the police went on strike. The army was called in to restore rder but used bullets to control the crowd, resulting in 33 deaths. Income tax roposals were withdrawn, and five ministries were abolished.

Continuing protests over rising fuel prices and the ownership of the country's aluable gas resources, as well as demands for autonomy from resource-rich rovinces, made Bolivia a tough country to govern. Sánchez de Lozada was orced to resign in 2003 and was succeeded by Carlos Mesa. Unable to do much etter, he too threw in the towel in 2005. One clear leader has emerged from the urgeoning social movements in Bolivia: socialist peasant leader and indigenous oca farmer, Evo Morales. His success in the 2005 elections has been crucial to he indigenous movement of Bolivia, and the country at last has a president vho is representative of the majority of the population. Morales has taken a lear stance against US influence in the region and has nationalized the coun-ry's gas reserves, which are the second-largest in South America.

Map on page 174

a Paz: the highest capital

f you're going to fly to Bolivia's unofficial capital, **La Paz ❶**, try to get a vindow seat. The views are extraordinary as the airplane sweeps across Bolivia's ighest mountain ranges and descends towards the city, which sits in a natural anyon. The one disadvantage is that some travelers arriving in the airport, at an ltitude of almost 4,000 meters (13,000 ft), are immediately struck by the nau-ea and headaches of *soroche*, or altitude sickness. However, the city is 400 netres (1,300 ft) lower than the airport, and a day or two of taking it easy is a ertain cure.

In such a magnificent setting, La Paz at first seems n ugly blur of orange brick and gray corrugated iron oof. But on much closer inspection, it is one of South merica's most unusual and lively cities. The streets f La Paz, made of slippery bricks, are steep and tir-ng in the thin mountain air. They meet at the **Plaza an Francisco** with its huge stone church containing statue of Jesus with a blue fluorescent halo.

The snowcapped **Mount Illimani**, at over 6,000 neters (19,000 ft), dominates the skyline from most arts of La Paz. The modern city center has a collec-on of shabby skyscrapers and broad streets often logged with traffic. The city's traditional center is le **Plaza Murillo**, where the Italianate **Presidential alace** is located – often referred to as the *Palacio Quemado* (Burnt Palace), twice gutted by inflamatory rowds since it was first built in the 1850s. Nearby is le modern **Cathedral**. The surrounding streets are le most atmospheric in the city: **Calle Jaén** is still obbled and without traffic, lined by preserved colo-ial buildings. Another atmospheric area is behind the hurch and monastery of San Francisco, near the pper end of Avenida Mariscal Santa Cruz. Dating om 1549, the carvings are rich and ingenious.

The café of the **Club de La Paz**, on the corner of venidas Camacho and Colón, is a cultural landmark. his antique wooden retreat has seen innumerable usiness and political deals, and was probably where

Elegant colonial streetlight in La Paz.

BELOW:
Bolivian girl.

A Night at the *Peña*

After a long day of sightseeing, the best place to head for is the local *peña*, or folk nightclub. Here, you can sit and enjoy the haunting music of the Altiplano while sipping a cold beer, glass of wine, or potent *pisco sour*, made from grape brandy.

Starting off at around 10pm, *peñas* are usually relaxed, informal bars which offer set musical programs. Up to a dozen groups can play on a single night, giving an idea of the range and variety of Andean music; while the rhythms of the Altiplano are related, every region has its own unique sound. A group from Potosí is quite different to one from the shores of Lake Titicaca, and different again to one from Cusco in Peru. The musicians are often accomplished mimics and the show generally includes a few comic turns, which can be quite hilarious, even if you don't understand the language.

In La Paz, one of the best *peñas* is the Naira at Sagárnaga 161, a dark and intimate venue with a fine repertory of musicians. Other well-known *peñas* are in the restaurants Los Escudos on M. Santa Cruz and La Casa del Corregidor on Murrillo 1040.

The basic instruments used are the single-reed flutes known as *quenas*, *zampoñas* (deep wooden pipes), drums, and rattles. The famous *charango* is a miniature guitar made from an armadillo's shell, with 15 strings with which the player creates a penetrating, tinny sound. Along with the Andean harp, the *charango* is an unusual example of the local culture mixing successfully with the Spanish. Stringed instruments were one of the few cultural innovations that the Andean peoples were glad to accept from Europe. The effect of these instruments is mesmerizing and evokes the loneliness and austerity of the bleak and harsh Altiplano. The music is traditionally played without vocal accompaniment, but in recent decades ballads – called *huaynos* – have been added, sung mostly in the Quechua or Aymará tongues, or in a mixture of native languages and Spanish. They often deal with the daily lives of *campesinos*:

> Do you want me to tell you
> Where I'm from?
> I'm from behind that hill,
> Amid the carnations,
> Among the lilies
> My sling is of Castilian fabric,
> And my lasso of merino wool:
> Very long-lasting,
> Very strong.

Others are much more progressive:

> The priest of Andahuaylas
> Keeps telling me to get married.
> Maybe he knows, maybe not,
> Where I went last night.

As an expression of Amerindian culture, the music has often had a mixed reception from the country's rulers. On radio, it must compete with modern pop, as well as salsa and samba. At its worst, it has "crossed over", producing Western songs on Andean instruments – even *Rock Around the Clock* on panpipes. But as native cultures are increasingly gaining acceptance, the presence of Altiplano tunes is definitely growing. ❏

LEFT: *zampoña* player, La Paz.

many of Bolivia's coups were hatched. It was a favorite hangout of Klaus Barbie before he was arrested in the early 1980s and returned to France for trial as
a Nazi war criminal.

Witches and markets

The real attaction of La Paz is the street life. Narrow alleyways stretching up the
hillside behind the Plaza San Francisco are generally packed with brightly
dressed Bolivian *campesinas* selling blankets, nuts, herbs and – for the *gringos* –
woolen jumpers with llama motifs. Near here is the famous **Mercado de
Hechicería**, or Witchcraft Market, where elderly ladies sell magic charms for
every possible occasion. You can pick up a small bottle full of colored pieces of
wood and oil which, depending on its contents, will give good luck with love,
money, or health. A somewhat macabre market specialty is the dried llama
fetus, traditionally buried in the foundations of a new building to bring good fortune to the occupants. Also available at many markets are plaster figures of the
native household god Ekeko, a red-nosed grinning character who is believed to
bring prosperity. During the Alacitas Fair, at the end of January, you can buy
miniature versions of something you wish for – houses, sheep, or even tiny airline tickets – and Ekeko will grant you the real thing before the year ends.

When visiting these markets, food turns out to be one of La Paz's most unexpected attractions. Street vendors sell papaya milkshakes, spiced chicken and
rice, fried trout caught in Lake Titicaca, or pieces of heart with hot nut sauces
skewered on a wire. The markets near Plaza San Francisco have a particularly
good range of delicacies, served by ladies grown large on their own cooking.
Take a seat at one of the booths for tea in the early afternoon and watch Boliv-

Map on page 174

Bolivian folk musicians have penned many unforgettable tunes, including El Condor Pasa, which became a huge hit for Simon and Garfunkel in the 1970s, and more recently, the lambada.

BELOW: *cholas* (indigenous women of the city) selling vegetables.

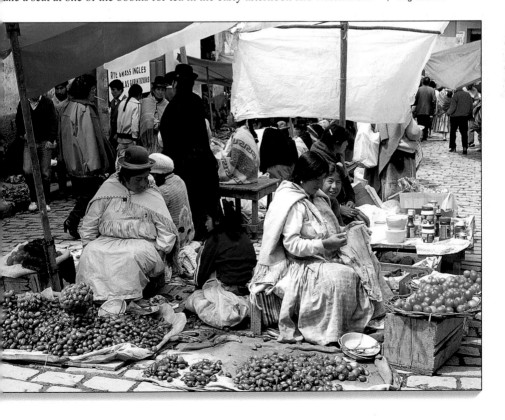

ian life go by. Later on, a potent *chicha* (fermented maize drink) might be mor
appropriate, or the excellent local beer. Non-beer drinkers should try a *chufla*
made from *singani*, the local spirit.

La Paz has an unusual collection of museums, such as the **Museo Murillo** o
Calle Jaén, in an old mansion owned by one of the country's greatest heroes
Pedro Domingo Murillo, who led an unsuccessful revolt against the Spanish i
1809 and was hanged for his efforts. There is a good collection of colonial fur
niture and a room devoted to medicine and magic. In the same street, the **Muse**
del Litoral has artifacts from the War of the Pacific, which deprived Bolivia o
its only access to the sea. A defiant emblem over the cashier reads: "Bolivia Ha
Not Lost and Will Never Lose Its Right to the Pacific." The **Museo Nacional de**
Arte, in the 18th-century baroque palace of the Count of Arana, near the cathe
dral at Calle Socabaya 432, has colonial and local paintings, and the **Museo**
Nacional de Etnografia y Folklore, in the palace of the Marquis of Villaverde
Calle Ingavi 915, has good Ayoreo and Chipaya exhibits.

Beyond the city

La Paz is the perfect base for exploring the Bolivian highlands. The easies
excursion is to the **Valle de la Luna ❹** (Valley of the Moon). Only 11 km (
miles) from downtown La Paz in distance, but light years away in appearance
this is a bizarrely eroded hillside full of pinnacles and miniature canyons. Know
technically as "badlands", its desert formations are constantly shifting and ca
be explored for hours.

Chacaltaya ❸, an hour and a half by bus from the city center, is the world'
highest developed ski area. The ski slopes, at between 5,200 and 5,420 meter

*Flute playing in the
mountains.*

7,000 and 17,780 ft) above sea level, are definitely only for those acclimatized to the altitude. For those less interested in snow sports or who tire quickly at such dizzy heights, the peak still provides some spectacular views of the Andes.

Most visitors to La Paz use the opportunity to visit the Bolivian side of nearby Lake Titicaca *(see page 168),* the great high-altitude expanse of water shared with Peru. One easy excursion is to the small village of **Copacabana** , famous for its miracle-working Dark Virgin of the Lake, the patron saint of Bolivia. An image of the Virgin was taken to Rio de Janeiro in the 19th century and the village later found itself giving its name to a Brazilian beach. The Bolivian Copacabana is a quiet and relaxing place, where visitors can stroll along the lakeside or loll in one of the many fish restaurants. But it comes alive during its fiestas, when the Virgin is paraded through the streets, a copious amount of alcohol is consumed, and new buses and trucks are solemnly blessed with beer poured over their hoods.

Map on page 180

Copacabana is a 3-hour bus trip from La Paz, and there are plenty of reasonably priced hotels and hostels. Festivals of the Virgin are held February 1–3, May 23, and the first week in August.

A boat trip to the lush and idyllic **Isla del Sol** (Island of the Sun) is well worth it. The sacred rock is where the Incas believed that their founding parents, Manco Capac and Mama Ocllo, emerged from the waters of Lake Titicaca at the call of the sun god. The Inca Utama Hotel and Spa and **Andean Roots Cultural Complex** is an oasis on the lakeshore at Huatajata, which provides a fascinating insight into the culture, lifestyle, and values of the native Andean people.

Glimpses of an ancient civilization

The splendid ruins of **Tiahuanaco** *(see page 22),* located on the southern tip of Lake Titicaca, are easily accessible from La Paz. This site is fast becoming one of the most important in South America. Tiahuanaco has a magnificently carved Gate of the Sun, the Acapana Pyramid, and chambers cut from stone with

BELOW: baptismal goods for sale, Copacabana.

faces staring from the walls. For those who would like to learn more abou
the ruins, many of the finds are now housed in La Paz, in the **Museo Nacion.
de Arqueología** (located on the corner of Federico Zuazo and Tiwanaku streets

Down to the valley

Sweeping down from the Andean heights near La Paz to Bolivia's steamin
Amazon basin is the lush, subtropical region known as the **Yungas**. The com
bination of a warm climate with magnificent mountain views has made the zor
a favorite for short visits from the capital and for the growing number of trekke
now flocking to Bolivia.

The Yungas – the name means "hot valleys" – is in a completely differer
climatic zone to the Bolivian capital, less than 100 km (60 miles) away on th
bleak, barren Altiplano. The drive from La Paz is one of the most spectacular i
South America, going over a high-altitude mountain pass to dive into ferti
valleys with drifting tropical mists, ancient Inca terraces, and abundant frui

*The Yungas valley
from Coroico.*

At 1,500 meters (5,000 ft) above sea level, the small town of **Coroico ❷**
the zone's main commercial center. Coroico itself is little more than a tidy mai
square surrounded by a few cheap restaurants and hotels. But there are plen
of tranquil walks in the dripping green countryside near the town, beyond th
plantations growing coffee, coca, and bananas. The gentle strolls provide spe
tacular views of snow-capped mountain ranges on the horizon leading to jungl
covered valleys, as well as to several rivers for swimming. The best views of th
Cordillera Real are from the little church located above the town, at the top o
Cerro Uchumachi. Also worth a visit is the **Mothers of Clarissa Conven**
where the nuns make peanut butter, biscuits, and quite drinkable wine.

BELOW: llama
traffic, Yungas.

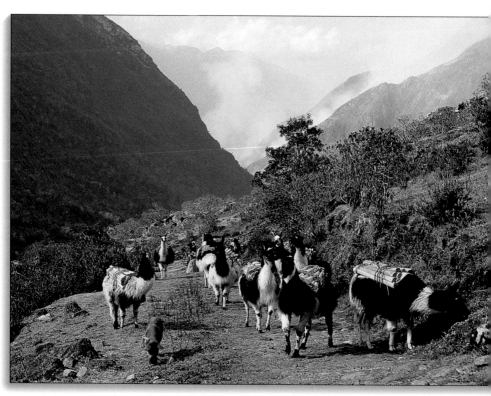

The nearby towns of **Sorata** and **Chulumani** ❸ are equally relaxing places
visit, with small guesthouses and walks. The roads to both places are mag-
ficent and Sorata in particular is said to have the most beautiful setting in
ɔlivia. A day hike from Sorata leads to the bat-filled **San Pedro Cave**, or the
ɔre energetic can embark on the Mapiri Trail, a strenuous eight-day expedi-
ɔn. Less adventurous spirits will be content with strolls through the flower-
led valleys that locals insist was the original site of the Garden of Eden.

Map
on page
174

ɔlivia's "Inca Trail"

ɔroico is a starting point and a goal for three popular treks, none of which
quires any special experience. A four-day hike begins at **La Cumbre**, the
ghest point of the road from La Paz to the Yungas, and follows an ancient
ca road that is in better repair than the path to Machu Picchu in Peru, though
lacks any sites as magnificent as the Inca ruins along the way.
Starting in the freezing and treeless heights, this path quickly descends into
e more lush and habitable Yungas. Most walkers advance slowly at first,
ısping in the thin mountain air and rhythmically plodding over the chilly pass.
t this altitude, there are no signs of human habitation. But further into the
ılleys, small villages begin to appear, which are often inhabited by numerous
ɔlping dogs but few people. More villagers can be seen walking along the path
lower altitudes, usually Bolivian women weighed down with sacks of pota-
ɛs or sticks. Finally the Inca path gives way to rough, landslide-prone Bolivian
ɔads, where passing trucks head to the town of Coroico.
The second trip, a favorite for adrenaline-junkies, is the 64-km (40-mile)
ɔwnhill cycle ride from La Cumbre to Coroico. Following the road that plunges
ɔ00 metres (16,000 ft) provides 5 km (3 miles) of
ɔrilling gravity-assisted mountain biking.

Gold mining in the Tipuani Valley has major environmental consequences. Deforestation, caused by felling trees for mine shafts, threatens biodiversity through habitat loss and causes land-slides and flooding.

BELOW: devil dancer in the *Diablada* parade, Oruro Fiesta.

ne Gold-Diggers' Trail

nother trek begins where the last left off, in Coroico.
ıking a road back into the mountains, the trail runs
rther down into the **Beni Jungle** along the so-called
ɔold-Diggers' Trail". It follows the **Tipuani Valley**,
region first fossicked by the Incas. They exhausted
l the surface gold, which was used for ornamental
ırposes in their temples and art. Today thousands of
ɔlivians have tossed in their old lives in cities to try
eir luck in the jungle, and are now digging tunnels
the hope of instant wealth.
The trail once again follows an ancient Inca road,
is time mossy and crumbling, through a beautiful
ndscape of jungle-clad mountains and dramatic
ɔrges. Locals still use the trail today as a kind of
ghway. Residents come panting down the mountain-
de after trips to the capital carrying portable cassette
ɛcks and non-stick frying pans. It passes many small
ining communities that can only be reached on foot,
ke the village of **Fátima**, put together from bamboo
ıd corrugated iron only a few years ago.
The path ends at the hot and dusty town of **Guanay**
ɔ, a rather insalubrious Amazon outpost. From Gua-
ıy there are buses that will take you back to Coroico
ıd La Paz.

Heading south: Bolivia's most famous fiesta

The town of **Oruro** ❺, 230 km (143 miles) south of La Paz, originally came to prominence as a mining town, but its mines are now redundant. Its past is remembered in the **Museo Etnográfico Minero**. Other places to visit include the **Casa de la Cultura**, a former residence of tin baron Simón Patiño, **Museo Antropológico** (ethnic history), and the **Museo Mineralógico** (minerals).

Oruro is best known today for its annual fiesta, **La Diablada**, the most famous in Bolivia, held eight days before Ash Wednesday. The celebrations begin the night before. At dawn on the big day, eager spectators take their places early, huddling against the cold mountain winds. Soon the street vendors are out in force, selling cans of beer. Older people turn up their noses at tinned drinks, preferring a more potent breakfast of *chicha*, the local maize beer. By 10am the crowd is ready for the Devil Dance.

Satan and Lucifer lead a procession of hundreds of dancing devils in fantastic outfits, leaping and pirouetting along the steep roads. Other dancers are dressed as pumas, monkeys, or insects. The lead is soon taken by China Supay, the Devil's wife, who tries to seduce the Archangel Michael with her wiles.

Some dancers dress as the Incas, in headdresses shaped like the condor, while others appear as black slaves brought over by the Spaniards, clanking through the streets in chains. Bolivian girls in pink and black miniskirts bounce along the steep streets, dancing with men dressed as giant white bears. The procession ends up at a football stadium, where dancers perform two masques. The first is a re-enactment of the Spanish Conquest, performed, naturally enough, as a tragedy. In the second, the Archangel Michael defeats the forces of evil with his flaming sword, taking on the devils and the Seven Deadly Sins. The result is

BELOW: preparing for the procession at the Festival of Jesús, La Paz.

nnounced by the Virgen del Socavón, the patroness of miners, and the dancers nter a chapel to chant a hymn in Quechua.

Despite the Christian gloss over the proceedings, the Diablada is a pagan cer-mony of thanks to Pachamama, "Earth Mother", to commemorate the struggle between the forces of good and evil. The conquering Spaniards were only able to convert the Amerindians superficially, changing a few names of deities to fit the formulae of the church. The *diablada* survived and grew during colonial times as an expression of the locals' frustration. The Europeans sat on their elegant balconies and looked on, while the subjected peoples were allowed their annual dose of freedom – an act of rebellion that became a safety valve.

Central city

Bolivia's third-largest city, **Cochabamba ⑥**, 160 km (100 miles) east of Oruro, lies in a fertile area known as Bolivia's granary, at an altitude of 2,400 meters (9,200 ft). This city is an intriguing mix of old, entrenched tradition and burgeoning new energy. The heart of traditional Cochabamba revolves around the **Plaza 14 de Septiembre**, with its typical mélange of elegant and imposing edifices, street vendors, busy office workers, and the more elevated personages, defiantly braving the cloying weather in wool and tweed. Notable buildings include the **Cathedral** and the colonial churches of **Santo Domingo** and **San Francisco**. In the evening, trendy bars and pizza restaurants around **Avenida España** fill with young people with disposable incomes. Out in the wealthy northern suburbs there are some unexpectedly snazzy office buildings, restaurants, and shopping malls, a world away from the gently decaying city center.

Tin baron Simón Patiño left his mark on Cochabamba in the form of the

Map on page 174

Llama fetuses and other fetishes are sold in street markets all over Bolivia.

BELOW: yet another bus breakdown.

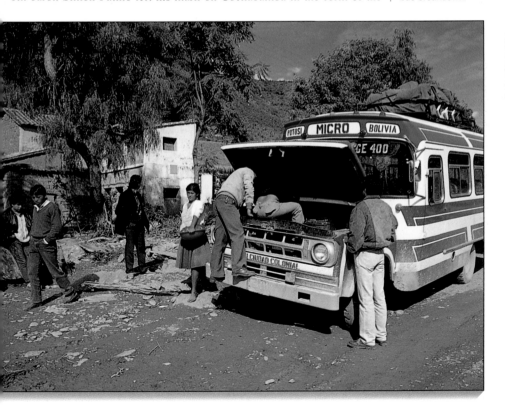

Palacio de Portales, built between 1915 and 1925 – all the furniture wa: imported from Europe. The **Museo Arqueológico** has an excellent selection o pre-Columbian artifacts dating back to 15,000 BC.

Just south of the city center, perched on a hill, the **Heroínas de la Coronilla** monument commemorates the female independence fighters who defended Cochabamba from Spanish forces in 1812. East of the city center, at the end o Avenida de las Heroínas, a statue of Christ stands atop the **Cerro San Pedro**

There are a number of Inca ruins in the vicinity of Cochabamba, and though none rival Machu Picchu or Tiahuanaco, they are worth visiting. **Inkallajta** described as the "frontier post of the Inca Empire", is an extensive site located on a turn-off from the old Cochabamba–Santa Cruz road. If you don't have your own transport, you may well have difficulty finding someone to take yo there; however, there are some guided tours available. **Inka Rakay**, 27 km (17 miles) west of Cochabamba, is better known for the wonderful views o the Cochabamba Valley than for the ruins themselves.

Along the Río Mamoré

Puerto Villaroel ❼ is the departure point for boats heading north to Gua yaramerín on the Río Mamoré. It's a cozy little village where everyone seem to know everyone else, and from **Ivirgazama** (last opportunity for river trip pers to purchase mosquito nets and hammocks) the road becomes a dirt track **Trinidad ❽**, in the heart of the Bolivian Amazon, is the capital of Ben province, with airport connections to Cochabamba and La Paz. The **Laguna Suárez**, 5 km (3 miles) away, is a popular wildlife-spotting and rest spot Wildlife can also be seen at **Chuchini**, 17 km (11 miles) from Trinidad

Chuchini has an archeological museum displaying remnants of the ancient Beni culture. The 300-km (200-mile) trip along the Río Mamoré to Guayaramerín ❾ takes three or four days. This bustling frontier town at the northern tip of the country is split by the river. The Brazilian side is known as Guajará-Mirim. The Bolivian side is an incongruous mix of dusty back-streets and brash duty-free shops selling perfume, jeans, and flashy electronic goods.

Riberalta ❿, three hours away by bus, is a pleasant, slow-paced and friendly little town, with a cluster of low-key restaurants grouped around the main plaza, ideally placed for perusing the town's social circuit. Towards dusk, motorbikes begin to trundle around the square. Once an important river port, since the road to La Paz was constructed, Riberalta's significance has declined.

It is possible to catch a boat between Riberalta and **Rurrenabaque** ⓫ along the Río Beni but, as boat traffic has declined since the construction of a road link, you'll probably have a long wait. However, the road is unsurfaced and can be a very sticky experience, especially during the rainy season – be warned. Rurrenabaque is a very pretty small town that has been enjoying a tourist boom due to its lush rainforest location, which makes it an ideal center for jungle and pampas expeditions and boat trips along the Beni and Tuichi rivers. The town also has some good restaurants and abundant low-budget accommodation.

The Oriente and Bolivia's official capital

The city of **Sucre** ⓬, 600 km (370 miles) southeast of La Paz, is Bolivia's official capital, although much government business is based in the big city on the

Map on page 174

BELOW: barges on the Río Mamoré, Trinidad.

GENTLY DOWN THE STREAM

Taking a river boat trip is one of the best ways to sample real Bolivian life. But be warned – if bucket toilets and tummy troubles give you nightmares, this is definitely not the trip for you! Barges chug up and down Bolivia's Río Mamoré from Puerto Villaroel to Guayaramerín on the Bolivia-Brazil border, delivering fuel and fruit. Bookings are informal – ask around in the village of Puerto Villaroel and people will tell you if a boat is due to leave. If you're in luck, it will have room for passengers. The most important things to bring with you are a mosquito net, hammock, and binoculars – beds may be in short supply. It's also a good idea to bring food and water, as supplies of these may be limited too. There may be occasional trading trips to jungle villages along the river bank, but passengers are not always taken along.

Don't expect any cruise-style entertainment either – you have to find your own way to fill the days. This is not as difficult as it might initially seem – you can catch up on your reading, chat to the crew and polish up your Spanish or Quechua, as well as doing a bit of bird-watching or dolphin-spotting. At dusk, if the weather is clear, find a comfortable spot on deck, lie back, and prepare yourself for a truly star-studded evening's entertainment.

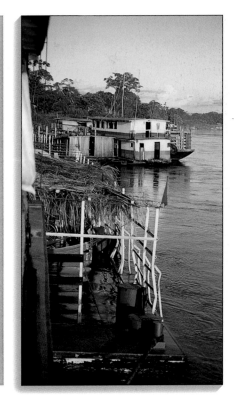

Coca Leaves

To the outside world, the small green coca leaf is best known as the raw material for cocaine. But in the highlands of Peru, Bolivia, and Ecuador, it has been part of Amerindian culture for more than 4,000 years. Coca leaves are on sale in any mountain town market. Ask at a café for *mate de coca*, and you will get a hot, refreshing drink of coca tea, said to be the best cure for *soroche* (altitude sickness).

Some three million South Americans chew coca regularly, adding a little bicarbonate of soda to get the saliva going. It gives energy and dulls the senses against cold. Miners chew up to 1 kg (2.2 lb) a day.

Coca is used at every stage of life. Before giving birth, a woman chews the leaves to hasten labor and ease the pain. Relatives celebrate the birth by chewing the leaf together. When a young man wants to marry a girl, he offers her father coca. When somebody dies, *mate de coca* is drunk at the wake and a

small pile of leaves is placed in the coffin. Local *yatiris* (soothsayers) use coca to tell the future, after scattering the leaves over a woolen blanket and reciting a prayer.

Coca was first cultivated in the Andes around 2,000 BC. Three millennia later, the Incas turned its production into a monopoly – just one more way to control the population. Its use was restricted to royalty, priests, doctors, and the empire's messenger runners, known to travel up to 250 km (150 miles) a day aided by chewing the leaves.

By the arrival of the first Europeans, the Incas had relaxed their monopoly on coca and its use had spread beyond their empire. Italian explorer Amerigo Vespucci, arriving in the Caribbean in 1499, noted with distaste that the islanders "each had their cheeks bulging with a certain green herb which they chewed like cattle." But within months of Pizarro's arrival at Cusco in 1533, he found some of his own men secretly chewing coca.

The Catholic church first tried to ban coca chewing, denouncing it as "the delusion of the devil." They quickly changed their tune when it was found that Amerindians needed it to survive the brutal conditions in colonial mines and plantations. To keep the captive labor force under control, the church then went into the coca business itself.

Coca was almost unheard of in Europe and the United States until the mid-1800s, when Parisian chemist Angelo Mariani marketed a wine made from the leaf. Immensely popular, this *Vin Mariani* quickly inspired several American soft drink companies to produce drinks based on coca.

At the same time, cocaine was first being developed. It was quickly taken up by such luminaries as Sigmund Freud, who called it a "magical substance". Sir Arthur Conan Doyle wrote of his fictional character Sherlock Holmes regularly partaking of cocaine. But moves were already afoot to ban the drug.

Scientists agree that there are no dangers in chewing the leaf, nor is it addictive, but because of its association with cocaine, coca leaves are banned in most countries. Taking home just a strip of coca leaf chewing gum or a coca teabag could get you into trouble. ❑

LEFT: bags of coca leaves, commonly seen at Bolivian markets.

ltiplano. Sucre is a small, elegant city of great historical significance. Notable ⊪ildings around the **Plaza 25 de Mayo** include the **Casa de la Libertad** (open ɑily), where Bolivia's declaration of independence was signed, and the **Cathe-ʀal**, with the nearby **Museo de la Catedral** (open Mon–Sat). The city has ⊪any interesting religious buildings, including the churches of San Miguel, ɑn Francisco, and Merced; and the Convento de San Felipe Neri. The Fran-ʂcan monastery of La Recoleta and its museum are on top of the Cerro Dalence ⊪ll to the southeast of Sucre, and afford excellent views of the city. There is also Natural History Museum and the very interesting **Museo de Arte Indígena** ʂUR (Textile Museum; San Alberto 413; open Mon–Sat), which displays Boli-ɑn textiles woven from llama and alpaca wool. Some 5 km (3 miles) south of ⊪e city, the **Castillo de la Glorieta** was built in a mixture of European styles ⊮ the Argandoña family.

Traditional textiles can be purchased at the typically Andean village of ɑrabuco, 65 km (40 miles) east of Sucre, which is renowned for its weaving. ⊃uth of Sucre is the Cordillera de los Frailes mountain range, with trekking, ⊃ck paintings, and hot springs. Dinosaur bones have been found at **Cal Orko**, km (4½ miles) from Sucre (guided tours to see them are offered in Sucre). Che ⊓uevara memorial tours are also available in Sucre, visiting some of the loca-⊃ns the revolutionary passed through on his final journey, including the small ⊪lage of **La Higuera**, where he was killed.

Some 500 km (300 miles) east of Cochabamba is **Santa Cruz** , Bolivia's ⊃omtown. Its first, shortlived boom came from rubber in the late 19th century. ⊪e current growth spurt was encouraged by a government-led "March to the ɑst" from the 1950s and has been powered by petroleum and tropical lowland ⊣ops like soybeans, sugar, rice, cotton, and coca.

ɑnta Cruz is not a popular tourist destination, though ⊣does have some interesting museums and a rich eth-⊣c mix due to the numbers of people who swarmed to ɛ city to take advantage of its economic success. ⊪here is a sizable Japanese community and a strong ⊓dean cultural presence, with *peñas* and an abun-ɑnce of nightclubs and karaoke bars. Santa Cruz is ⊓ked by rail to Brazil and Argentina – a journey that best described as an endurance test.

ity of silver

ɛrched at 4,200 meters (13,780 ft) above sea level the shadow of a cursed mountain, **Potosí** is ⊣cated in the southwest of Bolivia, 550 km (340 ⍳les) southeast of La Paz. It is the highest city of ʂ size in the world, and was built in this inhos-⊪table location by Spanish conquistadors for just ɑe purpose: silver mining. Today, Potosí is only a ⍳adow of its former self – during the 1600s it was large as London and many times more opulent. ɛvertheless, anyone visiting Bolivia should make ɛ journey to this remote Andean city. Not only is one of the least-touched colonial cities on the con-⍳ent and a World Heritage Site, but it has become, ⍲ many, a symbol of South America's fate, illus-ɑting that the richest regions in colonial times tend be the poorest today.

In 1967 the hero of the Cuban revolution, Che Guevara, was hunted down and killed in eastern Bolivia, where he was trying to incite the campesinos to rise in revolution.

BELOW: entrance to the Casa de Moneda, Spain's New World mint, Potosí.

"As rich as a Potosí"

Appropriately, **El Cerro Rico** (Rich Hill) is always visible from the city'
streets. The Incas had known that there was silver in the bare red mountain bu
did nothing to exploit it. The Spaniards, however, were quick to begin mining
soon discovering that the hill held the largest silver deposit the world had eve
seen. A frontier city was quickly created on the bleak mountainside, with con
quistadors and missionaries flocking from Spain to win a slice of the fantasti
wealth. Local Amerindians were press-ganged to work in the mines, dying b
the thousands in horrific conditions.

Even today, people in Spain use the phrase "as rich as a Potosí" when they try
to describe an unimaginable fortune. The city's churches were built with silve
altars and the lavish feasts of Spanish nobles glittered with the precious meta
Even the horses were said to be shod with silver in Potosí. When the silver gav
out, and the Spaniards left, the city survived on tin mining. Now tin is almos
worthless, and Potosí has become a fascinating relic.

Testimony to the former riches are the scattered crumbling villas, stone carve
doorways and forgotten abbeys of the city. Ancient houses teeter from bot
sides to nearly meet in the middle of narrow, winding streets. Potosí is sti
crowded with masterpieces of colonial architecture and artworks blending the
styles of medieval Europe and pre-Conquest South America.

Potosí's most impressive building, considered one of the finest examples o
Spanish civil construction in South America, is the **Casa Real de Moned**
(open Tues–Sun). First built in 1542 and reconstructed in 1759, it was used a
a mint by the colonizers. Now a museum, it has rooms full of religious art, col
lections of colonial coins, and the original wooden minting machines onc

BELOW: Tarabuco festival.

orked by African slaves. Guided tours take up to three hours to work through he many exhibits, which contain anything from altars removed from collapsed hurches to relics of Bolivia's foreign wars. One of the prize displays is a pair f iron strongboxes used to transport silver from the New World to Spain, using o less than 15 locks to secure them, while a huge gallery makes a valiant, but till incomplete attempt to provide portraits of the country's many presidents. Wear plenty of warm clothes, as the museum is like a refrigerator inside.

Many of Potosí's churches are crumbling into disrepair – in fact, some are angerously close to collapse. A stroll through the city will take you past **San Francisco**, **La Compañia**, and **San Lorenzo**, as well as the **Cathedral** and **Cabildo** (the town council) in the main plaza. Wandering through the town, ook out for old mansions such as the **Casa de las Tres Portadas** on Calle Bolivar 19–21 and the **Crystal Palace** at Calle Sucre 148–56.

A city drained of its wealth

Potosí is much more than a collection of ruined colonial buildings. Many of he Andean Amerindians in the area live in a way that has changed little over he centuries. The **Town Market** is a fascinating place to explore, full of women selling produce and butchers carrying whole animal carcasses over heir shoulders – usually covered in flies and with the beast's hairy tail still angling from the meat. But there are few signs of the city's past wealth. The poorest parts of the city, closer to the Rich Hill, were traditionally occupied by miners and their families. A monument to the Bolivian miner has een set up in one of the squares. The mining unions of Potosí and Oruro, nce the most powerful force in Bolivian politics, were all but destroyed

Map on page 174

TIP

As Potosí is more than 4,200 meters (13,780 ft) above sea level, it's essential to acclimatize to the altitude with a day or two of relaxation around the city before you expose your lungs to a trip down the mines. Asthmatics should avoid them altogether.

BELOW: Cerro Rico, Potosí.

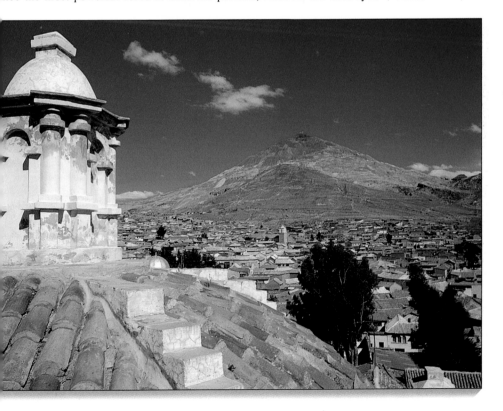

with the collapse of tin prices in the 1980s. There are few mines in operation these days, and unemployment stalks the streets. The wealth of Potosí proved a curse that is still with the indigenous population today. The city which helped finance the economic development of Europe in centuries gone by has slid deeper into Third World oblivion.

Realm of the Devil

Deep in the heart of Potosí's Rich Hill, dust-covered miners laugh with the Devil. Chewing coca leaves in a candlelit recess full of putrid air, they pay their respects to a small horned statue, the perceived owner of the silver beneath the ground. The miners visit El Tío – "the Old Fellow" – every day to leave a drink or burn a cigarette for luck. "El Tío has always liked tobacco," joke the miners, "but these days he only accepts filter tips."

Miners' shrine to El Tío, Potosí.

The image of the Devil in the Incarnación mine was first made 300 years ago by Amerindian slaves press-ganged by the Spanish to dig silver in Potosí. Shockingly, working conditions in the mines have changed little since those days. With the collapse of the tin market in 1985, the state mines of Cerro Rico were closed, but since then Bolivian miners have been re-opening old shafts to find the silver that the conquistadors left behind. The digging is being carried out in such a primitive and dangerous fashion that many miners accept their work as a kind of death sentence.

BELOW: mining in 18th-century conditions, Potosí.

Every day at dawn, the miners gather outside the mines on El Cerro Rico. The mountain that once held the world's greatest silver deposit is now a giant slag heap, an unnaturally symmetrical peak riddled with more than 5,000 shafts.

Inside a mine in Cerro Rico

There are several private mines still operating, to which guides from the city will bring visitors for a small fee. Most people bring a few packets of cigarettes to share with the miners as they spend the first hour of their day sitting in the cold sun, chatting and chewing coca leaves, which have been in use long before the Incas to ward off hunger and fatigue.

Visiting a mine is absolutely not for asthma sufferers or those not acclimatized to the altitude. Claustrophobics won't like it either – you need to crouch just to enter the mouth of the tunnels, while the miners' antique carbide lamps barely dent the darkness.

Ancient wooden shaft supports often sag in the middle. Stalactites hang from the rough walls of the tunnel near its mouth, but as the mine descends into the mountain, polar cold shifts to subtropical heat. Many of the shafts can only be passed on hands and knees. The air becomes thick and stale. Workers from the last shift become visible down cracks, stripped to the waist and hacking away with picks.

There are no power tools and no engineers in these mines. Blasting is done with dynamite bought in the supply store in Potosí, and the miners simply withdraw around a corner as the charge goes off. Each worker keeps the ore he finds himself. Miners on the lowest levels must climb long ladders to the surface with sacks of rocks on their backs.

The real enemy here is silicosis, caused by fine dust gathering in the miners' lungs. Within a few years of entering the pit, many feel a heavy weight on their chests. A few years later, they die coughing blood. Little wonder that tradition holds the metals of Potosí to be the property of the Devil, or that the miners give El Tío his daily cigarette for luck.

Group tours lasting four to five hours are organized by recognized guides. Put on your old clothes and take a handkerchief to keep out the dust. A helmet and lamp will be provided. Donations to the miners' cooperative are appreciated.

Lake district with a difference

In the west, near the frontier with Chile, is one of Bolivia's most popular tourist destinations. The **Salar de Uyuni** is said to be the largest salt lake in the world, at 10,500 sq km (4,055 sq miles). More desert than lake, it's an eerie sight, lying 3,653 meters (11,985 ft) above sea level – bring plenty of warm clothes, as temperatures can plummet at this altitude. Also don't forget sunglasses as the sun reflection on the salt can burn your eyes. There is accommodation available in the town of **Uyuni** ⓰, as well as the Salt Palace Hotel, which is out on the flats and built entirely of salt. Tours of the area can also be arranged from Potosí or Sucre, and most include the option of visiting **Laguna Colorada**, a bright red lake patronized by pink flamingoes that lies 346 km (215 miles) southwest of Uyuni, and **Laguna Verde**, a chilly aquamarine lake at 5,000 meters (16,400 ft) above sea level. Other attractions in the area close to the Chilean border include geysers at Sol de Mañana and hot springs at Aguas Termales Chalviri. Transport is available here to cross the border to San Pedro de Atacama. ❑

TIP

Be prepared for basic conditions in and around Uyuni. Accommodations have little or no heating, hot water, electricity, or plumbing. However, to compensate, the views over the salt lake are stunning.

BELOW: salt mining, Uyuni salt basin.

ECUADOR

Despite being one of the smallest South American countries, Ecuador has plenty of attractions: smoldering volcanoes, rainforest reserves, Amerindian markets and, of course, the Galápagos Islands

Maps on pages 198 & 200

cuador is one of the easiest and most rewarding countries to explore in South America. Small (just 283,500 sq. km/110 sq. miles) but geographically varied, Ecuador's incredible natural diversity has made it the focus of worldwide biological research. The country has more species of plants (25,000) and birds (over 1,500) than the United States, which is 34 times larger. Sadly, these precious ecosystems are being degraded by a rate of deforestation higher than any nation in South America (280,000 hectares/692,000 acres per annum), but INEFAN, the Ecuadorian National Park Service, with the help of national and international conservation organizations, currently protects 17 percent of the total landmass in national parks and ecological reserves. In addition, 97 percent of the Galápagos Islands' landmass is protected and a marine reserve protects the waters surrounding them. For a developing nation, these conservation efforts are admirable.

Outdoor activities are Ecuador's biggest tourist draw. Within a day's drive or flight from the capital city of Quito you can experience virgin Amazon jungle, snow-capped peaks, tropical sandy beaches, and Darwin's Galápagos Islands. Outfitters are set up for mountaineering, trekking, jungle canoe trips, mountain biking, rafting, paraskiing, scuba diving, and horseback riding.

Eight active volcanoes periodically erupt, spewing columns of ash and melting glaciers that cause mud flows to destroy Sierran villages. When the Andes are uplifted along geological faults from the coastal plain, powerful earthquakes can shake the hillsides. An earthquake in 1987 broke the trans-Andean oil pipeline in several places, crippling the national economy for six months. Landslides are common during the rainy season, closing roads. Floods due to El Niño in 1982–83 and 1997–98 virtually paralyzed coastal communities.

But Ecuadorians have a tremendous capacity to bounce back and rebuild their country. The tradition of the *minga* (an obligatory community work project), inherited from the Incas, continues to draw citizens together to overcome the challenges of nature and political and economic turmoil.

PRECEDING PAGES: Zumbagua market. **LEFT:** Mount Sangay eruption. **BELOW:** reveler in the Mamá Negra parade, Latacunga.

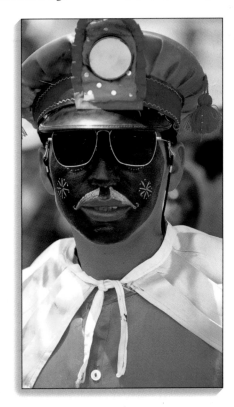

nation in movement

Although the country is traditionally divided into four regions – Sierra, Coast, Oriente, and Galápagos – these regions blend at the margins to form a rich mosaic. Perhaps most telling of Ecuador's identity is the flow of goods and people between regions. Trucks filled with *plátanos* (green bananas) daily climb the cloud forests of the western slope of the Sierra to stock Quito's cool open-air markets, while sacks filled with endemic varieties of potatoes are transported down to the hot and humid barrios of Guayaquil. The

The important Inca sun god Inti is often subtly portrayed in religious colonial art, and in return the Catholic celebration for Saint Peter is associated with the Inti Raymi festival (winter solstice).

Oriente pumps vital oil exports through a pipeline which crosses the Andes to tankers docked at the port city of Esmeraldas. It is not uncommon to see a colorfully dressed highland *otavaleño* on the coast selling woven goods, as well as a coastal *moreno* (Afro-Ecuadorian) on a bus on the Pan-American highway offering traditional homemade *cocada* (coconut candy).

The majority of Ecuadorians are Catholics but there is a growing number of Protestants (now estimated at more than 10 percent), due to missionary effort which began after freedom of religion was guaranteed in 1945. Pre-colonial indigenous religions are rarely practiced in their pure forms except in isolated pockets in the Oriente, but elements are incorporated into modern Christianity.

Pre-Inca civilizations

In the 10th century AD, the Caras – forefathers of the modern *otavaleños (see page 202)* – settled in the Quito area. They built an observatory to mark the solstices, and identified the equator as "the path of the sun". They were animist

ho worshiped the sun, and believed the moon to be inhabited by humans.
heir economy was based on weaving, and the law required women to spin
ool whenever possible, even when walking mountain trails.

Their successors were the Duchicela dynasty, who established the powerful
ingdom of Quitu, which was eventually conquered by the Inca Tupac-
'upanqui. Ecuador soon played an important part in the collapse of the Inca
Empire (see page 26), with the execution of the Inca Atahuallpa by the Spaniard
'rancisco Pizarro. While Pizarro plundered, his lieutenant Sebastián de Benal-
ázar battled northward to the city of Quito. Arriving in late 1534, he found the
ity in ruins: Rumiñahui, Atahuallpa's general, had destroyed and evacuated it
ather than lose it intact to the Spaniards. Benalcázar refounded Quito on Decem-
er 6, 1534. Rumiñahui was captured, tortured, and executed the following month.

Ecuador was initially ruled by the Spanish as a province of the viceroyalty of
'eru, and was the site of the first cultivation of wheat and bananas in South Amer-
ca. Colonial administration was based on the *encomienda* system, which was pre-
erved after independence in the form of huge estates or *latifundios* owned by a few
f Ecuador's wealthiest criollo families. The injustices of Spanish rule prompted
everal violent uprisings. The first of these was the so-called Alcabalas Revolution
f 1592–93, when the populace, with the support of the lower clergy, rebelled
gainst increased taxes on food and fabrics. The reprisals were brutal.

Land reforms were not enacted until 1964, freeing the indigenous popula-
ion from compulsory agricultural labor. Often, however, it was the most unpro-
uctive land which was redistributed, and many haciendas (ranches) remained
ntact, governments being reluctant to attack the wealthiest and most powerful
lass, the landowners.

Map on page 198

BELOW: Spanish engraving of conquistadors on the march.

The first president of Ecuador, Juan José Flores, arranged with his successor Rocafuerte, to alternate occupancy of the presidency, but then broke the deal, retained control of the army, and bribed Rocafuerte into exile. Finally ousted in 1845, he organized a Spanish invasion of Ecuador which was only averted by Great Britain's intervention. National politics since then have been turbulent: two of the best-remembered presidents, Moreno and Alfaro, were assassinated.

Stumbling through the 20th century

Twentieth-century Ecuador experienced mainly military rule, the last period of which was from 1972–79. In 1978, the army drew up a new constitution and an election was held the following year. Ecuador became the first South American country to return to democracy after the military era that engulfed most of the subcontinent during the 1970s, but corruption has been a recurrent theme.

León Febres Cordero, a Conservative elected in 1984, was kidnapped by troops loyal to a general who was in jail for attempting two coups. Febres secured his release after just 11 hours, by granting the general an amnesty. Elections in 1988 brought to power President Rodrigo Borja Cevallos, a Social Democrat who boosted the tourist trade and lowered inflation. Such trends continued under his successor, Sixto Durán Ballén, of the Christian Social Party, who introduced an

Girl from Esperanza.

unpopular privatization program. Many people were surprised that Abdalá Bucaram, "El Loco" (the Crazy One), was elected in 1996. The corrupt Bucaram was ousted in February, 1997, after thousands marched through the streets demanding his impeachment. In 1998, Jamil Mahuad of the Popular Democracy Party was elected as president and the new constitution came into effect. Mahuad concluded peace with Peru in October 1998, but an economic downturn

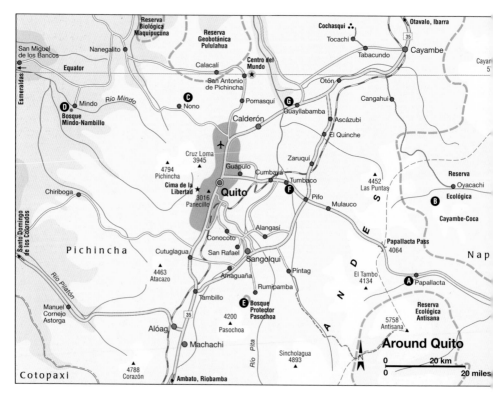

Around Quito

Maps
on pages
198 & 200

roded his popularity and in 2000 he fled as thousands of protesters stormed the Congress Building. Power was ceded to the vice president, Gustavo Noboa, who faced radicalized protestors and an even worse economic crisis. Soon afterwards, the sucre was replaced by the US dollar as the official currency.

Ecuador's economy has been much improved by low inflation and foreign investment in oil exploration and production. However, many Ecuadoreans have felt no benefit from the recovery. In 2005, a state of emergency was declared in two oil-producing provinces as protestors demanded that oil revenues be used to fund local development. Many Ecuadorians have migrated overseas in the past decade, forced to find work and better opportunities in the US and Europe. Many regularly send money back to their families and this income is now an important source of foreign revenue. In 2002 a former coup leader, Lucio Gutiérrez, won the presidential election, but, in 2005, when the Supreme Court dropped corruption charges against two former presidents, the public outcry forced him into exile. In November 2006, a left-of-center nationalist, Rafael Correa, became president.

Quito: Ecuador's expanding capital

Modern **Quito** ❶ spreads north and south into the intra-Andean valley each year, gobbling up rural farms. Most visitors stay in the **Mariscal** neighborhood, north of **Parque El Ejido**, where old Quito meets new, as the city's old colonial center is more pleasant to explore than the polluted modern sprawl. Hotels, restaurants, and stores bulging with handicrafts line **Avenida Amazonas** and nearby streets.

La Casa de la Cultura housing the **Museo del Banco Central** (open Tues–Sun), just off Parque El Ejido, is Ecuador's most comprehensive museum, with pre-Columbian treasures and ornate gold, along with republican, colonial, and

BELOW: Quito's
modern district.

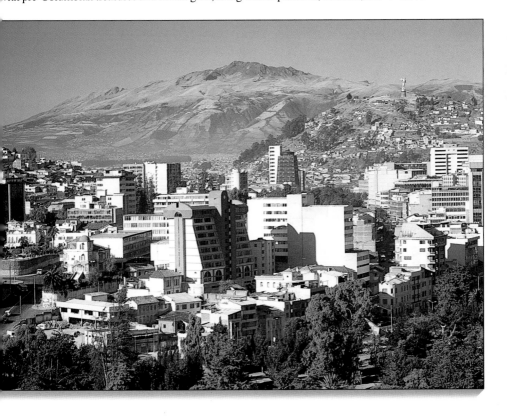

The Otavaleños

Otavalo is a modern miracle of economic achievement that grew out of colonial oppression. Forced to become weavers by the Spanish, about half of Ecuador's *otavaleño* people are today involved in weaving, which has made them the most prosperous indigenous group in Ecuador, possibly in all of South America.

Otavalo lies betwen Quito and the Colombian border. There are expatriate communities in Colombia, Brazil, and Spain. They export their fine-quality textiles to the United States, Canada, and Europe, while the bulk of their business remains in South America.

The modern *otavaleños* are descended from the Cara tribe, which expanded from Colombia to the Ecuadorian sierra about 1,000 years ago. The Cara established trade links with neighboring tribes, and bartered cotton and blankets, along with dogs and salt, in exchange for *achiote* (a plant from which dyes are extracted), parrots, and monkeys. The

arrival of the Incas in the late 1400s marked the beginning of 500 years of colonization and imposed labor and beliefs. After 17 years of fighting, the Inca Huayna Capac took Caranqui, the Cara capital, and massacred thousands of its inhabitants. Many Cara were transported to Peru, while loyal Inca subjects were settled on Cara territory. The Incas introduced coca and llamas, an excellent source of wool, but their rule was too shortlived to seriously influence *otavaleño* culture.

Under the Spanish, the *encomienda* system was established in Otavalo, putting Spanish settlers in control of an area and its indigenous inhabitants. The first weaving *obraje* (workshop) was set up in the 1550s with 500 workers, some as young as nine years old. Modern tools were introduced and within 50 years the Otavalo *obraje* was the most productive in Ecuador. *Otavaleños* labored 14 hours a day manufacturing cloth, woolen blankets, and rope for export. In 1648 an *obraje* in Peguche was closed, because the number of suicides among workers had grown to alarming proportions. The *otavaleños* were forced to learn Spanish to facilitate their conversion to Christianity, although their Catholicism today incorporates ancestral beliefs.

Land reforms enacted in Ecuador in 1964 abolished the *wasipungo* system, based on enforced indigenous labor. The first store selling woven products opened in Otavalo in 1966, and within a dozen years there were 75. Weaving has decentralized from the savage *obrajes* and is now a cottage industry. Over the years, the ingenuity of the Otavalo weavers has brought them worldwide fame.

Every Saturday morning, the usually quiet streets of Otavalo teem with life. By 9am Market Square, known as Poncho Plaza, is a feast of colors and textures: rolls of cloth, thick blankets, tapestry wall hangings, chunky sweaters, long patterned belts or *fajas,* and *cintas* – tapes the women use to bind their long hair. Most *otavaleño* textiles are made of sheep wool, though some alpaca sweaters can be found. The mechanization of the modern textile industry, potentially disastrous for the *otavaleños*, has been compensated by tourism and an emphasis on quality goods produced naturally. ❑

LEFT: an *otavaleña* displaying her wares.

modern art. Rivaling this is the smaller **Museo Guayasamín** (open Mon–Fri) in the Bellavista neighborhood. Oswaldo Guayasamín, Ecuador's most renowned painter *(see page 63)*, displays his bold portraits of indigenous people and his collection of pre-Columbian artifacts.

Back down the hill, fast-food joints, shopping malls, and trilling cellphones are evidence of the Ecuadorian middle-class fascination with American culture. Quito has a selection of international restaurants, folkloric ballet shows, and salsa bars.

Old Quito: a walking tour

Old Quito displays Spanish colonial architecture at its finest. Walls of brilliant whitewash, deep blue railings, and green tile rooftops dazzle the eye, reminiscent of a period when the city was a peaceful provincial capital. Earthquakes in 1587, 1768, and 1859 caused severe damage to many churches, but nevertheless there are still 87. In 1978, UNESCO declared Old Quito a World Heritage Site. In recent years the old town has been renovated and is now a pleasant place to stroll and admire the architecture. At night the plazas and churches are illuminated.

The Spanish past blends with modern cultural migration as members of Ecuador's many ethnic groups make Quito their home. Life on colorful **Calle Cuenca** contrasts with the city's relative affluence. Black women sell tropical fruits, while an indigenous newspaper vendor with a baby at her breast cries "Comercio, hoy!" in a nasal refrain. Above it all stands the church of **San Francisco**, the first major religious construction in the continent and the spiritual heart of the city. The creaking wooden floor contrasts with the spectacular baroque carvings and the statue of **Our Lady of Quito**, a fine example of the "Quito school of art", blending Spanish and Moorish techniques with the indigenous imagination.

Map on page 198

Statue of the Virgin, Panecillo, Quito.

BELOW: the Plaza de la Independencia, Quito.

From San Francisco, it is a short walk through the clothes market on Call Cuenca to **La Merced**, which contains paintings depicting scenes from Quito' past: Sucre riding gloriously into battle, volcanoes erupting, and suspiciously docil Amerindians being converted. Two blocks away is the **Plaza de la Independen cia**, where the heroes of 1809 are immortalized. Today, *quiteños* sun themselve read the morning newspapers, and put the swarming shoeshine boys to work.

The **Palacio de Gobierno** (Presidential Palace) has traditional guards in rec gold and blue 19th-century-style uniforms, and a mural by Guayasamín depic ing Orellana's descent of the Amazon. The adjacent **Cathedral**, finished i 1706, is where Ecuador's illustrious lie, including Sucre. Among its collectio of paintings is the *Descent From The Cross* by Caspicara, perhaps coloni Ecuador's best indigenous artist.

One block south of the church of **San Augustín**, where the first declaration c independence was signed, is the pedestrian thoroughfare **Calle Eugenio Espej** Nearby is the magnificent **La Compañia** (open daily), built by the Jesuit between 1605 and 1768. Containing an estimated seven tons of gold, it i Ecuador's most ornate church. The remains of the *quiteña* saint Mariana de Jesu lie beneath the solid gold main altar, and there is a bizarre collection of coloni art: one painting graphically depicts the punishment reserved for sinners in Hel with the most unpleasant fate reserved for adulterers and fornicators.

From 1828 until his death in Colombia two years later, Sucre lived a bloc from here: his house, the **Casa de Sucre Museo Histórico** (open Tues–Sat' affords a glimpse of period aristocratic home life. A statue of Sucre occupies th Plaza of Santo Domingo, opposite the church of the same name, which is bes seen at night when it is floodlit. Inside is an altar to St Judas, patron saint c

Corn on the cob sculpture, Quito.

BELOW: interior of the lavish church of La Compañía.

SPECTACULAR TRAIN JOURNEYS

Rail travel began in Ecuador in 1910, when the lin between Quito and Guayaquil opened, reducing to tw days a former nine-day trek along a mule path. Today, how ever, only short tourist rides survive.

The three-hour train ride south from Quito to El Bolich station, near Cotopaxi National Park, offers good views the Andean peaks and lush farmland before ascending t the high *páramo* (grasslands). A more reliable option is th Chiva Express, a bus-cum-railcar service to Cotopaxi whic runs on Tuesdays, Thursdays, and Saturdays. A highlight to ride on the roof of the train. This is operated by Metro politan Touring and lunch is included before the return jou ney to Quito.

The train ride over the "Devil's Nose" from Riobamba Sibambe is a popular day out. Cushions can be hired if yc are feeling adventurous and want to ride on the roof. Train run on Wednesdays, Fridays, and Sundays for a scenic si hour return trip, though the service has frequent disruption The "Devil's Nose" switchback is one of the world's mo impressive feats of railway engineering.

Metropolitan Touring offer extended excursions on t Cuenca or Guayaquil, in which a landscape of patchwor fields of potatoes and corn give way to tropical lowland desperate causes", where satisfied worshipers have posted "thank you" notices. One of the best-preserved colonial streets is **Calle La Ronda**, south of Plaza Santa Domingo. A quiet, narrow, cobbled lane, it is lined with 16th-century houses with overhanging balconies and heavy grilled doors. This brings you to the **Bridge of the Black Vultures**, where you can climb to the Virgin of Quito at the summit of **El Panecillo** (Little Bread Roll), with sweeping views of the valley and, on a clear day, the peaks of **Pichincha** and **Cayambe**, to the west and east respectively.

The **Sierra** stretching out before you are actually two mountain ranges (Western and Eastern cordilleras) divided by a series of central valleys running north–south. The major highland cities are spaced along the Pan-American Highway in these valleys, 2,000–3,000 meters (6,500–9,800 ft) above sea-level, and are blessed with temperate climates. This beautiful patchwork of fields is very productive due to rich volcanic soils and little variation in air temperatures. The hot lowland plains are intensely farmed by modern methods, mainly for the huge flower export industry.

The steep hillsides above the valley floor are owned by Quechua indigenous cooperatives, working small parcels of land, which tractors could never till, with hand tools. Their crops of potatoes, carrots, beans, wheat, and corn supply 75 percent of Ecuador's needs. Above are the cold, windswept paramos (alpine grasslands), home to grazing horses, cattle, and sheep. Still higher, the craggy and glaciated volcanic peaks that dominate the skyline are home to some of the few remaining Andean condors, which share them with mountaineers.

Excursions near Quito

The main road to the Oriente climbs to the continental divide at the headwaters of the Amazon basin. The village of **Papallacta** Ⓐ is located below the pass. Here you will find thermal-spring pools surrounded by lush cloud forest. The area is also known for some of the country's best fresh trout, introduced from North American stock. *Quiteños* escape here on the weekends for walks or horseback rides in the nearby **Cayambe–Coca Ecological Reserve** Ⓑ.

Toward the coast, two hours by bus from Quito, are **Nono** Ⓒ, **Tandayapa**, and **Mindo** Ⓓ, villages that are becoming favorite birding spots. Private reserves and lodges have been set up to cater for visitors keen on exploring the forests. **The Bosque Protector Paso-choa** Ⓔ (contact Fundación Natura, at República 481 and Almagro, Quito, tel: 503385, for excursions) is a pleasant nature reserve southeast of Quito. Some of the last intra-Andean cloud forest is protected on the slopes of the ancient volcano. Native trees and plants thrive on the rich volcanic soil and are home to 120 species of birds. A half-day hike on Ilaló, near the valley suburb of **Tumbaco** Ⓕ, is worth it for the views of northern Ecuador's main peaks.

North of Quito

Some 24 km (15 miles) north of Quito is the **Centro del Mundo** (middle of the world) monument, which marks the equator. Here you can straddle the equator

Map
on page
200

TIP

Take a taxi to the summit of El Panecillo – but don't go alone as numerous thieves are at work on the way up.

BELOW: bargaining for a cow.

*In 1917, a local
weaver started to
copy the famous
Scottish tweed. His
commercial success
led to the worldwide
recognition of the
weaving skills of the
otavaleños.*

with feet planted in both hemispheres, an irresistable photo opportunity. Th
obelisk houses a museum with displays from different ethnic cultures of Ecuado
   The Pan-American highway heading north passes through the agricultur:
town of **Guayllabamba** , several hundred meters lower and much warme
than Quito, which produces crops of avocado and chirimoya (custard apple
Restaurants are full at the weekends with *Quiteños* who stop off for the town
specialty of *locro*, a hearty cheese and potato soup with optional avocado an
pork skin. The **Zoológico Metropolitano** (open Tues–Sun) here houses th
Galápagos tortoise, jaguar, monkeys, and the Andean spectacled bear.
   Further north, before reaching **Otavalo** ❷ *(see page 202)*, you pass near th
town of **Cayambe** ❸. This area is historically known for cheese-making, but th
flower industry has surpassed cheese factories in economic importance. Thes
large plantations can be toured, and a dozen roses costs about US$1. Cayamb
is also the jumping-off place for excursions to the climber's refuge on the flank
of **Nevado Cayambe** (5,790 meters/19,000 ft), the woodworking indigenou
community of **Oyacachi**, and the Inca ruins of **Quitoloma**.
   The oldest hacienda (farm estate) in Ecuador, **Guachala**, built in 1580, is ju:
outside Cayambe on the equator. In earlier times it was a textile factory producin
Scottish-style tweed. Several other important haciendas open to visitors are sca:
tered around the Otavalo area, including **Cusin** and **Pisanqui**, offering a glimps
into the wealth and privilege enjoyed by estate owners in the recent past.
   About 5 km (3 miles) from Otavalo is an ecologically constructed mountai
lodge, **Casa Mojanda**, with spectacular views from its adobe cottages of th
nearby volcano, **Cotacachi** (4,940 meters/16,220 ft). Beneath the volcano lie
Laguna Cuicocha, a collapsed caldera, now a lake filled with bright blue wate

BELOW: one of
the Lagunas de
Mojanda, near
Tabacunda.

In the villages surrounding Otavalo the cottage-crafts industry is flourishing. otacachi is most famous for its leather work, **Peguche** and **Agato** for their eaving, and **Iluman** for its double-sided ponchos and felt hats. To the north, **arra** is a pleasant colonial town with many inexpensive restaurants and hotels, nown locally as "La Ciuidad Blanca" (The White City) for its whitewashed alls and red-roofed colonial buildings. For a challenging but rewarding excursion, climb **Cerro Imbabura** (4,610 meters/15,120 ft), just south of town, with iews of surrounding villages. This peak was once glaciated, and Amerindians arvested ice from the slopes. Twentieth-century climatic change has melted way the glaciers. A few hours west by bus, the subtropical **Chota Valley** is the nly place in the Sierra that is populated by Afro-Ecuadorians.

On the road to San Lorenzo is the **Reserva Cerro Golondrinas** cloud forest. four-day trek descends from the paramo through pristine submontane cloud rest and farmland. Visitors will see the positive effects of the conservation fforts in the area, such as the orchid farms, tree nurseries, and reforestation pro-cts. At the Colombian border is **Tulcán ❹**, the provincial capital of Carchi, est known for cypress trees in the graveyard, which are elaborately carved to esemble animals, houses, and geometric figures. At **Reserva Ecológica El ngel**, nearby, you can see the giant *frailejón* plants, members of the daisy amily, standing out of the paramo vegetation up to 2 meters (6 ft) tall.

Tafí candy shop, Baños.

outh from Quito

eading south from Quito takes you along the "Avenue of the Volcanoes", with xcellent views of all the major peaks. Several haciendas have been converted to hotels, notably **La Cienega**, steeped in 400 years of history, and **San gustín de Callo**. The latter was originally built on e site of an important Inca palace and some Inca alls remain. From **Lasso** a dirt road heads up into **arque Nacional Cotopaxi**, which encompasses the eaks of Cotopaxi, Rumiñahui, and Sincholagua. otopaxi is one of the world's highest active volca-oes and attracts thousands of climbers to its 5,900-neter (19,350-ft) summit every year. At its base, aguna Limpio Pungo harbors Andean gulls, ndean lapwings, and the Andean fox. It is one of the est locations to observe paramo vegetation and recent olcanic features.

BELOW: Baños thermal baths, possibly the best hot soak in the country.

Just off the Pan-American highway on Thursdays at awn, the quiet village of **Saquisilí** comes alive with cuador's largest indigenous market. People from out-ying communities fill the streets and plazas with their ocal produce. A little further south is **Latacunga ❺**, estroyed three times by mud flows from Cotopaxi n the 18th and 19th centuries. In September the treets are filled with processions, dances, and fire-vorks in honor of the black-faced Virgin Mary, an vent known as **La Fiesta de la Mamá Negra**.

To the west is the Amerindian-populated village of **umbahua**, which hosts a colorful vegetable market n Saturdays. An hour's drive away is the starting oint for walks to the deep-blue volcanic lake of **Quilotoa**. This area is one of the few places where lamas are still employed as pack animals.

Map on page 198

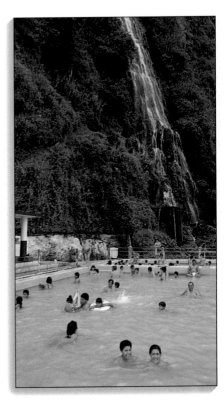

The capital of Tungurahua province, **Ambato**, was leveled by an earthquake 1949 and rebuilt with concrete buildings that lend a drab feeling to the city. Th is an important industrial and fruit-growing area. Between Baños and Amba lies the Quichua community of **Salasaca**, whose tapestries are sold throughout t country, including the Saturday Otavalo market. Salasaca's small outdoor mark is open on weekends, and you can see artists at work in their homes.

Hot springs and erupting volcanoes

Girl from Imbabura.

BELOW: Riobamba, beneath Mount Chimborazo.

Baños is a very popular tourist destination for Ecuadorians and foreigners alik Named after the thermal springs in town, it is graced with a semitropical clima but in August 2006 the **Volcán Tungurahua** (5,020 meters/16,470 ft) erupte and a number of small villages were covered in ash and destroyed. The town (Baños was spared but remains on "yellow alert". The **Basilica** houses a statu of **Nuestra Señora de Agua Santa** (Our Lady of the Holy Water). Baños is als a great place to shop for local handicrafts and experience hiking, rafting, jung trips, horseback riding, and mountain biking.

Further south, **Riobamba** 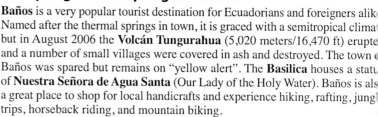 sits on the flanks of **Chimborazo**, the highe mountain in Ecuador (6,310 meters/20,700 ft) and starting point for rail trips the coast which pass through the town of **Alausí** ➐. Before the Inca perio Puruhua people lived in the region, but during Inca rule they were moved awa and people from northern Peru were ordered to move here. Today the region dominated by different indigenous groups and the variety of hats and trad tional dress reflects these strong cultures.

To the west of Riobamba is the expansive and remote **Sangay National Par** home to the mountain tapir and Andean spectacled bear, and the daily eruptin volcano **Sangay** (5,230 meters/17,160 ft). On the edge of the park is part of an old Inca highway that once ran from Quito to Cusco in Peru. Visitors can hike along the trail from **Achupallas** as far as the Inca ruins of **Ingapirca**, built in the 15th century to control the native Cañari living in the area.

Map
on page
198

The Pan-American highway continues south to **Cuenca** ❽, the third-largest city in Ecuador and formally the Inca town of Tomebamba. Most of the Inca stonework was destroyed by the Spanish and replaced by colonial architecture and cobbled streets. Today, patios, plazas, whitewashed buildings, and red-tiled roofs make Cuenca probably the most attractive Ecuadorian city to visit.

In February, when apples, pears, and peaches are ripe, young people come to Ambato from as far away as the coast for several days of parades and all-night dancing on the streets at Ecuador's largest festival, the Fiesta of Fruit and Flowers.

Nearby **Parque Nacional Cajas** with Inca ruins and more than 200 lakes is a popular retreat for fishermen and hikers. Since Cuenca draws its drinking water from Cajas it is well protected from environmental impacts. South of Cuenca live the indigenous people of **Saraguro** ❾, who have strong cultural pride. Their town has become a center of the indigenous political movement called *Pachacutek* (New Country). Here, men dress formally with short black trousers and women wear decorative shawls closed with a *tupus* (fastening pin). The sleepy town of **Loja** is the gateway to the southern Oriente and the Peruvian border. Quinine, the anti-malaria drug, was first exploited from the forests above the city in the 18th century, which led to their destruction.

Further down the valley, the village of **Vilcabamba** ❿ was made famous by the discovery in the 1960s of a large percentage of locals over 100 years old. Visiting doctors have suggested that a mild and stable climate, low stress levels, simple and healthy diets, and physical labor on small farms create this happy anomaly. Foreigners have since settled in the region, seeking longevity, and several ecologically and health-minded hostels have sprung up as a result.

Also in the vicinity is **Parque Nacional Podocarpus**, with a highland entrance at **Cajanuma** and rainforest entrance at **Bombascara**. Trails access the park and overnight camping is possible. An active environmental movement in Loja has kept multinational mining companies from moving in and causing deforestation and river poisoning. A spectacular mountain road goes to the town of Macará on the Peruvian border. This route to Peru is safer and more beautiful than the coastal crossing at Huaquillas.

BELOW: laden down in Cuenca.

The Oriente and the Amazon

The Ecuadorian **Oriente** is the upper Amazon basin east of the Andes, and is nowadays known as "the province of the future". It is a place of endless virgin rainforest cut by fast-flowing rivers and inhabited by jaguars, ocelots, anacondas, monkeys, tapirs, fish-eating bats, piranhas, and more than 450 species of birds. Travel in this region is easier than in neighboring countries, as distances are shorter and transportation quite straightfoward.

The indigenous inhabitants of the Oriente include the Siona, Cofan, Quichua, Quijo, and Huaorani tribes in the basins of the Napo, Aguarico, and Pastazo rivers to the north; and the Shuars, Ashuars, and Saraguros in the south. Colonization and oil development has affected the lifestyles of the tribes, and many traditions have died, such as those of the Shuar, who until

the 20th century would shrink the heads of dead enemies, and among whom th
ratio of men to women was estimated at one to two, due to constant warfare
Some of the Huaorani retain their ancient culture deep in the jungles borderin
Peru near the **Río Napo**. They hunt with spears, blowpipes, and poison dart:
keep harpie eagles as pets and watchdogs, and make fire by rubbing stick
together. Most of the Huaorani people do not welcome visitors, but some ar
turning to eco-tourism to protect their culture, and it is possible to spend tim
with the community of the village of Quehueri'ono by prior arrangement.

Several missionaries, including the Bishop of Coca, have been killed for at
tempting to encroach upon the Huaorani culture. Such disturbances of indige
nous life date from 1541, when Francisco de Orellana's expedition departe
Quito and stumbled upon the headwaters of the Río Napo. Towns such as Arch
dona and **Macas** were soon established as bases for conquest and for conve:
sion. Many were subsequently abandoned due to repeated attacks from th
indigenous people, but the gold prospectors, the Franciscans, and the Jesuits, dr
ven by fierce faith in their gods, gradually pushed back the frontiers.

*Shrunken head of a
Jívaro (former name
of the Shuar people).*

Oil and tourist booms

The loss of most of the Oriente to Peru following the border war in 1941 stirre
the government's attention, which was rewarded in 1967 with the discovery c
huge oil deposits near **Lago Agrio** ⓬. The face of the region has changed dra:
tically since then, with towns constructed overnight to provide services for th
booming oil industry, which quickly became Ecuador's main money-spinner. I
1989, Lago Agrio was made the capital of Sucumbios, Ecuador's 21st province
while in 1998 the new province of Orellana was created to its south.

BELOW: motoring
along the Río Napo.

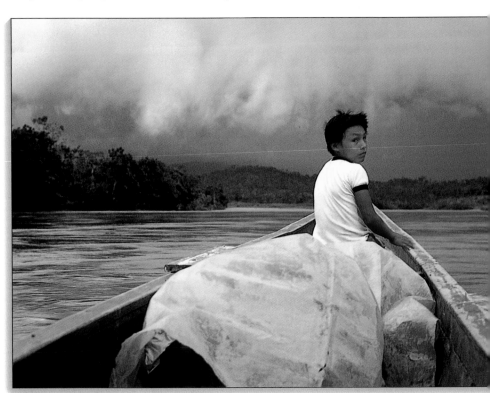

This influx of people has sent wildlife deeper into the forests. In areas on the ʌge of the Amazon Basin, there is little fauna left apart from birds and insects. ɔr those who are short of time, tours can be organized into the rainforest from ɪe small town of **Misahuallí**. These trips can give a good understanding of ɔw people living in the Oriente have adjusted to these outside influences.

The Napo flows on from Misahuallí to **Coca** ⓫ (officially named Puerto ɼancisco de Orellana), passing stilt houses with exotic menageries set in ramɪing banana patches. Farmers load fruit into their dugout canoes and then padɪe precariously off to market. The oil town of Coca itself has a seedy feel, miniscent of the frontier towns of the Wild West. Signs of oil development in ɪe area are obvious. Not too far from Coca however, pure rainforest abounds.

The Río Napo here is ever-widening, bordered on either side by a forest ɪnopy, thickest at the height of approximately 30 meters (100 ft), beneath ʌhich grows, in damp dimness, an astonishing assortment of ferns and wild mon trees with tiny edible ants living inside the stems. Above the canopy, the ɪant kapok tree stands out, the tallest Amazonian species, which can reach up ₀ 60 meters (200 ft) high and 40 meters (130 ft) around the base of the trunk. ɔcal people on the move seek shelter at night in the hollows between its roots. ɪ branches are cluttered with bromeliads, strangler vines, and belladonna.

Hidden in the forest, just off the River Napo, three hours downriver from ɔca, is Sacha Lodge. An elevated boardwalk heads through the forest, arriving ₐ a piranha-infested lagoon in front of the lodge. Resident naturalists and digenous guides venture into the forest with visitors on nature walks, canoe ɔats, or up into the 40-meter (130-ft) high observation tower to experience rest life high up in the canopy and maybe spot a sloth lazing atop his tree. ɪose to Sacha Lodge is La Selva, another well-run ɪdge and with good excursions to view wildlife.

The rewards of a very early morning boat ride to ℮ edge of **Parque Nacional Yasuni** may be the sight ⁻ flocks of macaws and parrots descending onto the ɪff by the river to feed on the minerals in the soil. ʌsuni is a national reserve created to protect and ɔnitor the incredible bio-diversity of this unique ɪnforest area. The comfortable Napo Wildlife Cenⁱ is situated in the Yasuni Reserve, operated by the ɪangu community. The birding here is excellent and ℮re are also black caiman and giant otters. The Tipuɪi River, a tributary of the Napo River, leads to the putini Research Station, where researchers and ecoɪrists wake to find groups of monkeys at their cabin ɪndow, exotic birds, and always the unnerving ɪance of a jaguar wandering through their camp. mazon cruises operate on the River Napo, aboard ℮ *Manatee Amazon Explorer*, a luxury vessel holdɪg 30 passengers. Kapawi Lodge is located on the ɪver Capahuari. It was built in partnership with the ɪhuar community and is accessible by small aircraft.

ɔastal Ecuador

ɪe tropical lowland west of the Andes has – along ɪth its inhabitants, who comprise half the nation – ℮n characterized as savage and uncivilized by ɔuntain dwellers, a place to be exploited. It is the

Map on page 198

The Spanish chronicler Cieza de Léon visited the largely ruined Cuenca in 1547 and found fully stocked warehouses, barracks, and houses formerly occupied by "more than two hundred virgins, who were very beautiful, dedicated to the service of the sun."

BELOW: feeding monkeys in a jungle resort.

traditional source of Ecuador's wealth, based on bananas, coffee, and cocoa. I late 1997 and early 1998, El Niño caused serious floods and extensive damage

Coastal Ecuador begins in the north with **San Lorenzo** 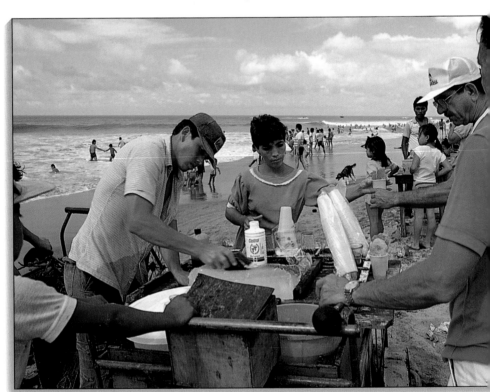 and its neighborin villages, collections of wooden stilt houses suspended in steamy, timeless isola tion amid twisting mangrove channels. It remains a ramshackle tropical tow with a Caribbean feel, pulsating with the beat of Colombian salsa. At **La Tola** on the edge of the San Lorenzo Archipelago, the coast road begins – a dust track through uninhabited swamps bursting with vegetation.

Esmeraldas , strung along the shore of the river of the same name, exem plifies urban coastal culture. This city is loud and vibrant late into the nigh Among a population that is chiefly mestizo and black, mountain *campesinos* i bowler hats sell fruit, Andean panpipes interrupt Caribbean dance music an techno rhythms, and Chinese restaurants serve sweet-and-sour.

Southwest of Esmeraldas are some of Ecuador's finest beaches. The road passe through **Atacames**, a small resort town that in recent years has become a nois party town, and on through **Sua**, a beautifully situated, friendly fishing villag finally ending at **Muisne** , with beaches as remote as they are alluring.

The main road south follows the river through cattle farms and plantations c bananas, palm oil, and rubber, rising 500 meters (1,600 ft) to **Santo Doming de los Colorados** . The Colorados, or Zatchila, inhabitants, who live mainl to the south of town, paint black stripes on their faces and wear their hair dye red with *achiote*, a plant dye, and cut in a bowl shape. They retain their know edge of natural medicine but dress traditionally only for special occasions.

Perhaps the most scenic of the lowland routes runs from Santo Domingo Manta , the calmest and prettiest coastal city. On **Tarqui beach**, local fishe

BELOW: crushed-ice vendor, Esmeraldas.

nen unload their catch of shark, dorado, eel, and the odd turtle, which are cleaned nd sold on the sand amidst an aerial frenzy of seagulls and vultures.

Manta is the gateway to the nearby Panama hat villages *(see below)*. Fine vickerwork furniture and sisal hammocks are also manufactured here. South of Manta is **Parque Nacional Machalilla**, one of the threatened dry tropical forests n the world. Now with national protection status, it is hoped that this unique for-'st with its bottle-shaped trees, the skyline dotted with kapok trees and more han 200 species of birds, will survive. The park entrance is just north of **Puerto** López ⓲, a small fishing town with unspoilt beaches. This is a good base to visit Machalilla and Isla de la Plata, an island with interesting bird life. From June hrough October humpback whales can be seen off the coast.

Panama hat maker.

South of the the central coast, all roads lead to **Guayaquil** ⓴, once the cen-'r of the Spanish regional shipbuilding industry and now Ecuador's largest and iveliest city, with approximately 2.8 million inhabitants. New technology and deas have always come first to Guayaquil: just as it had public streetcars and gas ighting before Quito, so it was the first city to realize independence in 1821, and as long been the bastion of progressive liberal thought. A pleasant walk goes long the extensively refurbished **Malecón Simón Bolívar** past **La Rotonda**, ommemorating Bolívar's meeting with San Martín; up to **Las Peñas**, the only xtant colonial district, and scenic **Cerro El Carmen**.

Shrunken heads from the Oriente, pre-Inca ceramics, colonial religious paint-ngs, and a changing modern art exhibition fill the **Museo Municipal**. The **Parque del Centenario**, where gymnasts and comedians perform, divides Avenida 9 de Octubre, the city's commercial heart. To escape the frenzy, grab a moment of tranquility in the city's botanical garden, **Parque Bolívar**.

BELOW: Panama hats for sale.

ECUADOR'S MOST FAMOUS HAT

Montecristi is the center of production of the Panama hat, a cottage industry that has protected the heads ' such notables as Teddy Roosevelt and King Edward VII. he hats are woven from the reed *Carludovica palmata*, ltivated locally and brought on horseback to craftsmen's mes. A top-quality or *superfino* specimen can change nds for up to US$1,000, and should be able to hold water hen held upside down. It should also fold up to fit into a p pocket without creasing. Weaving should ideally be ne at night or in dull conditions, and the process can ke up to three months.

The hats have always been produced in Ecuador, but were ipped worldwide from Panama, hence the misnomer. ade since pre-Columbian times, they caught on among e conquistadors, who were impressed by the headgear of e people of Manabí province. Soldiers fighting in the anish-American War of 1898 wore the hats, and the export arket to the US subsequently took off. They caught on in rope following the 19th-century World Exposition in Paris, many of Renoir's paintings illustrate. The hats were also big hit with US Prohibition gangsters, and the market aked in 1946. Since then demand has fallen, and some say at the production of *superfinos* will not survive much longer.

The Galápagos Islands

The first sighting by Europeans of the Galápagos Islands was in 1535. It is possible that the ancient Mantan, Incas and even Polynesians visited the islands which lie 1,000 km (600 miles) off the Pacific coast of Ecuador. From their European discovery until their incorporation into Ecuador in 1832, the islands served as a refuge for European and American pirates, whalers and sealers where they re-stocked supplies of firewood, water, and giant tortoises for meat which could remain alive for a year in ships' holds.

Just as the islands were undergoing permanent settlement, the *Beagle* dropped anchor in **San Cristóbal Bay** and the 26-year-old naturalist Charles Darwin strode ashore. Previous scientific expeditions had been mounted, but with Darwin's visit, the enormous biological and geological significance of the Galápagos islands was recognized. Although he stayed for only five weeks in 1835, Darwin made many of the observations upon which he based his theories of evolution and the mutability of species. He noticed 13 types of finch, each with different beak designed to collect its particular food.

The islands' romantic appeal was tarnished over the following century, when a penal colony was established on the island of **Floreana**. Conditions were harsh, administrators gratuitously cruel. The original colonists, some 80 soldiers whose crimes of insurrection had been pardoned, fled the island, leaving the prisoners to their fate. As recently as 1944, a colony was established on **Isabela** to which increasingly hardened criminals were sent. It was dissolved following a riot and mass escape, and in 1959, the islands were declared a national park.

The archipelago was designated a World Heritage Site in 1979 and a UNESCO World Biosphere Reserve in 1985. In December 2001, in an attempt to sto legal fishing and in recognition of the conservation issues, UNESCO declared the Marine Reserve around the islands a World Natural Heritage Site. Despite efforts to limit visitor numbers, the islands were placed on the UN's list of World Heritage Sites in danger in 2007.

There are 13 major islands, six small islands and 42 islets spread over an area of 80,000 sq. km (30,000 sq. miles). The land consists of lava resting on a basalt base, volcanic refuse produced by successive underwater eruptions which continue today. The islands have never been connected with the mainland, but emerged from the water individually over a million years. The violence of the geological past is most evident on **Isabela** with its chain of five volcanoes as high as 1,700 meters (5,600 ft). One of them, the **Sierra Negra**, has the second-largest crater in the world, measuring 10 km (6 miles) in diameter.

Seeds were transported accidentally by birds and aboard ships. Today the islands support almost 900 plant varieties, the most revered of which is the *palo santo*, found in abundance on **Isla Rábida ㉒**. There are six distinct vegetation zones ranging from low-level desert to the uppermost pampas; a walk up to the old sugar mill on San Cristóbal passes most of them.

On **San Bartolomé**, two sparkling horseshoe beaches are separated by a narrow strip of semitropical forest. From the island's summit, one of the best vantage points in the archipelago, the uninhabited volcanic wasteland of **Santiago** stretches away to the west. Within this desert is a freshwater spring. Flamingos dance around the nearby lagoon, and bury each other up to the neck in the coffee-colored sand of **Espumilla Beach**, and, near **Puerto Egas ㉑**, fur seals swim through an underwater tunnel between the open sea and two small, clear pools.

Author Herman Melville had a rather unromantic vision of the Galápagos Islands: "Take five-and-twenty heaps of cinders dumped here and there in an outside city lot; imagine some of them magnified into mountains, and the vacant lot the sea..."

BELOW: one of the famous iguanas.

Creatures of the sea

Some of the best snorkeling is done off far-flung islands like **Española** ㉔, the only place in the world in which the endemic waved albatross breeds. In **Gardner Bay**, flapping manta rays probably think you are just another sea lion, but the real sea lions know better, and an aggressive bull should be given right of way. The females and young are playful; they can recognize the 290 varieties of fish in the water, but a figure with a mask and flippers is still a curious sight.

The Galápagos are home to the world's only marine iguanas, and the island of **Fernandina** ㉕ holds the largest colony. As inquisitive as the two related land species, they are much more dragon-like with their scaly skin – which turns from black to blue and red during mating season – and the row of spines along their back. At one time land-dwellers, they can submerge for only a few minutes at a time, searching for algae; and upon re-surfacing, snort a salty spray into the air. Watching their antics beneath the smoldering **Volcán La Cumbre** which erupted in September 1988, is a truly primal experience.

Directly opposite Fernandina is **Urbina Bay**, and one of the few coral reefs in the archipelago. Fish of every color steer clear of the Galápagos penguin, the world's northernmost species. The entrance to nearby **Elizabeth Bay** is protected by a cluster of islands which penguins share with nesting pelicans. En route to Floreana, schools of sperm and killer whales cruise the deep waters, and bottle-nosed dolphins surf the bow waves of boats. At **Devil's Crown** ㉖, named after the jagged, truncated volcanic cone rising from the ocean, sea lions glide along strong currents, which make for adventurous snorkeling.

The beach on **Point Cormorant**, Floreana's most beautiful location, is dotted with olivine crystals, while the adjacent lagoons teem with flamingos.

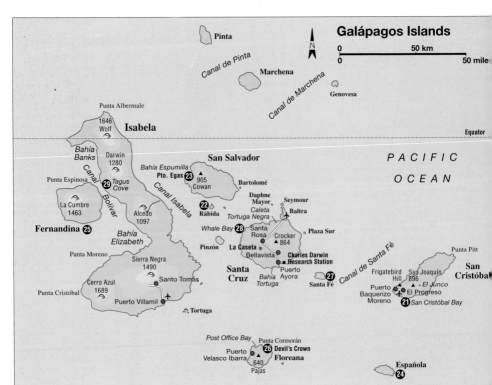

Around the point is the **Bay of Sharks** – its ring of pristine white sand is popular with nesting tortoises. The name refers to the relatively harmless white-tipped shark, which is found mainly here and off San Bartolomé. It is, along with the enormous and equally docile whale shark, the only kind in these waters. On land, the unchallenged king of the islands is the giant tortoise, which can live for 200 years and weigh up to 300 kg (600 lb). On rocky, sparsely vegetated islands like Isabela and Española, its longer neck and legs and saddle-shaped carapace enable it to reach higher to obtain food. These features are absent from the more cumbersome species inhabiting fertile islands like **Santa Cruz**.

The **Charles Darwin Research Station** was established on Santa Cruz in 1959, on the centenary of the publication of *The Origin of Species*. One of its most important programs is the controlled hatching of tortoise eggs, a necessary step since the introduction by early settlers of feral dogs, cats, goats, pigs, and rats. On **Pinzón**, not one young tortoise has been sighted for nearly 50 years. The feral species also destroy vegetation, but have participated in the evolutionary miracle of the islands in at least one respect: the goats on **Santa Fe** ㉗, in the absence of freshwater, have developed a taste for the sea, and now live on it.

In **Whale Bay** ㉘ on Santa Cruz, ceramic fragments conjure images of the buccaneer Henry Morgan with a blue-footed booby squawking on his shoulder. Pirates and whalers recorded their passage on the cliff faces of **Tagus Cove** ㉙ on Isabela: today the graffiti is seen mainly by flightless cormorants. A more recent ruin is the skeleton of an abandoned 1960s salt mine on Isla Santiago.

The Galápagos Islands are one of the few places in the world where animals still live relatively undisturbed, and nowhere are the forces of evolution more clearly displayed. Visitors should leave no scars. ❑

Map on page 216

Darwin encountered a "strange Cyclopean scene" on a San Cristóbal beach – two tortoises munching on cactus. One "gave a deep hiss, and drew in its head"; the other "slowly stalked away." Darwin became fascinated with the beasts, noting numerous subspecies.

LEFT: Sally Lightfoot crab.
RIGHT: stairway to heaven.

BIRDS OF THE GALÁPAGOS ISLANDS

From the marbled godwit to the black-necked stilt, the bird life on the Galápagos Islands, which taught us about evolution, is still rich, rare, and rewarding

Where else but on these small islands off the coast of Ecuador will birds come out to greet you? Life with no native predators has made the birds of the Galápagos fearless, which means that many of them are easy to spot. There are 58 resident species, of which 28 are endemic, as well as about 30 migratory birds. The sea birds are the most often seen: in the dry coastal areas you are likely to spot species of the booby family, the waved albatross – only found on the island of Española – and two flightless sea birds, the Galápagos penguin and the flightless cormorant. The best time to come is in winter (October to February) when most migrants are visiting, and birds are reproducing. Then, a serious ornithologist might observe 50 species in a week, and even a dilettante should be able to spot two dozen.

There are dangers in paradise, however: the introduction of domestic animals has been bad news. Some prey on the birds, others destroy or compete for their habitats. Farming on the inhabited islands also destroys habitats, and a natural phenomenon, the *El Niño* current, brings mosquito-borne disease and disrupts the food chain.

△ PEREGRINE FALCON
The endangered peregrine falcon *(Falco peregrinus)* originates in Canada and the US, and winters in South America. It is frequently seen on the islands of Española, Isabela, Baltra, and Santa Cruz. The world's swiftest bird, this falcon can reach speeds of 320 km/h (200 mph) when it is swooping to attack prey.

◁ GALÁPAGOS HAWK
The female Galápagos hawk *(Buteo galapagoensis)* is larger than the male of the species. While the males are monogamous, females will mate with up to seven males per season in order to ensure that breeding will be successful. The female and her males take turns in guarding the nest.

◁ BLUE-FOOTED BOOBY
The blue-footed booby *(Sula nebouxii excisa)* has a wonderful courtship ritual in which the male ostentatiously displays his brightly colored feet in order to attract a mate. Two or three eggs are laid and both of the parents share the task of incubating them. Once they have become independent, the young birds leave the islands and do not return to breed until some three years later.

THE SECRET OF DARWIN'S FINCHES

The finches of the Galápagos were vitally important in the development of Charles Darwin's ideas about evolution and the formation of species.

When he set off on his voyage around the world on HMS *Beagle* (1831–36), he believed, like most people of his time, in the fixity of species. But on the Galápagos he observed that 13 different species of the finch had evolved from a single ancestral group, and it was this (together with his observations of the islands' tortoises) which led to his contention that species could evolve over time, with those most suited to their natural environment surviving and passing on their characteristics to the next generation.

The main difference he noted between the finches was the size and shape of their beaks, leading him to conclude that the birds which survived were those whose beaks enabled them to eat the available food.

The 13 species of finch are divided into two groups: ground finches (pictured above is the large ground finch, *Geospiza magnirostris*) and tree finches, of which the mangrove finch, found only in the swamps of Isabela island, is the most rare. You are unlikely to see all of them on a short visit, but it's an enjoyable challenge to see how many you can spot.

◁ **VERMILLION FLYCATCHER**
The vermillion flycatcher *(Pyrocephalus rubinus)* is an attractive little bird and quite unlike any other bird to be seen on the Galápagos Islands. It has a high-pitched, musical song and builds a distinctive cup-shaped nest, on which the female incubates the eggs.

△ **FRIGATE BIRDS**
The magnificent frigate bird *(Fregata magnificens magnificens)* and its close relation, the great frigate bird, can be seen near the coasts of many islands. Both males and females have long forked tails and the male is remarkable for the red gular pouch which puffs in the mating season.

◁ **LAVA GULL**
The lava gull *(Larus fuliginosus)* is believed to be the rarest species in the world. It roosts on the shores of saltwater lagoons and builds solitary nests along the coast.

△ **BROWN PELICAN**
The brown pelican *(Pelecanus occidentalis urinator)* is a huge, cumbersome bird, which can often be seen following fishing boats in search of food.

THE TROPICAL GIANT

Laid-back tropical paradise, economic miracle,
or home of the hedonistic carnival – Brazil is
a heady mix of them all

Nearly half the South American subcontinent can be described in one tantalizing word: Brazil. Almost as big as the United States and home to 188 million people, Brazil is a world in itself – a sensuous giant that invariably becomes a part of everyone who experiences its pleasures. Brazil the geographic colossus is also a state of mind, one that loosens up even the most cautious of spirits who venture there. That's the power of the Brazilian *jeito*, or way. Relax, hang loose, improvize, and *nao esquente a cabeça*: don't get hot-headed, come what may.

There is a vibrancy to Brazil unparalleled elsewhere in Latin America; the country's cutting-edge innovations and penchant for fads have led some to call it "the California of South America." But for all its laid-back ethos, Brazil is also a dynamo of economic activity. The world's fifth-largest population produces the planet's ninth-largest economy. Virtually everything one buys in Brazil is made in Brazil. Cars crafted in São Paulo run on lead-free sugar-cane fuel (home-grown, naturally), and their compact-disc players made in the duty-free Amazon port of Manaus play tunes from the recording studios of Rio de Janeiro.

As the major port of entry, Rio *(see page 233)* is where most visitors get their first dazzling impressions of Brazil, with its beautiful beaches, sensuously rounded peaks, and world-famous carnival. But like the iceberg below its tip, there's much more to Brazil than Rio. Nearby is South America's and the southern hemisphere's largest metropolis, São Paulo *(see page 238)*. With 11 million people under its towering skyline, this is the country's powerhouse, the center of its massive commercial and industrial output. To the northwest lies Brasília *(see page 240)*, the pristine architectural wonder that sprang up from the wilderness to become the national capital. Beyond the triangle of political, cultural, and economic power formed by these three cities are slightly more subdued wonders: the stately colonial cities of Minas Gerais *(see page 241)*, living monument of the gold and diamond booms; the inviting beaches and rich Afro-Brazilian culture of the Northeast *(see page 244)*; the immense rainforests of the Amazon jungle that still cover more than half the country *(see page 254)*; the vast marshlands of the Pantanal, a naturalist's paradise *(see page 251)*; and the enormous waterfalls of Iguaçu *(see page 253)*. ❑

PRECEDING PAGES: coastal splendor, Costa Verde, west of Rio de Janeiro.
LEFT: Christ the Redeemer statue, Rio.

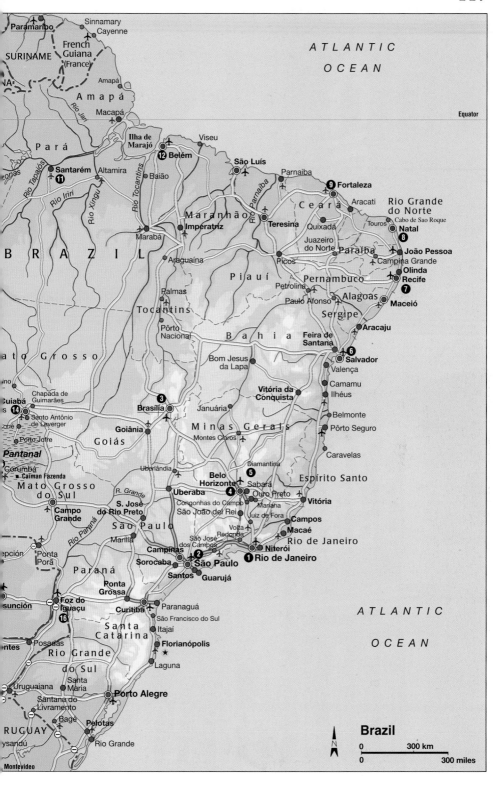

Brazil

0   300 km

0   300 miles

BRAZIL

*This vast country pulsates with life, from the rampant
fertility of the Amazon to the sensual delights of Rio and the
modern sophistication of São Paulo and Brasília*

Map on pages 226–7

Visitors can only hope to scratch the surface of this huge land, which still has vast unpopulated areas, and reveals its secrets reluctantly. It's worth making the effort, for there is much to discover, from the excitement of Rio de Janeiro and the gastronomic highlights of São Paulo to the majestic forests of the Amazon, scarred red by twisting rivers; and from the abundant wildlife of the Pantanal to the solitude of the arid northeastern "backlands". The past comes to life in the gold towns in the south of Minas Gerais, such as Ouro Preto, Tiradentes, and Congonhas. Harder to get to, but worth the effort, are places like the high plateaux of Bahia State, the Chapada Diamantina, where Brazil's second-highest waterfall tumbles from a mist-clouded plain.

The distance from the Andes to the Atlantic Ocean is almost 4,500 km (2,800 miles), and most of Brazil's attractions are a long way from the big cities, as well as from each other: the Iguaçu Falls is thousands of kilometers from balmy Belém in the north. But traveling around Brazil has become easier and cheaper, due to a price war between the country's airlines, some of them new low-cost carriers.

Travelers looking for warm water, white sand, and tropical beauty will be overwhelmed by the Brazilian coastline – the longest, and perhaps the most beautiful of any country in the world.

Conquering the interior

Brazil's interior was first penetrated by Europeans in the late 1600s. The first pioneers were Jesuits proseytizing to indigenous Guaraní, followed by Poruguese immigrants too poor to acquire land in the sugar-cane dominated coastal regions. These settlers pushed into what is now the state of São Paulo to raise cattle and plant subsistence crops. Like the wealthy sugar planters whose labor force was mostly black slaves, these farmers also sought bonded workers, so they organized expeditions to abduct Guaraní who inhabited the region. The Guaraní sought refuge in the Jesuit missions where indigenous peoples lived in educated, highly productive communities.

Despite their barbaric raids, the *bandeirantes* (so named because of the banners they marched under), have gone down in Brazilian folklore as brave pioneers who opened up what has become the country's most productive economic region.

Just when the world market for Brazilian sugar started to go soft around 1700, a new boom shook the country. This time it was gold and diamonds, discovered in the rugged hill country of Minas Gerais. Most of the gold was sent to the Portuguese crown, but enough remained to build the baroque cities of Ouro Preto, São João del Rei, and Sabará. The new treasures were shipped to Europe through Rio de Janeiro, putting the backwater

PRECEDING PAGES: Sugar Loaf Mountain dominates Rio's Guanabara Bay.
LEFT: exhibitionism at the Rio *Carnaval*.
BELOW: Ouro Preto.

port on the map, and by 1763 Rio had become so important that the Portuguese crown moved the capital there from the sugarcane and slave entrepôt of Salvador

Other booms followed, such as cotton. The biggest and most lasting boom, coffee, started in the late 18th century. The state of São Paulo was covered with coffee plantations as the craze for drinking coffee spread around the world. But coffee prices tumbled in 1930, and with them fell the government. Getulio Vargas, governor of Rio Grande do Sul, then seized the presidency and won Brazilians' hearts with his populist rhetoric and championing of organized labor. He established a corporate state apparently modeled on Mussolini's fascism, losing support after the fall of Hitler and Mussolini. Vargas resigned in 1945, but returned to office in 1951, before committing suicide in 1954.

Eighteen years of constitutional rule and steady economic growth followed, until the early 1960s. With the number of landless peasants increasing dramatically, land reform became an explosive political issue. The military responded to the growing unrest by seizing power in April 1964.

Birth of the "Brazilian Miracle"

The military's crackdown on leftists (many of whom were tortured and killed) and generous fiscal incentives combined to attract a flood of foreign investment. The Brazilian economy boomed, mainly enriching those who were already wealthy. Disenchantment with military rule grew as the economy took a nose dive in 1980, crippled by enormous bills for imported oil and public works projects, such as a rarely used Amazon highway. The last of a series of military dictator presidents stepped down in March 1985.

The new government of President José Sarney inherited a foreign debt of more than US$100 billion. Sarney, closely allied with the military, quickly lost political support as inflation which reached 1,000 percent in 1988, continued to ravage the economy.

Economic woes were accompanied by growing street crime. Such anti-social behavior is relatively recent in Brazil, and is widely considered a product of the huge influx of rural Brazilians into large cities since the 1960s. Some were attracted by jobs, but many arrived as refugees from droughts in the Northeast.

Progress for the poor is often limited by racial discrimination. Although Brazil has been called a racial paradise because of the high number of interracial marriages and an absence of open racial conflict, to be black in Brazil almost always means to be poor, and 40 per cent of the country's population is black. But whatever their color, there is little chance of a poor Brazilian becoming a rich one, unless they play soccer well.

From bust to boom

Few countries can have changed as much as Brazil since mid-1994, after the election of Fernando Henrique Cardoso as president. Inflation, then running at more than 3,000 percent a year, was halted by drastic measures, including the introduction of a new currency, the real. This set off a chain of events that are still transforming the country. Twelve to 15 million Brazilians joined the consumer society for the first time, causing food sales to surge and the demand for many other goods to explode. Credit, absent for three decades, became accessible, and millions went on a shopping spree, particularly for new cars, but as road building has not kept pace there is chronic congestion. In 2002, former metalworker Luis Inácio da Silva, popularly known as Lula, became Brazil's first left-wing president for 40 years. He has followed sensible economic policies while not defaulting on the country's US$250 billion public debt. As well as bringing food to 15 million needy people, he continued to meet IMF demands, and secured a series of several hundred billion-dollar loans. Lula was re-elected in 2006 and announced his intention to ensure an annual economic growth rate of 5 percent, while controlling inflation and government spending.

The Northeast has progressed rapidly, as factories relocate in search of cheaper labor. Stagnant state capitals such as Fortaleza, Recife, and Salvador, are being given a new lease of life, and neglected architectural gems are being restored.

Huge natural resources secure the country's future, but they bring responsibilites toward the environment, particularly in the Amazon region, where destruction has occurred on a massive scale. Disturbingly, "Avança Brasil" was announced in 2001. Already underway, the US$40-billion program will include the building of 10,000 km (6,215 miles) of highways, electric dams, and power lines in an attempt to industrialize the area. Indigenous peoples, particularly in the Amazon regions, still suffer daily threats and invasions of their homelands by fire, logging, and from settlers looking for homes away from Brazil's southern cities. Although President Lula has been criticized for his lack of commitment in protecting the rainforest, in June 2004 he announced the designation of four new national forests, covering around 400,000 hectares (1 million acres) of threatened land.

Monument to Juscelino Kubitschek, the driving force behind the creation of Brasília.

BELOW: crowded hillside *favela*, Rio.

Trouble in the rainforest

The conflict of interests over land use is exemplified in the remote western region of Rondônia *(see page 250)*, where settlers are pushing back the rainforest – and the people who have lived there for centuries. Two factors set off the land rush: first, changes in agriculture in Brazil's prosperous south made many peasants landless in the 1970s. Soaring world prices for soybeans convinced many coffee farmers to cut down their bushes and plant soybeans. Peasants who had sharecropped at the edges of the coffee plantations – assuring growers a stable workforce to harvest the beans – were no longer needed for the mechanized soybean harvest, and were forced to abandon their plots.

Second, the extension of the roadway BR 364 from the coffee regions of São Paulo state to Rondônia, the new Brazilian frontier, put into action the formula for peopling the Amazon enunciated by the Brazilian military, which then governed the country: "A land without people for people without land." Speculators cashed in, buying up enormous tracts for cattle ranches.

Brazil has a GDP of over US$900 billion, and nearly 70 percent of its exports are industrial goods – but the gap between rich and poor is still greater than almost anywhere else in the world. In most cities, unemployment has led to rising crime. Tourists can be targeted, and caution is needed, but things are not as bad as is often made out. A special police force guards tourists on many beaches.

Despite the pace of change, most Brazilians are well aware that the most important things in life are personal relationships, having fun, and making the best of what is available. Visitors will be impressed with their courtesy and friendliness, as well as their unflappable equanimity. Maybe it's because they have so many opportunities to let off steam – in carnival, music, and soccer.

BELOW: the glorious church of Glória, downtown Rio.

Rio de Janeiro, city of fun

Brazilians call **Rio de Janeiro ❶** *a cidade maravilhosa* – the marvelous city – and they have ample reason to do so. There's the city's stunning setting: flanked to the east by the enormous **Bay of Guanabara** and to the south by the Atlantic Ocean, Rio sprawls around and even up the sides of enormous granite peaks and down to wide sandy beaches. The result of this topsy-turvy topography is a city sculptured around the whims of nature, giving the urban landscape a look that can only be described as sensuous.

The six million people who live in and around Rio are known as *cariocas*, and they epitomize the casual, good-natured disposition associated with Brazilians. Part of the *carioca's* sunny outlook may derive from the smug satisfaction of living in a place most people only dream of, where it's possible to join the fun on the beaches for the price of a local bus fare. Another reason for their friendliness could be the open social scene of Rio. Unlike other big cities, where exclusivity heightens the appeal of social gatherings, in Rio people of all classes throng to public places for fun. The beaches are the biggest attraction, followed by soccer stadiums and carnivals. In Rio, it's sociable to down a *chopp* (draught beer) and chat with friends on the sidewalk; life is lived in the open air.

Cariocas have a reputation for few inhibitions and tremendous appetites. That image developed in part from the bacchanalian bashes of carnival, in part from the tantalizingly tiny beach attire favored by both genders. In Rio, you don't have to be gorgeous to be on display – just uninhibited. *Cariocas* are extremely tolerant (gay men seeking open minds flock to Rio from the rest of Brazil) and anyone can indulge in a little exhibitionism. Pleasure became Rio's main money maker after 1960, when the seat of government was moved from here to landlocked Brasília. Rio went from being the center of the Brazilian universe to a mere tourist attraction. It took a long time for the city to come to terms with its new identity, but *cariocas* take comfort in knowing that the politicians who moved to Brasília left their hearts in Rio.

From the airport to the city center

Most visitors' first encounter with Rio takes place at the sleek complex of Antonio Carlos Jobim International Airport. The airport, also known as Galeão, is located on an island north of Rio, and to the west is a massive swampy area known as the Baixada Fluminense, or fluvial lowlands, a poor, featureless area that is home to two-thirds of the city's inhabitants. The drive into the city from the airport passes Rio's port and the **Espaço Cultural da Marinha ❹** (Avenida Alfredo Agache; open Tues–Sun), one of Rio's principal museums, famous for its detailed model ships. Nearby is the **Museu Histórico Nacional ❺** (Praça Marechal Ancora; open Tues–Sun), which holds Brazil's national archives covering the period from 1500 to the proclamation of the republic in 1889.

The main thoroughfare through the heart of the downtown area, **Avenida Rio Branco**, is lined by sky-scraping banks, travel agencies, and the ornate 19th-century buildings of the **Teatro Municipal ❻** (which has a splendid ground-floor café with mosaic tiles).

BELOW: *cariocas* just want to have fun.

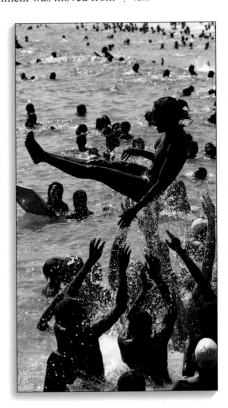

Maps
Area 226–7
City 232

Guanabara Bay from Sugar Loaf Mountain.

BELOW: snorkeling, one of the many outdoor sports available in Rio.

Across the street is the **Biblioteca Nacional** (the national library, with neo classical and Art Nouveau paintings on display) and the **Museu Nacional de Belas Artes ①** (open Tues–Sun), one of the country's foremost repositories of classic and contemporary Brazilian art, with around 16,000 works.

One of the best places to watch the action is on the plaza in front of the Teatro Municipal, an area known as **Cinelândia**. Come nightfall it's a mixture of polit ical campaigners, guerrilla theater, transvestites, and performers of *capoeira* (a stylized fight-dance with its own accompanying rhythms and music). On the other side of the Teatro Municipal is a wide pedestrian mall, **Largo da Carioca**, a favorite haunt of all manner of vendors and leather artisans.

For a flavor of what Rio was like before the skyscrapers crowded its skyline wander down the sidestreets off Largo da Carioca. Don't miss the stately Con feiteria Colombo at Rua Gonçalves Dias 32, with a mirror-lined tearoom down stairs and elegant dining room upstairs. *Belle époque* furnishings evoke the late 19th century, when Rio's intelligentsia used to gather here. Stroll down Rua da Carioca for hearty German food and *chopp* at the lively Bar Luiz, a downtown fixture for more than a century. Rising high above Largo da Carioca to the west is the **Igreja e Convento de Santo Antônio ⑤** (open daily), built between 1608 and 1780. Beside the main church is the lovely chapel of **São Francisco de Penitência**. To the south, on the other side of Avenida Republica do Chile stands Rio's cone-shaped **Catedral de São Sebastião**, finished in 1976.

Interesting neighborhoods

Nearby is the **Arcos da Lapa**, a towering 18th-century aqueduct that now serves as a bridge for the picturesque trolley cars, or *bondes* (pronounced "bon-jees" – so called because the system was funded by foreign bonds. The trolleys shuttle from a station by the ca thedral to the steep streets of **Santa Teresa ⑤**, to the west of the center. Known for its precipitous topogra phy and grand views, Santa Teresa is one of the most bohemian of Rio's neighborhoods. Be sure to see the **Chácara do Ceu** (open Wed–Mon) on Rua Martinho Nobre. This small museum has splendid views of the city and a great collection of Brazilian and European paintings, including works by Picasso, Braque, and Matisse. Take a detour to the northern suburb of Quinta da Boa Vista to the **Museu Nacional ⑤** (open Tues–Sun), the home of the imperial royal family from 1808 until the end of the monarchy in 1889. A throne room and reception rooms remain among an eclectic ethnographic and natural history collection.

Going south

Much of the shoreline between downtown Rio and the Bay of Botafogo, including Santos Dumont air port, home to the shuttle service to São Paulo, is the result of *aterro* (landfill). Toward the airport, inter national and Brazilian modern art is also on display in the exciting **Museu de Arte Moderna ⑪** (open Tues–Sun), off Avenida Infante Dom Henrique. South of the museum in the Parque do Flamengo is a tall stone monument built to honor Brazilians who died in World War II. There is a beach here but the polluted state of Guanabara Bay makes the water uninviting. Across the road, on a cliff, is the baroque **Igreja de Nossa Senhora da Glória ❶** and adjacent museum.

Emerging like a gigantic granite knee 400 meters (1,300 ft) from the waters of the entrance to Guanabara Bay is **Pão de Açúcar** (Sugar Loaf Mountain). Cable cars leave **Praia Vermelha** station every half hour to sweep visitors up the mountain via the Morro da Urca, with restaurant and amphitheater. To the west of Sugar Loaf begin Rio's legendary beaches. The first wide arc spans the neighborhoods of Leme to the east and Copacabana to the west, with Copacabana Fort at the western point. **Leme** is mostly residential and quiet. Rua Princesa Isabel, which divides Leme from Copacabana, is a favorite with prostitutes, and nightlife in the area is rather seedy. **Copacabana**, with 350,000 residents, is Rio's most densely populated neighborhood, and is a lively place to enjoy street celebrations at *Carnaval* and New Year's Eve. The **Praia de Copacabana** beach is magnificent, and stretches out almost a block to the water. It's floodlit at night, but stay close to the crowds on the sidewalk to avoid getting mugged. Tourists wandering by the water in the dark are considered "papaya with sugar" by petty thieves.

After Copacabana comes **Praia de Ipanema**, which connects at its western end with another beach, called **Leblon**. Both Ipanema and Leblon are much more attractive neighbourhoods than Copacabana, and altogether more pleasant areas for tourists to stay. Behind them to the north is the freshwater **Lagoa Rodrigo de Freitas**, a large natural lagoon surrounded by high-rises and restaurants.

South to the most unspoiled beaches

On the west shore of the lagoon are the **Jockey Club** race track and the **Jardím Botánico** on the street of the same name. Some 5,000 species of Brazilian plants

TIP

The best way to see the elegant 19th-century homes of Santa Teresa is to take one of the yellow streetcars that leave from the cathedral. Leave valuables behind, since the open-sided cars are vulnerable to pickpockets.

BELOW: garlic for sale in a Rio market.

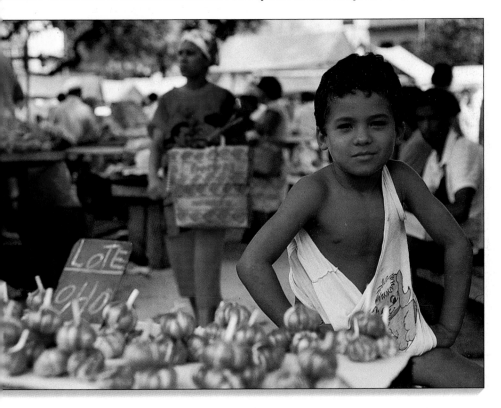

Carnaval!

Nothing else merits more preparation, more prolonged and devout attention, and a more lavish outpouring of private resources than the annual convulsion that has come to symbolize Brazil, for better or for worse. Extravagance, self-indulgence, exhibitionism, and a kind of gleeful innocence are the basic elements – qualities that color life in Brazil, albeit less intensely, the rest of the year. Streets normally clogged with vehicles are reclaimed by revelers on foot; macho men lasciviously parade in drag; laborers masquerade as 18th-century royalty; mothers dress up like babies; the wealthy watch the poor perform; people stay up all night and sleep all day.

Carnaval arrived with the Portuguese, a re-invention of the winter festivities of Europe. The celebrations are ostensibly the last shot at merrymaking before the 40 days of fasting that precede Easter (the name is believed to be a derivation of the Italian

carne vale, or farewell to meat). *Carnaval* in Brazil began as an aggressive spree of throwing water, mud, and flour at passersby. This still characterizes *Carnaval* in Bolivia and Argentina, but was banned in Brazil in the 19th century.

But the *Carnaval* that Brazil is renowned for did not become a tradition until the 1930s, when neighborhood groups began to compete. Samba *(see page 57)* has become the signature music of *Carnaval*. Today the competition between samba schools is akin to the rivalry between top sports teams. Most of the members come from the humblest of Rio's neighborhoods. Samba schools hold practice sessions for months before *Carnaval*, which are often open to the public. The moment of glory comes at the gates of Rio's mammoth samba stadium, the Sambódromo, designed by Oscar Niemeyer. Some 65,000 spectators can be seated along this kilometer-long parade strip to watch the samba schools go dancing by. If you can't get a ticket, you can see the schools line up outside on Avenida Presidente Vargas.

The best street dancing is in Salvador, where carousing hordes follow deafening sound systems. As is the case everywhere during *Carnaval*, it's best to dress minimally (shorts or bathing suits) to blend into the crowds and not attract thieves. Many travelers prefer *Carnaval* in the Northeast. In Recife the pre-eminent *Carnaval* music is *frevo*, which ignites passions, while in Bahia, and especially Salvador, *Carnaval* features the Trio Elétricos.

Less frenetic are the carnivals held in the cities of Olinda and Ouro Preto, and in Rio's outlying suburbs. Class lines dissolve as revelers hop down the streets in camaraderie fueled by generous amounts of beer and *cachaca* (sugar-cane brandy). *Carnaval* has moved off the streets and into the clubs recently, and this is where the most intense debauchery and exhibitionism goes on.

Not everyone in Brazil is wild about *Carnaval*. Many intellectuals sneer at the kitsch, wanton drinking, and lewdness. But for outsiders, there is probably no better time to see the Brazil of everyone's fantasies. ❑

LEFT: clothes serve a purely decorative purpose at Rio de Janeiro's *Carnaval*.

over the garden's 100 hectares (250 acres), and though some of the grounds have gone to seed, a visit is still a pleasure. Another natural adventure is the ride up the proverbially hunchbacked **Corcovado Mountain** on the impressive steep cog railway that leaves from Cosme Velho. An escalator takes passengers from the station to the summit, where there is a café. At the top, 710 meters (2,330 ft) above the ocean, towers Rio's trademark statue of **Cristo Redentor** (Christ the Redeemer). The road down from the statue wends through the **Parque Nacional da Tijuca**, a tropical reserve that includes 100 km (60 miles) of narrow, two-lane roads winding through the forest's thick vegetation, and with several breathtaking look-out points.

West of the sands of Leblon, sprawling up the sides of granite slopes, are two *avelas* or hillside shantytowns – **Vidigal** and **Rocinha** (the latter is the largest in South America). Their residents, who number hundreds of thousands, often endure precarious circumstances in order to live close to their jobs on the south side of the city. Rocinha tumbles down into **São Conrado**, a modern beachside suburb that is home to the city's hangliders and the beautiful Gávea golf course. Further along the coast, along a two-tier highway, is the start of "new" Rio.

Barra de Tijuca, or simply Barra, is a massive suburb that is already seen as the future of Rio. A little too American for some tastes, here you'll find the city's largest shopping malls and entertainment complexes sitting between modern, purpose-built condominiums that would not look out of place in Miami. Barra beach, at over 18 km (11 miles), is the city's longest and one of the most popular at the weekend. Beyond Barra are to be found a number of other beaches such as Prianha and Grumari that are relatively unspoilt and that help visitors to understand part of the awesome beauty that gives Rio its enduring magic.

Map on page 232

Trendy boutiques with artistic signs like this are plentiful in Brazil's many coastal resorts.

BELOW: flying down to Rio.

Close to Rio

The coastal route between Rio and São Paulo, a drive of 375 miles (600 km), i an attraction in its own right, being one of the planet's most stunning stretches o coastline. The Costa Verde, or Green Coast, includes **Angra dos Reis** (King' Cove), a bay with hundreds of tropical islands including Ilha Grande. There is als the colonial masterpiece of Parati, a coastal village that hosts some of Sout America's most important literary festivals. Closer to São Paulo are the resor areas of Ubatuba, Caraguatatuba, São Sebastião, Guarujá, and Ilhabela.

The coast to the east of Rio, known as the Costa do Sol (Sun Coast), als holds a number of attractions, most notably the extremely fashionable village o Búzios, that sits on a peninsula 200 km (125 miles) from Rio along with 2: beaches. Búzios is known for the beaches, charming inns, great restaurants, an its exciting and varied nightlife.

The most popular day trip from Rio takes visitors away from the coast and u in to the mountains north of Rio where the imperial city of **Petrópolis** is wait ing to be discovered. The region is also home to the **National Park of Serra do Orgãos**, an area that is extremely popular with walkers and trekkers.

Colonial Parati, on the Costa Verde between São Paulo and Rio de Janeiro.

BELOW: São Paulo.

São Paulo: Brazil's workhorse

The first thing that strikes most visitors to the city of **São Paulo ❷** is its shee enormity. Home to 11 million *paulistas*, as the city's natives call themselves, Sã Paulo's phenomenal growth shows no signs of abating. Already the city cover. nearly 2,600 sq. km (1,000 sq. miles), and it is ringed by mushrooming suburbs São Paulo is the center of Brazilian trade and industry. Two-thirds of the country' industrial goods are produced here, including nine out of 10 automobiles. "Sã Paulo works so that the rest of Brazil can play", *paulis tas* will tell you. Since its foundation in 1554, the cit has always attracted self-reliant individualists – it wa Brazil's equivalent of the Old West, and today proudl honors its old pioneers, the *bandeirantes*. Those who followed came from all over the world, especially in the 19th century, bringing industrious work habits. Mor recent immigrants have come from the drought-stricke states of northeastern Brazil. Poorly educated an unskilled, they often end up in the festering slums tha house a sizable percentage of the city's population.

São Paulo is not a place to spend your whole vaca tion, but it is well worth a visit. Its restaurants are a diverse as they are numerous – a reflection of the city's varied ethnic makeup – and the nightlife rival that of any other major cosmopolitan city.

Paulistas consider themselves trailblazers in the arts as well as industry. The pride and joy of the cit is the MASP, the **Museu de Arte de São Paul** (Avenida Paulista 1578; open Tues–Sun), with nearl 1,000 pieces originating from both Ancient Greec and contemporary Brazil, along with changing tem porary exhibitions.

Beneath the chaos

Perhaps the best way to explore São Paulo is by it. clean, fast subway network. Stop off at **Liberdade** home to the largest ethnic-Japanese community out de Japan. There are many inexpensive sushi bars in this area, and on Sundays there's a food and crafts fair at **Praça Liberdade**. Neighborhoods such as Jardim Paulista or **Jardim America** have tree-lined streets and mansions that provide respite from the downtown rush. Another favorite oasis is the lovely **Parque do Ibirapuera**, with curving pavilions designed by Oscar Niemeyer. Every even-numbered year, São Paulo hosts one of the world's largest international art shows, the prestigious Biennial, in a pavilion here. Linked to the pavilion by an undulating walkway is the **Museu de Arte Moderna** (open Tues–Sun), exhibiting work by Brazil's 21st-century sculptors and painters.

Not far away, on Rua do Horto, is the **Horto Florestal** (open daily), founded in 1896. A pleasant place to spend an afternoon, the park has a playground, picnic areas and the Pedra Grande viewpoint, offering a beautiful view of the north of São Paulo city. Inside the park is the **Museu Florestal Octávio Vecchi**, displaying a huge variety of native wood samples.

Whether or not you like snakes, the **Butantan Snake Farm** is a fascinating place. Some 54,000 snakes there are milked for venom daily, and serum is prepared for distribution throughout Brazil and the world. There is a museum as well, at Avenida Dr Vital Brasil 1500, in the Pinheiros district (open Tues–Sun).

At night, São Paulo has a wide variety of clubs and cafés to while away the hours. Live music is even more plentiful here than in Rio. There's also a counter-culture quarter, the **Bela Vista** (popularly known as **Bixiga**), centered on Rua 13 de Maio. There are few old buildings left in the city, but the **Teatro Municipal**, which has resident opera and dance companies, evokes the elegant days of 19th-century coffee barons. The city frequently hosts world-class performers – *paulistas* may be workaholics, but they demand the best in entertainment.

Map
on pages
226–7

Medical researcher and friend, Butantan Snake Farm.

BELOW: Butantan Snake Farm.

Brasília: futuristic capital

Rising out of the great scrubby expanses of Brazil's central *cerrado*, Brasília ❿ looks more like a gleaming extraterrestrial settlement than Brazil's nationa capital. Absent are the red-tile roofs, intimate passageways, and harmoniou pastel hues typical of Brazilian cities. Brasília is a cool, regimented architectura wonder, a "city of the future" that Brazilians are still trying to reconcile with the present. At 1,150 meters (3,773 ft) above sea level and more than 800 km (50(miles) from the coast, Brasília was built precisely because of its isolation from the great coastal cities. When Juscelino Kubitschek was elected president i 1955, he vowed that before he left office Brazil would have a new capital in it unpopulated interior, and he firmly believed that this capital would be a mag net to pull Brazilians away from their beloved coastline.

By 1956, work had already begun on Brasília. The city plan, drawn up b urban planner Lucio Costa, consisted of a central line of government building crossed by a curved arc of residential buildings – a layout that resembled th shape of an airliner. The architect chosen to design the structures was the Brazil ian Oscar Niemeyer, a one-time student of the great modern Swiss architect L Corbusier, with whom he collaborated in the design of the United Nations Head quarters building in New York. The project of Brasília was to incorporate all tha was new in materials and design. Work proceeded at a furious pace, and by it inauguration in April 1960, Brasília already had 100,000 inhabitants.

At this time, Brazil's automobile industry was quickly expanding, so Brasíli was designed with the certainty that everybody would get around in cars in th future. Wide thoroughfares sweep through the city, oblivious to the needs o pedestrians. With no sidewalks and few pedestrian crossings, Brasília has th country's highest pedestrian mortality rate. Its grass knolls are crisscrossed by red-earth paths created b Brazilians who still depend on their feet to get aroun

According to a popular joke, there are three great things about Brasília: its cool air, its enormous sky, and its air shuttle to Rio.

BELOW: Brasília's Foreign Ministry.

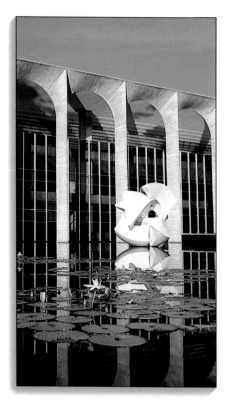

Modern wonder

Brasília is characterized by the graceful, pristine archi tecture of its public buildings. Down the hill pas the main bus terminal, the Eixo Monument (the Mon umental Axis) opens onto the **Esplanada do Ministérios** (Ministries Esplanade). Flanking the en of the Esplanade are Niemeyer's two finest building: the **Palácio Itamaratí**, housing the Foreign Ministr which floats in splendid isolation in the midst of reflecting pool; and the **Palácio da Justiça** (Ministr of Justice), whose six curtains of falling water on th exterior echo the natural waterfalls around Brasíli At the eastern end of the esplanade is the **Praça do Três Poderes** (Three Powers Plaza) – a dense fores of political symbols: the **Palácio do Planalto**, th **Supremo Tribunal Federal** (Supreme Court), an the twin towers and offset domes of the **Congress Nacional** – the building whose silhouette is the signa ture of Brasília. On the plaza proper is the sma **Museu Histórico de Brasília** (open daily). Inside a series of panels outlining the history of Brasília an the most memorable sayings of Kubitschek, whos powers of hyperbole must have rivaled his talent f construction.

In front of the Supreme Court is a blindfolded figure of Justice, sculpted by Alfredo Ceschiatti. Facing the Palácio do Planalto are the figures of *The Warriors* by Bruno Giorgi, a tribute to the thousands of workers who built Brasília. A note of whimsy is added to the plaza by Niemeyer's pigeon house, the **Pombal**.

The most recent addition to the plaza is the **Pantheon Tancredo Neves** – a tribute to the founding father of the New Republic, who died in April 1985 before he could be sworn in as president. Inside the darkened interior is Brasília's most extraordinary and disturbing artwork. The mural, by João Camara, depicts the story of an uprising in the 18th century led by Brazil's best-known revolutionary, Tiradentes (Joaquim José da Silva Xavier). Painted in seven black and white panels (rather like Picasso's *Guernica*), it is heavy with masonic symbolism.

The **Catedral Metropolitana da Nossa Senhora Aparecida**, at the western end of the Esplanada dos Ministérios, is a unique concrete building with a spectacular stained-glass domed roof. Three hundred meters (330 yards) away, on the northern side of the Eixo Monument near the Rodoviária, is the pyramid-shaped **Teatro Nacional** (open daily), where art shows and other exhibitions are held.

Minas Gerais: treasure trove of the Portuguese

Nestled in the steep hills north of Rio de Janeiro are some of Brazil's most beautiful colonial-era cities, in the large state of **Minas Gerais**, a mining region. In the 18th century it was the world's principal source of gold and today more than half the country's minerals and nearly all its iron ore come from here.

Belo Horizonte ❹, today's capital city of Minas Gerais, is neatly planned and a good base from which to explore the region. A hundred kilometers (60 miles)

Map on pages 226–7

Congress building, Brasília.

BELOW: the Parliament Building, Brasília.

Watching the world go by, Ouro Preto.

LEFT: colonial church, Minas Gerais.
RIGHT: sculpture by Aleijadinho, Congonhas do Campo.

to the south lies the most prized creation of Brazil's Golden Age, the beautifull preserved city of **Ouro Preto**. Its name comes from the gold encrusted wit black iron oxide that was discovered nearby, early in the 18th century.

The find set off a gold rush, and Ouro Preto soon became the colonial capita of Minas Gerais. The gold lasted more than a century, during which time Our Preto and several nearby cities acquired sumptuous baroque churches and man sions, the only lasting heritage of 1,200 tons of gold extracted during that era Thanks to the Brazilian Government's decision to declare the entire city a nationa monument in 1933, many of its colonial treasures are intact, and it has been mad a World Heritage Site by UNESCO. Cobbled streets wend through hilly quarter lined by well-kept colonial homes. Thirteen baroque churches gild the city o 25,000, many displaying the genius of the sculptor and architect Antônio Francisc Lisboa (1730–1814), better known as *Aleijadinho*, or Little Cripple. Afflicted b a debilitating disease, Aleijadinho sculpted some of Brazil's most beautiful an expressive statuary – with his hammer and chisel strapped to his wrists.

The self-taught artist almost single-handedly shifted the esthetics of th Golden Age from the boxish forms of mannerism to the sensuous curves o baroque. The most striking example is the exterior of the church of **Nossa Sen hora do Rosario dos Prêtos**, built by black slaves (there were insufficier funds to complete the interior). Nearby is the church of **Nossa Senhora d Pilar**, whose interior is a profusion of baroque carved angels and gilded wall At the center of town is the **Praça Tiradentes**, fronted by the imposing **Muse da Inconfidência** (open Tues–Sun). Just off the square is the church of **Sã Francisco de Assis**, an exquisite example of Aleijadinho's artistry and a repos itory of some of his most moving wood and soapstone figures. More of Ale dinho's work can be viewed at the impressive **Nossa Senhora do Carmo** church (open Tues–Sun), also on the plaza, and at the sacred art collection in the nearby **Museu do Oratório** (open Tues–Sun).

Ouro Preto has an important mining school, the sprawling **Escola de Minas**, which incorporates a mineralogy museum (open Tues–Sun), and there is an interesting gem museum in the imposing **Governor's Palace** nearby.

Treasures of stone

The colonial town of **Mariana**, just east of Ouro Preto, is another treasure left by gold barons who expressed gratitude for their good fortune by building extravagant churches. Work by Aleijadinho and Athayde can be found here, as well as a former beating post for slaves marked by a stone monument to Justice.

Some 30 km (20 miles) west of Ouro Preto is **Congonhas do Campo**, the site of Aleijadinho's greatest feat: his hauntingly beautiful soapstone carvings of twelve Old Testament prophets outside the majestic church of **Bom Jesus do Matozinho**, a shrine for pilgrims. There are also 66 expressive carvings in cedarwood of Christ's Passion by Aleijadinho and his students.

Located 100 km (60 miles) to the south, **São João del Rei** is a colonial city of 60,000 with three striking 18th-century churches. There is also beautiful pewterware made at a local factory. The railway station has been turned into a gleaming museum, the **Museu Ferroviário** (open Tues–Sat), a fascinating reminder of old-fashioned rail travel, with locomotives from 1880. Nearby is the silversmith village of **Tiradentes**, named after the man who agitated for independence from Portugal and was hanged in Rio de Janeiro on April 21, 1792, a date recognized as a national holiday. **Sabará**, 22 km (14 miles) east of Belo

Map on pages 226–7

BELOW: the colonial charm of Ouro Preto.

Horizonte, has fine examples of Aleijadinho's work in its church, as well a Oriental influences, brought by Portuguese Jesuits.

The least commercialized of all the colonial towns is the World Heritage Sit of **Diamantina** ❺, 284 km (175 miles) north of Belo Horizonte. Once the cen ter of a diamond boom, Diamantina was the birthplace of President Kubitschek founder of Brasília. The colorful **Nossa Senhora do Rosário** church was bui entirely by slaves, and the woodcarvings of the saints are black. The informa tive **Museu do Diamante** (Diamond Museum; open Tues–Sun) has a bac room in which grisly implements of torture used against slaves are kept.

Salvador and the Northeast

Brazil's Northeast is quite different from its prosperous south. The accent i different, the people are different, the food is more fiery, and the barren *sertã* (scrubland) is more like an African desert than tropical Brazil. For the essenc of the Brazilian mystique, one must go to where it all began: **Bahia**, the stat where Pedro Alvares Cabral established contact between Portuguese and nativ cultures in 1500. **São Salvador da Bahia de Todos os Santos** ❻ is Brazil's fir capital and is still the richest source of the country's cultural identity. Salvadc is where much of the food, religion, dance, and music that characterize Braz originated, where Catholic Portuguese culture blended with the beliefs an esthetics of the slaves who were brought from West Africa.

The 2.6 million inhabitants of Salvador, known as *baianos* (pronounced by ah-nooz) are known throughout Brazil for their laid-back, festive temperamer The city is convulsed by street celebrations most months of the year. *Carnav* is the biggest – it officially begins a day before carnival in the rest of the cou

Baiana girl.

LEFT: canoes on the Recife coast.
RIGHT: Largo do Pelourinho, Salvador.

Map
on pages
226–7

y. Salvador's carnival is entirely participatory – frenzied hordes of dancers
evel behind *trios elétricos* – floats laden with live bands and deafening sound
ystems. It is not for the faint-hearted, as the crowds often get unruly.

Rich heritage

The backdrop for all this revelry is a city with a rich heritage and a beautiful nat-
ral setting. Salvador is built mostly on a high escarpment overlooking a bay;
ne upper level of the city, where almost all the ancient buildings are found, is
nown as **Cidade Alta**. The **Terreiro de Jesus** square is home to three of Sal-
ador's most famous churches, the largest of which is the **Catedral Basílica**.
ising majestically from the adjoining square, **Praça Anchieta**, is one of the
orld's most opulent baroque churches, **São Francisco**. To the north side of
erreiro de Jesus, the **Museu Afro-Brasileiro** (open Mon–Fri) in the old med-
al faculty highlights the strong African influence on Bahian culture.

The **Pelourinho** neighborhood is full of pastel-hued 17th- and 18th-century
olonial buildings, considered by UNESCO the best examples in the New World.
Here you'll find practitioners of *capoeira*, a kind of foot-fighting martial art
riginally brought by slaves from Angola, performed to the rhythm of a tam-
ourine and the throbbing sound of a *berimbau*, whose single steel string
retched across a bowed stick resonates in a hollowed gourd. *Capoeiristas* per-
orm on the street for donations, but they also give shows during the evening at
cookery school and restaurant called SENAC (open Tues–Sat) on Pelourinho's
aza. Visitors will notice numerous women street vendors wearing flowing
hite lace dresses. They are known as *baianas*, and they sell the spicy and
weet specialties of Bahian cuisine.

TIP

Bahian cooking is
considerably more
spicy than elsewhere
in Brazil, and generous
amounts of coconut
oil – *dendê* – are used.
Seafood predominates,
and is often prepared
in succulent stews
called *moquecas*.

BELOW: *baiana* lace
dresses, Salvador.

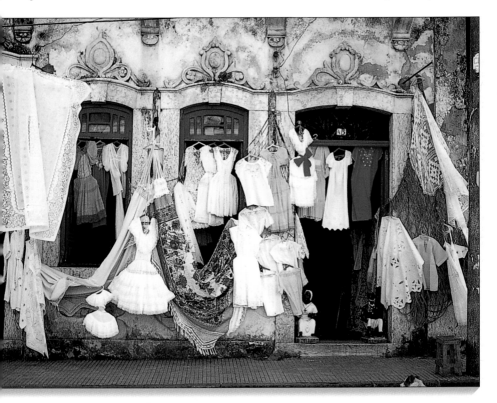

A famous Art Deco elevator called the Elevador Lacerda whisks you dow from near the Praça Municipal to the **Cidade Baixa** (Lower Town), which ha a big handicrafts marketplace called the **Mercado Modelo**. The white, lac decorated garments sold here are typically Bahian and the market is a live microcosm of Bahian life. Left from the market is the church of **Nossa Senho de Conceição de Praia**, which houses the image of Bahia's patron saint and the site of the annual religious procession held on December 8, one of the mo important feast days in Salvador's Catholic calendar. About 10 km (6 miles) the opposite direction stands the famous church of **Nosso Senhor do Bonfi** and another fascinating market, the **Mercado São Joaquim**.

Porto Seguro is the home of the sensual lambada *dance, which is taught by curvaceous women at a host of waterfront bars.*

Cidade Baixa is the departure point for schooners taking tourists around th bay, and for passenger boats to small towns in the vicinity, as well as the islan of **Itaparica**, where Club Med built its first installation in Brazil. Most of th island's 20,000 inhabitants make their living fishing, and the simple restauran serve delicious seafood. Be sure to try the marinated fresh oysters. Boats als leave for a two-hour cruise to **Morro de São Paulo**, a stunning series of islan dotted with trendy villages and pristine beaches. Accomodations are in charr ing and fashionable *pousadas*, the inns of Brazil.

Pristine beaches

Like Rio, Salvador is a city that lives at its beautiful beaches. The most acce sible from downtown is **Barra**, small but extremely popular. Bars near th beach are often jammed, and the fun continues long after sundown. Barra is at th tip of a long scalloped shoreline of beaches, most of them shaded by palms and wi grassy areas. The best are the farthest out from the city, **Itapoán** and **Piatã**. It's be

BELOW: the blood of a slaughtered chicken drips on an initiate's head during a *Macumba* ritual.

RELIGIOUS SPIRIT

Street intersections and meeting halls are places wh you may see *Macumba*, rituals practiced with var tions throughout the country. *Macumba* came with the W African slaves, and its phalanx of deities belongs to t traditions of the Yoruba-speaking peoples. The impositi of Christianity simply resulted in each of the saints taki a corresponding identity with a Yoruba deity.

Because street intersections form a cross, they a thought to be centers of power. Visitors are usually w come to watch *Macumba* rites, although photography forbidden. *Candomblé* is the kind of *Macumba* practic around Salvador, where slaves first disembarked. Dru ming is always an element and its hypnotic rhythms f quently plunge participants into wild gyrating trances. T happens at the sacred meeting places called *terrei* Devotees wear white to honor Oxalá, *Candomblé*'s equi lent to Christ and the highest of the deities.

In southern Brazil, another kind of *Macumba* flouris − *Umbanda*. It is a kind of white magic − good deeds a generosity are asked of the gods. It blends Catholicis *Candomblé*, and "Spiritism", a cult which started in Fra in the mid-19th century. People are believed to be visi by the spirits of deities during *Umbanda* sessions.

hit these beaches on weekends when there are crowds, both for safety and ≀cause there will inevitably be live music performed at local alfresco bars.

Some 80 km (50 miles) north of Salvador is **Praia do Forte**, an 11-km -mile) stretch of white-sand beach, bordered by coconut palms, that is very ₊pular with tourists. Also around 80 km (50 miles) north of Salvador, the ₊osta do Sauipe complex, opened in January 2001 at a cost of US$100 million, luxury complex of resort hotels and a championship golf course.

Ilheus, a coastal city 390 km (240 miles) south of Salvador, is a mixture of ₊odern and ancient architecture. The city is renowned for its lively carnival and ₊e lovely beaches nearby, and is the center for 95 percent of Brazil's cocoa ₊oduction. Further south down the coast is **Porto Seguro**, a tourist hub, where ₊abral and his explorers first set foot in Brazil. Other popular resorts along the ₊ast include Itacaré and Trancoso.

Inland from Salvador begins the enormous scrub region called the *sertão*, ₊quently parched by drought and a tableau of human misery. The *sertanejos* ₊o live there are often forced to leave to avoid starvation.

The heart of Bahia, however, is also where the **Chapada Diamantina** is ₊cated, one of Brazil's most beautiful national parks and a major attraction for ₊kkers. Gateway to the Diamantina Plateau is the colonial town of **Lençóis**, ₊hich dates from 1844 when diamonds were discovered in the region.

Map on pages 226–7

Hammock room only on the deck class of an Amazon steamer.

₊eyond Salvador

₊ahia is the southernmost part of a nine-state region collectively known as the ₊ortheast, home to a third of Brazil's population. The *nordestinos* have, until ₊ry recently, benefited least from Brazil's material progress. Those who live

BELOW: sunset over the River Amazon.

along the coastal regions of Bahia are predominantly of African descent, whi those living inland and to the north are a Portuguese/Amerindian mixture.

The Northeast has wonderful white-sand beaches where you can still fir fishermen using *jangadas*, an ancient precursor to the windsurf. The city **Maceió** has some of the most spectacular beaches. North of Maceió is **Reci** , one of the principal cities of the Northeast, with 1.4 million inhabitant Recife's beaches are protected by coral reefs, and the most popular is in th well-to-do **Boa Viagem** sector of the city. Located just to the north is **Olind** a beautifully conserved colonial gem designated a World Cultural Monument b UNESCO, while to the south is the popular resort town of Porto de Galinhas.

Further up the coastline is **João Pessoa**, the Americas' easternmost city. It very pleasant and brightly painted, with a wealth of baroque churches. Hug sand dunes distinguish the beaches of **Natal** ❽, capital of the state of R Grande do Norte. Outside the city are other oceanside enclaves, such as deligh ful **Touros** (95 km/60 miles to the north), and to the south, **Praia da Pipp**

Fortaleza ❾, the capital of Ceará, once drab and utilitarian, has benefite from the huge amount of capital that has flowed into the region in recent year using some of it to rebuild the seafront area, which now rivals Recife's B Viagem for elegance and liveliness. The city is a very popular destination f international tourists. Other popular destinations in the state of Ceará are Can Quebrada to the south, and Jericoacoara to the north, of Fortaleza.

The river ports: Manaus to Belém

The last thing you might expect in the middle of the Amazon jungle, 1,600 k (1,000 miles) from the sea, is a thriving port city. But **Manaus** ❿ was cut fro

he wilderness in the 19th century: where mad conquistadors once searched in
vain for gold, Brazilians found a modern El Dorado of rubber. Today, this
strange outpost is enjoying a new boom as a tourist destination and through
high-tech industries as one of the duty-free capitals of South America. Arriving
in Manaus by boat is dramatic, not because of the city, which is spread out on
low bluffs – but because it is the meeting place of two Amazon tributaries at an
8-km (5-mile) wide junction. The dark River Negro, which looks like fizzy
cola when riverboats churn it up, hits the yellowish River Solimoes, and the two
vast currents run side by side without mingling their differently colored waters.

The chaotic bustle of modern Manaus is a dim reflection of its past glory. In
1888 the pneumatic tire was invented, and Amazon rubber suddenly became
very valuable. For a brief, dazzling period, Manaus became the richest city in
the world. Pioneers flooded into the jungle, creating the boom town of fast
fortunes and grand gestures portrayed in Werner Herzog's film *Fitzcarraldo*.

Thousands of rubber tappers collected latex from isolated trees found deep in
the jungle, working as virtual slaves along the sinuous waterways of the Amazon, and the newly rich rubber barons, quaffing champagne and lighting their
cigars with US$100 bills, earned Manaus a name for extravagance and deca-
dence. When the rubber boom collapsed, Manaus fell into a torpor that was
only broken in 1967, when it became a duty-free zone.

The most famous and bizarre monument to the boom days is the grand opera
house, the **Teatro Amazonas** (open for tours Mon–Sat). Materials for this temple of art in the jungle were wholly imported from Europe: white marble from
Italy, iron pillars from England, and polished wood from France. The original
house curtain remains, painted with Grecian nymphs lolling in the Amazon

Map
on pages
226–7

*Toucan in the
Amazon.*

BELOW: sunset over
Manaus dockside.

SLOWLY DOWN THE AMAZON

Nothing quite matches the romance of taking a slow
boat down the world's greatest river. This vast water-
way is still plied by hundreds of vessels: from ocean-going
cargo ships to passenger boats. Your best bet is to take a
half-day trip from Manaus or Belém. Longer voyages are
not really geared for tourists and are just a means of
getting from A to B. Smaller, wooden vessels known as
gaiolas, or "birdcages", after the crowded mid-deck levels
where passengers pile over one another in hammocks, still
work the smaller tributaries from Manaus to Benjamin
Constant, on the border of Colombia, then onward into
Iquitos in Peru, and back. Finding one of these boats is
largely a matter of patience and luck. The smaller companies have no fixed schedules, and the only way to arrange
a booking is to wander around the port, talk to people, and
check out the boats for yourself. You'll no doubt be
approached by skippers or agents offering you space on
their boats. These can be relatively comfortable or crowded, noisy, and somewhat unhygienic. Food is basic, and
bottled water should be taken. Stops are made at jungle
villages, where the whole population turns out to watch
the boat unload beer, pass out a few letters, and take on a
cargo of bananas.

Anaconda crossing!

River. In its heyday, the opera house attracted such greats as the Italian tenor Caruso and today, fully restored, it can still pull in international names.

The old **port area** of Manaus is thriving. Wooden riverboats dump exotic cargoes while overhead circle black urubu birds. Ramshackle houses have been thrown up around the port on precarious stilts. A more imposing construction is the stone **Alfândega** (Customs House), dating from 1906.

For a glimpse of the lost Amerindian cultures of the area, head for the **Museu do Homem do Norte** (open Mon–Fri), on Avenida Sete de Setembro 1385, which gives a good idea of traditional lifestyles. There is even a "beach" near the **Hotel Tropical**, where braver swimmers can prove that the river is free of piranhas and electric eels which can so spoil a holiday.

The majority of visitors to Manaus use the city as a gateway to the Amazon proper. A good selection of lodges are located in the jungle that surrounds Manaus, and the transfer out to a lodge is an attraction in its own right. Most lodge programs cover two or three nights out at the lodge and include a number of activities that involve the region's diverse flora and fauna.

Beyond Manaus

Further down the Amazon towards the sea is the port of **Santarém ⓫**, at the confluence with the Tapajós River. Once a colonial fortress, Santarém today is a kind of Dodge City for half a million jungle gold prospectors, or *garimpeiros*. On the south side of the mouth of the Amazon stands proud, stately **Belém ⓬**, 145 km (90 miles) from open ocean. A city of more than a million inhabitants, Belém retains some of the graceful airs of its rubber-boom heyday. Its old town has colonial-era homes and churches and there's a fort nearby, now occupied by the Círculo Militar restaurant.

Belém's striking **Catedral de Nossa Senhora da Graça**, built in 1617, contains artworks in Carrara marble and paintings by the Italian de Angelis. Not far away is the dockside municipal market **Ver-o-Peso** (Check out the Weight), where fishermen bring their catches. Another landmark is the **Emilio Goeldi Museum**, with exhibits of native crafts from nearby **Marajó Island**. An interesting addition to the town is the Estação das Docas – imaginatively restored warehouses with tourist facilities and restaurants.

Rondônia: Brazil's Wild West

If you thought the days of the Wild West were over, consider **Rondônia**. At the beginning of the 1970s this Brazilian state was tree-tangled wilderness on the southern flank of the Amazon jungle, bordering Bolivia. It was home to just a few thousand hardy rubber tappers. Today, settlers have pushed their way pell-mell into almost every corner of Rondônia, hacking down the jungle and frequently enforcing their land claims with the squeeze of a trigger. In the 1980s nearly one-quarter of the Rondônian rainforest was destroyed, mostly by burning, to clear land for planting and cattle pastures. In the dry season, from May to October, a blanket of smoke hangs over the state as forests are incinerated. With the extension of roadway BR 364 from São Paulo to the capital of Rondônia, he riverport of **Porto Velho** ⓭, express buses carry peasant migrants directly to he new frontier. A ride up the highway in one of the local buses provides a evealing view both of frontier life and rainforest devastation.

Rubber tapping has all but been abandoned in Rondônia as the trees have disppeared, despite laws enacted for their protection. Some 300,000 Brazilians still urvive collecting the fruits of the forest – wild rubber, Brazil nuts, and resin. They now live mostly in the state of Acre, west of Rondônia on the borders of Bolivia and Peru. Key to their survival are their isolation and international pres-ures to protect their benign co-existence with the rainforest. Some protected reas called "extractive reserves" have been established for these jungle har-vesters. But as Brazil's population continues to grow faster than the new jobs, he pressures to clear the forest that have transformed Rondônia are likely to keep moving westward.

The Pantanal: bird paradise

An enormous wetland called the **Pantanal** is perhaps the most exquisite gallery of all for observing Brazilian fauna. Comprising 210,000 sq. km (81,000 sq. miles) of seasonally flooded swampland east of the Paraguay River on Brazil's western border with Bolivia, the Pantanal is home to more than 650 species of birds, 400 kinds of fish, and an abundance of reptiles and animals as well as 3,500 species of plants. There are white ibises, egrets, blue herons, green para-keets, pheasants, and the 2-meter (7-ft) tall white jabirú or tuiuiú stork.

During the rainy months (October to April) when waters are high in the north, the birds feed on fish in the southern sector. From May until September, they move to the shallower waters in the north. The best time to visit is in the win-

Ilha de Maracá, near Boa Vista.

LEFT: snappy sunbathers.
RIGHT: a red-necked Tuiuiú.

Unfortunate piranhas, Pantanal.

ter months of June, July, and August; January and February are infernally ho
and humid. When the waters recede from the northern Pantanal, wide sand
riverbanks are exposed and large alligators, called jacarés, like to bask in the su
on the sand. There are also ocelots, pumas, wild boar, jaguars, red lake dee
tapirs, and a large furry rodent, the capivara.

Exploring the swamps

Access to the Pantanal's edge is quite easy, but getting around inside is anothe
matter. **Cuiabá** ⓮, capital of Mato Grosso, is an attractive city that once enjoye
a gold boom, though it gets intensely hot here. Some 70 km (45 miles) north
east of Cuiabá there are cool waterfalls at **Chapada de Guimarães**, the sourc
of much of the water that enters the northern part of the wetlands. Just south o
Cuiabá is **Santo Antônio de Leverger**, on the edge of the marshland. From
Cuiabá you can transfer to the lodges and cattle ranches, or *fazendas*, within th
Pantanal. You can obtain ground transport, boats, flights, even hot-air balloo
rides at these lodges, for observing the wildlife. Fishing is permitted – piranha
are prized for their supposed aphrodisiacal powers – but hunting emphaticall
is not. The main attraction is **Baia Chacorore**, a huge shallow water basi
flocked with roseate spoonbills. Its banks literally crawl with alligators.

You can drive into the Pantanal along the partially completed **Trans
Pantaneira Highway**, which starts just outside the small town of **Poconé**, 10
km (63 miles) from Cuiabá. Vehicles can be hired here. The road is often roug
and sometimes floods, but it crosses many rivers (there are 126 bridges) an
provides a close-up view of wildlife. The road ends 145 km (90 miles) into th
Pantanal at Porto Jofre. Accommodations are available en route and at the por

BELOW: wildlife-
watching at the
Caiman Ecological
Refuge, Pantanal.

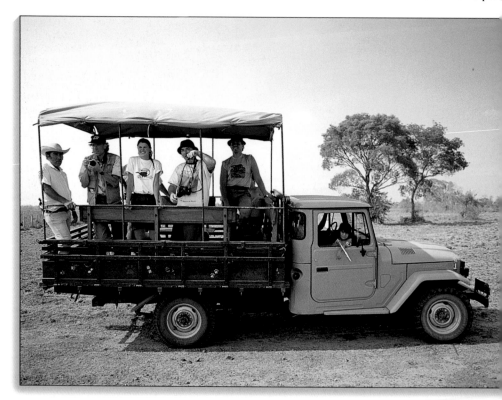

Although the Pantanal reaches up to the city limits of **Corumbá** ⑮, a border town on the southwest flank, local tours reveal little – much of the wildlife has fled to more remote areas. The best way to see the Pantanal is to arrange passage on cattle boats that penetrate more deeply into the area, or organize a trip to one of the lodges.

Map on pages 226–7

Iguaçu Falls and the Itaipú Dam

The famous falls, which link the Brazil, Paraguay, and Argentine borders, are described fully in the Argentina chapter *(see page 336)*. The closest Brazilian city to the falls is **Foz do Iguaçu** ⑯, near the junction of the Paraná and Iguaçu rivers. This frontier town has grown phenomenally in the past decades, due to the construction of the world's largest hydroelectric dam, the **Itaipú** (Guaraní for "Singing Rock"). It is well worth visiting, and is only possible on a guided tour. Built jointly by Brazil and Paraguay, it is powered by the waters of the Paraná River, which divides the two countries.

Armadillo, caught for the cameras only.

The south

The falls at Foz are the main attraction in the Brazilian south, but far from the only one. Others include the beach resorts close to Florianópolis; the mountain towns of Gramado and Canela close to Porto Alegre; the German-influenced towns in the interior of Santa Catarina that include Blumenau, and its Oktoberfest; and the scenic train ride between the port of Paranaguá and the model city of Curitiba. The southern coast close to Florianópolis attracts visitors interested in whale watching. The season runs from June through November and involves the southern right whales. ❏

BELOW: twilight flight, Pantanal.

THE RICHES OF
THE AMAZON RIVER

*The world's greatest river and largest rainforest,
in the heart of Brazil, is estimated to contain
one-tenth of the plant and insect species on earth*

The Amazon River is one
of the greatest symbols of
Brazil. It rises in the
snows of the Peruvian
Andes just a short distance
from the Pacific Ocean. It
then travels across the
heart of South America –
a distance of 6,570 km
(4,080 miles) – before it
flows out into the Atlantic
Ocean at the equator. It has about 15,000 tributaries, some of which, like the Araguaia and the
Madeira, are mighty rivers in themselves. Just
past Manaus, one of the most spectacular river
sights is the meeting of the "black waters" of the
Negro River with the "white waters" of the
Solimoes River, two other Amazon tributaries.
The Amazon has a heavier flow than any other
river, depositing in the ocean each year about
one-fifth of the world's fresh water.

At its mouth the Amazon is 300 km (185 miles)
wide, a labyrinth of channels and islands, one of
which has a greater landmass than Switzerland.
The water flows with such force that it is still
fresh 180 km (110 miles) out into the ocean.

RAINFOREST AND AMERINDIANS
The Amazon's network of dark, dense jungles has
often been referred to as The Great Green Hell. In
the west of the Amazon basin, it is still possible to
fly for several hours and see nothing below but a
carpet of tropical forest, broken only by rivers
snaking their way through the trees. The Amazon
has remained virtually unchanged for the past 100
million years, for it did not pass through the same
ice ages that altered other parts of the
world's landscapes. Some areas
are still inhabited by
indigenous groups who
have survived through
the centuries and have
never had contact
with the world outside
their own jungle.

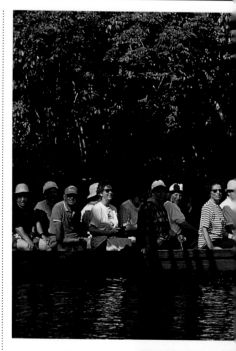

△ **AMAZON CRUISES**
A river trip along the
legendary Amazon, taking in
the sights, sounds, and
smells of the verdant jungle,
is one of the highlights for
many visitors to Brazil.

▷ **BLACK SPIDER MONKEY**
This delightful animal uses
its tail to swing from branch
to branch in the forest.

◁ **POISON ARROW FROG**
The poison from this
brightly colored frog
used to be extracted
by the Amerindians to use on
the tip of arrows.

△ **RIO MADEIRA**
Though just a tributary of
the Amazon, the Madeira
River itself flows over a
distance of more than 1,6■
km (1,000 miles).

DEFORESTATION IN THE AMAZON

Over the past 15 years, 245,000 sq. km (95,000 sq.miles) of the forest, about 5 percent of the Brazilian Amazon, have been destroyed. The rate of growth still exceeds the rate of destruction but the gap is falling, despite reforestation programs. In the 1960s and 1970s, in the east of the basin, the government built a vast network of roads, and cattle companies moved in, burning the forest to sow pasture. But ranching was not successful, for the soil, once denuded of the protective forest cover, quickly became barren.

Foreign timber companies demand the Amazon's hardwoods, now that the rest of the world's hardwood forests have been destroyed; and big grain farmers, cultivating genetically engineered soybeans, have moved here from the south of Brazil.

◁ **URUCU BERRIES**
Amazonian Amerindians treasure the Urucu tree. Its berries contain a red-colored dye that they use to paint their bodies and faces.

UNGLE LODGING
he eco-friendly Ariau
el guests can hear the
itching sounds of the
ical forest at night.

▽ **VICTORIA REGINA**
The indigenous water lily has enormous, circular leaves that can be up to 2 meters (6 ft) across.

△ **RUBBER TAPPING**
Thousands of families, living deep in the rainforest, still tap rubber trees for the latex.

▷ **TOUCAN**
This striking bird, a recognizable image of the Amazon forest, uses its huge yellow bill to crush the seeds it feeds on.

THE SOUTHERN CONE

Often considered the most European part of South America, this region contains some of its most cosmopolitan cities and starkly stunning scenery

El cono sur – the "southern cone" of Paraguay, Argentina, Uruguay, and Chile – makes up a geological and cultural unit quite apart from the rest of South America. Sparsely populated in pre-Columbian days by nomadic tribes, these countries today form the most ethnically and climatically European part of the continent.

European settlement came late to the south, with many areas unexplored until the late 19th century. The newcomers were from many places besides Spain, Portugal, and Italy. Small colonies remain here of Germans, Boers, Britons, and Swiss, all descendants of these pioneers. The attraction was the prospect of sudden wealth: several decades ago these countries were relatively affluent, riding on booms of agriculture and minerals.

Isolated Paraguay *(see page 265)* has no access to the sea, but its capital, Asunción, has become a bustling duty-free center – although horse-drawn carts still clatter through its streets, beneath statues of long forgotten generals. Most of the country is made up of the vast, sparsely populated Chaco lands *(see page 274)*.

Squeezed between the Pacific Ocean and the Andes mountains, ultra-narrow Chile *(see page 279)* covers a huge range of latitudes. Heading south from the northern Atacama Desert – one of the driest in the world – you pass through the moderate climate of the capital, Santiago *(see page 282)*, with its surrounding vineyards *(see page 284)*, to the snow-covered forests of the Lake District *(see page 291)*. Beyond that are the glaciers, peaks, and windswept fishing villages of Chilean Patagonia *(see page 295)*.

The republic of Uruguay *(see page 311)*, once dubbed "the Switzerland of South America" for its progressive political tradition, had enough money from beef to build a powerful social welfare state. Today, the country seems frozen in the 1950s. The capital, Montevideo *(see page 313)*, is a quaint city where hand-cranked automobiles still groan through the streets, while the country's beautiful beaches are mostly used by the wealthy from elsewhere in the world.

The second-largest country on the subcontinent, Argentina *(see page 321)* was at the beginning of the 20th century its richest by far. Things haven't gone quite as expected since then, and the elegant capital Buenos Aires *(see page 325)* is crowded with the crumbling Parisian relics of the boom days. Argentina sprawls over every climatic zone, with grassy northern plains where gauchos still ride *(see page 338)*, the subtropical province of Misiones *(see page 336)*, lush forests around Bariloche *(see page 339)*, the windswept, sheep-strewn plains of Patagonia *(see page 341)*, and at the southern tip of the continent, the chilly, mountainous island of Tierra del Fuego *(see page 344)*. ❏

PRECEDING PAGES: huge chunks of ice broken from the glacier melt in the Canal de los Tempanos (Channel of the Icebergs) at Glacier National Park, Argentina.
LEFT: traditional chaps: gauchos of northwest Argentina.

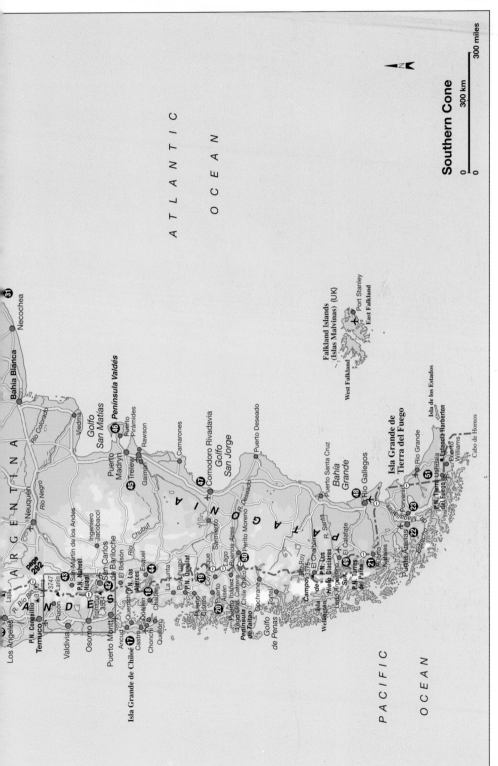

Southern Cone

0   300 km

0   300 miles

ARGENTINA

Los Angeles
Laja
R. Bío Bío
Lima
▲3747
Pucón
Lanín
P.N. Conguillío
Temuco
Valdivia
Osorno
Puerto Montt
Ancud
Castro
Chonchi
Queilen
Isla Grande de Chiloé
Quellón
Chaitén
Coyhaique
La Junta
Puerto Puyuhuapi
Puerto Cisnes
Puerto Aisén
Cochrane
Tortel
Caleta Tortel
Península de Taitao
Golfo de Penas
Isla Wellington
Puerto Natales

R. Río Bío Bío
3100
Neuquén
Río Negro
San Martín de los Andes
Ingeniero Jacobacci
Río Negro
El Bolsón
Esquel
R. Chubut
Sarmiento
R. Deseado
Perito Moreno
Buenos Aires
Lago Buenos Aires
R. Santa Cruz
El Chaltén
El Calafate
Campo de Hielo Sur
P.N. Los Glaciares
Lago Argentino
Río Gallegos
Bahía Grande

Bahía Blanca
Necochea
Río Colorado
Viedma
Golfo San Matías
Península Valdés
Puerto Madryn
Puerto Pirámides
Trelew
Gaiman
Rawson
Camarones
Comodoro Rivadavia
Golfo San Jorge
Puerto Deseado
Puerto Santa Cruz

PATAGONIA

A N D E S

P.N. Nahuel Huapi
San Carlos de Bariloche
P.N. Los Alerces
Querdín
Coyaiq
Chaitén
P.N. Puyehue

ATLANTIC OCEAN

PACIFIC OCEAN

Falkland Islands (Islas Malvinas) (UK)
West Falkland
East Falkland
Port Stanley

Isla Grande de Tierra del Fuego
Río Grande
Punta Arenas
Porvenir
Ushuaia
P.N. Tierra del Fuego
Isla de los Estados
Puerto Williams
Estancia Harberton
Cabo de Hornos
Magallanes
P.N. Torres del Paine

PARAGUAY

One of the continent's most intriguing nations, this is a land of Utopias and experimental communities, where the language of the original inhabitants shares pre-eminence with that of their colonists

Map on pages 260–1

Surrounded by Bolivia, Brazil, and Argentina, the small subtropical nation of Paraguay lies at the heart of South America. The River Paraguay divides the country into two distinct halves: the lush, fertile east, where most of the population lives, and the barren Chaco tablelands to the west, home to a few scattered settlements, Mennonite farmers, and nomadic Amerindians. The River Paraguay eventually feeds into the River Plate, linking the country historically and geographically to the other River Plate nations of Uruguay and Argentina.

"An island surrounded by land" is how exiled Paraguayan novelist Augusto Roa Bastos once described his landlocked native country. The phrase refers not only to Paraguay's physical remoteness but to a kind of psychic solitude brought about by wars, dictatorships, and a profound sense of ethnic unity. A visitor to the capital, Asunción, can't help noticing the profusion of monuments commemorating military rulers, crushing defeats, and Pyrrhic victories. Yet one is also struck by the tropical prettiness of the colonial city, and by the soft-spoken, gentle manners of Paraguayans, reminders that the Spaniards who first settled this region dreamed not of plunder but of founding an earthly paradise.

In a country where almost everyone is of part Guaraní descent, schoolbooks devote considerable space to pre-Columbian Paraguay. The Guaraní were the original inhabitants of what is now Asunción. Mainly farmers, they were also accomplished warriors who bore suffering stoically. Early Spanish chroniclers reported with horror that the Guaraní were cannibals, although this custom was apparently limited to the ritual eating of prisoners of war. Their language, in the words of one Spanish priest, was "one of the most copious and elegant on the globe", and it was used as *lingua franca* throughout the region.

Arrival of the Spanish

Asunción was founded on August 15, 1537, by Domingo de Irala, a man of letters who came seeking refuge from the miseries of the settlement at Buenos Aires and the rigors of the conquest. The Guaraní, who were also anxious for Inca gold, were eager to form an alliance with the Spaniards and gave them their daughters as tokens of good faith. The discovery that the Incas had already been conquered and plundered by Pizarro, and the lush life in Asunción, far from the sea and the watchful eye of the Spanish crown, induced Irala and his men to stay. The colonial farms were organized in a feudal manner, although intermarriage evened out the social hierarchy.

Fulgencio Yegros declared Paraguay's independence on May 14, 1811, and ruled along with a civilian lawyer named Doctor José Gaspar Rodríguez de Francia. Soon after independence Francia seized

PRECEDING PAGES: the Itaipú Dam. **LEFT:** guards at the Panteón de los Héroes, Asunción. **BELOW:** young Paraguayans.

Steam train waiting to depart from Asunción station.

BELOW: 19th-century etching of General Urquiza's Palace, San José.

power, and Congress named him supreme dictator for life in 1816. To protect Paraguay from the danger of annexation by Argentina or Brazil, Dr Francia closed the borders: no one was allowed in or out during his 24-year reign.

"El Supremo", as Francia was called, ruled by absolute decree. A learned man, initially a frugal and honest ruler, he grew deranged by power and isolation. At one point he ordered all the dogs in the country killed; he also decreed that none of his subjects could look at him in the street. At his death in 1840, no Paraguayan priest was willing to say a funeral Mass, and a priest was finally imported from Argentina. Paraguay was plunged into political chaos until the next dictator, Carlos Antonio López, was proclaimed in 1844.

López was an enlightened despot who re-opened the country to progress and sent students to Europe to study. But his son and designated successor, Francisco Solano López, was a weak and spoilt young man. Feeling that Paraguay's neighbors did not take his country seriously, he intervened in Uruguay's civil war, and quickly found himself at war with Brazil and Argentina as well. The ensuing War of the Triple Alliance was disastrous for Paraguay. The country was further ravaged by cholera, and López, at this point seriously unhinged, ordered the execution of hundreds of people, including his two brothers and scores of officers. Abetted by his Irish mistress, Elisa Lynch, he also executed his childhood sweetheart and other society ladies who had snubbed Madame Lynch. On March 1 1870, he was shot by one of his own generals after refusing to surrender. "I die with Paraguay," he exclaimed, which was almost literally true. After the war more than half the population of 525,000 were dead; of the survivors, only 29,000 were adult males. Paraguay was rebuilt mostly by women, who resigned themselves to a polygamous society as the Catholic Church looked the other way

Between the fall of Solano López and Paraguay's bloody Chaco War with Bolivia, the country changed presidents 32 times and endured two assassinations of presidents, six coups d'état, two revolutions and eight attempted revolutions. Paraguay won the Chaco War of 1932–1935, fought over a piece of barren land that was believed to contain oil and other mineral deposits *(see page 38)*, but once again the male population was devastated. A succession of dictators followed, until in 1954 the son of a German brewmeister, Alfredo Stroessner, seized power and ruled with an iron fist for nearly 35 years.

Map on pages 260–1

Winds of change

Stroessner played off one political faction against another while providing a sanctuary for fleeing Nazis and exiling, imprisoning, torturing, and killing rivals and opponents. In the all-pervading climate of corruption, Paraguay became notorious as a haven for smuggling, much of it in narcotics. Human rights activists and some of the country's artists and writers, notably the novelist and poet Augusto Roa Bastos and the artist Carlos Colombino, provided a moral center for resistance. Stroessner's regime brought some notable innovations, but in 35 years these developments may well have occurred without him. In the 1970s, the construction of a Brazilian-Paraguayan hydroelectric dam at Itaipú in eastern Paraguay stimulated land investment, expanded financial services, and provided thousands of jobs. The giant Paraguayan-Argentine hydroelectric project at Yacyreta, proposed in 1973, began operating in 1997.

On February 3, 1989, Stroessner was overthrown by General Andrés Rodríguez, his right-hand man and father of his daughter-in-law. Rodríguez promised a free press and a gradual return to democracy after the coup and his Colorado Party was elected into office in 1991. Gleeful Paraguayans took down the photographs of Stroessner, exiled to Brazil, that graced every shop window, changed the names of streets and towns, and decapitated statues of the former president. Since then Paraguay has been experiencing a process of democratic transition, marked by a new constitution, political and press freedoms, and regular elections. Paraguay has also joined the Mercosur common market, a development that upsets some of the more extreme nationalists but which has opened the country to foreign investors.

Offsetting these achievements are continuing wide disparities in wealth and an absence of land reform, not to speak of a pervasive military presence in national politics that surfaced in May 1996 in an attempted coup by the popular General Lino Oviedo. Despite these blemishes, democracy in Paraguay seems to be here to stay. Luís González Macchi was elected in 1999, representing the first coalition government in decades, while the ruling Colorado Party won the presidency again in April 2003, with Nicanor Duarte Frutos extending their run to over half a century.

The atmosphere of rather seedy militarism of the Stroessner years is brilliantly captured in Graham Greene's novel Travels With My Aunt.

BELOW: musicians perform with the traditional Guaraní harp.

Asunción: elegance and neon lights

Today, **Asunción ❶** matches the dynamism of most South American cities while retaining a sleepy elegance, with handsome colonial mansions rubbing shoulders with luxury boutiques, duty-free shops, and

A Bilingual Land

Spanish explorers in Paraguay, unlike other colonies, did not clash with the local population but blended to form a homogeneous, bilingual society. This was possible mainly because the local Guaraní had nothing the Spanish conquistadors wanted to steal. What the Guaraní did have to offer was a peaceful life in a fertile country.

It is difficult to say how much the notorious Guaraní "harems" kept by the Spaniards were fact and how much exaggeration for the benefit of their miserable compatriots in Buenos Aires, but it was true that a great deal of social mobility was achieved by intermarriage, and that the mestizo offspring were not considered marginal citizens.

Sociologists also cite the relatively high position of women in Guaraní society as a factor in the continuing status of the mother tongue. But perhaps the most decisive element in Paraguayan bilingualism was the missionary work of the Jesuits. Although the

Jesuits imposed Spanish on the Amerindians, they were impressed by the complexity and musicality of Guaraní, and produced catechisms and hymns in the native language. Ironically, as a result, the Guaraní neglected much of their original music. Nevertheless, Guaraní music still has a distinctive sound.

In 1624, the Jesuit priest Antonio Ruiz de Montoya created the first Guaraní dictionary and grammar, giving the language a written form and thus a better chance of survival.

During the dictatorship of Doctor Francia (1814–40), marriage between Paraguayans of pure Spanish descent was forbidden. This attempt to dilute the country's ruling class increased contact between the two cultures and their languages. Guaraní was considered a sort of homely argot rather than the speech of educated people, but its use became widespread during the War of the Triple Alliance, as a symbol of national pride and unity. On the battlefields of the Chaco War (1932–35) Spanish was banned and Guaraní was spoken, as a secret language. As a result, many older Paraguayans with little or no indigenous heritage speak Guaraní more fluently than Spanish.

In urban areas today, more than 70 percent of the population is completely bilingual; less than 12 percent speak only Spanish. In rural areas, the use of Guaraní still supersedes that of Spanish; 60 percent of the population speak only Guaraní. Before the 1970s it was rare for teachers to use Guaraní in the classroom, but changing ideas about bilingual education have made the new generation not only fluent but literate in Guaraní.

Novels and poetry are published in Guaraní translations; there are also theater productions, and television and radio shows in the language. The influence of Guaraní on the language of the conquistadors is notable even to those who don't understand Guaraní: the musical tones, the penchant for modesty and understatement – none of which are characteristics of Spanish.

But despite ever-present Guaraní melodies, and the 1981 Law of Native Communities guaranteeing Amerindians' rights over their lands and cultures, the social status of full-blooded Guaraní remains inferior. ❑

LEFT: a Guaraní woman sells handicrafts outside the Guaraní Hotel in Asunción.

Map on pages 260–1

eon lights. The **Plaza de los Héroes** is bright with butterflies and birds of par-dise. Many passers-by seem to have come directly from central casting: fruit endors with baskets on their heads, furtive black-market money-changers, the luster of helmeted military police investigating a broken water pipe.

Gone are the bright yellow electric streetcars that Stroessner revived after ne oil crisis of the 1970s. Gone too is the neon sign that flashed STROESSNER: EACE, WORK, AND WELL-BEING over the square, but its focal point is still the rnate **Pantéon Nacional de los Héroes**, which was built as a copy of Les nvalides in Paris. Inside are the tombs of the two López presidents, of two nknown soldiers, and a small urn containing what remains of the dictator Fran-ia. It's said that his bones were dug up and flung into the river by an angry mob.

But no matter how Paraguayans feel about their military governments, this is country that reveres soldiers; it's not at all unusual for passers-by to stop at this hrine and make the sign of the cross before the heroes' crypts. Diagonally cross from the pantheon are shop windows that display Chaco War memora-ilia. West of the Plaza de los Héroes, on Presidente Franco, is the **Casa de la ndependencia**, where independence was declared in 1811 and which nowadays ouses a museum with relics from the revolution (open daily).

he historic old town

he oldest part of the city can be reached by following Calle Chile down ward the River Paraguay. On a small bluff is the pastel **Palacio de Gobierno**. was built in the style of the Louvre by Francisco Solano López, who imported uch of the building's beautiful interiors and furniture from Paris. He did not ave much time to enjoy the palace since its construction was interrupted by the

The Palacio de Gobierno was designed by a British architect, Alonso Taylor. Having fallen out with his patron, Taylor was tortured in the palace base-ment but escaped with his life, unlike numerous other victims of "El Mariscal" López.

BELOW: stormy sky over Asunción.

War of the Triple Alliance. Further along El Paraguayo Independiente are the tree lined **Plaza Constitución**, the **Congressional Palace**, and the **Cathedral**, which has an excellent museum of religious objects. Opposite the Palacio is the 18th century **Manzana de la Rivera**, or Casa Viola. Once the headquarters for Stroessner's élite forces, it is now an innovative cultural center incorporating a museum of the history of the city, an art gallery, library, and bar. The Spanish Government paid for its renovation to mark the 500th anniversary of the "discovery" of America. A short distance further on are the **Aduana** (Customs House), the port buildings and the barracks, naval headquarters and old fortifications that provide eloquent testimony to the one-time status of Asunción as a frontier city with only the river separating its inhabitants from the wild lands of the Chaco. From a pier by the palace a tiny ferry takes passengers across to the island of **Chaco-i**.

Parks and plazas

East of the Plaza de los Héroes is another large and pleasant square, the **Plaza Uruguaya**, which was once the site of a famous convent and was renamed in tribute to the Uruguayan Government when they returned Paraguayan flags captured in the War of the Triple Alliance. There are some interesting bookshops in pavilions in the plaza, which also has stalls selling leather work, paintings, and other crafts. Handicrafts made by the indigenous Macá people in their settlements on the outskirts of the city can be bought here.

A short distance away is the **Estación San Francisco**, a relic of the López years which was designed by Alonso Taylor. Restored courtesy of the Spanish Government, the building is a Victorian gem, built largely of wood, but with cast- iron supports and a tower that was once the home of the station master. The

BELOW: Guaraní woman selling *chipas*, small cakes made from maize, in an Asunción market.

station used to be the terminus for the British-run track to Encarnación in southern Paraguay that ultimately linked to Buenos Aires. Nowadays occasional trains run to nearby Areguá on Lake Ypacaraí, pulled by wood-burning locomotives.

The Itaipú hydroelectric dam has given Paraguay the cheapest electricity in South America. World Bank loans for the project also enriched some Paraguayans beyond their wildest dreams. Some of their splendid houses can be seen if you take a trip along Avenida España. There are also some beautiful old colonial houses with wide verandahs and gardens of bottle brush and banana trees on this road, as well as the American Embassy, the library, and Stroessner's former home, now a museum.

Parque Carlos Antonio López, on the Avenida of the same name, provides a good view of the city from the Antonio López and Río Gallegos intersection. The **Jardín Botánico**, 7 km (4 miles) outside Asunción, which has its own zoo, is well worth a visit, as are the nearby **Museo de Historia Natural** and the **Museo Indigenista**, both former residences of the two López presidents.

A reservation of the Macá people, who were brought here from their home in the Chaco as a tourist attraction, is located across the river. They live in rather dismal conditions. Ironically, the best handicrafts are to be found in the middle-class suburb of **San Lorenzo** along the eastern highway, where the shop of the **Museo Boggiani** offers authentic and very beautiful artifacts made by the indigenous people of the Chaco.

Traveling east

The Mariscal Estigarribia Highway crosses Paraguay to the Brazilian border town of Ciudad del Este, formerly Ciudad Presidente Stroessner. By express bus the trip takes about four hours, but there are interesting stops along the first half of the journey. About 20 km (14 miles) east of Asunción is **Capiatá**, which was first settled by the Jesuits in 1640. It has an interesting church, which contains a 17th-century sculpture made by the Guaraní under Jesuit instruction. Some 10 km (6 miles) east is **Itagua**, famous for its production of *ñandutí*, or spiderweb lace, which is woven by hand into handkerchiefs, tablecloths, and hammocks and displayed by the weavers in stalls along Route 2. There is a museum and an annual festival in July.

The resort town of **San Bernardino**, 55 km (35 miles) from Asunción on Lake Ypacaraí, is a favorite retreat of prosperous Paraguayans and a center for water sports. The lake, immortalized in a hauntingly beautiful Guaraní song, measures 5 by 24 km (3 by 15 miles) and is an idyllic spot, surrounded by tropical vegetation. The resort town of **Areguá**, on the southern shore of the lake and terminus for the short steam train journey from Asunción, has many shops and stalls selling earthernware. **Caacupé ❷**, 24 km (15 miles) down the road from San Bernardino, is another popular resort and religious shrine. On December 8, pilgrims come to this town from all over Paraguay carrying heavy stones on their heads as penance. Nearby are the villages of **Tobatí**, which has pottery and woodcarvings, and **Piribebuy**, which has a fine church and an interesting museum. There are some lovely small resorts in the hilly, verdant countryside between Piribebuy and Paraguari near **Chololó**, where bathing is possible in refreshing streams.

Ciudad del Este ❸, on the Brazilian border, has been called South America's biggest late-night shopping center. It's a bustling, rather unattractive city with a makeshift boomtown air. Brazilians arrive by the busload to buy electronics, watches, and other imported goods in the huge air-conditioned malls. The city is also a magnet for con artists, who hawk everything from imitation perfume to "musical" condoms. More impressive is the nearby **Itaipú Dam**, one of the world's largest hydroelectric projects. Ciudad del Este is connected to the Brazilian counterpart city of Foz do Iguaçú *(see page 253)* by the **Puente de la Amistad** (Friendship Bridge), and is a portal to the famous falls of Iguazú *(see page 336)*. There are tours and public transport to Iguazú and Itaipú, but the Salto Monday Falls, 10 km (6 miles) out of town, are only accessible by taxi.

On the trail of the Jesuits

Most of the Jesuit *reducciones* were set up in the fertile regions of the high Paraná River, southeast of Asunción along Route 1. In **Yaguarón**, 48 km (30 miles) south of the capital, there is a Franciscan mission, built in 1640. The church is a jewel of the His-

A Paraguayan witticism has it that every sentence starts in Spanish and finishes in Guaraní. Another saying is that Spanish is the language of the head and Guaraní of the heart.

BELOW: shop till you drop in Ciudad del Este, Paraguay's consumer capital.

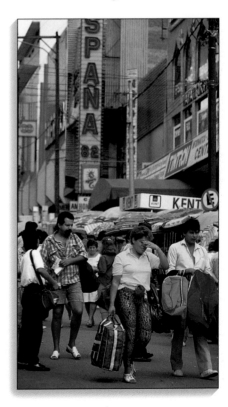

A Jesuit Utopia

In colonial times Paraguay encompassed parts of what are now Bolivia, Brazil, and Argentina. Within this vast area the Jesuit order created an administrative unit or province that achieved a semi-independent status. Like the Franciscans who preceded them, the Jesuits' primary mission was conversion. They insisted on the human value and dignity of the indigenous peoples and offered an alternative to the Spanish *encomienda* system *(see page 29)* that sought only to exploit their labor.

The Jesuits' first efforts at conversion started in 1587, one of the fathers being Thomas Fields, an Irishman from Limerick. The decision to gather the native population into settlements was made at a synod in 1603 and confirmed by Philip II of Spain in 1609. The following year, small parties of Jesuits began to travel into what was still largely unknown territory to Europeans. In the wild lands of the Chaco the Jesuits did no

better than the Spanish military expeditions that occasionally sallied forth from Asunción. With the Guaraní to the south and east of the city, they succeeded.

In the early years the Jesuit *reducciones* (missions) were threatened by the *mamelucos* or *bandeirantes*, slave raiders from Brazil. In 1629 thousands of Guaraní were forced to flee from the upper Paraná, but 12 years later a Jesuit-led army, drawn from the missions, put the *mamelucos* to flight. The missions then flourished. Ultimately the Jesuits gathered in around 150,000 Guaraní to 30 missions in a broad belt of territory on either side of the River Paraná, living by theocratic-socialist principles.

By the early 18th century the missions were thriving and were acquiring a reputation amongst European travelers as micro-Utopias. The Guaraní were farmers, herding cattle and sheep, and cultivating crops such as *yerba maté* (herbs for maté tea – *see page 315*). Some developed skills as fine craftsmen and sculptors. The Jesuit priests also found the Guaraní to be highly musical and introduced them to European idioms, to the harp and the guitar.

But the grand experiment in communal living was not to last. The Jesuits always had their enemies, and by the mid-18th century these included royal advisers in far away Madrid. In 1767 the Jesuits were expelled from the country and the Guaraní were left to fend for themselves, at the mercy of the slave raiders or absorbed into the *encomienda* system. Most of the greatest Jesuit churches were destroyed or fell into ruin, but the remains of the missions (some still in ruins and some restored) bear testimony to the achievements of the Jesuits in this region. This whole historic episode has also been powerfully reconstructed in the movie *The Mission*, starring Jeremy Irons and Robert de Niro.

Eight of the Jesuit missions were in what is now southern Paraguay, with the rest in the neighboring Argentine province of Misiones *(see page 336)* and Brazil. The missions are accessible from Asunción by Route 1 running southeast to Encarnación. ❑

LEFT: the imposing remains of a Jesuit mission in southern Paraguay.

ano-Guaraní baroque. Nearby is a museum dedicated to Doctor Francia. The first Jesuit ruins are at **San Ignacio Guazú ❹**, at Km 226. The **Museo Jesuítico** houses a fine collection of indigenous art from the missionary period. Route 4 runs west to **Pilar** and ultimately to **Humaitá**, near the junctions of the rivers Paraná and Paraguay, and whose garrison held out for three years during the War of the Triple Alliance.

To the northeast of San Ignacio is **Santa María de Fé**, established in 1669. It has a modern church and a museum that houses dozens of Guaraní-made carvings of saints and apostles. Sixteen kilometers (10 miles) south is **Santa Rosa**, founded in 1698. The church was destroyed by fire in 1883, but wooden carvings, a tower, and frescoes remain. These include a figure of the Annunciation, which is one of the great works of the Hispanic-American baroque. To reach the Jesuit ruins of **San Cosmé y Damián**, turn off Route 1 at Km 306 and travel 30 km (20 miles) south. Of particular interest is the sundial, which is all that remains of what was once a world-renowned astronomy center, built by Father Buenaventura Suarez and Guaraní laborers.

The city of **Encarnación ❺** was founded by the Jesuits on what is now the Argentinian (southern) bank of the River Paraná, and transferred to the present site on the northern bank in 1621. There is nothing left of the original Jesuit mission of Itapúa. The city, which is close to the **Yacyretá dam**, is a good center for exploring the Jesuit missions at Trinidad and Jesús de Tavarangue. Nearby are Japanese colonies which produce soybeans, vegetables, timber, maté, and cotton. About 30 km (20 miles) northeast of Encarnación is Paraguay's most splendid ruin, **Trinidad**. The sheer size of the mission, which has been declared a world heritage site by UNESCO, gives some idea of the scope of the Jesuit project in the New World. It was founded in 1706, relatively late in the Jesuit era, and the church was only finished in 1760, a few years before the expulsion of the Jesuits. There are many interesting features including a pulpit, carved in great detail. In addition to churches, Amerindian houses and crypts, there is a baptismal font and an impressive carving of the Holy Trinity, which was hollowed at the back so that a priest could hide inside and give an echoing rendition of the voice of God. Ten kilometers (6 miles) along a road north of Route 6 is **Jesús de Tavarangue**, founded by the Jesuits in 1685. Much of the site remains unfinished, as the Jesuits embarked on a massive building program seven years before their expulsion. The most remarkable surviving features are the three arched doorways built by Catalan architects in the Spanish *Mudéjar* style.

Traveling northeast

Less frequently visited than the populous eastern region, the northeast of Paraguay has a number of interesting and remote places to explore. Accessible by taking Route 2 from Asunción to Coronel Oviedo, then heading northward by Routes 3 and 5, is **Pedro Juan Caballero ❻**, a town located on the Brazilian border. Here travelers can cross into Brazil, or travel southwest to **Parque Nacional Cerro Corá**, scene of the last battle in the War of the Triple Alliance and the

Map on pages 260–1

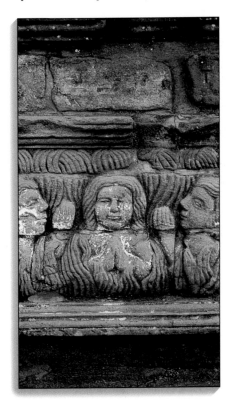

BELOW: detail of Jesuit architecture.

death of "El Mariscal" López. There are monuments to him in the national park, as well as some caves with intriguing pre-Columbian petroglyphs.

The River Paraguay provides an important route to the north. Some 300 km (200 miles) upstream from Asunción is **Concepción**, which is a significant port for trading with Brazil and has a good market. There is boat traffic further upstream which, depending on river conditions, may be used to reach some of the more remote places. Some of these places are also accessible by four-wheel drive from the Chaco. The ports on these stretches of the river, such as Puerto Casado and Fuerte Olimpo, can be reached by air or boat, and a ship, *Paraguay Cruise,* allows visitors to explore the **Pantanal** and the **Swamp of Nembucu**. Travelers on a tighter budget should ask for accommodation upon arrival if they wish to visit these intriguing but isolated small towns.

The vast expanses of the Chaco

This desolate region, which is extremely hot in summer and waterless for months at a time, covers 60 percent of Paraguayan territory but holds only four percent of the population. It was once the preserve of indigenous groups, including the Nivaclé and Lengua people, who now share the region with military personnel, Mennonite colonists, and other assorted migrants. There are a number of Catholic missions and large estancias (ranches), for this is cattle-rearing country. Unlike most of the Chaco, the Mennonite areas have good roads and facilities, and hotel accommodation is available in the towns. It is also possible to camp in the Chaco as long as you take everything with you – especially water. The Chaco is a paradise for ornithologists, with immense gatherings of birds after the rains.

BELOW: Mennonite furniture shop.

The **Low Chaco**, the region nearest Asunción, is a primeval terrain of marsh

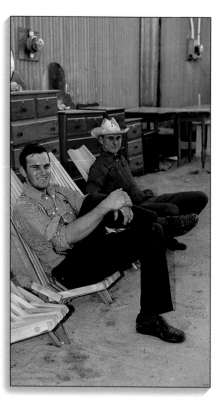

NEW SOCIETIES

The Chaco, like many remote regions, has attracted a number of unusual immigrant communities. Best known are the Mennonites, a strict Protestant Anabaptist sect, who began to arrive from 1927 onwards. They run their own banks, schools, and hospitals, and subsist on a co-operative farming system, and they can often be seen in 19th-century dress at markets in Asunción. Most speak a variety of old German known as Platt Deutsch.

Less well known is the settlement of Nueva Germania north of Coronel Oviedo. This was the site of a very different experimental community founded in 1886 by Elisabeth Nietzsche, the fanatic sister of the philosopher Nietzsche, and her equally fanatical anti-semite husband. Their plan was to found a pure Aryan colony, but the venture foundered as the colonists came up against the unforgiving realities of dense vegetation, intense heat, and torrential rains combined with a perplexing absence of ground water. Undaunted either by the rage of the duped colonists or by the suicide of her husband, Elisabeth returned to Germany where eventually she was able to greet Hitler as her true leader. The bizarre story is told in the book *Forgotten Fatherland: The Search for Elisabeth Nietzsche* by Ben Macintyre.

nd palm forest, and is used for cattle ranching. It is easily accessible by traveling over the river bridge from Asunción and then up the first few kilometers of the Trans-Chaco Highway to **Villa Hayes**. This small town is named after the 19th-century American president Rutherford B. Hayes, who arbitrated in Paraguay's favor in a territorial dispute after the War of the Triple Alliance.

At about Km 250 is **Pirahu**, which is a good place to stop and find out about road conditions. About 20 km (12 miles) further on is **Pozo Colorado**, the turning for Concepción, and at Km 415, **Cruce de los Pioneros**. All these places have restaurants and service stations, and Cruce also has a supermarket and a good hotel with an excellent restaurant.

About 50 km (30 miles) further along the highway, and off to the right, is **Loma Plata**, largest of the Mennonite towns. Further on, and also off to the right, is the Mennonite town of **Filadelfia ⓐ**, capital of the **Central Chaco**. Further north along the Trans-Chaco Highway, at Km 540, is **Mariscal Estigarribia**, a military post with facilities for the traveler. The paved road stops here. Further on, conditions can be very difficult, although the road does go all the way to Santa Cruz in Bolivia. It is possible to travel from Asunción to Bolivia by bus, especially in winter when road conditions tend to improve.

Further north is the **High Chaco**, a desert of thorn forests and military outposts. The roads are unpaved, and the land is rich with wildlife: jaguars, pumas, tapirs, and poisonous snakes, as well as a kind of wild hog, discovered in 1975, which was thought to have become extinct in the Pleistocene Era. The large, remote **Parque Nacional Defensores del Chaco** is difficult to reach and to travel around – enquiries should be made to the Dirección de Parques Nacionales in Asunción. ❑

Map on pages 260–1

BELOW: puma on the prowl in the High Chaco.

—

CHILE

This is a geographically diverse land, where you can experience the blistering heat of the Atacama Desert and chilling Patagonian winds, as well as beaches, lakes, mountains, and city delights

Map on pages 260–1

Snaking down the Pacific coast of South America from latitude 18 to 56, Chile covers a huge range of temperatures and landscapes. Squeezed between the Andes and the Pacific, never more than 355 km (220 miles) wide, this spaghetti-like strip of land extends over 4,300 km (2,700 miles) of coastline. Within its borders are the world's driest desert, lush expanses of forest and a spectacular array of glaciers and fiords. Stretched directly along the Pacific "ring of fire," Chile also has some 2,085 volcanoes, of which 55 are active. In parts of the country, earth tremors are an almost weekly occurrence.

In the north of the country is the arid and mysterious Atacama Desert, rising to more than 4,500 meters (14,760 ft) above sea level as it meets the Bolivian Altiplano. The northwest coast is distinguished by a range of expansive Pacific beaches and resorts. Chile's eastern boundary runs along the Cordillera de los Andes, which provides a mountain setting for Santiago, the capital city, placed right in the middle of the strip. South of Santiago the land becomes cooler, greener, and more alpine. Chile's Lake District has 12 great lakes and most of the country's active volcanoes. Further south, the coastline breaks up into islands, the largest being Chiloé, a rainy location steeped in regional folklore. In the far south of the country lie the remote territories of Chilean Patagonia, the glaciers and mountains of Torres del Paine National Park, and the subarctic regions of Tierra del Fuego.

The wild geography hasn't stopped Chile from becoming one of the continent's most developed nations. Travelers are often surprised by the efficiency of Chile's banking system, public transport, and services, though beneath the affluent surface are social and economic imbalances waiting to be redressed.

Chileans are renowned among Latin Americans for an unusual creative flair: Chilean folk musicians, poets, painters, and theater groups are followed in every country on the continent. And their reputation for legalizing (new laws are hawked in the streets of Santiago alongside chocolates and newspapers) and business acumen has earned Chileans the somewhat facetious label as "the English of South America."

The traditional hospitality of Chileans, noted by travelers from the 18th century on, is even more evident today. After years of dictatorship, Chileans have welcomed the influx of foreigners as a sign of support for their democracy.

PRECEDING PAGES: Torres del Paine National Park. **LEFT:** harvest time in the Lake District. **BELOW:** Cerro Santa Lucia, Santiago.

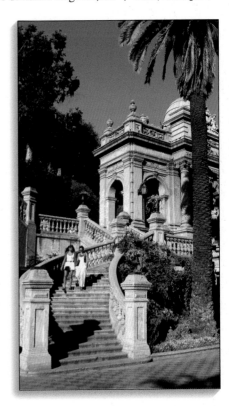

Socialism to fascism

Chile made few headlines on the world stage until 1970, when the country's first ever elected socialist government came to power under Salvador Allende, in spite of efforts by the right and the United States to subvert the process. The narrow margin of victory lim-

ited Allende's power, but his reforms to improve the standard of living for th
poor initially worked: wages increased, land was redistributed, and jobs wer
created. But opposition mounted from the middle and upper classes, terrified o
revolution, and from the left, who considered Allende too soft on the middl
class. Fearing nationalization, local and foreign capital fled. Production decline
while demand increased, spurring rampant inflation. The right and the US Gov
ernment plotted to oust Allende, financing a 1972 truckers' strike. The trucker
were soon joined by shopkeepers and professionals. But Allende's Unidad Pop
ular won 44 percent of the seats in the March 1973 congressional elections.

In the early hours of September 11, 1973, the Allende government fell in
bloody storm as troops surrounded the presidential palace, congress, newspape
offices and party headquarters. Some working-class barrios were strafed. The ai
force bombed the Presidential Palace, where Allende committed suicide. Thousand
of "subversives" were herded into concentration camps, and a military junta tool
over, declaring a state of siege and declaring that Marxism would be eradicate
from Chile. At least 2,500 people (some estimates say 10,000) were killed.

The leader of the coup, General Augusto Pinochet Ugarte, ruthlessly crushed th
opposition; dissidents – and many innocents – were imprisoned, tortured, exiled
or murdered. But in 1988 the tide finally began to turn against Pinochet; a refer
endum on his presidency was announced for October 5. Voters were registered
exile was abolished, and a state of emergency in effect since 1973 was lifted. Th
majority of the seven million Chileans voted "No", resulting in a resounding defeat
Pinochet accepted his fate, announcing that elections would be held in 1989.

The new government took office on March 11, 1990, but Pinochet kep
cronies in eight seats in the Senate and remained head of the army. Confidenc

*Museo de Bellas
Artes, Santiago.*

BELOW: Changing of
the Guard at La
Moneda, Santiago.

nd democracy slowly returned, helped by an "economic miracle", which made debt and hyper-inflation seem like problems of the past. Events came full circle in 1993 when the center-left Democratic Coalition's Eduardo Frei, son of the 1960s president, was elected president. In March 1998, Pinochet retired as head of the army but, as a former president, he was entitled to a life seat in the Senate, which he took up amid a wave of street protests. However, in October of that year, he was placed under house arrest during a visit to London pending his extradition to Spain on torture charges. He was finally released in early 2000 on health grounds and allowed to return to Chile. After several strokes, Pinochet died in 2006, never having faced trial.

In 2000, Ricardo Lagos, a socialist, took office as Chile's president, heading the third term of the centre-left coalition that has governed Chile since 1990. Lagos aimed to combine economic growth with greater social justice, but his government was initially overshadowed by high unemployment, forcing it to concentrate on short-term relief, rather than long-term social reform. In 2004, divorce was legalized, despite fierce opposition from the Roman Catholic Church, and in 2005, Pinochet's political constitution was reformed, restoring the president's right to dismiss military chiefs.

In 2006, Chile gave South America its first popularly elected woman president, Michelle Bachelet. However, her government had a difficult start as different sectors, encouraged by the high price of copper, Chile's main export, demanded increased social spending and higher wages. This highlighted one of Chile's most important challenges – to improve an income distribution that, despite almost two decades of solid growth, remains one of the most unequal in Latin America.

Map
on pages
260–1

LEFT: colonial reflections, Santiago.
RIGHT: President Michelle Bachelet.

On duty at Plaza de la Constitución.

statue of the Virgin, Cerro San Cristóbal, Santiago.

Santiago, Chile's sophisticated center

The conquistador Pedro de Valdivia is said to have forgotten his tortuous journey to Chile from Peru when he gazed upon the valley at the point where the Mapocho and Maipo rivers descend from the Andes on their journey to the Pacific Ocean. Surrounded in all four directions by hills and mountains, Valdivia knew he had found the right place for a settlement. Today, the conquistador might not recognize **Santiago ❽**, the smoggy home to 6 million of Chile's 16 million people, but it has a charm unmatched in South America.

Valdivia marked the center of Santiago with the **Plaza de Armas** (1541). I served as a market and a place of public hangings. Today, this clean, tree-lined square is a haven for old men, shoeshiners, vagrants, and lovers. The **Correo Central** (1882), which houses the most efficient postal service in South America, has an impressive iron skylight that illuminates the central corridor. Next door, the excellent **Museo Histórico Nacional** in the Palacio de la Real Audiencia traces Chile's history from its pre-Columbian roots to the present. On the west side of the square is the country's largest church, the **Cathedral** (1748–1830), with an impressive baroque interior.

Two blocks away on Calle Catedral is the **Congreso Nacional** (1876), a neoclassical structure that was home to Chile's legislative branch until it was closed in 1973. The high courts are across the street. The imposing **Palacio de la Moneda** (1805) is four blocks south on Calle Morandé. It originally served as the mint, but later became the presidential palace, where President Allende died in the 1973 military coup. On the south side of the palace, lies the recently renovated Plaza de la Ciudanía and, underneath the square, the **Centro Cultural Palacio la Moneda** (open Tues–Sun), a beautifully designed arts center.

Paseo Ahumada, a pedestrian precinct linking Plaza de Armas to the **Avenida Libertador Bernardo O'Higgins**, is the heart of Santiago, offering a human collage of businesspeople, street vendors and moneychangers. Across the Alameda, the city's major east–west artery, is the imposing, chalky-red **Iglesia San Francisco** (1612). The church has interesting touches of Arab influence, remnants of the Spanish. Alongside is **Barrio París-Londres**, where mansions from the 1920s border sinuous streets. Uptown from Ahumada, three blocks along Calle Augustinas, and past the 17th-century church of San Augustín is the **Municipal Theater** opened in 1857 and one of the finest on the subcontinent. Plays, concerts, and other cultural events are held around the small, dimly lit **Plaza Mulato Gil**.

Green spaces beneath the Andes

Santiago's founders were careful to include green spaces. Valdivia founded the city while standing atop one of its present-day parks, **Santa Lucía**, a small hill topped with terraces and a replica castle, which offer a view of the downtown area. **Parque Forestal** follows the course of the Mapocho River (corresponding to metro stations from Puente Cal y Canto to Baquedano). Large trees line winding footpaths which betray the park's narrow confines. The **Museo de Bella Artes** is here, a copy of the Petit Palais in Paris, with a fine collection of works by Chilean artists.

The **Parque Metropolitano** covers four hills towering 800 meters (2,600 ft) over Santiago. A funicular railway goes to a terrace on the peak, commanding a view of the whole city when the smog is not too thick. There is a statue of the Virgin Mary, two pools, a zoo, a botanical garden, and a wine-tasting center that offers the best of Chile's vineyards. A cable car descends half the length of the hill, to Calle Pedro de Valdivia in the *barrio alto*. Strolls or horseback rides around the expansive **Parque O'Higgins** (Metro Line 2) became stylish for city dwellers when it opened in the late 1800s. **El Pueblito** is a replica of a typical southern village, but rather tacky.

Bellavista is the cultural heart of Santiago, the night-time haunt of artists, writers, and people who go to see and be seen. Dimly lit streets are sprinkled with raucous cafés, art galleries, and restaurants, while roving theater troupes, musicians, and hippies peddle their work. At night, tables spill from bars along **Calle Pío Nono**, Bellavista's main street. On the side streets, quaint homes with flowering gardens, eccentric details, and sculpted balconies weave an intriguing architectural quilt. The house where poet Pablo Neruda created many of his greatest works is on Calle Fernando Márquez de la Plata.

Mercado Franklin (four blocks east of Metro Franklin) is a weekend flea market that winds for several blocks through an abandoned slaughterhouse. Four blocks north of the Plaza de Armas along the Mapocho River is the colorful fresh food center **Mercado Central**. High fashion is also available in Santiago at a reasonable cost. Uptown, the **Alonso de Córdova** area, off Avenida Vitacura, is an affluent neighborhood with several chic boutiques and swanky stores. **Parque Arauco** (Avenida Kennedy 5413) and **Alto Las Condes** (Avenida Kennedy 9001) are fashion malls on the upper-east side of the city.

Map on pages 260–1

BELOW: vineyard harvest.

Wine Country

The conquistadors introduced vineyards to Chile in the 16th century to supply the symbol of Christ's blood for the Catholic communion. Small wineries were nurtured on haciendas in the Maipo Valley throughout the colonial period by patrons doing their bit for the church. Today wine is one of Chile's finest products – its purpose rarely spiritual – and an increasingly popular export even to wine-soaked Europe.

The first commercial vineyard was established in 1851 when Silvestre Ochagavía brought French vine stock to the Maipo Valley. Mining magnates built extensive irrigation projects, and the vineyards spread further from the river banks. The valley's lime-heavy soil, elevation, and dry climate were ideal for producing world-class wines. Chileans boast that when French vines were destroyed by phylloxera, a grape pest, in the late 19th century, their vines were rushed across the Atlantic to replenish the stricken vineyards. The

larger labels outgrew the confines of the valley in the early 1900s and new wineries sprung up near Los Andes and Rancagua. However, it wasn't until the 1980s that Chilean vineyards began to export and embarked on a process of modernization to adapt their heavy, full-bodied wines – with the strong tannin taste that Chileans were used to – to the lighter and fruitier unblended wines (varietals) that are more popular in the US and Europe. Exports expanded rapidly and today there are vineyards from as far north as La Serena to Chillán in the south. The Casablanca Valley between Santiago and Valparaíso, discovered as a wine-growing area only 30 years ago, now produces some of the country's best white wines.

The vendimia, or harvest, takes place between early March and mid-April – the further south the vineyard, the later the picking starts. In recent years, the vendimia in Santa Cruz, in the Colchagua Valley, has won acclaim for the quality of its tastings and activities, but there are also similar festivities in other areas.

Many vineyards are open to the public, although off-season visits are usually limited to the bottling plant, the original cellars – some of them, like those of the Santa Rita winery, near Paine, built by the Spaniards in the 18th century – and the grounds of the winery. A number, including several in the Casablanca Valley, also have excellent restaurants.

Vineyards close to Santiago include Concha y Toro, Chile's largest wine producer, which has its main center an hour's drive south of Santiago in Pirque and can also be easily reached by taking the metro to Puente Alto. A tour of the plant and old family estate might be included in a weekend trip to the nearby Cajón del Maipo, but booking is advisable (tel: 476 5269 or www.conchaytoro.cl). The beautiful Santa Rita vineyard, just off the Panamerican Highway 35 km (22 miles) south of Santiago, is well worth a visit. Tours can be booked on tel: 362 2520 or www.santarita.cl. The Cousiño Macul winery, one of the oldest in Chile, is a quiet haven in the Andean foothills and about 45 minutes drive from the city center. For visits, tel: 351 4100 or www.cousinomacul.cl ❑

LEFT: vats in a Chilean bodega.

around Santiago

The lofty Andes, the tranquility of rural valley communities, and the cool breezes of the coast are all within a few hours of the capital by car or bus. On the eastern end of the city at the foot of the Andean mountains is **El Pueblito de los Dominicos**. A creek meanders through the small village, around a cluster of adobe huts with thatched roofs. The sounds of craftsmen at work drift from the workshops where they produce leather, ceramics, and metals. In nearby **Lo Barnechea**, people still ride horses around the village, and each weekend vendors set up an antiques fair in the shadow of the adobe church.

Above Lo Barnechea, **El Arrayán** has become a refuge for city dwellers who have built comfortable and breezy homes on the Arrayán River valley. The **Santuario de la Naturaleza** park follows the narrow Arrayán Canyon.

Santiaguinos venture to the **Cajón del Maipo** on weekends to take afternoon tea, nibble on *empanadas* and *kuchen* (strudel) and relax in little towns and trails along the 60-km (40-mile) canyon. The valley has distinct characteristics. A sinuous road leads from **Puente Alto** southeast, against the current of Maipo and its tributaries, to finally reach its source near the 5,000-meter (16,600-ft) extinct volcano **El Morado**. Arid peaks with names like **Punta Negra**, **Peladero**, **Lomo del Diablo**, and **Yerba Buena** meld with the changing day's sun, turning from green and brown in the day, to blue, pink, orange, and red before disappearing at dusk. The narrow valley floor is lush and intensively cultivated with vineyards and pasture land. Hiking, swimming, camping, and climbing are practiced in the area, and there are many picnic areas close to the road.

San José de Maipo, 25 km (15 miles) from Puente Alto, was founded in 1791 when miners discovered silver in the surrounding hills. Its adobe homes

Enjoying a beer at the rodeo.

LEFT: the Baños de Colina.
RIGHT: action at Valle Nevado.

and central square pay homage to the past. At **San Alfonso** (Km 40) there is hiking and camping at **Cascada de las Ánimas** facing the canyon wall. The road forks at **San Gabriel** (Km 47) where the mountains darken and the air grows thinner. **Lo Valdés** (Km 70) is on the southern fork of the road, a veritable oasis on the semi-arid slopes of the Morado volcano. The Refugio Alemán is a pleasant inn near extensive trails for exploring the snow-capped peaks surrounding the area. Nearby, **Baños de Colina** are natural hot springs in a small valley with magnificent views of the Andes and the valley below.

South of Puente Alto across the boulder-strewn Maipo River ravine is **Pirque**, birthplace of Chile's oldest wines *(see page 284)*. The **Reserva Nacional Río Clarillo** is in the midst of a semi-arid area where the best of indigenous cacti and flora flourish. In colonial times, Spanish aristocrats used to take vacations on the sandy shores of **Laguna de Aculeo**. The lake fills a valley 60 km (37 miles) from the capital, in a wooded mountain setting. There are camping facilities, hotels, and several restaurants along the shore, but the lake has become contaminated due to its heavy use for motorized water sports. Twenty years ago the government built a dam where the **Tinguiririca** and **Cachapoal rivers** meet, forming the **Rapel Lake**, which provides waterskiing, swimming, and fishing.

Fit and healthy in Arica.

BELOW: dry vineyards, Valle del Elqui.

Skiing in the Andes

The omnipresence of dizzying Andean peaks makes Chile one of the finest ski centers in the world, with challenging runs that can be enjoyed from June to September. Four resorts are within sight of Santiago. Farellones-Colorado and La Parva are ski villages above El Arrayán, just 50 km (30 miles) from Santiago along a sinuous road with 50 hairpin bends (access is controlled in winter and drivers are only allowed to head up there until noon). Valle Nevado, set in a remote valley above Farellones, is a posh resort built in 1988 by the owners of Les Alpes in France. There are three luxury hotels as well as apartment blocks, and ten lifts to slopes as high as 3,670 meters (12,000 ft) above sea level. Portillo is one of the most famous resorts in South America, 2,850 meters (9,350 ft) above sea level in an Andean pass 7 km (4 miles) from the Argentine border at Mendoza.

Pomaire, 60 km (35 miles) southwest of Santiago, has become a part of nearly every Chilean household. Dark clay scraped from the Mallarauco Hills is hand-shaped into pottery and sculpture, and fired in large rustic stone ovens to be sold in the dozens of adobe homes along the town's dusty main street.

The Pacific coast

Algarrobo, 140 km (87 miles) west of Santiago, became a resort in the late 1800s and is known for its calm seas and elegant vacation homes. It has also become an important yachting center, hosting international competitions. Nearby **El Quisco** is a tranquil town with wide beaches complementing a small fishing port and yacht club. **Isla Negra**, 4 km (2½ miles) to the south, is hidden within a cool pine forest, its rocky coast battered by great swells. Poet Pablo Neruda's home, the inspiration for many of his works, is on a bluff above the sea. It is now a museum (open

Map on pages 260–1

Tues–Sun; tours arranged through the Neruda Foundation in Santiago, tel: 777-8741, or at Isla Negra, tel: 35 461284, or it can be visited independently).

The port of **Valparaíso ⑨**, 120 km (75 miles) west of Santiago, is an enchanting town where a map is unnecessary and wandering is bliss. It is split between the geographically flat port area and 17 *cerros* (hills) that tower above the bay. The picturesque port is host to a strange brew of sailors, prostitutes, vagabonds, and tourists. The *cerros* are an impressive maze of colorful homes, winding streets, narrow alleys, rickety *ascensores* (funiculars), hidden plazas, and treacherous stairways that cling delicately to the precipitous slopes. **Muelle Prat**, dating from the 16th century, is the oldest part of Valparaíso's port. To the west, at **Caleta El Membrillo**, fishermen unload their catch near weathered *picadas*, small shacks where the freshest seafood in the city is served. The historic center of the city was declared a World Heritage Site by UNESCO in 2003.

Rickety rides

Valparaíso's *ascensores* are the best guide to the upper city. For a few pesos, these romantic wooden carriages make harrowing ascents to the neighborhoods high on the *cerros*. Ascensor Artillería (1893) first ran on coal, and goes to Paseo 21 de Mayo, providing a fantastic view of the bay. **Paseo Yugoslavo** is a promenade that winds along Cerro Alegre, among homes and gardens dating back to the early 1900s. Alegre is reached by the Ascensor El Peral.

Ascensor Concepción (1833) is the oldest elevator, reaching a neighborhood dating to the 19th century. Homes along **Paseo Atkinson** are simple wooden structures with zinc facing that creep up the mountainside. **Iglesia Anglicana San Pablo** (1858) was built by British immigrants. The **Ascensor Polanco** on

BELOW: traveling in style, Viña del Mar.

the eastern side of Avenida Argentina, built in 1915 and now a National Mon ument, is a feat of engineering. Reached by a narrow tunnel, it rises vertically through the heart of the hill, before emerging into daylight at the top of a towe that is connected to the hill top by a suspended walkway.

A road along seaside cliffs leads 9 km (5 miles) south to **Laguna Verde**, a small fishing village set in a cove, with a long, unspoiled white beach. **Quintay** 45 km (28 miles) from Valparaíso, is a modern resort. It has an expansive beach with fine white sand.

Viña del Mar, the garden city, is a cosmopolitan Pacific resort, with a spicy mix of beaches, lush gardens, and nightlife. Viña is taken over in the summe by Chileans and Argentines who crowd the expensive nightspots and bask on it golden, albeit crowded beaches. A century ago Viña was the retreat for affluen *porteños* (people from the port area) from Valparaíso. They built mansions with large gardens that later became the city's parks.

The **Quinta Vergara** is Viña's most elegant park, filled with exotic plant from around the world. The **Palacio Vergara** (1908) was built by Viña' founders and today houses the **Museo de Bellas Artes** (open Tues–Sun). The **Anfiteatro** hosts the International Festival of Song in February. **La Plaza Jose Francisco Vergara** is the palm-filled center of old Viña with the neoclassic **Club de Viña** (1910), **Teatro Municipal** (1930), **Hotel O'Higgins** (1935), and the **Casa Subercaseaux**, now a hotel, on its borders.

Pedestrian precinct **Avenida Valparaíso** is a magnet in summer, with cafés shopping malls, and an artisan fair. At the end of the street is **Cerro Castillo**, a hill sprinkled with late 19th-century mansions and terraces overlooking the bay Calle Alamos winds up the hill, past Castillo Brunet and the presidential palace Avenida Peru is a misty promenade following the shore north of the hill. The **Casino Municipal** is the premier gambling house on the Pacific side of the continent, where the rich play for high stakes. The promenade continues along Avenida San Martín, bor dering long beaches that are mobbed by tourists i the summer months.

Reñaca, 8 km (5 miles) north, is the chic place to be in high season (January and February). Its mile long beach lies below a cliff side full of fashionabl apartments and smart hotels, which are accessible b little trams and stairways. The sleepy fishing villag of **Horcón** is the center of Chile's counter culture. I is set on a rocky peninsula 40 km (25 miles) north o Viña del Mar, in the midst of a eucalyptus forest, with a small wharf and colorful skiffs towed in and out o the water by teams of horses.

Northern deserts

Northern Chile has a mysticism that sets it apart. Th 2,074 km (1,289 miles) from Santiago to Arica seem silent, a landscape sprinkled with whitewashed adob villages marooned in the **Atacama Desert**. Traditio bends the rules of Catholicism, and visits by extra terrestrials find their way into the folklore.

Arica , in the far north, is right on the threshol of Peru. The streets are filled with markets and store catering to Peruvian and Bolivian smugglers. Aric

TIP

On a visit to El Tatio Geysers, bring aspirin with you and lots of water to drink to ease the effects of altitude – headaches and nausea are common at this height. At the geysers, take great care not to tread on thin ground.

BELOW: Arica.

is also known for its beautiful beaches and nightlife. **Plaza Aduana** provides cool respite from the desert sun. Nearby is **Catedral de San Marco** (1876), a wrought-iron sanctuary designed by Gustave Eiffel. The **Morro de Arica** is a huge mountain with magnificient views of the city, the Pacific, and the desert. A museum in an old fortress recalls the battle for Arica during the War of the Pacific (1879–83), when the city was won from Peru. Several travel firms offer day trips east to **Lago Chungará**, near Bolivia, a magnificent if harrowing journey to 4,400 meters (14,500 ft). The emerald lake is surrounded by snowy peaks that rise high above the shoreline. The town of Chungará is located in **Parque Nacional Lauca**, where alpacas, vicuñas (deer-like llamas), vizcachas (large hares), and white geese with black-tipped wings perambulate along the road.

Spectacular landscape

Calama ⓫, 603 km (375 miles) south of Arica, is a mining center servicing the massive Chuquicamata copper mine, 16 km (10 miles) away. Wisps of sulfur vapor from the mine linger among its bars, cheap hotels, and restaurants. Tours of the open-pit mine are available. Three hours on the sinuous road to Bolivia is **Géiseres del Tatio**, an impressive field of scalding geysers at an altitude of 4,300 meters (14,108 ft). The geysers are at their most exuberant at sunrise.

The pleasant village oasis of **San Pedro de Atacama** ⓬, 93 km (58 miles) southeast of Calama, was the most populated Atacamanian town in pre-Columbian times. It was conquered by the Incas in 1450, and by Pedro de Valdivia in 1540. The beautiful **Iglesia de San Pedro** (1641) is constructed of the same white adobe as most of the town. Next door is the impressive **Museo Arqueológico** (open daily), with a fine collection of pottery, mummies, and

Map on pages 260–1

Typical Chilean textiles, Lauca National Park.

BELOW: Valle de la Luna.

Church mural depicting conquistadors as Roman centurions, Parinacota, Lauca National Park.

BELOW: wooden house, Lake District.

ancient Amerindian vestments. Nearby is **Pukara de Quitor**, a mountain-side stone fortress built by the Atacamanians during the Inca siege.

In the distance are lofty snowcapped volcanoes, including **Licancábur**, at 5,900 meters (19,357 ft) the highest in South America. Not far from the village is the enormous **Salar de Atacama** salt basin, as well as the **Valle de la Luna** (20 km/12 miles on a very bumpy road), a mysterious desert valley endowed with supernatural qualities and ringed by jagged, white peaks which contrast with the ochre valley floor. At twilight its formations turn brilliant colors.

West of **Copiapó** ⓭ are **Caldera** and **Bahía Inglesa**, which comprise three successive bays with long, unspoiled beaches and year-round warm water. **La Serena** ⓮, a colonial city founded in 1543 as a trade link en route between Santiago and Lima, Peru, is known for its 30 distinctive churches. Remodeled in the 1950s, it is now one of the most attractive towns in Chile. The **Iglesia San Francisco** (1627) on Calle Balmaceda has a baroque facade, with interior *Mudéjar* details. The **Mercado La Recova** has a good selection of regional crafts.

Tongoy (48 km/30 miles south of La Serena) is a summer resort on a high peninsula overlooking the Pacific, with expansive, white beaches. Along the Elqui River is the narrow, serpentine **Valle del Elqui**. This lush refuge is famous for its clear blue skies, dry mountain air, steep arid mountains, and intensely cultivated pastures and vineyards that are the source of the national liquor, pisco. **Monte Grande** ⓯, a small village along the river, is where the Nobel Prize-winning poet Gabriela Mistral spent her infancy. Her tomb is on the road to Cochiguaz and her birthplace in **Vicuña** is now a **museum** (open daily). There are a number of communes in the area whose inhabitants practice meditation in what is considered to be a focal point of mystical energy.

South to the Lake District

The Lake District is a land of extreme beauty, a seemingly endless succession of lush alpine valleys, low Andean hills, and snow-covered volcanoes. The outstanding scenery is reflected in the bitter-cold waters of the lakes, which were formed by the abrasive retreat of glaciers that once covered the region. Roughly half of the region's population lives in the cities, making a visit to the area a euphoric escape from the bustle of urban life. It's hard to believe that this natural paradise was once forbidden to outsiders. The Mapuche people wiped out every foreign settlement south of the **Río Biobío** at the end of the 16th century, and remained undefeated until the 1880s.

Concepción ⓰, Chile's second-largest city (pop. 396,000), on the banks of the mighty Biobío, was little more than a garrison town until 1818, when Bernardo O'Higgins declared Chile's independence there. The downtown area is best explored on foot on the streets near the plaza. Four blocks south is **Parque Ecuador**, which winds up **Cerro Caracol** (Snail Hill) for a good view of the city. North is the **Universidad de Concepción**, founded in 1919.

About 15 km (9 miles) north of Los Angeles, deep within a wooded Andes valley, the town of **Salto del Laja** is the gateway to the Lake District. The frigid waters of the Laja River slice through some of the most beautiful scenery in Chile, before plunging 35 meters (115 ft) into a deep, rocky canyon, which is eternally bathed in a foggy mist. Within sight of the valley are four volcanoes that rise high above the forest.

The road east snakes through huge pine forests, nearing the mountains as the valley narrows and the terrain becomes semiarid. Huge lava fields lie nearby, flanked by mountain cypress. **Parque Nacional Laguna del Laja** is located in

Map on pages 260–1

BELOW: Villarrica Volcano.

a narrow valley. In the center is a 200-meter (650-ft) high volcanic cone that holds **Laja Lagoon**, and to the right is the desolate cone of **Laja Volcano**. Three of the four lakes in **Parque Nacional Conguillío** (110 km/70 miles northeast of Temuco) were formed by the depressions in lava fields spewed out by the **Llaima Volcano** (3,125 meters/10,253 ft) within the past 50 years. The narrow valley is covered with arucaurias up to 1,200 years old, plus oaks and cypresses.

Turbulent landscape

Villarrica ⓐ is a major resort on the shore of the 176-sq. km (68-sq. mile) **Lago Villarrica**. Its blue waters change hue as the sun falls, reflecting the perfect cone of the Villarrica Volcano. The lake is scarred by eruptions from the still-active volcano, which glows like the end of a giant cigar at night. The first European colony at Villarrica was beseiged by the Mapuche in 1598, and collapsed without survivors in 1602. The colony was not re-established until 1882. There is a Mapuche museum near the tourist office at Villarrica. The resort village of **Pucón ⓑ**, further east along the lake, is a summer haven for affluent Chileans. **Parque Nacional Villarrica**, on the steep slopes of the volcano, is a bizarre mix of untouched forest and barren lava fields that seared through the woods during an eruption.

Slender **Lago Caburga ⓒ**, 24 km (15 miles) to the east, was formed when lava flows were blocked by the precipitous, densely wooded valley. Three pristine lagoons are hidden in the small valley, and several hot springs, fed by volcanoes, gush from the ground.

Lakes Calafquén, Panguipulli, Pellaifa, Neltume, Riñihue, Pirihueico, and, in Argentina, Lacar, are collectively known as the **Seven Lakes**. This little-known

BELOW: street musicians, Valdivia.

area wasn't really settled until the late 1800s, due to its remote setting and harsh winters. **Lican Ray ⓓ** was built for tourists on a wooded peninsula overlooking Calafquén Lake. It is said to have the nicest beach in the area and is a magnet for vacationing Chileans in summer. **Panguipulli ⓔ**, a small, picturesque town on the banks of the lake, has an interesting Capuchin mission and church. A road leads to the tip of a wooded peninsula, with sandy beaches on the lake. Nearby, **Salto del Huilo Huilo** crashes down a deep vine-covered gorge into the River Fuy, producing an eternal rainbow.

German settlements

One of the first Spanish settlements in Chile was **Valdivia ⓕ**, located at the confluence of several waterways in the Valdivia Estuary. The streets follow the sinuous rivers, and **Calle General Lagos** near the waterfront and lively port still has remnants of the architecture that German immigrants brought with them in the 19th century. The **Museo Histórico y Antropológico Mauricio van de Maele** (open Tues–Sun) on **Teja Island**, chronicles the German migration. Nearby is the **Austral University**, with a large campus. Valdivia was heavily fortified by the Spanish after 1600 to guard against Mapuche invasions. Tours are available to see the forts along the river.

The nearby city of **Osorno ⓖ**, 990 km (615 miles) south of Santiago, is the center of a cattle region. It lies east to west across the Rahue River, surrounded by azure-green pasturelands nourished by abundant rainfall. The city was settled by German farmers, its shingled wooden homes and streets with names like Buschman, Amthauer, and Francke reminiscent of a distant past. **Calle Bulnes** has good river views. Try to catch the morning **Feria Ganadera**,

Map on page 292

BELOW: on the waterfront at Valdivia.

Wooden boat and fishermen's houses, Puerto Montt.

BELOW: fishing boats, Puerto Montt.

Chile's largest cattle market, where burly *campesinos* haggle over animals. **Lago Puyehue** (60 km/37 miles east) is a popular fishing and camping spot. The **Casablanca**, **Puyehue**, **Puntiagudo**, and immense **Osorno** volcanoes are all within sight of the lake's waters. Near the eastern shore are the **Puyehue Hot Springs**, known for their therapeutic qualities. On the road to the Casablanca Volcano, through lush virgin forest, is **Aguas Calientes** (hot springs).

Picturesque towns creep up to the edge of **Lago Llanquihue** and the perfect cone of the snow-capped Osorno Volcano is eternally reflected in its frigid waters. **Puerto Varas** , at the southwest tip of the lake, is an immaculate town created in 1854 to handle lake commerce to Puerto Montt. Today it is a thriving stop-off point for tourists who like to gamble in the casino at **Gran Hotel Puerto Varas** on the shore. **Frutillar** , on the western lakeshore, is filled with interesting German homes with meticulous gardens, and has a peculiar claim to fame: the world's southernmost palm tree. In February it hosts the **Semanas Musicales de Frutillar**, a music festival renowned throughout the subcontinent.

On the eastern shore is **Ensenada** , a tiny village set in the shadow of the Osorno Volcano and surrounded by lush forest cut by lava flows. About 12 km (7½ miles) east, the rapids of the **Río Petrohué** are broken by strange lava formations comprised of thousands of black volcanic stones, reminders of an ancient eruption. Further east is **Lago Todos Los Santos**. There are daily boat excursions along the length of the lake to **Peulla** , a magnificent journey along shoreline mountains covered in dense virgin forest and, from here, it is also possible to cross to Bariloche in Argentina.

The road south from Ensenada to Cochamó is a journey through an area of great wilderness beauty. **Cochamó** is a tiny village on the estuary, a branch off to the Pacific through spectacular fiords that rise up to 1,500 meters (4,900 ft) straight out of the water. At Cochamó you can hire fishermen to give you a tour of the estuary in a skiff, where it's easy to spot seals, 30 kg (70 lb) groupers, and even whales.

Puerto Montt was founded in 1853 by the adventurer Vicente Pérez Rosales, with a handful of German immigrants intent on settling Llanquihue province. The area mushroomed when the railroad arrived, 60 years later. Today the city is a grimy port, gateway to Chiloé and the Patagonia frontier. Despite its size, Puerto Montt has a small-town feeling, with many homes of northern Germanic design: wooden, with pitched roofs, ornate balconies, and shingles well weathered by the region's eternal drizzle. The cathedral in the central square is the city's oldest building, made of redwood. Puerto Montt faces the Reloncaví Sound, and a walk along the waterfront is a good introduction to the city.

Angelmó, a contiguous fishing port, is a jewel of maritime activity. Cafés on the pier offer fresh *erizos*, *locos*, and other cold-water seafood, and burly fishermen mend their nets by the skiffs on the shore. The pier is lined with artisan shops that sell a wide selection of woolen goods and woodcarvings. Young boys will row you across to **Isla Tenglo** ⭕, where you can walk around its fishing communities.

Traditional wood-tiled church, Chiloé.

The rugged south: Chilean Patagonia

South of Puerto Montt, the land and sea become one as the country breaks into a maze of islands, fiords, rivers with myriad tributaries, lakes, and wooded mountains with trees a thousand years old. Chilean Patagonia is a place of forbidding, intense beauty that has escaped the ravages of man.

BELOW: chopping wood, Chiloé.

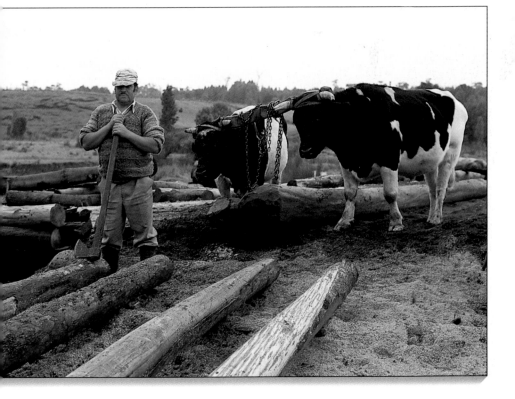

The island of **Chiloé** ⟨17⟩ emerges just out of sight of Puerto Montt, a romantic place filled with picturesque villages, a hundred tiny enchanted islets, misty waterways, and little wooden homes. Chiloé is steeped in fishing tradition, and the magic of its culture attracts trekkers in search of the customs, legends, and folklore of its friendly people. It is home to lively dances like the *cueca* and *vals*, local dishes like *curanto*, drinks like *chicha de manzana*, and myriad legends, festivals, and rituals all its own. Somehow it has held on to its oldest traditions.

The island is known for its wooden *capillas* (chapels) with distinctive shingled steeples and porticos. Sixteen of these are UNESCO World Heritage Sites as they are the only Latin American example of a rare form of ecclesiastical wooden architecture. Many of the chapels are in poor shape, but are being repaired with international support.

Ancud, with narrow streets packed with wooden commercial buildings from its heyday, is a bustling port. The **Museo Azul de las Islas de Chiloé** (open Jan and Feb daily, Mar–Dec Tues–Sun) contains exhibits on Chilote culture and mythology, and the **Fort of San Antonio**, the last Spanish garrison to surrender to the independent Chilean Republic in 1826, offers a spectacular view on a clear day.

Castro (founded in 1567), on the shores of a protected fiord, is one of the oldest cities in Chile. The **Iglesia de San Francisco de Castro** is an unusual wooden cathedral on the plaza. On the outskirts of Castro, the **Museo de Arte Moderno** (open Nov–Feb Tues–Sun) shows some of Chile's best contemporary art in a prizewinning building in the traditional Chiloé style. In February the **Festival Costumbrista Chilote** is a marvelous display of island culture. At the waterside, fishermen park their skiffs beside rows of *palafitos*, houses on stilts.

Quellón is famous for its soft, gray ponchos, which are very resistant to the rain because the wool used for making them is raw and still full of natural oils.

LEFT: guanacos, Paine National Park. **RIGHT:** Chinook salmon.

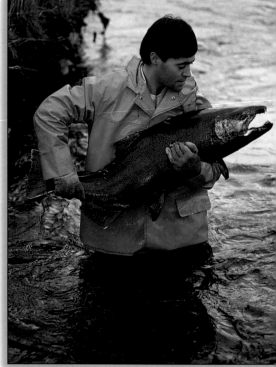

Nearby **Dalcahue** is famous for its Sunday artisan fair, where fine woolen sweaters can be found. **Chonchi** (26 km/16 miles south of Castro) is built on a cliff face overlooking the water. There is a nice church among several colorful large houses with well-kept gardens. Heading southward, **Queilén** is a picturesque town on a narrow peninsula with beaches at each end, and elegant old homes dating back to its founding as an immigrant colony in 1900. Ferries leave from **Quellón** (not to be confused with Queilen), the southernmost port.

South to the end of the world

South of Chiloé lies the remote Aisén region, where visits still give the sensation of penetrating a new frontier. The Carretera Austral winds through the largely uninhabited archipelago in the far south for almost 1,000 km (600 miles). The region is still largely untouched by humans, save a few fishermen and farmers. It is an amazing landscape where rocky cliffs drop into lush river valleys and dense jungles are bordered by glaciers. **Chaitén** ⑱ is a coastal town with food, lodging, and good ocean and mountain views, which is accessible by a six-hour ferry journey from Chonchi or by road (160 km/100 miles, including two ferry crossings). **Santa Bárbara**, 11 km (7 miles) north, is a picturesque fishing village with a wide beach.

The south is a contrasting mix of lush forest, waterfalls emerging from icy cliffs, glaciers, and valleys flanked by the icy slopes of the Andes. From Santa Lucía the road follows the Río Frío along a wooded valley, reaching **La Junta** at the confluence of three rivers, from where there are excursions to the picturesque **Lago Rossellot** and **Lago Verde**. The road continues to **Lago Risopatrón** and **Termas de Puyuhuapi**. Nearby **Parque Nacional Queulat**

Visit the park, get the badge.

BELOW: wild scenery at the end of the world.

has amazing views of the *ventisqueros* (glaciers). **Puerto Cisnes**, to the south,
is a small beachside village that was colonized by Germans and Italians in th
late 19th century. Heading inland, **Coyhaique** is a large town, and a goo
jumping-off point for exploring the region. Founded in 1929, it is largely a gov
ernment and military center. The **Museo Regional de la Patagonia** (ope
Mon–Fri) is a good introduction to the region's history. South of the city the lan
turns rugged, with trees giving way to weathered scrub. Steppe grasses begin t
appear, buffeted by incessant winds. The area was settled by ranchers who mad
their fortunes with enormous *fundos* (ranches).

Puerto Aisén, to the south, was founded to service the ranches in 1914. I
the region is **Laguna San Rafael**, a pristine lake which is only accessible afte
a journey through fiords and archipelagos. The lake is enclosed by the **Sa
Rafael Glacier**, which sends huge blocks of 20,000-year-old ice crashing int
the water as it makes its way to the sea. A number of firms offer cruises ther
from Puerto Montt. About 120 km (75 miles) south of Coyhaique is **Lago Gen
eral Carrera**, South America's second-largest lake. It juts into Argentina, wit
views of the vast pampas to the east. On the Chilean side it is bordered by ba
ren, rocky mountains eroded by glaciers. Several towns have lodgings along th
shore, including **Puerto Ibáñez**, and **Chile Chico**.

Torres del Paine

Down at the far south of the Andes mountain chain, **Torres del Paine Nation
Park** is one of the newest nature reserves in South America, a 2,400-sq. k
(927-sq. mile) uninhabited wilderness. Aficionados agree that the unique phys
ical formations of the Paine (pronounced *pie-nay*), crowded with glaciers, lake

LEFT: a cargo boat
in the Southern
Ocean.
RIGHT: produce for
sale, Punta Arenas.

gnarled Magellanic trees and animals, offer the most magnificent walking in the world. The best time to be there is between December and April.

The jumping-off point for the national park is **Puerto Natales ㉑**, a small, sleepy town set beside the Ultima Esperanza Gulf, with numerous hotels, and restaurants serving the local specialty, king crab. Tour boats head out from Natales to nearby glaciers. Not far away is a huge cave where the remains of a prehistoric Milodon sloth were found several years ago.

But most people visit Puerto Natales to arrange a trip to the Paine. Several times a week (every morning in summer), vans and buses make the three-hour drive along a rough dirt road to the park. The trail winds through mountain passes before descending to the foot of the Andes, providing the first view of the **Cuernos del Paine** (Horns of the Paine): twisted pillars of gray granite dusted with snow, invariably surrounded by billowing clouds. As everywhere else this far south, weather in the Paine can be unpredictable, even in summer. The famous **Torres del Paine** (towers) are even more spectacular than the Cuernos, but are often obscured by the harsh, incessantly windy weather. Accommodations can be found at the Hostería Pehoe on a lake and the Posada Rio Serrano.

Several day trips can be made from these bases, as well as more ambitious walks. The park has over 250 km (150 miles) of tracks, including a seven-day circuit. Along the way are *refugios* or shelters, often scanty wood and corrugated-iron structures that barely keep out the elements – sleeping bags and cooking gear are essential. Those who complete the full seven-day circuit will, weather permitting, be rewarded with extraordinary views of snow-covered peaks, turquoise lakes, and lush valleys. The trails are lined with orange, red, and purple flowers. Much of the park is lushly forested, although a worm plague

Map on pages 260–1

Freshly caught centolla, king crab.

BELOW: tree bent in submission to the Patagonian wind.

Map on pages 260–1

Bowsprit of the Lonsdale, wrecked near Punta Arenas.

BELOW: Fuerte Bulnes, near Punta Arenas.
RIGHT: guanacos in Torres del Paine National Park.

killed many trees in the late 1990s and, more recently, there was a bad fire. Walks pass the accessible **Grey** and **Dickson glaciers**.

Most routes allow walkers to see plenty of animals, most commonly the guanacos: unlike camelids in other parts of South America, they appear unafraid of people and can be easily photographed from up close. Although the weather can turn from fair to foul and back again within minutes, the memories of the park will last well after your clothes have dried. Many people who go for a day end up staying a week: the liberating sensation of being in one of the most remote and untouched wilderness areas on earth is worth savoring.

The remote Magallanes

The southernmost province of Magallanes is a solitary place with names like Porvenir (Future) and Ultima Esperanza (Last Hope) that try to shake the feeling that you have reached the end of the world. This is where the tip of South America has crumbled into myriad islands as the land, sea, and ice mingle. The forbidding nature of the territory is reflected in the names of some of the islands, which include Madre de Dios and Desolación.

Punta Arenas ㉒ is a port city on the rolling hills above the barren, wind-swept steppe on the Straits of Magellan. This is a peculiar part of the world: the sky looks bigger here, and people seem distant and less open to outsiders, while the sun glares through the damaged ozone layer. Punta Arenas is known for its monuments to the Yugoslav settlers and ranchers who pioneered the region. The **Museo Regional de Magallanes** (open daily), provides a fascinating trip back to the days before the Panama Canal opened, when the city boomed as ships called in on their journeys round the cape. **Cerro La Cruz** has good views of the city and across the straits to Tierra del Fuego.

Tierra del Fuego, an island of inhospitable terrain across the straits from Punta Arenas, was discovered as Ferdinand Magellan struggled to make the passage to the Pacific in 1520. In the late 19th century the land was settled by a few immigrants from Yugoslavia and England who came to start sheep ranches, and cash in on the 1881 gold rush. The wooded mountains and peat bogs on the western side are cold and snowy in the long winter; the rainforests to the east are warmer and wetter; and the wind never ceases on the treeless pampas facing Punta Arenas.

Porvenir ㉓, settled primarily by Yugoslavs, is the largest town on the island. The **Museo de Tierra del Fuego** (open daily) is connected to the municipal buildings on the main plaza, with historical photographs and a Fuegian mummy discovered in the nearby countryside. You can take a ferry across the straits from Punta Arenas to Porvenir docks, where a sign gives the distance to every port in Chile, as well as to the former Yugoslavia.

The town itself is quiet and sleepy, little changed since the late 19th century. A road continues to the Argentine side of the island (*see page 344*) toward the icy waters of Cape Horn passing the southernmost piece of inhabited land on earth, and south along the Chilean side of the island. ❑

EASTER ISLAND

*Visiting this tiny Pacific outpost means a long flight from Chile,
yet each year many visitors make the journey to wonder
at its mysterious monolithic figures*

idden in the endless wastes of the Pacific, nearly 4,000 km (2,500 miles) from the coast of Chile, the small remnant of volcanic rock named Easter Island was once the most isolated place to live on earth. But in recent decades the Polynesian culture that left behind huge and inexplicable statues has drawn increasing attention from around the world. Where once only one ship a year made the visit to the island, today flights arrive regularly from Santiago. This tiny triangular South Seas outpost measures just 24 km (15 miles) across and has a population of only 4,500, but there is a lot to explore. Easter Island has a wonderful raw, unspoiled beauty with windswept coastlines, gentle, treeless hills, and a lush interior. Golden beaches and coconut palms are in short supply.

Archeologists now believe that Easter Island may have been first populated as long ago as 400 AD. The Norwegian adventurer and archeologist Thor Heyderdahl argued in his famous book *Aku-Aku* that the inhabitants came from South America, noting resemblances between the island culture and that of Tiahuanaco in Bolivia *(see page 181)*. But most academics today agree that the first settlers came from Polynesia, bringing sweet potato, sugar cane, and bananas to the fertile ground of the island. Left in total isolation for centuries, the settlement prospered and spread. Its people created not only the remarkable stone *moai*, but also the *rongo rongo* script, the only writing system known in all Polynesia and the Americas.

The first Europeans arrived on Easter Sunday in 1722, giving the island its name. Dutch Admiral Roggeveen spent a day ashore, recording (unlike later accounts) that the statues were upright, the lands were neatly cultivated, and "whole tracts of woodland" were visible. The population may have been as large as 12,000.

Turbulent times

The picture changes in later descriptions. European explorers in the late 18th century noted that many of the statues had tumbled, little land was under cultivation and there were only a thousand people. The most likely explanation for the island's decline is that the population of Easter Island had outgrown its resources; the food supply failed, the forests were felled and soil began to erode. Without wood for canoes to escape from the island, fighting and cannibalism broke out, and the *moai* were toppled.

The people of Easter Island were to endure further suffering in the 19th century, when whalers and slave traders came to call. Of one thousand islanders taken as slaves to the guano islands off Peru in 1862, only a hundred were released alive, of whom only 15 survived the return journey, bringing smallpox to wreak further havoc in the community. By 1871, only 175 islanders remained. Today, some

LEFT: one of many *moai* statues.
BELOW: *moai* in the old volcanic quarry of Ranu Raraku.

Young Easter Island man in traditional dress.

4,500 people live on the island, but many were born on the mainland, o Chilean ancestry. The airfield, opened in 1967, increased tourism, and i 1988 the airstrip was extended to become an emergency landing strip fo the space shuttle, thrusting the island into the technological age. In the earl 1990s Kevin Costner brought a Hollywood film crew to the island to produc the historically creative film *Rapa Nui*. Despite being a monumental flop, th film brought a surge of tourist traffic to the island in its wake. Rapu Nui i the indigenous name of the island, much of which is a national park and World Heritage Site.

The mysterious *moai*

No one knows the true story behind the *moai,* but they are thought to hav been symbols of gods and ancestors. They were carved from around 900 AD out of the soft volcanic rock forming the sides of **Rano Raraku** crater, wher some 400 incomplete pieces remain, many as high as 5.5 meters (18 ft) – th largest is 21 meters (69 ft) tall. Each probably took a year to complete. Onc finished, the *moai* was cut out of the quarry and transported to a family bur ial platform called an *ahu,* some being given red stone "topknots". The fam ily dead were usually placed in a vault beneath the *moai,* which was probabl believed to transmit *mana,* or power, to the living family chief. All of th standing *ahu moai* that can be seen now have been re-erected in moder times. In the period of the tribal wars, all the *moai* were toppled, presumabl to break the *mana* of the family chief they protected.

The most famous of the *moai* are the standing sentinels embedded in th ground on the southern slope of Rano Raraku. These haughty-looking statue

BELOW: the *moai* of Ahu Akiví.

remain eyeless: *moai* were only given coral eyes once they were raised on *ahus*, at which time the *mana* began to work. Most of the sites can be reached by bicycle or horse if you're happy to spend a couple of hours passing through marvelous countryside, but make sure you bring water with you.

The "Bird Man" cult

The most geologically spectacular place on Easter Island is the volcano **Rano Kau**, with its steep crater and multicolored lake. The ruined village of **Orongo**, sitting on steep cliffs above the crashing sea and three foam-washed islands, is surrounded by rocks with "Bird Man" carvings: a man's body is drawn with a bird's head, often holding an egg in one hand. Fortunately, we know quite a lot about the Bird Man cult, as it continued up to 1862. It involved a strange rite that probably began in the period of the wars. The basis of the cult was finding the first egg laid by the *Manu Tara*, or sacred bird, each spring.

The chief of each tribe on the island sent one chosen servant to Moto Nui, the largest of the islets below Orongo. Swimming across the dangerous waters, the servants or *hopus* spent a month looking for the first egg. On finding the egg, the successful *hopu* plunged into the swirling waters with the egg strapped to his forehead, swam to the mainland, and climbed the cliffs to Orongo. The *hopu's* master, named Bird Man for the year, would be given special powers and privileges. Today, there are more than 150 Bird Man carvings in the area, overlaid with fertility symbols. Nearby are markings and stones that have been interpreted as forming part of a solar observatory, where on the summer solstice the sun can be seen rising over Poike peninsula – one more mysterious attraction on this beautiful and fascinating island in the Pacific. ❑

 Map on page 303

TIP

Motorbikes, jeeps, and horses can be rented. Guided tours by four-wheel drive are highly recommended. You won't cover every single site in just one day's tour, but you'll see the most important ones.

BELOW: Easter Island women.

JUAN FERNÁNDEZ ISLANDS

The location of the true story that inspired the fictional Robinson Crusoe, these little-known Pacific islands are also home to some fascinating and unique species of plants and animals

BELOW: the fictional Robinson Crusoe.

Named after Spanish navigator Juan Fernández, who discovered them in 1574, the Juan Fernández Islands owe their notoriety to a classic novel written by Daniel Defoe. Their place in history was set when Scottish mariner Alexander Selkirk was marooned on Isla Mas a Tierra, now officially known as Isla Robinson Crusoe, for four years in 1704. His experience provided the inspiration for Daniel Defoe's classic tale, *Robinson Crusoe*.

The three Juan Fernández islands – Isla Robinson Crusoe, Isla Alejandro Selkirk, and Isla Santa Clara – lie 650 km (400 miles) off the Chilean mainland. The whole archipelago is a national park and World Biosphere Reserve. Reaching them today can seem as complicated as it was for Selkirk to get off them 300 years ago. Unless you travel on a pre-arranged tour, flights to the islands from Santiago are irregular, to say the least. Winter rains flood the dirt runway, limiting air traffic to the months of October through April.

The flight to Isla Robinson Crusoe is followed by a one-and-a-half hour journey in an open fishing boat to the township of **San Juan Bautista**. On a fine day the water is clear and blue, with schools of fish zigzagging below and the obese Juan Fernández seals sunning themselves by the shore. The boatmen often smoke succulent lumps of freshly caught cod and share them around with bread and water. The township of San Juan Bautista, where almost all of the archipelago's 600 inhabitants live, is located roughly where Selkirk spent his enforced leisure time. Set beneath forest-covered fists of stone with their peaks always lost in the gray mist, it consists of a few unpaved streets, a bar, a soccer field and a small cemetery with ship's anchors above many of the graves. With just a handful of automobiles, the only noise is the never-ending howl of the wind.

In Selkirk's footsteps

The classic hike from town follows Selkirk's path to **El Mirador** – the lookout used by the marooned sailor every day to scan the horizon on both sides of the island. Start early, at about 8am, to arrive before the mists roll in. The path runs through crops of introduced eucalyptus into higher forests of indigenous trees. It also passes the remains of an old Spanish fort as well as a turn-off to a rock bearing sailor's graffiti from 1866 – a ship and a giant fish.

The trail becomes a corridor through rainforest before revealing a knife-shaped peak. In the saddle of the mountain is the only place to see both sides of the island: lush, green Juan Bautista to the east; dry brown swirls and jagged peaks on the northern side of the mountain. A plaque was erected here by a British warship in the 19th century commemorating Selkirk's ordeal. It has more recently been joined by a small memorial from one of the mariner's descendents from Largo in Scotland. On the return journey, call in at the **Caves of the Patriots**, where 300 pro-Spanish soldiers fled in 1814 after Chile's declaration of independence. Unlike Selkirk, they couldn't stand the wind and rain in their huge, damp caves, so gave themselves up. Back on shore, a number of other caves vie for the title of Selkirk's home, although for most of the time the mariner lived in his own handmade huts.

Within the town is the local office of CONAF, the island's national park service, financed mostly by European funds. The center operates to protect the unique flora and fauna of the area that put the island on the UNESCO Biosphere Reserve list. The plant life is unusually varied on the island, with 101 endemic varieties including a range of enormous ferns, many of which look as if they would be at home in Dr Seuss books. Of the unique animals, the red hummingbird is the most famous for its needle-fine black beak and silken feather coverage. CONAF spends most of its time trying to eradicate threats introduced by humans: everything from mulberry bushes to the wild goats and feral cats descended from Selkirk's days. Rabbits were once a problem, but have been controlled by paying a trapper to catch and sell the animals on a daily basis (the islanders thought this a more humane solution than introducing the disease myxomatosis).

Biologists on the islands regularly turn up new finds: recently, a fern called *Dendroseries macranta* that had not been sighted since 1907 was found.

But one of the real pleasures of any visit is just taking a seat by the wharf and watching the world go by, sipping on a beer and chatting with the islanders. Prepare to eat your fill of the local lobster too, as there may be little else on the menu – delicious for the first few days but palling by the end of your stay. ❑

The local delicacy is langosta de Juan Fernández – *a lobster, which is also shipped to the Chilean mainland.*

BELOW: Isla Santa Clara.

URUGUAY

Map
on pages
260-1

*'his tiny nation, wedged in between Argentina and Brazil, has been
a pioneer of social reform. It retains flavors of colonial opulence
and rural frontier life, as well as elegant beach resorts*

ong known as the Switzerland of South America, owing to its size, its
democratic tradition and its dependence on the banking sector, Uruguay
■ and its capital, Montevideo, are often seen virtually as one. This is not so
rprising, given that the country covers an area of just 186,000 sq. km (72,000
. miles) and that more than half of its population of 3.5 million is located in
ontevideo, the rest being spread among attractive coastal towns and the inte-
r of the country, dedicated to cattle, sheep, rice, and fruit production.
Successive colonial wars decimated Uruguay's indigenous Charrúa popula-
n; the population today is made up principally of the descendants of Italian
d Spanish immigrants who arrived in the late 19th and early 20th century, as
ll as a black or mixed-race minority descended from former slaves and Brazil-
i immigrants. Usually seen as less formal than the Argentines, the Uruguayans
e of similar ancestry, though as a small and family-based society they are
o less open in their social relations, in particular with foreign visitors.
Although Uruguayans tend to use Argentina as a reference point (they call them-
lves *Orientales*, or Easterners, as opposed to the Argentines to the west), there are
me marked differences between Montevideo and Buenos Aires. One is Monte-
leo's racial mixture. In the 19th century, rumors of fair treatment attracted eman-
pated slaves from Brazil and Argentina. The army
ered them a familiar regimented life, and many joined
e infantry, which considerably reduced their numbers.
uguayans claim to have no racial prejudice, but blacks
d to occupy the bottom rungs of the economic ladder.
Another difference from Argentina is Uruguay's
ong secular tradition. The Catholic church plays no
le in government, and holidays all have secular
mes: Christmas is Family Day and Easter or Holy
eek is Tourism Week.
Uruguay claims to host the world's longest carnival,
ld in Tourism Week (Easter) – it may be a little
re sedate than the Rio version, but it is a good place
see *Candomblé*, which evolved from rituals and
ditions brought by African slaves. The country also
s a long tradition of tango, with many tango stars
rn in the country. Tango Week is in October.

iilding a nation

e Portuguese were the first Europeans to settle the
gion, founding the city of Colonia in 1680. In 1726,
ain established a colony in Montevideo; the two
untries battled over the area until Spain won pos-
ssion in 1726. In 1815, José Gervasio Artigas led
uguay to independence, becoming leader of the
uguayan nation, but wars with Brazil postponed
l independence for 10 years *(see page 31)*. Artigas
s eventually forced into exile in Paraguay. For the

PRECEDING PAGES:
house of the painter
Paez Vilaró, Punta
del Este.
LEFT: gaucho with
maté gourd.
BELOW: Colonia del
Sacramento.

next 50 years, civil wars raged between two political forces: the Blanco (Whites) and Colorados (Reds). Initially feuding factions, they would eventually evolve into Uruguay's major political parties. In 1872, in the interest of beef exports, peace was established by ceding the Blancos' influence to the countryside and the Colorados' to the city, a division that remains to this day.

Montevideo is said to be a corruption of a Galician sailor's cry: "Monte vi eu!" (I saw a hill!).

The social revolution

José Batlle y Ordóñez is usually credited with forging the model of civic order that Uruguay became during the first half of the 20th century. Batlle (pronounced *Ba-zhay*) studied in Paris, and returned to Uruguay full of enlightened ideas. He became a political journalist, fearlessly attacking the country's dictators, founded his own newspaper, *El Día*, in 1886, and gradually made his way into politics. He was elected president for the first time in 1903.

On a four-year sojourn in Europe between presidential terms, Batlle was impressed with the Swiss social legislation and state-operated industries. In his second term, he legalized divorce, abolished the death penalty, and established an eight-hour workday. He also forbade naming public buildings after saints. His 1918 Constitution provided complete freedom of the press, the prohibition of arbitrary arrest, and decreed that prisons were for reform, rather than punishment.

After his death in 1929, Batlle's reforms had succeeded in liberalizing both parties. The widespread peace and prosperity of the past decades prevented even the conservative moneyed classes from objecting to the advance of social security and workers' rights. A coup d'état in 1933 temporarily halted progress, but a 1942 Constitution provided explicitly for universal health, accident, and unemployment insurance, and gave illegitimate children the right to inherit.

BELOW: an early 19th-century view of Montevideo harbor.

End of the welfare state

Map on pages 260–1

The collapse of Uruguay's wool and beef economic base in the late 1950s produced a crisis in the country's welfare system and a boom in poverty and unemployment. This in turn facilitated the rise of the guerrilla group Tupamaros in the 1960s and, in 1973, the rise of a repressive military government. During 12 years of dictatorship, one in every 50 Uruguayans was arrested at some point for supposed subversive activity. One in every 500 was sentenced to six years or more in prison, and some 400,000 fled into exile. Following the return to civilian government in 1985, Uruguay enjoyed comparatively high living standards and a relatively equitable distribution of wealth. But the country's banking system has become increasingly uncompetitive, and no industry has yet arisen to replace the declining demand for wool and beef exports.

Elections are held every five years, and voting is compulsory. Jorge Batlle of the center-right Colorado Party was elected as head of state and government in 2000. Tax increases, among other measures, were implemented soon afterwards in an effort to prevent neighboring Argentina's financial crisis from entering Paraguay. In 2005, for the first time in Uruguay's history, the two traditional political parties failed to win the presidency. Instead Tabaré Vázquez, a medical doctor, was elected on behalf of the left-wing Broad Front coalition. He has tried to restore the Uruguayan state's role as provider, and internationally has aligned himself with President Lula da Silva in Brazil, and Néstor Kirchner in Argentina.

The government of President Vázquez, a renowned oncologist, has banned smoking in public places, the first Latin American country to do so. This is a major public health initiative, in a country where one-third of the population smoke.

Montevideo and the coast

To visitors it can seem as if all roads in Uruguay lead to the beach – not so surprising given that the country has one of the most attractive coastlines in the continent. Even the capital, **Montevideo ㉔**, is noted for its long beaches, and virtually all the country's principal tourist destinations are on the coast, linked by the *ruta interbalnearia* (interbeach route) running from Montevideo to Chuy, on the Brazilian border. Visitors who have had enough of the beach may want to head into the country and enjoy a slice of rural Uruguayan life on an estancia (ranch), sampling Uruguay's famous beef and wine. Rural activities range from horseback riding to wild boar hunting.

The most pleasant way to travel to Uruguay is to cross the River Plate from Buenos Aires. There is a choice of hydrofoil, catamaran, or ferry bus, taking between three and four hours. From the decks, the low hill that gave Montevideo its name comes slowly into view. Landing in Montevideo harbor and walking through the musty customs office may give you the sensation of going back in time. Cobbled streets are jammed with scooters, cyclists, and pedestrians. Uruguay's high import duty on automobiles has filled Montevideo's streets with vehicles that would be considered antiques elsewhere. (Uruguayan auto mechanics are said to be among the best in the world.) The rural air is reinforced every August with a farm show, held in the **Parque Prado**.

With a population of nearly 2 million, Montevideo is the only town of any size in Uruguay. Economic hard times have given it an elegantly shabby look,

BELOW: make do and mend in Montevideo.

Colorful hand-woven landscape.

although ceremonial occasions such as afternoon tea are as important as they are in Buenos Aires, as is the perpetual ritual of maté *(see page 315)* – you'll see people with their maté gourd and thermos of hot water on buses and in bank lines.

The best place to begin a tour of Montevideo is at the **Plaza Cagancha** (also called Plaza Libertad) on the main thoroughfare, Avenida 18 de Julio, named after the day in 1829 when Uruguay was finally freed of Argentine and Brazilian control. You'll find the main tourist office on Plaza Cagancha offering brochures and free city maps. Avenida 18 de Julio runs downhill past the **Gaucho Museum** at No 998 (open Mon–Sat), with its eclectic collection. The street leads to the city's main square, **Plaza Independencia**. To the left is an unattractive skyscraper known as the **Palacio Salvo**, which is, mysteriously, a beloved landmark for Montevideans. To the right is the Art Deco **Hotel Victoria** and in the middle of the square is the subterranean tomb and equestrian statue of General José Artigas. Also worth visiting are the cream-colored **Government House**, now used only for ceremonial purposes, and the jewel-like **Teatro Solís**, an exact copy of the Teatro María Guerrero in Madrid. Now renovated, the theater was established in 1856 and is still operating, making it one of the oldest theaters in the Americas.

Into the Old Town

BELOW: Plaza de la Independencia, Montevideo.

The archway at the west end of Plaza Independencia is part of the city wall that once protected Montevideo against its many invaders. It marks the entrance to the **Ciudad Vieja**, or Old Town, a neighborhood of narrow, winding streets and early 20th-century buildings. The heart of the Old Town is **Plaza Consti-**

ución. Here is the old *cabildo*, or town hall. Like the **Cathedral**, also in the square, it's been renovated but retains its colonial appearance. The cathedral dates from the beginning of the 19th century and is the oldest building in the city. The *cabildo* has a good **Museo de Historia** dedicated to the history of the city, containing clocks, furniture, and portraits. **La Bolsa** (the Stock Exchange), the **Banco de la República**, and the imposing **Aduana** (Customs House) are all north of the plaza and worth a look. Also intriguing is the **Palacio Taranco**, on the Plaza Zabala, the former home of a wealthy merchant who imported every stick of furniture and even the marble floors from France.

Following Calle Piedras down to the waterfront leads to the **Mercado del Puerto**, a lively market with a series of open-air restaurants at one end. The market is only open in the afternoons; it's as much about atmosphere as the produce on sale, and Saturdays are particularly lively.

From the old town there is a view across the port to the **Cerro**, the 139-meter (456-ft) hill that gave the city its name, topped with a lighthouse and fort.

A city of beautiful beaches

If the weather is good, try to visit one of the city's clean white-sand beaches. It also has two lovely parks of historical interest. The **Prado** is located northwest of downtown (follow Agraciada north from 18 de Julio) in a neighborhood where some of Uruguay's grand old houses still stand. It was once the property of a 19th-century financier named José Buschental, who built a 40-hectare (100-acre) estate here and married the niece of Emperor Dom Pedro II of Brazil. He brought fish from Asia as well as exotic plants and animals from around the world. This area has a statue of Buschental, as well as 800 varieties of roses.

In 1939 the great German battleship Graf Spee was sunk a couple of kilometers off Montevideo; its anchor can be seen in the port. The city stadium was built using metal plates from the leviathan's salvaged bulkheads.

BELOW: enjoying maté in the traditional way.

SHARING A MATÉ

Everything stops for maté in Uruguay – in fact, so important is this stimulating brew that many Uruguayans carry their own DIY maté kit around with them at all times. This usually consists of a drinking gourd known as a *culha* or maté, sometimes decorated with silver, containing *yerba* (dried leaves); a *bombilla* (drinking tube), which has a strainer at one end; and a hot-water flask.

Maté, or *yerba* maté, is brewed from the leaves of an evergreen plant, *Ilex paraguariensis*, which is related to the holly and grows wild in Paraguay and southern Brazil. The drink was popular with the Guaraní people in pre-Columbian times, and the leaves were first cultivated on a large scale by the Jesuits.

Maté is now an integral part of the culture of Uruguay, Paraguay, Argentina, and Brazil, with the gourd often shared between friends or family. Each guest drinks from the gourd and passes it back to the host to be refilled in turn.

Maté is usually drunk plain, but sometimes lemon juice, sugar, or even milk are added. Iced maté is also very popular. *Yerba* maté has diuretic and anti-rheumatic properties, and maté teabags are available in many northern hemisphere health shops.

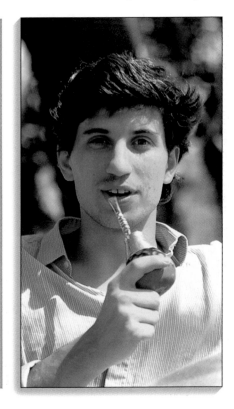

Parque Rodó, just behind the city's **Playa Ramírez** beach, is resplendent with palms, eucalyptus, and native *ombú* trees. It was named after José Enrique Rodó, one of the most prominent 19th-century South American writers, whose most famous work, *Ariel*, influenced a generation of intellectuals.

Promenades and smart hotels

In summer, many Buenos Aires political news articles are datelined Punta del Este – Argentina's movers and shakers are all at the beach.

The metropolitan beaches stretch east as far as **Carrasco**, a fashionable suburb with streets shaded by big trees and houses that belong to the few well-to-do people left in Uruguay. The rather run-down old casino still opens every season and is now undergoing a long-overdue face-lift. Montevideo's international airport lies just beyond Carrasco, 14 km (9 miles) from the city center.

Beyond Carrasco, the highway turns inland, but smaller roads branch off to the beaches. At Km 42, shortly before Atlántida, is the **Fortín de Santa Rosa** an 18th-century fortress converted into a hotel with a virtually private beach and an excellent restaurant. **Atlántida**, 45 km (28 miles) from Montevideo, is surrounded by a windbreak of cypress and eucalyptus. The beach also has a casino golf course, and tearoom. Just beyond Atlántida is **Piriápolis**, a pretty town on a curving bay with an old-fashioned promenade dominated by the imposing Argentino Hotel, a 1920s spa with mineral baths, stained-glass windows, and an elegant solarium where you may sip the curative sulfur-flavored water.

BELOW: an *asado* (barbecue) at the port markets.

The most famous beach on the Uruguayan coast is **Punta del Este** 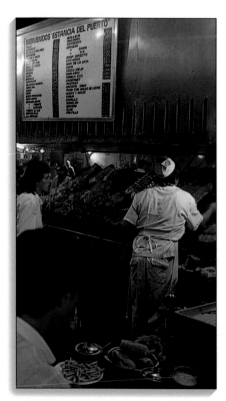, a jet-set-studded peninsula that attracts well-heeled Argentines as well as a fair share of international celebrities and European royalty. Prices at "Punta" make this primarily *porteño* resort an exclusive one. The peninsula has two long and beautiful beaches: the Atlantic one is more windswept than the tranquil bay side. Those who don't share the Argentine herd instinct might find Punta more attractive off-season, when hotel rates go down and cool autumn breezes clear the sand of body-to-body sunbathers.

North of Punta del Este, the Uruguayan Atlantic coast is rich with gorgeous seascapes and deserted white-sand beaches. Along the coastal highway toward Brazil, it's worth stopping at the 18th-century Portuguese fortresses of **Santa Teresa** 26 and **San Miguel** 27, now beautiful national parks and popular bird sanctuaries, and **Punta del Diablo**, an attractive fishing village with a number of small restaurants offering excellent seafood.

European communities

West of Montevideo are some interesting European settlements. **Colonia Valdense** was settled by Waldensians from the Piedmontese Alps, and **Colonia Suiza** is a small Swiss enclave, also known as **Nueva Helvecia**. Some 50 km (31 miles) west of Colonia Valdense is the 17th-century Portuguese town of **Colonia del Sacramento** 28. Colonia retains more of its original flavor than most cities in the region, partly because little has happened here since the Portuguese founded it as a rival to Buenos Aires in 1680, although in recent years many Argentines have bought land and houses here.

Sights to see in the old quarter include the **Museo**

Map
on pages
260–1

Español (Calle San José; Fri–Wed 11.30am–5pm), in a restored 18th-century viceroy's mansion; the **parochial church**; and the **Museo Portugués** (Plaza Mayor; Thur–Tues 11.30am–5pm), which has an excellent collection of mahogany and Cordoban furniture, and military uniforms. Narrow cobbled streets lead toward the river, where you can walk along the promenade to the remains of the colonial fortifications. A couple of miles further out stands a grandiose bullring, which has not been used since Uruguay outlawed bull-fighting at the beginning of the 20th century. A hydrofoil connects Colonia with Buenos Aires.

North along the River Uruguay

For Uruguayans, a trip up the River Uruguay is the patriotic equivalent of an American tourist's pilgrimage to New England. The small, tidy villages where nothing appears to be happening were at one time the crucibles of Uruguayan independence. About 30 km (18 miles) up the river from Colonia is **La Agra-ciada**, where the famous "Thirty-three Orientales" *(see page 31)* landed from Argentina and organized a battalion to expel the Portuguese from Uruguayan soil. A statue to General Lavalleja, the patriots' leader, is on the beach.

The port of **Fray Bentos** commemorates revolution of a different kind in its **Museo de la Revolución Industrial**. Fray Bentos was the site of the country's first meat extract factory. **Paysandú** ㉙, further upriver, is the town where Artigas led his followers when they fled Spanish rule in Montevideo. Today it's a popular spot for stalking the delicious *pez dorado* game fish. It's also where **Artigas Bridge** crosses the Uruguay River to Argentina. North of Paysandú are the remedial hot mineral springs of **Termas de Daymán** and **Arapey**. ❑

Browsing for bargains at the Sunday Tristan Narvaja fair.

BELOW: the fashionable Parque Hotel, Montevideo, c. 1920.

ARGENTINA

*Low prices and new-found stability make Argentina a
perfect destination, from passionate Buenos Aires to the
furthest reaches of its vast territory*

Map
on pages
260–1

T he second-largest country in South America and the eighth-largest in the
world, geographical magnitude is not the only grand aspect of Argentina. The
country is characterized by large cities, large ranches, large open spaces,
even large steaks. In the early 20th century, Argentina was one of the world's
richest nations and seemed set to become the Texas of South America. But instead,
the country became notorious for political drama and military dictatorships.

Argentina has always been heavily oriented toward its capital, Buenos Aires,
with the city sometimes described as a giant's head on a dwarf's body. Most of
the country's economic, political, financial, and industrial activity is focused on
the Buenos Aires area, implying that the distribution of wealth and resources is
extremely skewed. Despite periodic economic and political crises, many Argentines live well, enjoying restaurants, museums, and theaters. Throughout the
country, the urban middle class has its nearby beach, lakeside resort, ski center,
or mountain village retreat.

Argentina covers a range of latitudes, from the subtropical northeast, with
Jesuit ruins and the imposing Iguazú Falls, to the Andean northwest, changing
abruptly from barren mountains to lush greenery, with the colonial architecture of Salta and the sugar-producing province of Tucumán. Central Argentina
is characterized by spectacular mountain scenery,
vineyards, and impeccable urban planning in Mendoza; green mountains and lakes in Córdoba; and
attractive beach resorts in Buenos Aires province. In
the south, bleak oil towns co-exist with Welsh communities, pseudo-Tyrolean architecture, pretty towns
surrounded by snow-capped mountains and lakes, and
magnificent glaciers in the far south. All have a well
developed tourist industry with good transport links,
accommodations, and food.

PRECEDING PAGES:
late afternoon on
the pampas.
LEFT: pedestrian
mall of Lavalle,
Buenos Aires.
BELOW: tango hero
Carlos Gardel.

The people of Argentina

Argentines are known for strong localist tendencies
and a capacity to disdain those from the rest of the
subcontinent, tempered by a genuine instinct to be
hospitable. While the *porteños* (inhabitants of Buenos
Aires – literally "people of the port") see their city as
more sophisticated and cosmopolitan than the rest of
the country, many provincial cities – Tucumán, Mendoza, and Córdoba – have large populations of
second- and third-generation descendants of European and Arab immigrants, and are far enough away
from the capital to have developed an exciting cultural, artistic, and academic life of their own.

Very few indigenous peoples remain, with small
groups of Guaraní, Colla, Toba, and Wichi in the far
north and Mapuche in the south, marginalized by the
so-called "European" culture of Argentina.

Porteños, gauchos, and caudillos

In the 18th century, when Buenos Aires was thriving as a smuggling center, fortunes began to be made in cattle hides and mule breeding, and indigenous people were forced back from the pampas. Huge tracts of land were set aside for a few Spanish families, whose names would recur again and again as the power-brokers of Argentina. For 70 years after independence in 1816, civil wars raged, with Buenos Aires trying to impose central rule over local strongmen (caudillos), and their armies of gauchos – mestizo horsemen from the pampa *(see page 338)*. The most famous caudillo was Juan Manuel de Rosas, who rose from the chaos of civil war in 1829 to become governor of Buenos Aires province and de facto ruler of Argentina. Rosas is remembered for his reign of terror, enforced by secret police, and his nationalist policies, enabling Argentine goods to compete against foreign trade. After 23 years, he was thrown out and his supporters massacred. His protective tariffs were dismantled, and the country was flooded with foreign goods, while the civil wars resumed.

It was not until 1886 that the final step toward nationhood was made, when Buenos Aires was separated from its province and declared the capital of Argentina. The country's leaders were eager to appear cultured and urbane, notably Domingo Sarmiento, who divided the world into "civilization" – represented by all things European – and "barbarity": the caudillos, gauchos, and Amerindians. Codes were introduced to control the gauchos. General Julio Roca embarked on a "Conquest of the Wilderness" in the 1870s to open up the pampas and Patagonia. Any indigenous person in his path was killed, the rest herded into reservations. Cultivation of the pampas exploded to keep up with the new demand for beef. Railways were laid and Argentina was soon outstripping its rivals, Australia and Canada, in agricultural advances.

BELOW: a 19th-century painting of a gaucho and his *china*.

The immigrants arrive

Thousands of laborers were needed to keep the boom going. Before 1880, only a trickle of foreign workers stayed in Argentina. Overnight they became a flood. Most were poor peasants from northern Italy, with the next largest group coming from Spain. But Argentina's boom wealth was not shared among these new arrivals, and Argentina remained the property of around 200 close-knit families known as "the oligarchy". The result was a distortion in ownership that has stunted the country's growth and political life.

As the economy expanded, the new-found importance of Buenos Aires allowed it to shed the Hispanic colonial atmosphere and become an expression of all things French. The 16th-century street plan was cast aside and streets widened into grand avenues lined with marble footpaths, cafés, and jacaranda trees. But political and economic inequalities began rising to the surface. Protest movements against the oligarchs' grip produced the middle-class Unión Cívica Radical, forerunner of today's party of the same name. While tensions grew in the 1920s, Buenos Aires became the cultural mecca of South America. The rich indulged in tango parties and balls rather than worry about social ills. Then the Great Depression hit. Nobody was surprised when, on Sep-

Map
on pages
260–1

ember 6, 1930, the Argentine military marched into the Presidential Palace to take power under General José Uriburu. It was the first of many interventions.

The age of Perón

The military handed power over to a series of conservative governments in the 1930s, allowing the oligarchy to run the country as if nothing had changed in 40 years. Then, in 1943, a group of young army officers staged a successful coup. One of the figures in the new government was a man who founded a movement that still dominates Argentine politics: Juan Domingo Perón. Perón joined the army at 16, and became an ardent admirer of Mussolini while serving as military attaché in Italy. Perón took the post of Secretary of Labor and started to organize trade unions and to champion disenfranchized and unprotected workers. He was joined by the beautiful actress, Eva Duarte. The daughter of a peasant, Evita shocked high society but was worshiped by the working class for her passionate speeches on their behalf. Thanks to her, women got the vote and a public health service was developed.

Perón became president in 1946, nationalized industries, and started social welfare programs, while Eva toured Europe in jewels and couture dresses as if she were royalty. She died of cancer in 1952 at the age of 33, but the Vatican resisted calls for her canonization. The Perón magic quickly began to wear off: the cost of living was rising, government spending was out of control, and corruption rife. When it was rumored that Perón would distribute arms to the trade unions, the military struck, bombing the Presidential Palace and forcing Perón to flee on a Paraguayan gunboat. His supporters were purged from every level of government, and even mentioning Perón's name in public was banned.

BELOW: Eva and Juan Perón.

Lighthouse, Buenos Aires harbor.

BELOW: dancing on water, at Plaza Lavalle, Buenos Aires.

The "dirty war" and war with Britain

Despite the repression, Peronism lived on through 18 years of incompetent military and civilian rule. When full democratic elections were allowed in 1973, Peronist candidates won easily – and invited the aging founder back from exile in Spain to become president once again. Returning in triumph to Buenos Aires, Perón promptly died, leaving the presidency to his third wife, a cabaret dancer known as Isabelita. Argentina's economy nose-dived again, guerilla fighting began in the mountains in Tucumán, and terrorists began letting off bombs and kidnapping prominent figures. The military let the situation drag on until they had popular support for a coup in 1976. Then they began a "dirty war" to purge Argentine society of everyone suspected of left-wing sympathies. As many as 30,000 people were kidnapped, tortured, and secretly executed in the campaign.

But in 1982, with inflation reaching record levels and poverty growing, President Galtieri decided to distract attention by taking the Falkland Islands (Las Malvinas to the Argentines; *see page 350).* The possession of these windswept rocks had been contentious since the British annexed them in 1833. After a brief, bloody war (during which British Prime Minister Margaret Thatcher rejuvenated her electoral prospects on the back of her zeal to counterattack while the UN was still negotiating a peaceful solution) the Argentines were defeated and the humiliated military were forced to call democratic elections in 1983.

Radical candidate Raúl Alfonsín won the presidency and guided the country into a new democratic era. In 1989 the Judicialist (Peronist) party's candidate Carlos Menem won the presidential elections by a landslide. Menem imposed a series of draconian economic reforms and reformed the constitution to allow for his re-election.

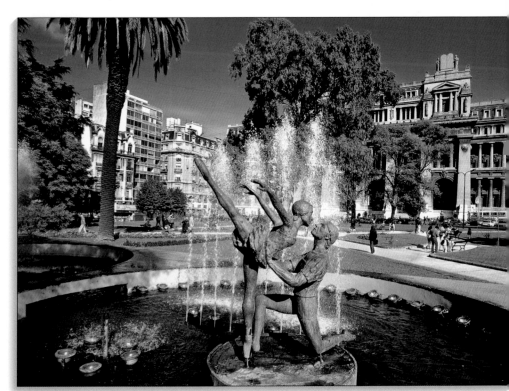

Recession and poverty

In 1998, Menem proposed further reforms to allow himself a third term, despite repeated allegations of corruption, but in October 1999 his 10-year tenure as president ended when Fernando de la Rúa, representing the Radical Civic Union, was elected. The recession rapidly worsened and poverty and unemployment rose sharply, with jobless rates at 25 percent and around half the population below the poverty line. One in four children was suffering from malnutrition – in a country capable of feeding 10 times its population.

The country was on the verge of imploding financially, politically, and socially. Bank accounts were frozen, and in December 2001 President Fernando de la Rúa resigned after 27 people died in food riots. Three days later Adolfo Rodríguez Saa was named interim president; he resigned a week later. On January 1, 2002, congress elected Peronist senator Eduardo Duhalde as caretaker-president. Days later, the government devalued the peso, ending 10 years of parity with the US dollar. Three months later, banking and foreign-exchange activity were suspended. Argentina seemed close to economic meltdown.

In 2002, the country defaulted on a US$800m debt repayment to the World Bank, after failing to secure IMF aid. Peronist governor Néstor Kirchner won the presidential run-off vote in 2003 when his rival, former President Carlos Menem, withdrew from the race. Accusations of fraud forced Menem to flee to Chile – a familiar South American scenario – but he returned in 2004 when arrest warrants were canceled. Under President Kirchner, Argentina regained its political and economic stability. The country paid off short-term IMF loans, and settled with many of its foreign creditors. Kirchner adopted more traditional Peronist policies, and took several key industries back into public ownership. At the end of 2007, Kirchner stood down as president, leaving his wife Cristina Fernandez de Kirchner as the Peronist candidate for the presidency. She won the election by a wide margin in the first round, and in December 2007 became Argentina's first elected female president.

Map on pages 260–1

Buenos Aires: a sophisticated city

Few countries are so gripped by their capital cities as Argentina is by **Buenos Aires** ㉚. Everyone and everything that passes through Argentina must at some stage come to "the Paris of South America." Sprawling over the flat, empty pampas, by the shores of the muddy Río de la Plata (River Plate), Buenos Aires flaunts its European heritage. It is a city of immigrants who always intended to return home, but still find themselves, somewhat uncertainly, in a remote land. But it is also a city with a creative energy that can put New York to shame. In good times or bad, you can see people of all ages enjoying a meal in a restaurant, lining up for a movie, or in deep discussion in a café.

Porteños are a special breed, renowned for their contradictions. Obsessed with style, they turn their city into an open-air fashion parade. They are in love with the theater, public debate, and the spectacle of politics. Privately, the dramas of the mind exert an endless fascination: Buenos Aires has more psychiatrists per head of the population than Manhattan.

BELOW: the Obelisk on Avenida 9 de Julio, the widest street in the world.

Beef and Red Wine

Long before arriving, you will have heard that Argentina is a carnivore's paradise. Although it is exported to many parts of the world, the best beef is consumed at home with an almost religious reverence. Until recently Argentina's fine wine was one of the country's best-kept secrets, with very little being imported overseas, despite being the world's fifth-largest producer. Today, Argentine wines are being appreciated on dinner tables worldwide. Taken together, a cut of beef with a bottle of red are both a simple meal and part of a gastronomic ritual that goes to the heart of the country's traditions.

Steak preparation is regarded as an art, and the *parrillas* (steak houses) on every corner in Buenos Aires can seem more like temples to beef than restaurants. The most extravagant have meat in their windows being cooked in traditional gaucho fashion, with whole carcasses crucified on metal crosses around a mound of coals. Others have

stuffed cows flanking the doorways, and over the tables are posters illustrating the cuts. The most expensive and leanest cut is the *bife de lomo*, roughly equivalent to a sirloin steak in other countries. The popular *bife de chorizo* is cut from the rib near the rump, while a *bife de costilla* is a T-bone.

In a class of its own is the *tira de asado*, which is a strip of rib roast usually large enough to feed two. The *parrillada* is a portable grill of mixed cuts, including plenty of offal and sausages – for the most committed carnivores. *Vacio* comprises the bottom part of what in the US is designated as sirloin, porterhouse, and the flank, and is the juiciest of all cuts. *Matambre* is shaped like a Swiss roll with a vegetable and hard-boiled egg filling. Often served cold, it can be an appetizer, or eaten inside French bread.

If you like your beef rare, order it *jugoso*; medium, *a punto*; and well done, *bien hecho*.

Steaks at an Argentine restaurant are unlikely to be sullied by vegetables, gravy, or sauces. The most common accompaniment is a salad, which can vary from lettuce and tomato to a giant mixed extravaganza with artichokes and eggs. For those whose taste buds require a little more than salt and flesh, order the *salsa chimichuri*. This oregano and spice mix is traditionally a gaucho's favorite. The flavor is considered so strong that asking for it often gets a grunt of respect from the most sombre waiter – although the spices are unlikely to surprise most foreign palates.

Argentina is the sixth-largest consumer of wine in the world. Grown near Mendoza and the drier stretches of the north near Salta, wines are both absurdly cheap and amazingly good. *Vino común*, served in jugs, is at the rougher end, but you will appreciate any of the inexpensive bottled *vino fino* on the wine list. Around 50 types of wine are produced; many European grapes are used, but Malbec and Torrontes are the local varieties. One positive thing to come out of the economic collapse is an increase in exports from the country's chief wine-growing region: Mendoza. And the US is one of the biggest foreign consumers. ❑

LEFT: meat is rarely off the menu in the restaurants of Buenos Aires.

A slice of Europe

Buenos Aires was founded more than 400 years ago, but it was virtually re-created at the end of the 19th century. Riding the beef boom of the 1880s, the city's Hispanic colonial buildings were leveled and replaced in the image of Paris. It was a time of tremendous wealth: Buenos Aires was a world center of fashion and high art, the cultural mecca of the Americas. But cracks were already appearing, and no sooner was the city built than the decline began. This sense of faded grandeur makes it a fascinating place to wander through. Buenos Aires is not so much a city of sights as of atmospheres, where the main pleasure is to stroll through the neighborhoods, stop for a coffee, stroll on again and absorb the everyday flavor of a city that seems to exist in a world of its own.

Map on page 329

El Centro

The center is carved up by wide avenues, lined by jacaranda trees and magnificent buildings that nobody has ever had the money either to knock down or restore. Bulbous cupolas protrude from roofs, windows are framed by statues of Greek gods, and hidden inside are chandeliers and marble stairways.

The natural spot to start is at the pedestrian walkway of **Florida**, which is crammed at every hour of the day with *porteños* trying to catch glimpses of themselves in window reflections as they pass. It is lined with boutiques selling Argentina's famous leather goods, although shoppers should control themselves until reaching the cheaper **Avenida Santa Fe** at the **Plaza San Martín**, where a dramatic statue commemorates one of the only heroes in Argentine history who commands universal respect. The better shops in Florida are also at this end, between Avenida Córdoba and Santa Fé. Intersecting Florida is another pedestrian mall, **Lavalle**, with movie theaters, bingo and video-game halls, restaurants, and bargain stores, and which can clog with people at night.

The colorful houses of La Boca, Buenos Aires.

BELOW: presidential guards on parade, Buenos Aires.

The presidential palace is called the **Casa Rosada**, (Pink House), for the tint of its masonry. It stands in the **Plaza de Mayo**, where guards in blue uniforms strut and parade, surrounded by schoolchildren. White headscarves painted on the ground commemorate the Madres de la Plaza de Mayo, who for many years after 1980 marched here every Thursday to demand information from the authorities about their "disappeared" children.

To the east of the Casa Rosada are the recycled 19th-century brick warehouses of the old port of Buenos Aires, now the smart area for working and eating out. An oasis of sun and silence at the edge of the bustle of the banking district, the **Puerto Madero** dockland development is an ideal place for a late afternoon drink on the promenade overlooking the water. At the other end of the plaza is one of Buenos Aires' few colonial buildings, the **Cabildo** or municipal palace. Inside this whitewashed edifice, which now houses a museum, the city's independence from Spain was declared in 1810. Next door is the **Catedral Metropolitana**, where General José San Martín is buried. The grand **Avenida de Mayo** stretches from here to the **Palacio del Congreso**, which looks like the White House in Washington DC. On the way, it crosses the **Avenida 9 de Julio**, which despite being

TIP

San Telmo's major event is the Sunday antiques market in the main square. Here you can scour hundreds of stalls for unique memorabilia of Argentina's past while live jazz is played in nearby cafés and buskers tango in the streets.

BELOW: looking for a gramophone? Try San Telmo.

the widest avenue in the world, manages to be clogged with traffic at most hours of the day. The street's crowning glory is the **Obelisco**, a rather tasteless phallic object around which the city revolves.

The nearby **Avenida Corrientes** is the show business heart of Buenos Aires, lined with bright lights, Art Deco theaters, and movie-theater palaces from the 1920s. Argentines prefer to eat dinner very late, and the restaurants along this street can be packed until 2am, while on Saturday night, the last movie session does not even begin until 1.30am. Corrientes is also noted for its dozens of bookstores, which are crowded with browsers until the early hours of the morning. The **San Martín Cultural Center** hosts art exhibitions, film festivals, and photographic displays.

A few blocks northeast, on Plaza Lavalle, is the sumptuous **Teatro Colón**, one of the world's great opera houses. A performance here should not be missed, if only for the experience of sitting back in wooden armchairs with plush velvet padding, looking out over six gilded tiers and gallery boxes. Guided tours are given daily of the theater's three floors of underground workshops and the small museum commemorating appearances by such greats as Melba, Nijinsky, Pavlova, and Caruso.

Café society

To understand Buenos Aires, try to do as the *porteños* do: spend as much time as is humanly possible in the *confiterías* or cafés of the city, watching the world go by. To the *porteño*, Buenos Aires is mapped out not by streets, landmarks, or barrios, but by key places to sit, write, think, and observe.

Two of the city's oldest and most venerable *confiterías* are located within walking distance of this area. The Ideal, on Suipacha, near Corrientes, was where the once sizable British community in Buenos Aires met for high tea every afternoon. These days you can still have tea and cakes surrounded by polished wood, brass, and marble pillars. Possibly the most famous of the *confiterías* is the Tortoni, on Avenida de Mayo and Piedras. In the 1920s it was the hang-out of bohemians such as the writer Jorge Luis Borges, listening to tangos, experimenting with cocaine, and debating politics. Its red leather chairs, sparkling mirrors, and chandeliers have changed little since that time, and every Friday night older patrons gather in a back room to hear the tango again.

Map below

Remnants of the colonial city

For a taste of Buenos Aires as it used to be, head for the artistic barrio of **San Telmo Ⓐ**, south of the Plaza de Mayo. During the 1700s it was the riverside hub of the city, with one third of its population black. Its cobbled streets are lined by low buildings, tango bars, and antiques shops.

The most surprising thing about the working-class suburb of **La Boca Ⓑ** is the sudden splash of color in an otherwise reserved city. Coming to life in the mid-19th century as the home for Genovese dock workers, this barrio by the river is famous for its houses of corrugated iron, all painted in different dazzling tones. The 20th-century Argentine painter Benito Quinquela Martín was a leading influence in the suburb's use of color, and his home has been turned into a gallery for his paintings of dock workers. By night, La Boca has a series of gaudy restaurants where bands play renditions of kitsch classics.

Colonial streetlight.

The city's upper crust fled to the **Barrio Norte** in the 1870s when yellow fever hit Buenos Aires. Today it is the most elegant and refined of barrios, where old ladies in minks sit under oak trees at outdoor cafés and business-

BELOW: colorful La Boca.

Dance of Passion

L oneliness and despair, jealousy, and homesickness – all are themes of tango, Argentina's most famous musical tradition. The accompanying dance is a demonstration of strutting Latin machismo: passionate, erotic, and flamboyant. So closely associated with the history of Argentina, tango is said to be a distillation of the national character. Where Brazil has the exuberant samba, *porteños* listen to the melancholy tango. True or not, the tango lingers throughout Buenos Aires like a perfume from another age.

The origins of tango can be traced to the slums of Buenos Aires at the end of the 19th century, where cultures from around the world were meeting – discharged soldiers from Argentina's civil wars, descendants of African slaves, and boatloads of Italian and Spanish immigrants. Overwhelmingly male, the new arrivals gathered in the bars and brothels. They shared the loneliness of exiles, mixing their national music to create the haunting

tango sound. The dance was invented before lyrics were introduced, usually performed by two males waiting in line at the local bordello.

Before long, the tango was gaining popularity amongst the *porteño* working class. By the early 20th century, the wheezing sound of the *bandoneón* (concertina) had been added to the guitar, flute, violin, and piano of tango ensembles. Writers even began putting their names to tangos. Only the snobbish upper classes kept aloof from the new rhythm, preferring to keep to their waltzes and polkas.

When the tango reached Europe, mothers in Edwardian England tried in vain to stem the popularity of the sensual dance, with its thrusting hip movements and intertwined limbs. Kaiser Wilhelm of Germany banned his staff from performing it. But for the rest of Europe, tango was the rage. And once the dance had succeeded in the salons of Europe, the Argentine upper crust accepted it wholeheartedly, agreeing with the French that it must be the very essence of Latin style.

In 1917, the little-known singer Carlos Gardel recorded the tango *Mi Noche Triste*. Almost overnight, the handsome figure became the first great tango star whose voice was heard around the world. Although arguments continue as to whether Gardel was born in France or Uruguay, he is remembered in Argentina as *El Pibe del Abasto* – the kid from the Abasto district of Buenos Aires. He became a movie star in Argentina, his place in the local pantheon assured when he was killed in an airplane accident in 1935 – as though Gardel were living out a tango himself. Today, new techniques are used to improve his old recordings, and in Buenos Aires they say: "Every day he sings better."

Tango fell into a lull in the 1950s until it was pushed in new directions by *tanguistas* like Astor Piazzola. Trained in classical and jazz music, he led a revival with his new, energetic arrangements. In the 21st century, tango is enjoying an extraordinary renaissance. At the beginning of the 1990s, it was only danced by aging locals in half-empty venues. Today, it is an exciting, fashionable pastime, practiced by trendy youths in steamy, underground dancehalls. ❑

LEFT: singing tango on the street, San Telmo.

men in European suits arrogantly order waiters about. The neighborhood is built around a giant walled cemetery, the **Recoleta** . Hundreds of ornate marble crypts contain the remains of the city's wealthiest families, with giant angels and grim reapers adding to the unsettling effect. The nation's great leaders, as well as their enemies, are buried here. The barrio is also home to the city's range of *albergues transitorios* – hotels rented out by the hour – where, overlooking the Recoleta necropolis, local denizens can steal a few hours of sensory gratification.

When the urban rush becomes too much and you feel the need for a view and fresh air, head for the **Costanera Norte**. A promenade runs along the brown Río de la Plata, where on a clear day you may be able to pick out the coast of Uruguay in the distance. Fashionable *parrillas* (grillhouses) line the road on the other side of the walkway, for when the exercise loses its charm. In October or November, a classic day can be spent at the polo by heading out to **Palermo** playing fields.

An alternative day-trip venue is the **Tigre Delta**, a weekend refuge for *porteños* of all ages for more than a century. Trains and buses are plentiful from central Buenos Aires, taking passengers to the quiet, tree-lined rivers and canals within an hour. Wooden ferries leave for destinations further into the delta, where French restaurants and guesthouses retain the genteel atmosphere of the 1930s.

Beaches, lakes, and mountains

About five hours' drive from Buenos Aires are the Atlantic coastal resorts of Mar del Plata, Villa Gesell, and Pinamar. **Mar del Plata** ⑪ is also accessible by air

To the disgust of the Argentine old wealth, the Recoleta's most famous occupant is the daughter of a provincial nobody – Eva Perón. Thousands visit her tomb every year, in a crypt of black marble which has a single rose before it.

BELOW: Mar del Plata.

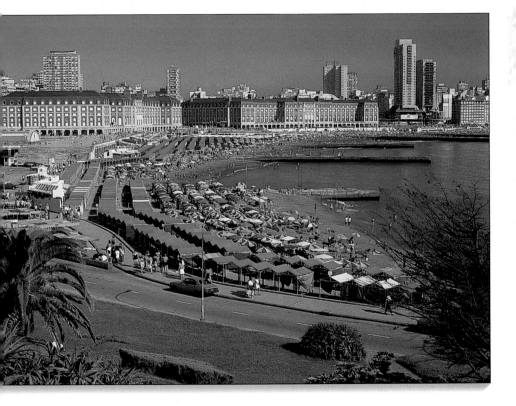

in about 30 minutes from Buenos Aires. By far the largest of the country's seaside towns, it has an enormous quantity of hotels at all prices, all of which fill up from mid-December to mid-February.

This very attractive city is the country's most popular resort, and has a long *rambla* (pedestrian area) along the coast, beginning at its famous casino. The beach becomes heavily overpopulated in summer, but suburban areas are reasonably peaceful throughout the year. There are many *confiterías* and restaurants serving excellent seafood, and a good variety of movie theaters and nightclubs. Further north on the coast, **Villa Gesell** and **Pinamar** are much smaller and more peaceful. Both towns have open spaces and wooded areas, in addition to their beaches, Pinamar being the more exclusive of the two, with more nightlife.

West to the land of wine and sun

The city of **Córdoba ㉜**, some 700 km (435 miles) northwest of Buenos Aires, is one of the country's cultural and religious centers, known for the number of lawyers and seminaries it houses. The university is one of the oldest and most distinguished in Argentina, and the city offers both well-preserved colonial architecture – especially in religious buildings – and an active modern urban life.

The lakeside resort of **Villa Carlos Paz**, a former German enclave which still slightly resembles a Bavarian village, lies 36 km (22 miles) west, in the green sierras of Córdoba. Villa Carlos Paz is often crowded with visitors in summer and is famous for its busy nightlife. Here, there is a wide range of hotels and restaurants, as well as beautiful scenery and access to the Sierra. To the north are **Cosquín**, a smaller town which hosts the National Folklore Festival every January, and **Río Ceballos**, a quiet place to enjoy the mountains and rivers, and to walk in the Córdoba range, which is less rugged than the Andes. All these towns are easily reached by excursions from Córdoba city.

BELOW: ceiling of Córdoba Cathedral.

Southwest of Córdoba, on the Chilean border, **Mendoza ㉝** is more a tribute to hard work and ingenuity than to Argentina's natural scenery. An arid province at the foot of the Andes, Mendoza attracted Italian and French settlers in the late 19th century who, with encouragement from the progressive provincial government, installed irrigation methods that allowed the province to become one of Argentina's principal agricultural zones. Known as "the land of sun and good wine," Mendoza is the country's principal area of wine production and vineyards, although its prosperity is also based on its significant oil reserves.

Mendoza is not as architecturally interesting as cities like Córdoba, due to earthquake devastation. However, it is by far the cleanest and tidiest city in Argentina, and full of trees planted to dispel the desert image. To the west of the city is the huge **Parque San Martín**, with hill-side views of the city, a lake, horse-drawn carriage rides, the local university, and a monument to San Martín, whose famous Andes crossing to Chile began at Mendoza. Public buses and organized tours go to the bodegas (wineries).

From the central plaza an attractive pedestrian precinct leads past the provincial legislature to **San Martín**, the main street. The attractive **Plaza España** was donated to the city by the Franco government in the 1940s and displays a beautiful collection of Spanish tiles, as well as an example of the Mendozan obsession with fountains, lawns, and trees. Mendoza is the base for a number of outdoor activities, including pony trekking and skiing, though the most exclusive center for skiing is the **Las Leñas** resort, roughly 400 km (250 miles) southwest of the city. Mendoza is also the base for committed mountaineers to explore the high peaks of the Andes, with Aconcagua (6,962 meters/22,840 ft) the highest of all.

Northern traditions

The north is the only part of the country where indigenous people still survive in significant numbers. The region gives visitors a fascinating glimpse into Argentina's colonial past and the Andean countries just across the border. It was here that the first Franciscan monks settled, coming south from Peru and building whitewashed chapels in the desert.

Tucumán ❸, 90 minutes from Buenos Aires by air or about 16 hours by bus, is known as the "cradle of independence," because Argentina's freedom from Spain was declared in the **Casa de la Independencia** in 1816. Nightly son et lumière shows are held here. On the **Plaza Independencia** is the neo-French style government house and the **Cathedral**. Nearby are the churches of **San Francisco** and the **Virgen del Rosario**. Near the main plaza, on and around Avenida 24 de Septiembre, are various crafts shops and a number of restaurants offering excellent regional specialties. The tourist office and the **Museo Folklórico** (open daily) are also on Avenida 24 de Septiembre.

Leaving Tucumán by bus or car for Tafí del Valle, the road winds through mountainous terrain with subtropical foliage, rivers, and waterfalls, as well as

Map on pages 260–1

Jesuit church tower, Alta Gracia.

BELOW: Argentina's arid north.

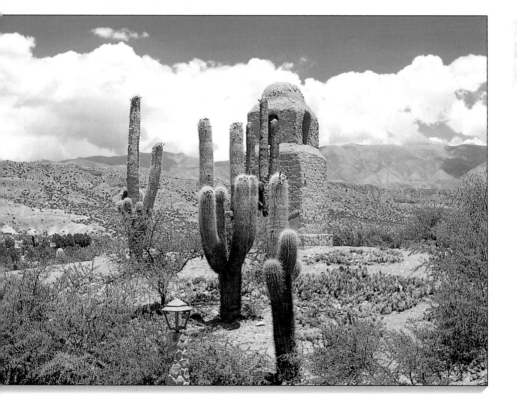

the El Cadillal reservoir near Tafí, an attractive mountain village favored by *tucumanos* for summer holidays. To the north of Tafí, the mountains become dry and moonlike before arriving at Quilmes, the well-preserved remains of an Amerindian village (open daily 9am–6pm) dating back to the 11th century. Some 20 km (12 miles) further north is Amaicha del Valle, the only village in Argentina where indigenous people hold the title to their ancestral lands. The Fiesta de la Pachamama (Mother Earth Festival) is held here in February. Santa María, 10 km (6 miles) away, is an attractive place turned boomtown by the nearby Bajo La Alumbrera gold and copper mine. About an hour beyond Santa María is Cafayate, a pretty town surrounded by wineries. The scenery between Tucumán and Cafayate (about a six-hour drive) is among the most breathtaking and varied in Argentina.

Colonial churches and markets

Salta ㉟ is an open, relaxed town that can be used as a base to explore the surrounding provinces. Neo-colonial buildings line the straight streets that head toward the mountains, often little more than outlines obscured by dust. The center of town is an unexpectedly green plaza with well-preserved Spanish and Italian-style buildings. Most of the city's best colonial buildings are on La Florida and Calle Caseros, which has the **Casa Uriburu**, housing a colonial-era museum (open Tues–Sun); the Iglesia de San Francisco; the Convento de San Bernardo; and the **Cabildo** (City Hall), housing the **Museo Histórico del Norte** (open Tues–Sun). Most of the rooms are devoted to European-Argentine heroes from the Wars of Independence, with paintings of their deeds alongside medals, vests, and gloves. The Amerindian section, covering the Incas and their customs,

BELOW: corn on the cob for sale.

contains a dry and poorly explained collection of pots and pans. For an altogether different view of the city, take the cable car up to Cerro San Bernardo.

The north of Argentina is saturated by religion but visitors to Salta may be surprised by the number of churches and statues dedicated to San Francisco. The **Cathedral** contains the town's pride and joy: the Virgin and Cristo del Milagro, statues carved in the 16th century and credited with miraculous powers. The ship carrying them from Spain was wrecked, but the figures were washed up on the Peruvian shore. Then in 1692, an earthquake in Salta was dramatically halted when the statues were paraded in the streets. The simple, almost childlike figures are almost lost in the huge baroque altar. Across the aisle, the faithful pray before a life-sized effigy of Christ fresh from the cross, complete with vast holes in his chest and a virtual fountain of fake blood. Depictions of suffering in colonial religious art had to be horrific if they were to impress indigenous people as worse than their own lives.

For a change of pace, one of the most exciting trips from Salta is to take *El Tren a las Nubes* – the Train to the Clouds. Due to the height at which the train travels it is quite common to see clouds under its bridges. Fully equipped with a dining car, this poetically named service leaves Salta for a spectacular journey through nearby mountains. It climbs through the barren **Quebrada del Toro** across steel span bridges to the small town of **San Antonio de los Cobres** at 4,000 meters (13,000 ft) in the Andes, to its highest point at **Abra Chorrillos** (4,475 meters/14,680 ft) and then to the Chilean frontier at **Socompa** ㊱. The whole trip takes almost 15 hours, crossing 29 bridges and 13 viaducts in all.

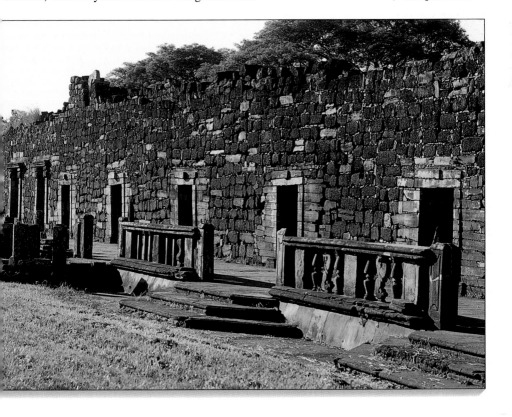

Map on pages 260-1

Toward the Bolivian frontier

A highway heads north from Salta to **Jujuy** ㊲. The population becomes more indigenous the closer you get to the Bolivian border, while the road gets rougher, the houses poorer, and the religious imagery stranger. Tiny chapels can be seen in the most remote villages. One of the most curious, in **Uquaia**, contains the *Angeles Arcabuceros*: a painting of angels dressed as 17th-century musketeers.

The road climbs to over 3,000 meters (9,800 ft) and the countryside dries out completely along the *quebrada* (gorge) of the **Río Grande**. Odd land formations appear: some mountains are sharp triangles, others seem to spill like molten lava, while others look like decayed ants' nests. The sides of the gorge range in color from purple to yellow: near the village of Purmamarca is the famous "hill of seven colors", while nearby **Tilcara** boasts a pre-Columbian fortress and is home to many potters and weavers. The town of **Humahuaca** ㊳ is almost in Bolivia. In early afternoon it becomes an empty dust bowl, with winds sweeping from the valleys to cover everything with orange powder. The only sound comes from the 16th-century church. The town has several guesthouses and restaurants, and is not far from the extensive archeological site of **Coctaca**, whose mysteries are still being unraveled.

BELOW: Jesuit ruins, San Ignacio Miní.

Humahuaca is dominated by a huge iron monument to Argentina's 19th-century war of independence. An artistic sleight-of-hand has given the fierce figures staring down over Humahuaca Amerindian faces.

Misiones and the Jesuit ruins

Sticking out like a crooked finger from the northeast of Argentina, the subtropical province of **Misiones** boasts some unexpected associations. Graham Greene used its wet and steamy towns as the setting for his novel *The Honorary Consul*, where expatriate Britons and South American revolutionaries accidentally meet. More recently, the award-winning movie *The Mission,* which was shot in the area, publicized the province's 18th-century Jesuit empire.

A visit to the region usually begins in the provincial capital of **Posadas ❸❾**, which is accessible from Buenos Aires by daily flights. The town has a Paraguayan handicrafts market and several museums. A highway escapes north from the town into the rich green countryside, kept lush by regular downpours. The road follows the flood-prone **Río Paraná**.

It was in this same region in the 1600s that the teams of Jesuit priests began setting up their mission stations *(see page 272)*. At their height in the 18th century, they housed 100,000 of the local Guaraní people, studying, growing grain, and carving musical instruments which became renowned in the finest courts of Europe. Today, the ruins of the greatest Jesuit mission at **San Ignacio Miní ❹❶** (open Mon–Fri, 7am–7pm, with a nightly son et lumière show), just a two-hour drive from Posadas, are announced by the unfortunate marriage of a piece of Jesuit art caught in a concrete military bridge, designed by a former province governor. The grounds themselves are more tastefully kept. Bus loads of visitors wander among the old Jesuit living quarters and cathedral, decorated with indigenous carvings of celestial beings and stars. Outside, the priests' gravestones bear simple messages: "Here Lies Father Juan, a good man." Other Jesuit ruins can be found nearby, mostly overgrown by jungle. Sitting amongst these shattered relics of their religious empire, it is difficult to contemplate the experiment that flourished here for over 150 years. While indigenous people in the rest of South America were being brutally exploited on plantations, here they were working and learning in a system that has earned the praise of many modern socialist writers. The Jesuit priests distributed grain according to need, and arranged indigenous armies to keep out slave traders.

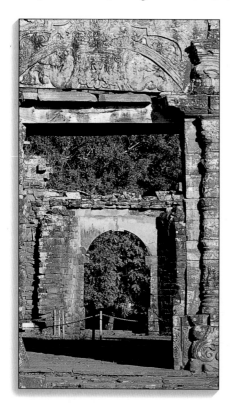

BELOW: Jesuit ruins, San Ignacio.

Only when the Jesuits were expelled was the fatal flaw of the system revealed. The priests had ruled a paternalistic order, never training the Amerindians to run it themselves. With the Jesuits in exile, slave traders were more successful, the crops failed, and the Guaraní people fled back into the jungle. Today, their descendants have returned to the ruins – selling plastic flutes and feathers to tourists.

Iguazú Falls

The other great attraction of Misiones is a few hours further up the highway to the border with Brazil: the magnificent **Cataratas del Iguazú ❹❶**. The falls can be reached from the commercial center of **Puerto** guazú. This spectacle is one of South America's most extraordinary sights. Vast torrents of water thunder over the various cascades with such force that most visitors wear waterproof raincoats for protection from the violent spray. The falls are divided between Brazil and Argentina – while the Brazilian side is most spectacular, the Argentine side is more pleasant to explore – but to see them properly one must visit both sides. If attempting to do so in a day (which is possible, with some effort – and don't forget your passport), it's best to start out on the Brazilian side. Though more removed from the falling waters, the Brazilian vantage point gives a much more panoramic view of the immense cascade. The light there is best in the morning for photographers.

The Brazilian side also gives the best views of the most spectacular section of the falls, the roaring **Devil's Throat**. Fourteen falls combine forces in their 100-meter (330-ft) fall, pounding the water below with such force that there is constantly a huge rainbow-spanned cloud of spray hovering above them. Swallows make their nests under the roaring waterfalls. A catwalk on the Brazilian side, reached by a winding foot trail and an elevator, gives more intimate views. Helicopter rides are also available but disturb local wildlife.

Cacique birds' nests.

A stop at the Argentine interpretive center can provide much useful information about the falls and surrounding flora and fauna. A train service takes visitors to the start of two walking trails, which explore the Argentine falls, including one that takes visitors over the water rushing into **Devil's Gorge**. It's also possible to climb down a series of trails and stairways to the river below, where a short (recommended) boat trip takes visitors to the island of San Martín, making a pass close to one of the falls. The climb back up is strenuous, and should be attempted only by those in good shape.

BELOW:
Iguazú Falls.

The Gaucho

Scattered through the estancias of the Argentine hinterland are horsemen wearing a uniform from the country's distant past: black Spanish hats, woven Amerindian shawls, baggy pants known as *bombachas,* and carrying deadly knives called *facones.* They are the last descendants of a breed of South American cowboys, the gauchos.

From the early days of Spanish settlement, individuals disappeared to the countryside and mixed with the local population. Fleeing criminals, escaped slaves, and deserting militiamen lived at the fringes of society and were known as *la gente perdida:* the lost people. They developed their own harsh, nomadic lifestyle on the pampas, taming wild horses to ride and slaughtering escaped cattle, while learning how to hunt with the skillful use of lassos and the *boleadores*: three balls connected by ropes that could wrap around the legs of any running target. Soon known as

gauchos – the name may have derived from the local word for "orphan" – they had a growing reputation for gambling, horsemanship, and knife fighting. Women, called *chinas*, played a subsidiary role in this macho lifestyle. Often kidnapped from settlements, they raised children in small huts indistinguishable from those of the indigenous population.

But in the late 18th century, large tracts of pampas land was distributed to prominent *porteños*. Fences were put up in the grasslands and gauchos were seen as little better than cattle thieves. Many grudgingly signed up as ranch hands, working for subsistence wages on the lands they once roamed.

When the British took Buenos Aires in 1806, many gauchos were pressed into the army. After independence, they joined up with the private armies of provincial caudillos, who allowed them to indulge in their usual drinking, gambling, and knife fighting for several decades without undue molestation. But as the era of civil wars drew to a close, the days of the gaucho were numbered. New codes were introduced to regulate their movements, dress, drinking habits, and diet.

Soon the gaucho was a symbol of the backward, chaotic Argentina that the statesmen of Buenos Aires wanted to destroy. Gauchos were described by Domingo Sarmiento as "biped animals of the most perverse stripe" whose carcasses were only good to fertilize the earth. Barbed-wire fences hindered their movements still further – the gaucho was being eliminated as a distinct social grouping.

As this was happening in the 1870s, José Hernández wrote in two parts his classic epic poem, *The Gaucho Martin Fierro*, which lamented the passing of the wild frontier past.

By 1926, when the second great literary work on gauchos appeared, *Don Segundo Sombra* by Ricardo Güiraldes, the gaucho was nothing more than a literary memory. This does not mean to say that there are not glimpses of their lost culture in the Argentina of today. In the furthest reaches of the country, on remote farms in Salta and Patagonia, hands still wear traditional gaucho dress – even if they are as likely to be driving a Land Rover as riding a horse.   ❑

LEFT: gaucho on a Buenos Aires estancia.

Map on pages 260–1

The Argentines have created a national park adjacent to the falls, where there s a jungle trail posted with information, and a bird hide overlooking a swamp. A trek through the park can take most of the day. In the evening, catch a bus to **Puerto Canoas**, where the day's dying light heightens the beauty of Devil's Gorge as swallows dive into their nests in the walls behind the tumbling water.

Iguazú Falls are best visited in fall and spring – summers are intensely hot and the busiest time for tourists, while the water level drops considerably in winter. There are hotels on both the Brazilian and Argentine sides. Near the falls a marker shows the point at which Paraguay, Brazil, and Argentina all converge.

The only sight capable of crowning the Iguazú experience is **Moconá Falls**, where the River Uruguay falls into itself in a fault more than a kilometer long, not far from the Brazilian town of **Tenente Portela**. For a panoramic view, take a ferry to Brazil from the Argentine town of **El Soberbio**. Boat trips are on offer in the same town for those craving a close-up white-water view.

Iguazú means Great Waters in Guaraní – a fitting name for the most spectacular waterfalls in the western hemisphere. Taller than Niagara Falls by 20 meters (65 ft) and twice as wide, Iguazú Falls consists of 275 cascades over a gulf of nearly 3 km (2 miles).

Bariloche: Switzerland in the Andes

Strategically placed between the towering Andes and the plains of Patagonia, for six months of the year **San Carlos de Bariloche ㊷** is a booming vacation resort with a unique alpine flavor. Summer (December to March) brings hordes of travelers enjoying walks amongst the lush forests, spectacular glaciers, and mountains of the surrounding Lake District. Later, the winter snows (June to September) bring South America's select set of affluent skiers to the Andean slopes, filling Bariloche's restaurants by night with raucous fireside carousing. The remaining neglected months of the year are perhaps even more delightful: in spring, the valleys of the Lake District are filled with flowers and greenery, while fall brings the slow shift of the forest colors to red, orange, cinnamon, and ochre.

The alpine atmosphere attracted Swiss, German, and Austrian settlers at the end of the 19th century. Today the town itself is a reproduction of a Tyrolean skiing village. Many of the buildings are designed like chalets, while the streets are full of chocolate shops and restaurants offering Swiss fondue, trout, and roast venison. But the real attraction is the surrounding countryside. Bariloche's setting, by the shores of **Lake Nahuel Huapi**, surrounded by jagged brown mountains, is spectacular. In the distance you can spot the towering **Mount Tronador**, the highest peak in the region at 3,554 meters (11,660 ft).

Begin your visit by going to the **Patagonian Museum** near the **Civic Center** (Tues–Fri 10am–12.30pm and 2–7pm, Sat 10am–5pm). It relates the region's history from the days when indigenous nomads roamed the countryside, covered from head to toe in animal grease for warmth, to the arrival of the first white pioneers. Outside in the square is a statue of General Roca, leader of the desert campaign which led to the virtual extermination of local tribes.

Dozens of tour companies offer visits to the surrounding attractions – alternatively, you can hire a car in Bariloche to explore the dirt roads and byways of this magnificent region on the border of Chile. The *circuito chico* or "short circuit" runs out along Lake

BELOW: St Bernard dogs in front of the Centro Cívico, Bariloche.

Ski school plaque, Bariloche.

BELOW: Lake
Nahuel Huapi and
Cerro López.

Nahuel Huapi to the Hotel Llao Llao. Refurbished and reopened after years o
neglect, it reflects the glory of its heyday in the 1940s. Boats run from the dock
of Bariloche to **Isla Victoria**, whose myrtle forests are said to have inspire
some of Walt Disney's advisers when drawing backgrounds for *Bambi*. Con
tinuing around the circuit is the path to **Cerro López**. In summer, the peak ca
be climbed to a refuge run by Club Andino, where hikers can stay overnight. O
a clear day the summit offers spectacular views over the lakes and mountains o
the region to Chile. Day trips can also be taken from Bariloche to **Cerro Tron
ador**, **Cerro Catedral**, **Cerro Otto**, and the waterfalls of **Los Cesares**. Th
region is world-famous for its trout fishing from November to March, and i
summer there is sailing and windsurfing on the lakes.

Exploring the wild countryside

Also passing through some of the world's most magnificent scenery is the so
called route of the seven lakes, which winds along the border with Chile.
leads to the small town of **San Martín de los Andes ⓭**, a more up-marke
tourist destination than Bariloche, often used as a base for hikes, camping trip
and skiing. The return trip over the **Córdoba Pass** runs through the lowe
regions of Neuquén province, much drier and closer to the Patagonian waste
Fingers of stone protrude from thorny expanses, in what one English traveler i
1920 compared to the prehistoric *Lost World* imagined by Scottish novelist S
Arthur Conan Doyle. Many of the estancias or ranches of the region are still ru
by the descendants of foreigners and worked by Chilean peons (farmhands) o
weather-beaten gauchos, whose ponchos, knives, and *bombachas* are definite
ly not worn just for tourists.

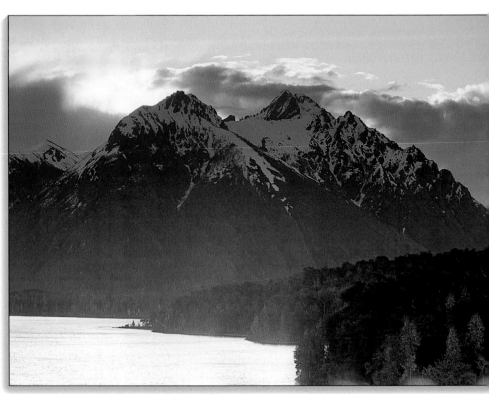

For a longer excursion, an overnight trip can be made to **El Bolsón**, once a hippy refuge of the 1960s, now a tourist and fishing resort with a twice-weekly handicrafts market. Further south, a road cuts through the serene **Cholila Valley** to **Esquel ㊹**. First settled by the Welsh, it is now the base for visiting **Parque Nacional Los Alerces** and the gateway to the **Chubut Valley**. The national park, dotted with lakes and crossed by streams, features walking trails and horseback riding opportunities. Standing by the shores of the lake is **Estancia Nahuel Huapi**, founded by a Texan cowboy named Jared Jones in 1889. The house, which is still standing, was a refuge for Butch Cassidy and the Sundance Kid, on the run from the Argentine authorities, having brought their Wild West ways to the new frontier of Patagonia in the early 1900s.

Wild, windswept Patagonia

Way down at the chilly southern end of South America, Patagonia has for centuries been a byword for the remote and the strange. But today Patagonia is linked to Buenos Aires with daily flights, and by bus for those with enough time to fully appreciate the size of this flat, empty plain that takes up one-third of the country's landmass. Heading south, the rich cattle country dries out and becomes divided into sheep stations. As recently as the 19th century some of these ranches were bigger than small European countries, with their owners ruling like royalty.

First stop is the city of **Trelew ㊺**, surrounded by dry bluffs and dusty scrub. Thousands of Welsh colonists came here after 1865, fleeing their homeland, where their culture and language were being repressed by the English, to set up a "Little Wales" in the middle of nowhere. Despite some early disasters, the colony began to succeed. The Welsh used their irrigation skills to make the

Map on pages 260–1

BELOW: a Welsh tea house in Gaiman.

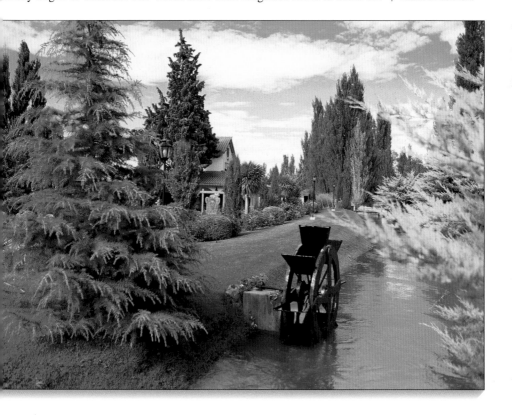

desert bloom, and soon Patagonian wheat was winning prizes at international shows. Welsh was spoken in the streets and taught in the schools. But by the beginning of the 20th century, things were going awry in Trelew. The Argentine Government had imposed its authority on the town and many Spanish-speaking immigrants, attracted by the Welsh success, had arrived with their families. Floods devastated the area's crops. Many settlers left for Canada or Australia, but the core of the community stayed on, their Welsh nationalism slowly being diluted by intermarriage with Spanish speakers.

Today, Trelew looks much like other provincial Argentine towns, although the street signs are still in Welsh. Echoes of its origins can be found in the old Hotel Touring Club, with cracked windows and an antique wooden bar full of old men playing chess on quiet afternoons. Many of the town's elders still speak in their native Welsh to one another, using Spanish when necessary. For a taste of the Welsh colony as it once was, take a half-hour bus ride to the village of **Gaiman**. Built around the irrigation canals that converted the desert into an oasis, Gaiman has a number of Welsh teahouses serving up Welsh cream pastries to passing visitors. A small museum located in the old railway station is well worth a visit.

Whales and frontier towns

Easily reached from Trelew is the famous **Península Valdés** ⓐ, which contains some of the world's most spectacular wildlife. Charles Darwin spent weeks here on his famous journey in the *Beagle*, and today tourists come to watch the sea lions yawning by the rocky shore and hundreds of penguins wandering in lines to the sea. During September and October, enormous right whales can be seen throwing up their tail fins as they mate dramatically offshore.

The Portuguese explorer Fernando Magellan, the first European to see Patagonia, reported it to be full of dog-headed monsters and natives with steaming heads.

BELOW: rounding up sheep, Patagonia.

Flying south from Trelew, the Patagonian plain below looks increasingly desolate. Towns like **Comodoro Rivadavia** ❹❼, once center of an oil boom, and **Río Gallegos** ❹❽ 3,000 km (2,000 miles) south of Buenos Aires, are devoid of rural charm. Unfortunately, because most flights pass through here, many travelers end up spending a night. Nothing much has happened since 1905, when Butch Cassidy and the Sundance Kid held up a bank on the main street.

Changing to a small propeller-driven plane in Río Gallegos, a one-hour flight cuts west across the plains to the foothills of the Andes and some of the most magnificent scenery in South America. The village of **El Calafate** ❹❾ is surrounded by snowcapped mountain peaks and sits next to **Lago Argentino**, which seems to be full of turquoise milk rather than water. This remote village is enjoying a boom as the stepping-off point to the huge blue glaciers wedged in the forest-covered countryside nearby.

The most famous is **Perito Moreno** ❺⓿, in a national park of the same name, a 50-meter (160-ft) high wall of ice which cuts through a lake. It cracks and growls throughout the day, with enormous chunks of ice regularly falling from its side to send waves of water thundering to the shore. The glacier is still advancing in four-year cycles. Blocking off part of the lake, the water level rises until the glacial wall collapses in a spectacular scene lasting several hours.

From Calafate you can visit the sheep estancias of Argentina's deep south, where the occasional gaucho figure still works. Sheep-raising is a key industry in Patagonia, and between October and January, traveling teams of workers arrive for the shearing season. **La Anita** became notorious in 1921, when the whole of Patagonia was paralyzed by a strike of farmhands, known as *peones*. The organizer was a young Spanish anarchist named Antonio Soto, who had

Steaks for an asado.

Map on pages 260–1

BELOW: the Perito Moreno glacier.

wandered through the country from Buenos Aires to Patagonia. The mostly British *estancieros* called on the government for help, and the army ended the strike, with bouts of shooting followed by mass executions. One of the biggest of these was at La Anita – although it has since changed hands, and hardly anybody remembers where the 200 or so workers are buried.

Located a few hours from Calafate is the **Parque Nacional Fitzroy**, where you can pass from the windswept plains to lush and wet forest amongst the snowcapped Andes. Hikes through the park cross mountain streams and landscapes reminiscent of Scottish moors. Clouds are constantly billowing overhead, but on a good day you can often catch a glimpse of Mount Fitzroy, a sheer knife of granite that is a favorite with fearless mountaineers.

Tierra del Fuego: last stop before Antarctica

It is the forbidding image of Tierra del Fuego that paradoxically lures travelers to the southernmost tip of South America. It was named "land of fire" by Magellan, who saw mysterious fires in the darkness when first passing the island.

For centuries afterwards, Tierra del Fuego was feared by sailors for the icy Antarctic winds that blew their ships toward jagged rocks. Few of them considered **Ushuaia** ⓯, the world's most southerly town, an attractive refuge from the storms. Over the years it progressed from a primitive whaling station to a prison colony where Russian anarchists lived out their last days. Today, the land at the end of the world can be reached by daily flights from Buenos Aires. Ushuaia is no longer the wild and wooly outpost it once was, but more an odd blend of modern tourist center, Klondike-style boomtown, and the gateway to one of the world's last great wilderness areas.

BELOW: penguin colony at Punto Tombo, near Trelew.

The northern half of the island is flat sheep-farming land – much like the rest of Patagonia – but the south is rugged and thickly forested. Approaching Ushuaia by plane is suitably dramatic, since the town is surrounded by snow-capped claws of granite. The dominating peak, **Mount Olivia**, would suit a Walt Disney wicked witch for its mist-shrouded and vaguely evil appearance. The weather lives up to Tierra del Fuego's reputation: even during the 20 or more hours of summer daylight, it shifts erratically from cold drizzle to perfectly cloudless skies, with the only constant being a gusty southern wind.

Ushuaia itself is far from being a picturesque pioneering town. It is home to a large naval base, government offices, and stores for imported goods. Houses with decorative cornices built by prisoners are still scattered in the older part of town and have a somewhat Russian flavor. They are intermingled with modern concrete structures, imported Swedish prefabs, and hundreds of small, wooden shanties. Usable land is in short supply in the area hemmed in by mountain and sea; new houses climb the mountainsides and many people live in poor conditions. Nevertheless, subsidized building and improvements are going on everywhere. The main street is like an open-air department store, with duty-free electronic goods being offered. One of the town's claims to fame is the Bank of Tierra del Fuego, which is the world's first financial institution to have a branch in Antarctica.

Housed in a former prison, the **Museo Marítimo** and **Museo del Presidio** (daily 9am–8pm) provide an interesting glimpse into the town's role as a penal colony. The **Beagle Channel**, on which the town sits, was named after the boat that carried Charles Darwin here in the 1830s for his famous wildlife studies. Boat trips can be taken on the channel past mountains dropping sheer into the water, circling islands populated by penguins or sea lions.

Map on pages 260–1

BELOW: Ushuaia, the world's southernmost town.

Map on pages 260-1

At one time Argentina had 80 million sheep and was one of the world's largest wool producers. Today, there are only 30 million.

BELOW: a group of Ona Amerindians, before they were wiped out by settlers.
RIGHT: sleepy elephant seal.

Windswept wilderness

Parque Nacional Tierra del Fuego is the main attraction of Ushuaia because of its easily accessible wilderness area. The walking here is simply magnificent, following the spectacular coastline to lakes and glaciers. The park preserves the sense of being at the end of the world, with paths that wind around spongy moss oozing cold water, past tough shrubs and thorny bushes and trees that the wind has bent 45 degrees. The path to **Bahia Ensenada** passes an encouraging altar to the Virgin of Luján, Argentina's patron saint of travelers. There is a camping ground at the rocky beach, where you can breakfast on sweet calafate berries. Stepping stones lead to **Bahia Lapataia**, where you can pick fresh mussels from the sea. A picturesque narrow-gauge train will take you into the Tierra del Fuego National Park along a route formerly used to transport prison inmates to cut timber for houses.

Just three hours' drive from Ushuaia along a winding dirt road is **Harberton** *(see below),* the first estancia on Tierra del Fuego. Founded by the Rev. Thomas Bridges in 1888, it is open to tourists, with guides in English and Spanish. Harberton is worth visiting not just for its history but for the beauty of its setting. Surrounded by trees and flowers, perched above the blue Beagle Channel, it seems like the calmest place on earth.

Back in Ushuaia, shops are full of books on the local Ona people, but they are dull, anthropological works written as if they were still wandering around the countryside. The rumors of murders are denied or forgotten, with only a few scraps suggesting the contrary: a ledger showing that only women and children were brought back from raids; a photo in a Liverpool newspaper showing a mass grave found by police. The final certainty of the destruction of these tribes is that the only fires now burning in Tierra del Fuego are from the oil rigs off its coast. ❏

A GRISLY PAST

The good Reverend Thomas Bridges spent much of his time in Harberton in the late 19th century working with the Ona people and writing a dictionary of their complex Yaghan language. To his dismay, he could see before his death that the lists of words would soon be the only monument to those who spoke them. As the British writer Bruce Chatwin noted, Darwin's theory of "survival of the fittest" was put into brutal practice in the 1890s. The indigenous people of the area, who had lit the fires that Magellan saw, occasionally killed and ate the sheep brought onto their land by European settlers. The newcomers decided to remove this "pest" en masse. Official records show that most of these people died of disease, but the folk memory persists of active resistance, battles, and massacres.

The most grisly tale is of white bounty hunters being paid £1 sterling per pair of Amerindian ears. Old-timers tell of such gruesome characters as the Scotsman Alex MacLennan, nicknamed the Red Pig, famous for his drunken ravings about killing indigenous folk. The Englishman Sam Hyslop, who is credited with gunning down 80 people of the Ona tribe, was caught by Amerindians and flung from a cliff.

THE FALKLAND ISLANDS

These tiny, windswept islands in the South Atlantic were at the center of a violent international conflict in the 1980s. Now peace has returned to the sheep pastures and penguin colonies

PRECEDING PAGES: windswept solitude in the Falkland Islands. **BELOW:** Magellanic penguins.

Some 500 km (300 miles) off the coast of Argentina, the Falkland Islands (Las Malvinas to Argentines) offer the type of treeless, windswept, austerely beautiful landscapes similar to the Orkney and Shetland islands in Scotland. Attempts have been made to plant trees with little success. Like Scotland, the islands offer four seasons in one day, with sun, wind, and rain coming and going in a matter of minutes; also similar to Scotland are the hills and valleys uncharacteristic of flat Patagonia. There are southern desert-like landscapes, tall grass, and wild flowers, though in places the scenery is marred by signs warning of minefields left over from the 1982 war (some 17,000 mines remain in certain areas hidden beneath sandy beaches).

With an area of some 12,000 sq. km (4,633 sq. miles), the islands have a population of around 3,500 *kelpers* (residents, universally of British origin), with 500,000 sheep, plus penguins, geese, whales, elephant seals, and sea lions for company. Some 1,500 *kelpers* live in the capital, **Port Stanley**, known as Puerto Argentino to the Argentines who claim sovereignty over the islands. The few hundred youngsters who live outside the capital attend school by radio; teachers visit for two weeks each year. There is a monthly mail service to and from England.

Disputed territory

The Falklands and South Georgia Islands have been in British hands since 1833, although Argentina has been firm in demanding sovereignty for over a century, on the grounds that the islands were taken from Spain by the British and that after Argentine independence from Spain, they should technically have reverted to Argentine territory. Claims by various European powers had always been doubtful and frequently shifting since the first reported sightings of the uninhabited islands in the late 16th century, although since its independence Argentina has never wavered from its claim that "*las Malvinas son Argentinas*." The area became strategically important to the rest of the world only in the latter part of the 20th century, with the realization that the islands offer a claim both to Antarctic territory and to offshore oil deposits that have become increasingly exploitable with modern technology.

The 1982 war between the UK and Argentina followed an invasion first of South Georgia and then of the Falklands by troops sent by Argentine dictator Leopoldo Galtieri. The war brought about the deaths of 655 Argentines, many of them conscripts, and 255 British soldiers. Thereafter, the attitude of the *kelpers* to Argentine sovereignty claims hardened still further, not unnaturally, with distrust of Argentine politicians reaching new heights. Communications with Argentina were cut off, and it was not until July 2000 that a joint declaration between the Argentine and British governments was enforced, permitting Argentines to visit the islands. Prior to this, only relatives of the fallen soldiers were allowed occasional visits to Darwin Cemetery, near the site of the battle of Goose Green, where the remains of an Argentine fighter plane lie.

Despite the traumatic experience of the invasion and the emphatic rejection of post-war Argentine overtures by the *kelpers*, the economic life of the islands improved after the war, not just because of oil exploration. A permanent garrison of some 2,000 troops has been based in Mount Pleasant since that time, an airport, hospital, and secondary school have been installed, and average annual income is now around US$20,000, a 700 percent increase over pre-war levels. Economic life centers on fishing – this includes fishing licenses to foreign ships operating in the islands' 240-km (150-mile) exclusion zone; agriculture; and services, especially tourism, which benefits from the spectacular wildlife. Agricultural lands were subdivided and sold by the Falkland Islands Development Corporation after the war, and are now in the hands of local farmers.

Direct travel between Argentina and the islands is still limited but flights are available in Chile. Cruises are also available from Uruguay in spring and summer. Port Stanley is a picturesque town noted for its Englishness, with neatly painted houses framed by lawns and flowerbeds, and three churches. Port Stanley has various types of accommodation to offer visitors, including two hotels, and a few guesthouses, lodges, and self-catering cottages. There are restaurants and bars, but no theaters. It also has virtually the only trees in the islands, brought from abroad and laboriously protected from the winds which constantly batter the islands. The port, with its windbreak hill backdrop, steadfastly faces the treacherous Southern Ocean and the still visible wreckage of old fishing vessels. ❑

The islands took their English name from the Falkland Sound, named after a British peer in 1690. Seventeenth-century French seafarers named the islands Les Isles Malouines ("Malvinas" in Spanish) after their St Malo home.

BELOW: Carcass Island settlement, Falklands. **OVERLEAF:** heading for home, Ecuador.

TRAVEL TIPS

CONTENTS

Getting Acquainted

In South America, temperature depends greatly on altitude above sea level, and temperate climates can be found among mountain landscapes away from the coast. Hot temperatures tend to prevail throughout the year in the lowlands, mainly along the coast. The **Colombian highlands**, for example, have moderate weather all year round, while the coast is tropical. The only seasons here are wet and dry, varying by region.

Venezuela has a tropical climate with average temperatures of 27°C (80°F). Four climatic zones are represented within its boundaries: hot, mild, cool, and cold.

The rainy season lasts from mid-May until the end of October, but showers may fall in December or January. In Caracas, the January average temperature is 18.6°C (65°F), rising to 21°C (70°F) in July.

Peru's coastline has average temperatures of 14–27°C (58–80°F), while in the highlands – or sierra – it is normally cold, sunny, and dry for much of the year, with temperatures ranging from 9–18°C (48–65°F). The rainy season in the sierra is from December to May. The jungle is hot and humid with temperatures ranging from 25–28°C (77–82°F).

Lima alone suffers from the climatic condition the Peruvians call *garúa* – a thick wet fog that covers the city without respite from April through November.

Ecuador's regions each have a distinct climate. The coast is hottest and wettest from January to April. The mountains are driest and clearest between June and

September, and in December. The Oriente is usually inundated with rain between June and August, followed by a drier season until December. As on the coast, however, a torrential downpour is never out of the question.

In **Bolivia**, the average temperature in the highlands – the most popular area to visit – is 10°C (50°F). Rain falls heavily in summer (November through March) here, but winter (May through November) is very dry. The average temperatures in La Paz are 6–21°C (42–70°F) during summer and 0–17°C (32–63°F) in winter.

In **Brazil**'s jungle region, the climate is humid equatorial, with high temperatures and humidity, and heavy rainfall all year round. The eastern Atlantic coast of Brazil, from Rio Grande do Norte to the state of São Paulo, has a humid tropical climate, also hot, but with slightly less rainfall than in the north and with summer and winter seasons. Most of Brazil's interior has a semi-humid tropical climate, with a hot, rainy summer from December to March and a drier, cooler winter (June to August).

Part of the interior of the northeast has a tropical semi-arid climate – hot with sparse rainfall. Most of the rain falls during three months, usually March–May. The average temperature in the northeast is 24–27°C (75–80°F).

Brazil's south, below the Tropic of Capricorn and Rio de Janeiro, has a humid subtropical climate. Rainfall is distributed regularly throughout the year and temperatures vary from 0–10°C (32–40°F) in winter, with occasional frosts and snowfall (but the latter is rare) to 21–32°C (70–80°F) in summer.

Paraguay has a subtropical climate. Summers (December to February) are very hot and humid; spring and fall are milder. In winter (June to August) temperatures can drop to around 5°C (41°F) but it never snows.

Chile's central valley (Santiago, Valparaíso, Viña del Mar) has a Mediterranean climate with summer

(January and February) averaging 30°C (82°F), and winter (June and July) 10°C (50°F). Evenings are cool and it rains in winter but the weather is generally pleasant.

In the Atacama Desert, the days are very hot and the nights extremely cold. The Lake District has a pleasant temperate climate, but winds can be chilly. The mountains are cold and it rains a lot. Patagonia is almost always cold. Fog, rain, and high winds are not uncommon even in the summer.

In **Uruguay** fertile grasslands alternate with wooded hill country and lush river valleys. The climate is temperate. Winter (June, July, and August) can be quite cold and damp. Spring (September through November) and fall (March through May) are pleasant; summers (December through February) are hot but tempered by the cool Atlantic breezes.

Most of **Argentina** lies within the temperate zone of the southern hemisphere. The northeastern part is very humid and subtropical but has mild winters. The pampas are temperate while the southern part of the country has colder temperatures and rain most of the year.

Rainfall varies in the humid pampas (which comprises the province of Buenos Aires, and some of the Córdoba and La Pampa provinces) from 99 cm (39 inches) in the eastern parts to about 51 cm (20 inches) near the Andes.

Consult your local public health service before leaving home and be sure to get a certificate for any vaccination you have. The most common illnesses are picked up from contaminated food and water, so you should pay particular attention to what you eat and drink.

The quality of tap **water** in much of South America is unreliable. You are advised to drink only bottled water, or to take purifying tablets.

Hepatitis, picked up from contaminated food and water, is common, and all travelers should get immunized against the disease.

Malaria occurs in jungle areas of South America, so you should take anti-malaria tablets if you are visiting any part of the Amazon.

Yellow fever, transmitted to humans by mosquitoes, is prevalent in the whole of South America except Chile, Argentina and Uruguay. You are therefore advised to seek immunization. A yellow-fever shot protects you for 10 years, but is effective only after 10 days, so plan ahead. You may be asked to show your yellow-fever vaccination certificate if arriving from a country where yellow fever is endemic.

Your physician or, in the UK, the Medical Advisory Service for Travellers Abroad (MASTA), tel: 0906 8224100, will advise you about other tropical diseases that may be endemic in the area you are visiting – such as dengue fever and Chaga's disease. All travelers should check that they are inoculated against tetanus, typhoid, and polio.

You should take some form of remedy for **stomach upsets** and **diarrhea**, which is likely to be the main complaint of most travelers. Immodium is a popular travel companion, but note that this medication treats the symptoms and not the cause.

The other main cause of illness is the **heat**. Have respect for the power of the tropical sun: wear a hat and be sure to drink plenty of fluids.

Travelers planning to spend time in the Andes should be aware of the dangers of **altitude sickness** *(soroche)*. Anyone arriving by air in La Paz, for example, is likely to need several days to acclimatize.

Acute mountain sickness (called *puno*) is totally unpredictable – even the fittest people can be affected – and the only solution is to go back to a lower altitude as fast as you can. If you must continue, rest for a few days, drink lots of fluids but do not smoke or consume any alcohol.

Security and Crime

The crime rate is generally high in South America, although risks can be minimized by taking a few basic

precautions. Jewelry should not be worn and large amounts of money and expensive watches should be kept out of sight. Wear a money belt when traveling. Keep an eye on your possessions at all times and make use of hotel safes whenever possible (but always take a verified list of what you have deposited). Do not leave valuables in cars. Avoid walking alone and in deserted areas after dark. Never carry packages for other people without checking the contents.

Colombia is part of a major drug-smuggling route, so it is particularly important that you do not carry packages for other people. Be guided by advice before you leave home about which areas are safe.

The crime rate in **Venezuela**, particularly in Caracas, is high. You should not walk alone in narrow streets in downtown Caracas after dark and it is strongly recommended that you do not travel by car at night, particularly in the countryside where, should you have an accident or breakdown, the risk of robbery and other crimes is much greater.

Petty crime is rife in the urban centers of **Peru**. Pickpockets and thieves are common in Lima and Cusco and are amazingly adept at slitting open shoulder bags, camera cases, and knapsacks. Officials also warn against dealing with anyone approaching you in your hotel lobby or on the street, allegedly representing a travel agency or specialty shop.

A special security service for tourists has been created by Peru's Civil Guard. They are recognizable by a white braid across the shoulder of their uniforms and can be found all over Lima, especially in downtown areas. In Cusco, all police have tourism training. The tourist police office in Lima is in the Museo de la Nación, Avda Javier Prado Este 2465, San Borja, tel: 01-225 8699. In Cusco: Calle Saphi in the Delegación de Policía, two blocks from the main square, tel: 084-249 652.

Traveling alone and after dusk is not advisable. Don't hitchhike. For journeys overland choose well-

known and established bus companies. Carry your passport at all times. For specific inquiries, contact your embassy.

The US State Department and the British Foreign Office both publish detailed information on all South American countries and offer advice to travelers. Their websites are, respectively:
US: http://travel.state.gov
UK: www.fco.gov.uk

Money Matters

Traveler's checks in US dollars are the safest and most convenient form of currency, acceptable all over South America. Sterling and other currencies are not worth bringing (unless you are visiting French Guiana, whose currency is the euro, or the Falkland Islands, where sterling is used).

Changing money. You can change money in banks, *casas de cambio* (exchange bureaux) and larger hotels; *casas de cambio* usually give the best rate of exchange. Take checks and cash in a variety of large and small denominations since exchange rates in some countries can change dramatically overnight; and bring only notes in optimum condition as some exchange bureaux can be sniffy about old notes. It is worth bringing

Photography

Digital photography has taken over most of South America, just like the rest of the world, and there are places to print photos or record them onto a CD in most shopping centers and downtown areas of larger cities. Film is still available in larger centers, although it can be expensive.

Note that it is forbidden for military sites (including ports, transport terminals, and bridges) to be photographed. It is best to ask permission if you are unsure.

Many people, particularly from indigenous cultures, are sensitive about having their portraits taken, so always ask permission first.

a pocket calculator as some rates of exchange run into the thousands.

Cash. You will always need to carry some cash with you, of course, and should think ahead if you are traveling into a rural area for some time. But try not to exceed the amount covered in your insurance policy.

Credit and debit cards are also widely accepted, with ATMs (cash machines) located in most cities. In Brazil, cards are more convenient to use than traveler's checks. Before leaving home, memorize your PIN number, and check handling fees and cover in the event of loss or robbery. Many establishments also add their own supplementary charges.

See the separate Money section under each country for more detailed information.

Finally, it is worth remembering the much-quoted advice: pack half the clothes you think you'll need, but twice the money.

Shopping

Much of South America's best bargains are still to be found in the local markets, particularly in the Andean countries, where prices are low and the choice of goods extensive. Jewelry, textiles, jumpers, ponchos, and leather goods are all widely produced. A certain amount of haggling with traders is expected but be careful not to go too far; think of your income compared to theirs.

Venezuela's craftsmen hold a prestigious position because of the variety and quality of their workmanship. Outstanding Quibor ceramics have pre-Hispanic origins, molded using styles and techniques handed down through the generations. Baskets, hammocks, hats, and other products made from vegetable fibers can be found in the towns and villages along the east coast. Beautifully woven ponchos, colorful blankets and caps are sold by the Andean people while craftsmen of the *llanos* (prairies) sell four-string guitar-like musical instruments called *cuatros* as well as harps and mandolins.

Bolivia likewise produces a wide range of craft work, including tapestries, woolen clothing, and wooden sculptures. And **Peru** is also known for the quality of its handicrafts, as well as its bargain gold, copper, and silver items. A good range can be found in the *artesanías* markets in Lima. **Argentina** offers a wide variety of craftwork, from silver and leather to alpaca wool ponchos.

Colombia specializes in emeralds and leather goods, but if you're looking for a number of different gemstones, **Brazil**'s tremendous variety is unmatched, and prices are low. If you're not an expert gemologist, it's wise to buy from a reliable jeweler. The leading jewelers operating nationwide are H. Stern and Amsterdam Sauer, but there are other reliable smaller chains. The top jewelers have shops in the airports, shopping centers, and in most hotels. Leather goods, especially shoes and bags, are another good buy in Brazil; the finest leather comes from the south.

Chile's open, import-oriented free-market economy offers a selection of just about anything you want to buy, but also produces some fine copper ornaments and lapis lazuli jewelry.

Ecuador is renowned as the home of the Panama hat and also for its colorful balsa wood carvings, as well as tapestries, leather goods, and embroidered textiles from Otavalo market and other outlets. **Paraguay** is famous for its *ñandutí* (*Guaraní* for cobweb) lace, used to decorate bedcovers, tablecloths, blankets, etc. Other good buys are guitars and harps, gold and silver filigree jewelry, tooled leather, and ponchos of cotton and wool.

Be careful when buying wool as vicuñas are an endangered species and selling vicuña wool is against international law.

Planning the Trip

Getting There

BY AIR

Argentina
From Europe: Aerolíneas Argentinas, Air Comet, Air France, Alitalia, Avianca, British Airways, Iberia, KLM, Lufthansa.
From/via US: Aerolíneas Argentinas, American Airlines, Continental Airlines, United.
From Australasia: Aerolíneas Argentinas.

Bolivia
From Europe: LAN.
From/via US: American Airlines.

Brazil
From Europe: Aerolíneas Argentinas, Air France, Alitalia, Avianca, British Airways, Iberia, KLM, LAN, Lufthansa, TAM, TAP, Varig.
From/via US: American Airlines, Continental Airlines, Delta, TAM, United.

Chile
From Europe: Aerolíneas Argentinas, Air France, Air Comet, Avianca, Iberia, KLM, LAN.
From/via US: American Airlines, Delta, LAN.
From Australasia: Aerolíneas Argentinas, LAN, Qantas.

Colombia
From Europe: Air France, Alitalia, Avianca, Iberia, Air Comet.
From/via US: Aerolíneas Argentinas, American Airlines, Avianca, Continental Airlines.

Ecuador
From Europe: Air France, Air Comet, Avianca, Iberia, KLM, LAN.

Air Passes

If you are planning to cover large distances and time is short, consider buying one of the air passes that most Latin American airlines offer, covering one or a combination of countries. These passes can work out cheaper than buying individual flights locally. The cost depends on the number of flights, the season, and the region they cover. It is best to speak to a tour operator, who will help you find the pass most suited to your travel plans. However, because bargain flights can be bought from budget airlines now, air passes do not represent quite such good value as they used to.

From/via US: American Airlines, Avianca, Continental Airlines, LAN.

French Guiana
From Europe: Air France.
From/via US: Air France, Surinam Airways.

Guyana
From Europe: British West Indian Airlines, British Airways, or Virgin Atlantic connecting with LIAT or Caribbean Star.
From US: British West Indian Airlines, North American Airlines, Universal Airlines.

Paraguay
From Europe: Aerolíneas Argentinas, Iberia.
From/via USA: American Airlines, LAN.

Peru
From Europe: Aerolíneas Argentinas, Air Comet, Air France, Avianca, Iberia, LAN, KLM.
From/via US: Aerolíneas Argentinas, American Airlines, Avianca, Continental Airlines, LAN.

Suriname
From Europe: Surinam Airways, British West Indian Airlines, KLM, Martinair.
From/via US: Surinam Airways.

Uruguay
From Europe: Aerolíneas Argentinas, Iberia, LAN.
From/via US: American Airlines, United.

Venezuela
From Europe: Air France, Alitalia, Avianca, Iberia, LAN, TAP.
From/via the US: American Airlines, Avianca, Continental Airlines, Delta.

Tour Operators

In the United Kingdom
Latin American Travel Association, produces a useful guide to South America and lists all the main travel companies who operate there. Tel: 020 8715 2913, www.lata.org
Dragoman Overland, adventure group tours. Camp Green, Debenham, Stowmarket, Suffolk, IP14 6LA, tel: 01728 861133, fax: 01728 861127, www.dragoman.com
Exodus, adventure group tours. Grange Mills, Weir Road, London SW12 0NE, tel: 0845 863 9600 (admin/reservations), 020 8673 0859 (brochures/trip notes), fax: 020 8673 0779, www.exodus.co.uk
Explore Worldwide, adventure group tours. Nelson House, 55 Victoria Road, Farnborough Hants GU14 7PA, tel: 0870 333 4001, fax: 01252 391110, www.explore.co.uk
Journey Latin America, flights, tailor-made itineraries, escorted tours, and adventure trips. 12/13 Heathfield Terrace, Chiswick, London W4 4JE, tel: 020 8747 3108 (flights), 020

Arriving by Boat

An unusual alternative to flying is to join a cargo ship in England and travel by sea. For further information contact Strand Voyages, 257 Strand, London WC2R 0HS, tel: 020 7010, fax: 020 7010 9292, www.strandtravel.co.uk

8747 8315 (tours), fax: 020 8742 1312, www.journeylatinamerica.co.uk
South American Experience, flights and tailor-made itineraries. Welby House, 96 Wilton Road, London SW1V 1DW, tel: 0845 277 3366, fax: 020 7821 4001, www.southamerican experience.co.uk
STA, specialists in student and under-26 fares, tours, and hotels, with 400 branches worldwide. Tel: 0871 230 0040, www.statravel.co.uk
Trailfinders, long-haul flights and tailor-made holidays. Tel: 0845 054 6060, www.trailfinders.com
Trips Worldwide, specialists in tours to the Guianas. 14 Frederick Place, Bristol BS8 1AS, tel: 0117 311 4400, fax: 0117 311 4401, www.tripsworldwide.co.uk

In the United States
South American Explorers' Club Tel: 607 277 0488, fax: 607 277 6122, www.saexplorer.org

What to Pack

Take light summer clothes if you are heading for tropical zones. Note that shorts and very skimpy tops are frowned upon in churches. In the highlands, a sweater should suffice in the evenings. Take plenty of layers of warm and waterproof clothing if you are heading up into high mountain areas. Pack some high-factor sunscreen and lip salve, and remember to take a hat. A money belt is handy to avoid carrying all your money in one place. Don't forget rechargeable batteries and a recharger for any electrical equipment.

Argentina A – Z

Getting Acquainted

Area 2,780,400 sq. km (1,074,000 sq. miles)
Capital Buenos Aires
Population 38 million
Language Spanish
Currency Peso ($)
Weights & measures Metric
Electricity 220 volts
Time zone GMT -3hrs, EST +2hrs
Dialing code 54 (Buenos Aires +11)

Government & Economy

The Republic of Argentina has a federal system, with 24 provinces and a strong central government, headed by a president.

Argentina was once one of the world's richest farming economies with agriculture and livestock

Embassies/Consulates

The following are in Buenos Aires:
Australia: Calle Villanueva 1400, tel: 4779 3500, fax: 4779 3581, www.argentina.embassy.gov.au
Canada: Calle Tagle 2828, tel: 4808 1000, fax: 4808 1111, www.dfait-maeci.gc.ca/argentina
Ireland: Avda del Libertador 1068, 6th floor, tel: 5787 0801, fax: 5787 0802.
New Zealand: Carlos Pellegrini 1427, 5th floor, tel: 4328 0747, fax: 4328 0757.
UK: Calle Luis Agote 2412, Recoleta, tel: 4808 2200, fax: 4808 2274, www.fco.gov.uk
US: Avda Colombia 4300, tel: 5777 4533, fax: 5777 4240, http://buenosaires.usembassy.gov

Public Holidays

- **January 1** New Year's Day
- **March/April** Good Friday
- **May 1** Labor Day
- **May 25** Commemoration of First Government
- **June 10** Malvinas Day
- **June 20** Flag Day
- **July 9** Declaration of Independence
- **August 17** Death of San Martín
- **October 12** Columbus Day
- **October 10** Día de la Tradición
- **December 8** Annunciation Day
- **December 25** Christmas Day

providing 50 percent of export earnings, and the country is virtually self-sufficient in oil. However, Argentina suffered a severe economic decline in 2000/2001, which, together with high-level political corruption, poverty, and unemployment, brought the country to the verge of imploding financially, politically, and socially by 2002. In November of that year Argentina defaulted on an US$800m debt owed to the World Bank, having failed to secure IMF aid. Since then Argentina has regained its economic and political stability, but the peso is only worth a third of its previous value.

Visas

Visitors to Argentina must have a valid passport; a visa is not necessary for citizens of the EU, US, Canada, Australia, and New Zealand, who can stay for three months. Those wishing to extend their trip past the 90-day limit can try leaving the country and returning to get a fresh stamp. This usually works, but is frowned upon if done regularly, and the provision of a stamp is at the discretion of the border guards.

Money

Casas de cambio will usually accept traveler's cheques. ATM dispensers are fairly widespread and major credit cards are widely accepted. US dollars, in cash, are often accepted in small denominations.

Getting Around

From the Airport

Ezeiza International Airport (EZE) is the arrival point for all foreign travelers. It is about 40 minutes from downtown Buenos Aires. There are buses to the center of the city every 30 minutes (although they can take up to 2 hours), and plenty of taxis, as well as the **Manuel Tienda** minibus service.

By Air

Traveling by air within Argentina is via the local airlines, which are **Aerolíneas Argentinas** and **Lineas Aereas del Estado** (LADE), serving mostly Patagonian destinations.

Jorge Newbery Airport, also known as Aeroparque, is used for flights within Argentina and bordering countries.

Confirmation 24 hours before your flight is strongly recommended. There is a departure tax of around US$18 on leaving the country.

By Sea

Few cruise ships call at Buenos Aires. Traveling to Uruguay on the ferry is a pleasant and inexpensive trip. Contact **Buquebus** in Buenos Aires, tel: 4316 6500, www.buquebus.com. There are boat connections between Uruguay and Argentina: Tigre to Carmelo and Montevideo to Carmelo. Ferry services run to Colonia from Darsena Sur and a hydrofoil service runs between Montevideo and Colonia several times a day during the summer. The English-language daily, Buenos Aires Herald, has listings of all sailings to Argentina.

By Bus

Buses are an excellent way to get around Buenos Aires, which is a very large city. They are usually prompt and inexpensive, but avoid them during the rush hour as the lines are very long. Bus stops are located throughout the whole city. The number and destination are clearly marked. Long-distance travel on buses is also available. A huge, modern bus terminal is located in Retiro. Information on destinations can be obtained there from the different companies.

Bus services are available from Chile, Bolivia, Paraguay, Uruguay, and Brazil. Large air-conditioned buses are usually used for long-distance overland travel, but travelers must remember to be vigilant to ensure personal safety.

By Rail

With the exception of a few tourist services, passenger services around the country are virtually non-existent since the government privatized the network in 1994. Trains do run to the suburbs of Buenos Aires, however. There are four main train terminals in the city: **Retiro**, tel: (011) 4311 8074. For services to Delta Tigre, Capilla del Señor, and Bartolomé Mitre. **Constitución**, tel: (011) 4304 0028. For local trains. **Federico Lacroze**, tel: (011) 4553 5213. For excursions on a Scottish 1888 Neilson steam engine. **Once**, tel: (011) 4861 0043. For travel around Buenos Aires province. The journey from Olivos to Tigre on the Tren de la Costa (tel: 011-4732 6000, www.trendelacosta.com.ar) offers great views of the River Plate.

By Road

Traveling by car is possible. Most of the roads are paved but cautious driving is absolutely essential. Speed limits are posted and should be followed closely.

The **Automobile Club of Argentina** in Buenos Aires on Avda Libertador 1850, tel: 802 6061/ 7061, is very helpful and can provide maps and useful information.

Media

The main local papers are *La Nación* and *Clarín*. The English-language paper is the *Buenos Aires Herald* and there's a free tourist information paper, the *Buenos Aires Times*. There are newspaper and magazine stands throughout the capital, selling these and some foreign papers and international magazines.

By Taxi

These can be easily recognized in Buenos Aires – black with a yellow roof – and are readily available 24 hours a day. The meter registers the fare. Be careful when paying and make sure you receive the correct change. A small tip *(propina)* is expected.

By Subway

The subway system, better known as the Subte, is the fastest and cheapest way to get around Buenos Aires, and is the oldest in South America, built in 1913. Trains run daily 5am–10pm and tickets cost 30¢ flat fare per journey. The rides take no more than 25 minutes, and the waiting is between three to five minutes. The artwork at some of the stations has an interesting history: many of the painted tiles were baked by artisans in Spain and France in the early 20th century.

Medical Services

Health care in Argentina is good. Hospitals have trained personnel who have studied at home and abroad, and there are excellent specialists in most of the medical fields. Medical equipment is very costly, but all efforts are coordinated in order to maximize benefits. In some sections of the country, the hospitals may not have up-to-date equipment, but what is available is adequate for an emergency.

Emergency Numbers

For general emergencies, dial **101** for the **police**, who can advise

There are five TV channels, and cable TV is available. Most of the programs are brought in from the US and some from Europe. Many drama series are locally made.

Radio stations carry a variety of programs. The BBC runs from 5pm to about 12.30am. A number of stations play international pop, tango music, and talk programs.

Remise Taxis

Remise taxis are private cars that can be rented, with a driver, by the hour, day or any other time period. Fares normally work out much cheaper than those charged by ordinary taxis.

A list of *remise* offices can be found in the telephone directory, and staff in your hotel should be able to provide information too.

about other emergency services in the area. For the **ambulance** service, dial **107**. For medical emergencies in the Buenos Aires area, you can contact the following: **British Hospital**, Calle Perdriel 74, tel: 4309 6400. **Children's Hospital Pedro Elizalde**, Calle M.Oca 40, tel: 4307 5553 **Ricardo Gutiérrez**, Calle Gallo 1330, tel: 4962 9247. **Hospital de Clínicas**, Calle Córdoba 2351, tel: 5950 8579.

Business Hours

Offices open Mon–Fri 9am–6pm, and banking hours are Mon–Fri 10am–3pm. Stores normally open Mon–Fri 9am–8pm, but you'll often find that they close for several hours in the middle of the day.

All government agencies and banks close on public holidays.

Postal Services

The main post office in Buenos Aires is on Calle Sarmiento 189, and operates Mon–Fri 8am–8pm. Other small post offices are found throughout the city. Hotels are the best source of stamps.

Telecommunications

Telephones

Telephone services are run by *Telecom* in the north and *Telefónica Argentina* in the south. Phone cards are available. Domestic calls can be made from public telephone boxes using coins or cards. In main cities the **Centros de Llamadas** offer good telephone and fax services.

International public phones have a DDI sign. Many telephone offices send international faxes. In Buenos Aires you can make international calls and send faxes from the communications office on Avda Corrientes 705. Open 24 hours.

There are three cellular phone companies in Argentina: **Movistar**, **Personal**, and CTI. All charge around the same. The cheapest way to use a cellphone, if coming from abroad, is to bring your phone and buy a SIM card once in Argentina. They cost around US$10 and can be purchased at cellphone shops in cities around the country.

Internet

Email and Internet can be accessed at internet cafés *(locutorios)* all over Buenos Aires.

Useful websites include:
www.grippo.com.ar (in Spanish)
www.liveargentina.com (in six languages, and easy to use)
www.bue.gov.ar (the government's official website for tourist information in the capital)
www.economist.com/cities (up-to-date information on cultural and political events in the capital)
www.estanciasargentinas.com (information on *estancias* throughout the country)
www.museos.buenosaires.gov.ar (comprehensive guide to the museums in the capital).

There are *casas de turismo* (tourist offices) in most big towns in Argentina. Buenos Aires has the following offices and services:

The **National Tourist Office** is at: Calle Santa Fe 883, tel: 4312 2232, fax: 313 6834, www.turismo.gov.ar. Open Mon–Fri 8.30am–10pm, Sat 9am–7pm. Other tourist information centers are found at: Diagonal Norte/Florida, Galerias Pacifico, Retiro Bus Station, Ezeiza International Airport, and Jorge Newbery Airport. In these booths travelers can obtain maps of the city and a bilingual (Spanish and English) tourist information newspaper, the *Buenos Aires Times*; it offers

Travel Agencies

ASATEJ, Calle Florida 835, 3rd floor, Office 315, Buenos Aires, tel: 4311-8700, fax: 4311-6150, www.asatej.com. Primarily aimed at students, but there's no age limit. Bright and cheerful office with noticeboard brimming with items for sale, travel news, travelers seeking companions.
Eurotur, Calle Viamonte 486, Buenos Aires, tel: 4312 6077, fax: 4311 9010, www.eurotur.com. Tours, transport and accommodations for individuals and groups. English spoken; highly professional and recommended.
Eves Tourismo, Calle Tucumán 702, Buenos Aires, tel: 4393-6151. Helpful and efficient for travel in Argentina and abroad.
Kallpa Tour, Calle Roque Sáenz Peña 811, 1st floor, Office D, Buenos Aires, tel: 4394-1830/1860, fax: 4326-2500; www.kallpatour.com. Specialists in trekking, horseback riding, and cultural tours.
Swan Turismo, Cerrito 822, Buenos Aires, tel: 4129 7926, www.swanturismo.com.ar. Long-established, high quality, specialist travel agency, which organizes trips throughout the country.

complete listings of what is happening in the city. A booklet of shopping, dining, and entertainment listings can be found in most hotels.

The provinces of Argentina have offices in Buenos Aires offering tourist information and a ready supply of pamphlets about events, attractions, hotels and restaurants, etc. All the offices are located in the center of town and can be easily located. Look in the phone book.

Religious Services

Argentina is predominantly Roman Catholic. The main cathedral is the Catedral Metropolitana, at Rivadavia and San Martín. The city is also home to the largest Jewish

community in South America. One of Once's well known synagogues is Yesod Hadat, located on Lavalle 2449. Buenos Aires has the largest mosque in Latin America, donated by the late King Fahd of Saudi Arabia. The Centro Cultural Rey Fahd provides a school, library, and meeting place and is situated at Avda Bullrich 55 and Cervio.

Where to Stay

Buenos Aires (011)
Carsson, Calle Viamonte 650, tel: 4131 3800, www.hotelcarsson.com.ar. Faded, charming elegance. $$$
Claridge Hotel, Calle Tucumán 535, tel: 4314 7700, fax: 4314 8022, www.claridge-hotel.com. Old-fashioned British style. $$$
Faena Hotel and Universe, Martha Salotti 445, Dique 2, Madero Este, Puerto Madero, tel: 4010 9000, www.faenahotelanduniverse.com. This swish new BA landmark caters to your every need. $$$
Five Cool Rooms, Honduras 4742, between Armenia and Malabia, Palermo Viejo, tel: 5235 5555, www.fivebuenosaires.com. Stylish and minimalist. Some rooms come with balconies and jacuzzis. $$$
Gran Hotel Colón, Calle Carlos Pellegrini 507, tel: 4320 3500, fax: 4320 3507, www.colon-hotel.com.ar. Rooftop pool. $$$
Gran Hotel Hispano, Avda de Mayo 861, tel: 4345 2020. Housed in a colonial building and popular with budget travelers. $$
Marriott Plaza Hotel, Calle Florida 1005, tel: 4318 3000, fax: 4315 3008, www.marriottplaza.com.ar. For the rich and famous with the renowned Plaza Grill. $$$
Orly Hotel, Calle Paraguay 474, tel: 4312 5344, www.orly.com.ar. Basic rooms, good location. $

Hotel Price Guide

Prices for a double room including continental breakfast:
$ = US$30 – inexpensive
$$ = US$30–50 – moderate
$$$ = US$50 plus – expensive

Posada Palermo, Salguero 1655, between Soler and Paraguay, Palermo, tel: 4826 8792, www. posadapalermo.com.ar. A rustic-feeling retreat in the city. **$$$**

Sheraton Buenos Aires Hotel & Towers, Calle San Martín 1225, tel: 4318 9000, fax: 4318 9353, www.starwoodhotels.com. Magnificent view over the river and port. **$$$**

Waldorf Hotel, Calle Paraguay 450, tel: 4312 2071, fax: 4312 2079, www.waldorf-hotel.com.ar. Modern; near shopping streets. **$**

Puerto Iguazú (03757)

Sheraton Iguazú Resort & Spa, tel: 491 800, www.starwoodhotels.com. Located in Iguazú national park, offering a magnificent view of the falls. With all facilities including golf course. **$$$**

Las Orquídeas, Ruta 12, Km 5, tel: 420 472, www.orquideashotel. com. Comfortable and inexpensive, outside the city in a beautiful location. **$–$$**

Mendoza (0261)

Hotel Aconcagua, Calle San Lorenzo 545, tel: 520 0500, fax: 420 2083, www. hotelaconcagua.com. A few blocks from the main shopping area, with modern architecture, pool, and air-conditioned rooms. **$$$**

Hostería Puente del Inca, Ruta 7, Las Heras, tel: 4380 480, fax: 438 0477. Secluded, within sight of Aconcagua. **$$**

Bariloche (02944)

Edelweiss Hotel, Avda San Martín 232, tel/fax: 445 500, www. edelweiss.com.ar. A large hotel with sauna, fitness rooms, and a good restaurant. **$$$**

Hotel Tronador, Ruta 237, Km 19, Bariloche, tel: 468 127, www. hoteltronador.com. Small lodge-type hotel with excellent food, fishing, horseback riding, hiking, and beautiful surroundings. In front of the Mascardi Lake, southwest of Bariloche. Open Nov–April. **$$**

Salta (0387)

Hotel Regidor, Buenos Aires 8, tel: 431 1305. Good value and good facilities. Comfortable. **$**

Hotel Salta, Buenos Aires 1, tel/fax: 431 0740, www.hotelsalta.com. Traditional hotel with wooden balconies and all amenities, situated in the main square. **$$$**

Vieja Posada, Salta 70, tel: 422 251, www.viejaposada.com.ar. Nice rooms and an enchanting vine-covered courtyard. **$**

Ushuaia (02901)

Cabo de Hornos, Calle San Martín and Rosas, tel: 422 313. Clean and comfortable. **$$**

Del Glaciar, Camino Glaciar Martial, Km 3.5, tel: 4893 1346, www. hoteldelglaciar.com. Four-star hotel above the city. **$$$**

Las Hayas Resort Hotel, Camino Glaciar Martial, Km 3, tel: 430 710 18, www.tierradelfuego.org.ar/ lashayas. Five-star hotel set on a hill with great views, spa, and minibus to the city.

Calafate (Lago Argentina) (02908)

Hotel La Loma, Calle B Roca and 15 Febrero, tel: 491 016, www.lalomahotel.com. In the National Glacier Park, with 27 rooms, centrally located with lovely views. Open Oct–April. Several languages spoken. **$**

Córdoba (0351)

Hotel Windsor, Buenos Aires 214, tel: 422 4012. Great hotel with a rooftop pool as well as sauna and fitness facilities. **$$**

Hotel Felipe, San Jerónimo 279, tel: 425 5500, www. hotelfelipe.com.ar. Centrally located near Plaza San Martín. **$$**

What to Eat

Hotel breakfasts are rarely very exciting, and you'll do better to head for a local *confitería* or bar. A traditional breakfast includes *café con leche* (white coffee) and *medias lunas* (croissants, smaller and denser than the French variety). Other types of pastry *(facturas)* are usually also available. Good *confiterías* in the center of Buenos

Aires include the **Florida Garden** (Calle Florida and Paraguay) and the wood-paneled **Richmond** (Calle Florida near Corrientes). Breakfast is usually available from 8am.

Argentina is well known for its beef. The typical meal will begin with *empanadas* (meat pastries, although the filling will vary according to the region), *chorizos* (pork and paprika sausages) or *morcilla* (pork-blood sausages), and an assortment of *achuras* (sweetbreads). For the main course, excellent meat dishes such as *bife de chorizo* (T-bone steak), or *tira de asado* (grilled ribs) are the most popular choices, accompanied by various salads. To finish off, try a *flan* (custard), topped with *dulce de leche* and some whipped cream.

Restaurant Guide

Prices for a three-course meal for two, including house wine:
$ = less than US$20
$$ = US$20–40
$$$ = US$40 plus

Eating in Buenos Aires

The scope of this guidebook does not allow a listing of restaurants from all parts of Argentina, so the list below focuses just on Buenos Aires, where there is a vast choice. It is possible to eat out every day of the year and still not savor the cuisine of all the recommendable restaurants in the city. Dining out in Buenos Aires is a delightful experience. Food, wine, and service are usually excellent.

Eating out is a favorite pastime of the locals *(porteños)*, but the menu is not the only attraction. Restaurants are a place to socialize, to see and be seen, and share a bottle of wine until the early hours of the morning. Nevertheless, *porteños* take eating seriously. A list of recommended eateries follows, but don't be afraid to try any clean, well-lit place that catches your fancy. The food is almost always fresh and well-prepared in a simple southern European style.

Restaurants in Buenos Aires open for lunch at noon, and for dinner around 8pm. But no one dines out in the evening before 9pm, with restaurants really coming alive between 10pm and 11pm. At weekends, restaurants stay busy long after midnight.

Regional Argentine

El Ceibal, Calle Güemes 3402, tel: 4823 5807; Cabildo 1421, tel: 4784 2444. Great place to try specialties from northern Argentina, including *humitas* (tamales), *locro* (corn chowder), and *empanadas*. **$$**.

Parrillas (Steakhouses)

El Mirasol, Avda Alicia Moreau de Justo 202, tel: 4315 6277. Upscale *parrilla* in posh Puerto Madero district. Elegant atmosphere, reservations recommended. **$$$**

El Palacio de la Papa Frita, Avda Corrientes 1612, tel: 4374 8063. Inexpensive and popular. **$$**

La Chacra, Avda Córdoba 941, tel: 4322 1409. Huge portions. **$$$**

La Estancia, Calle Lavalle 941, tel: 4326 0330. Classic grillhouse in the heart of the city. **$$**

La Veda, Calle Florida 1, tel: 4331 8680. Dark wood paneling, excellent peppered steak, tango dinner show most evenings. Reservations recommended. **$$$**.

Los Troncos, Calle Suipacha 732, tel: 322 1295. Excellent meat and fruity wines at bargain prices. **$**

Munich Recoleta, Calle R.M. Ortíz 1879, tel: 4804 3981. Popular for nearly 40 years, for the lively atmosphere and great steak. Reservations are not accepted. **$$**

Popular Eateries

Bárbaro, Calle Tres Sargentos 415, tel: 4311 6856. A BA landmark, a charming, old-world version of the hole-in-the-wall bar, a great place for a simple midday meal or for music, beer, and bar food in the evening. **$**

La Casa de Esteban de Luca, Calle Defensa 1000 and Carlos Calvo, tel: 4361 4338. In the heart of San Telmo, in a colonial-style building. Popular Sunday lunch after the San Telmo fair. **$**

Pippo, Parana 356, tel: 4374 6365. No frills but great atmosphere and unbeatable prices. Try a *bife de chorizo* (T-bone steak), or a bowl of *vermicelli mixto* (pasta noodles with pesto and bolognaise sauce). **$**

Restaurant Dora, Calle L. Alem 1016, tel: 4311 2891. An upscale version of a popular eatery with rave reviews on the enormous steaks and simple seafood dishes; a downtown "don't miss." **$$**

Te Mataré Ramirez, Calle Paraguay 4062, tel: 4831 9156. An excellent, original, international assortment of dishes, located in Palermo. It specializes in dishes with "aphrodisiac" qualities. **$$–$$$**

Theaters & Concerts

The theater season in Buenos Aires usually opens in March, with a large number and variety of plays on offer. Check the local paper or with your hotel for the current and best shows available. Open-air concerts, held in the city's numerous parks, are very popular on hot summer evenings.

Teatro Colón: Most of the world's renowned performers are well acquainted with this magnificent theater. It has a capacity for 3,500 people, with about 1,000 standing. The acoustics are considered to be nearly perfect. Opera and ballet are two of the favorite programs for the season. The local ballet company is very good and many of its members go on to become international figures. The Colón also has a magnificent museum, where the theater's history and mementos are stored. A guided tour of the theater and the museum can be arranged by calling 4378 7100. Tours: Mon–Sat 11am–4pm, Sun 11am–3pm. Tickets are for sale at the box office on Calle Tucumán. Closed Jan and Feb.

San Martín Theatre: Calle Sarmiento 1551, tel: 4371 0111,

offers plays and musicals, and free music performances and exhibitions in the foyer. Check the local paper for performances.

Nightlife

Buenos Aires is often labeled the city that never sleeps, but the same applies to most large towns outside the capital. Argentines are creatures of the night – it is customary to have your evening meal between 10pm and midnight and then go out to socialize. Most restaurants do not close until after 2am, whilst some in the bigger cities are open all night. Cinemas are also open late, with the last showings at around midnight.

For those wanting to sample the bar and club scene be prepared to begin your night at 2am and party until daylight. Buenos Aires has a major club scene, which is internationally renowned. Lots of the best DJs from around the world come and play here.

Bahrein, Lavalle 345 and Reconquista. Open from midnight, Tues, Wed, Fri, and Sat. One of the most popular night spots in the city. Different types of music on different floors.

Mint, Avda Costanera Rafael Obligado and Sarmiento, Costanera Norte. Open Feb–Dec Fri and Sat from 1.30am. One of the more extravagant options available, playing techno and house. Friday is the most popular evening.

Millón, Paraná 1048, between Marcelo T de Alvear and Santa Fe. This capacious bar has been built inside a stately town mansion. The interior design is very cutting edge and it has a gorgeous garden.

Bar Seddón, Defensa 695 and Chile. Open Tues–Sun from 5pm. A cozy, traditional Buenos Aires bar. It is often fairly quiet during the week but full on weekends, when they play live music.

Sports

Trekking

There are many tour operators in Las Heras, Mendoza, which

Tango Shows

A good tango show can be found almost everywhere, but the best are in Buenos Aires. It is best to reserve for the following venues:
Casablanca, Calle Balcarce 688, tel: 4331 4621. Excellent show, prices include drinks.
La Ventana, Calle Balcarce 425, tel: 4334 1314. Small, atmospheric venue, with good food and excellent show, featuring both tango and folk music from around South America. Inclusive show and meal, with pick up and drop off from your hotel.
Michelangelo, Calle Balcarce 433, tel: 328 2646 Mixed repertoire of tango and folk music and dance, in atmospheric former monastery.

specialize in climbing and trekking tours. One of the best is **Servicios Especiales Mendoza**, Calle Amigovena 65, 5500 Mendoza, tel/fax: (0261) 424 4721.

Skiing

The main ski resorts in Argentina are the **Cerro Catedral Complex**, located near Bariloche; **Valle de las Leñas**, in the south of Mendoza province; **Los Penitentes**, a small resort near the town of Mendoza.

There are also a number of small facilities located throughout the southern provinces, including one in Tierra del Fuego and another near Esquel. Package tours tend to keep down the costs of a ski vacation.

Horseback Riding

A weekend in the Pampa makes a relaxing excursion. Within a couple of hours' drive are many estancias (ranches) that offer horseback riding, *asados* (barbecues) and displays of gaucho (cowboy) skills. Some also have rooms and offer inclusive packages.
Estancia La Bamba in San Antonio de Areco (115 km/70 miles from Buenos Aires) offers comfort and

tranquility. In this peaceful location, with beautiful scenery, the Aldao family has converted the estancia into a country inn, with all the facilities to make a stay comfortable and memorable.
Tel: 011-4732 1269, www.la-bamba.com.ar
Estancia El Carmen de Sierra is an historical building in Arrecifes, 170 km (106 miles) from Buenos Aires, offering accommodations, horseback riding, and a swimming pool. Tel: 011-4311 9603
Estancia Los Patricios, on Ruta 41 near San Antonio de Areco, is a beautiful ivy-covered estancia with riding, golf, swimming pool, local music and folk dancing, barbecues in a barn, and accommodations. Tel: 02326-453 823, www.lospatricios.com

Shopping in Buenos Aires

The best-known, and the most touristy, shopping street in the Argentinian capital is **Florida**, with Avenida Santa Fé coming a close second. You'll find the most expensive boutiques in **Recoleta**, the most exclusive part of Buenos Aires, primarily along **Avda Alvear**, **Quintana**, **Ayacucho**, and small side streets.

For antiques, try the historic barrio of **San Telmo**, which has a fair every Sunday. The plaza is surrounded by stalls that sell an array of objects, from cheap to outrageously expensive. Around the plaza are many antiques stores.

Buenos Aires also has a number of factory outlets (far from the city center), where a large selection of good-quality merchandise is available at low prices.

Alternatively you could go to one of the many shopping malls (known simply as *shoppings*). **Patio Bullrich** in Recoleta (Libertador 750) offers a selection of chic stores, whilst the enormous **Paseo Alcorta** (Salguero 3172), **Alto Palermo** (Avda Santa Fe 3253), and **Solar de la Abadía** (Acre 940) offer a vast range of shops, from high end to cheaper options.

Bolivia A – Z

Getting Acquainted

Area 1,100,000 sq. km (424,200 sq. miles)
Capital Sucre is the legal capital but La Paz is the effective capital.
Population 8.6 million. Seventy percent live in and around La Paz, Oruro, and Lake Titicaca. About two-thirds are of pure indigenous stock, most of the rest are mestizos, or mixed Spanish and local descent, locally referred to as *cholos* and *cholas*. About 1 percent are of African heritage, and a fraction of pure European and Japanese descent.
Languages Quechua, Aymará, and Spanish
Currency Boliviano = 100 centavos
Weights & measures Metric
Electricity 110 volts in La Paz, 220 volts elsewhere. Check first.
Time zone GMT -4hrs, EST +1hr
Dialing code 591 (La Paz +2)

Government & Economy

The president is elected by popular vote every four years under the 1967 constitution. The country is divided into nine departments, each controlled by a delegate appointed by the president. Evo Morales was elected president in 2005 following a period of popular discontent. As the first indigenous president, he represents the interests of the majority of Bolivians.

La Paz is the seat of the government and congress, although the supreme court sits in the small city of Sucre, the legal capital.

Bolivia is the poorest country in South America. More than half the population subsist on agriculture.

Until the collapse of prices in 1985, tin was the major export earner for the country. Today, Bolivia still mines gold, silver, and zinc. Natural gas is exported. The biggest money-spinner is coca growing – it employs thousands of peasants and contributes an undetermined but significant sum to the economy.

Visas

Citizens of the US and most European countries do not need visas (but must fill out a tourist card on arrival); Australians, New Zealanders, and most Asians do. At the border, the guards will grant entry for between 30 and 90 days. The office for visa extensions is at Avda González 240. On departure, a US$20 tax is levied.

Money

Exchange your money in either banks or hotels as there is a lot of false currency in circulation. Ask for low-value Bolivian banknotes and only carry small amounts with you. Credit cards are not always accepted outside of major hotels and restaurants. Visa cash advances are possible from the Banco de La Paz in the capital, and most banks in cities have ATMs.

Getting Around

From the Airport
El Alto, at some 4,000 meters (13,000 ft) above sea level on the

Tour Agencies

Most tour companies offer trips all over the country. For information on trekking and lists of recommended mountaineering guides, contact: **Club Andino Boliviano**, Calle México 1638, La Paz, tel: 2312 875.

For trekking and adventure tours, **Andes Expediciones**, Avda Camacho 1377, Edificio Saenz, 3rd floor, Oficina 1, La Paz, tel: 231 9655/220 2983 is one specialist agency.

Altiplano above La Paz, is the highest international airport in the world. Taxis to the center take about 30 minutes and cost US$8. **Cotranstur** minibuses also go to various points downtown, for about US50¢ (but allow about 1 hour because of all the drop-offs).

By Air
Domestic airlines LAB, TAM, and **AeroSur** cover routes between most major towns and cities. Fares are fairly cheap and, if time is short, it is worth flying to avoid a back-breaking bus journey, especially from La Paz to Potosí (you can fly to Sucre then take the four-hour bus journey to Potosí). **Crillon Tours** offers a comfortable minibus connection that can be arranged in La Paz – their office is at Avda Camacho 1223, tel: 233 7533, www.titicaca.com

By Bus
The bus network in Bolivia is well-developed, being the main form of public transportation for most Bolivians. The quality of service, however, depends on the conditions of roads (of which only some 5 percent are paved) and the terrain covered. Luxury services run between La Paz, Cochabamba, and Santa Cruz; there are quite rough services to Potosí. A wide choice of services are available to Coroico and Copacabana. Toilet stops are few and far between, and the facilities very basic.

Most travelers enter Bolivia via Lake Titicaca in Peru. Many firms offer minibus connections between Puno and La Paz. Crillon Tours *(see above)* offers a luxury hydrofoil service both ways across the lake, with a stopover on the Island of the Sun, a meal in Copacabana, and a visit to the Museum of the Altiplano, with audiovisual displays, which gives an excellent introduction to Bolivia. If you are taking this route, you may have to change buses at the border.

It is also possible to travel from Argentina by land, crossing the frontier at La Quiaca and continuing by bus or train – a slow but fascinating journey.

Truck Transport

To really get off the beaten track, trucks are the standard transport in the Andes. These are usually dilapidated, high-sided vehicles, with only a tarpaulin to protect you from the elements. They are often used by locals going to market, so you are likely to share your space with sacks of fruit and vegetables, or livestock (and in some cases slaughtered carcasses too). Most trucks leave early in the morning, from the market areas; timetables are unreliable and fares highly variable (though usually about half the equivalent bus fare); best to ask locally. A Bolivian truck journey is not the fastest, but will certainly be an experience to remember.

By Train
Trains run from Oruro to Villazón and Potosí. This is a long journey, so worth paying for a pullman seat if available. Tickets can be bought in advance but schedules change frequently and delays are common.

From Brazil, the so-called **Tren de la Muerte** (Death Train) comes up from Corumbá on the edge of the Pantanal to Santa Cruz. Tickets can be up to 50 percent cheaper at the station than from a travel agent, despite agents' scare tactics. It is advisable to get on the train as soon as it is possible to do so. The train is not particularly comfortable and can take anything from 12–40 hours to reach its destination.

There are train and bus links to and from Chile and Argentina.

By Taxi
For longer distances within La Paz, taxis are probably the best way to get around, either privately to go anywhere in the city for about US$1.40, or caught as *colectivos*, sharing with passengers along a fixed route for about US25¢ each.

Medical Services

Make sure you have medical insurance that will provide you with private medical cover.

Major hotels have doctors on call. The **Clínica Alemana** in La Paz (Calle 6 de Agosto 2821, tel: 243 3676), and the **Clínica Americana**, Avda 14 de Septiembre, Obrajes, tel: 278 3510, are competent and well-run.

Business Hours

Most businesses function Mon–Fri 9am–noon and 2–6pm; banks generally close at 4.30pm.

Embassies/Consulates

Canada: Victor Sanjinés 2678, Sopocachi, tel: 241 5141.
UK: (also represents New Zealand): Avda Arce 2732, tel: 243 3424, fax: 243 1073, www.britishembassy.gov.uk/bolivia
US: Avda Arce 2780, Consulate on Avda Potosí, tel: 243 0120, fax: 243 3900, lapaz.usembassy.gov

Newspapers

In La Paz, you can choose from the conservative daily *El Diario*, the independent dailies *Hoy*, *Los Tiempos*, *Ultima Hora*, or *La Razón*, or the weekly, English-language publication the *Bolivia Times*. Other cities have their own local papers.

Postal Services

The main post office in La Paz is at Avda Mariscal Santa Cruz and Oruro, open Mon–Sat 8am–10pm, Sun 9am–noon. The outbound mail is quite efficient. The poste restante *(lista de correos)* keeps letters for three months.

Communications

Telephones
Telephone calls can be made by satellite to the US and Europe. You can call from your hotel, which is the most expensive option, or the **Entel** offices in La Paz, Edificio Libertad, Calle Potosí and Ayacucho 267. Public telephones, found in all major cities, are the cheapest option. Phone cards can be bought in various

denominations. All telephone numbers dialed nationally must be prefixed with the local dialing code: 2 (La Paz and Potosí); 3 (Santa Cruz and Panolo); or 4 (Cochabamba and Central region).

Internet
Internet access is widespread, although not always reliable. Useful websites include: www.bolivia.com, comprehensive information, in Spanish only; www.boliviaweb.com, tourist information in English; www.titicaca.com, created by Crillon tours, information in 4 languages.

Hotel Price Guide

Prices for a double room including continental breakfast:
$ = US$50 – inexpensive
$$ = US$50–100 – moderate
$$$ = US$100 plus – expensive

Where to Stay

La Paz (2)
Presidente, Calle Potosí 920 and Sanjines, tel: 236 7193, fax: 235 4013. Situated downtown. Heated indoor pool, solarium, gym, sauna, conference facilities. **$$**
Radisson Plaza Hotel, Avda Arce 2177, tel: 244 1111, fax: 244 0402, www.radisson.com. North American hotel chain; traditional style. **$$$**
Residencial Rosario, Calle Illampu 704, tel: 245 1658, fax: 245 1991, www.hotelrosario.com. Highly recommended; lovely colonial building, with a café and its own travel agency, running local tours and bus connections to Puno in Peru, and Chile (*Turisbus*, tel: 245 1341, fax: 245 1911). **$**

Potosí (2)
Hostal Colonial, Calle Hoyos 8, tel: 622 4265, www.hostalcolonial.potosi.com. Rooms of various sizes arranged around a pretty courtyard; terrace has views over Cerro Rico. **$**
Hostal Libertador, Calle Millares 58, tel: 622 7877, www.hostal-

libertador-potosi.com. Has the luxury of heated rooms and corridors, plus sun terrace with good views over the colonial rooftops and mountain. **$**

Sucre (4)
Hostal Libertad, Calle Aniceto Arce 99, tel: 6453 101. Café, *en suite* rooms, open 24 hours. **$**
Colonial Hotel, Plaza 25 de Mayo 3, tel: 6454 709. Three-star hotel; all rooms have a/c, TV, and terrace. **$**

Copacabana (2)
La Cúpula, Calle Michel Pérez 1–3, tel: 862 2029, www.hotelcupula.com. Lovely hotel with a friendly atmosphere and distinctive Moorish-style architecture. **$**
Hotel Rosario del Lago, Calle Rigoberto Paredes/Avda Costanera, tel: 862 2141. Right on the lake and very attractive. **$**

What to Eat

Bolivian food varies by region. Lunch is the main meal of the day and many restaurants offer an *almuerzo completo* or three-course fixed menu. Staple foods of the highlands are potatoes, bread, and rice. Meats are highly spiced. Trout from Lake Titicaca is excellent.

Where to Eat

La Paz (2)
Casa del Corregidor, Calle Murillo 1040, tel: 236 3633. International and local dishes. Folk music. **$$**
El Arriero, Avda 6 de Agosto 2535, tel: 232 2708. Claims to serve the best meat in the world. **$$$**
Los Escudos, Edificio Club de la Paz, tel: 322 028. Local food and live music. **$$**

Restaurant Guide

Prices for a three-course meal for two, including house wine:
$ = US$50 – inexpensive
$$ = US$50–100 – moderate
$$$ = US$100 plus – expensive

Hare Krishna, Pasaje Jauregui, 2262. Reasonably priced vegetarian food. Popular with travelers. **$**
Wagamama's, Pasaje Pinilla 2557, tel: 2434 911. Fish and sushi and other Japanese specialties. **$**

Potosí (2)
El Mesón, Plaza 10 de Noviembre, tel: 622 3807. Historic restaurant with wide-ranging menu. **$**

Sucre (4)
Restaurant Sanga, Calle Tarapaca 161, tel: 642 2547. Recommended vegetarian food. **$**

Drinking Notes

The usual tea, coffee, and soft drinks are readily available in restaurants and cafés, as is the *mate de coca* in tea bags.

Bolivian beer, brewed under German supervision, is surprisingly good. The favorite drink of everyday Bolivians is *chicha*, the potent maize liquor produced near Cochabamba. The local spirit *singari* is diluted with lemonade to make a very drinkable *chuflay*. Keep in mind that altitude intensifies the effects of alcohol – both the intoxication and the hangover. Also remember that most Bolivians drink to get drunk.

Nightlife

La Paz has several *peñas* (folk clubs). Try the most popular, **Peña Naira**, on Calle Sagárnaga, tel: 2325 736, just above Plaza San Francisco, open every night, with a US$5 cover charge. Others are at the **Casa del Corregidor** and **Los Escudos** (*see Where to Eat section above*).

Where to Shop

The **artisans' market** in La Paz is on Calle Sagarnaga, between Mariscal Santa Cruz and Isaac Tamayo, and has a vast selection of craftwork. Most shopping takes place in markets. Vendors give a price and expect a bit of gentle haggling.

Brazil A – Z

Getting Acquainted

Area 8,512,000 sq. km (3,285,600 sq. miles)
Capital Brasília
Population 188 million. Over half the population are white or near-white, 11 percent are Afro-Brazilians and the rest are of mixed race.
Language Portuguese
Currency Real (plural, reais*)*
Weights & measures Metric
Electricity Mostly 127 volts; 220 volts in Brasília, Florianópolis, Fortaleza, Recife, and São Luis; 110 volts in Manaus.
Time zone Major cities and eastern half of country GMT -3hrs (EST +2hrs); Mato Grosso and the north GMT -4hrs (EST +1hr); Acre and western Amazonas GMT -5hrs (EST).
Dialing code 55 (Brasília +61, Rio de Janeiro +21)

Government & Economy

Brazil is a federal republic with 27 states, each with its own legislature. The federal government exercises enormous control over the economy. The head of government is the president, who has extensive powers and exercises more control over the nation than the American president does over the US. Luiz Inacio Lula da Silva became the country's first left-wing president for 40 years in 2002, and was re-elected in 2006.

Brazil is almost self-sufficient in food and is the world's largest producer of coffee. It has huge reserves of metals and minerals and well-developed technology-based industries. The gap between rich and poor is huge.

Visas

If Brazilians need a visa in advance to visit your country, you will need a visa in advance to visit Brazil. US citizens need to apply for a visa in advance; European Union citizens do not. Your airline or travel agent will be able to tell you if you need a visa; or contact a Brazilian consulate or embassy.

If you do not need a visa in advance, your passport will be stamped with a tourist visa upon entry. This usually permits you to remain in the country for 90 days. If you apply for a visa in advance, you have up to 90 days after the issue date to enter Brazil. Upon entry, you will get a tourist visa allowing you to stay in Brazil for up to 90 days.

Customs

You will be given a declaration form to fill out on the plane before arrival. Customs officials spot-check half the "nothing to declare" arrivals.

Money

Using ATMS is the easiest way to obtain foreign currency, and they are found throughout Brazil at the following banks: Banco do Brasil, Bradesco, HSBC, Itaú, and Unibanco. You can exchange foreign currency at banks, hotels, and tourist agencies. If you can't find one of these, some travel agencies will change your currency, although this is, strictly speaking, an illegal transaction. The few hotels that exchange travelers' checks generally give a poor rate.

Banks will not exchange *reais* or traveler's checks into foreign

Boat Trips

Short sightseeing or day-long boat tours are available in cities located on the coast or on major rivers. Many towns have local ferry services across bays and rivers and to islands. Schooners and yachts, complete with crew, may be rented for an outing.

currency. The only exception is the Banco do Brasil. You cannot get traveler's checks cashed into dollars.

Stores in major shopping areas and most hotels and restaurants accept Visa and MasterCard/Cirrus cards. Most hotels will also accept traveler's checks. You can pay with US dollars in many stores.

Getting Around

From the Airport

Most visitors arrive in Brazil through the international airports in São Paulo or Rio de Janeiro. The easiest and safest way to get from the airport to your final destination (and this is true of all Brazilian airports) is to take an official airport taxi, for which you pay a fixed rate in advance according to your destination. The rates will be posted clearly above the taxi company desks and you can pay by credit card or cash. Airport taxis are usually air-conditioned, and larger and more comfortable than standard city taxis. If you do choose to take a regular taxi, check out the fares posted for the airport taxis so that you will have an idea of what is a normal rate. If your flight coincides with rush hour, there is every chance the airport taxi will be cheaper than a regular taxi.

Brazilian airports are also well connected to their city centers and main hotels by regular bus services – both executive air-conditioned buses and standard buses.

By Air

Brazil has a good network of domestic flights provided by established companies such as **Varig** and **TAM**, as well as budget airlines such as **Gol**, **BRA**, **Ocean Air**, **Trip**, and **Web Jet**. All of the larger lines fly extensive routes throughout the country and have ticket counters at the airports and ticket offices in most cities. At smaller airports in the more remote cities, these may only be manned shortly before a flight.

There are extensive shuttle services between Rio and São Paulo (with flights every half hour), Rio and Brasília (flights every hour) and Rio and Belo Horizonte (usually about 10 flights per day). Despite the frequency of flights, a reservation is still a good idea.

By Bus

Comfortable and punctual bus services are available between all major cities, and to several other South American cities, including Asunción (Paraguay), Buenos Aires (Argentina), Montevideo (Uruguay), and Santiago (Chile). While it is a good way to see the countryside, distances are huge, you sit in a bus for several days and nights, and the landscape is not continuously fascinating. Nevertheless, buses on longer routes will stop for meals at regular intervals. Some luxury (*leito*) overnight services are available between large cities that include on-board service and blankets. On some routes, there may be just one bus per day (such as the Rio–Belém route, a 52-hour trip) or just one or two per week.

By City Bus

The larger cities have special air-conditioned buses connecting residential areas to the central business district, including routes from airports and bus stations, that pass by many of the larger hotels. You will be handed a ticket as you get on. Take a seat and an attendant will come around to collect your fare.

Regular city buses are entered through the back door (often quite a high step up) and after paying the *cobrador*, who will give you change, you move through the turnstile.

Theft is common on crowded buses, particularly in Rio and São Paulo, even in daylight. Avoid the rush hour, don't carry valuables, keep shoulder bags in front of you, and your camera inside a bag. Avoid attracting attention by speaking loudly in a foreign language.

By Subway

Rio and São Paulo both have good, although not extensive, subway services. Lines radiate from the city centers and are extended by bus links. Maps in the station mean you can find your way without needing Portuguese.

Medical Services

If you need a doctor while you are in Brazil, your hotel should be able to recommend reliable professionals. Many of the better hotels even have a doctor on duty. Your consulate can supply you with a list of physicians who speak your language.

Check with your health insurance company before traveling – some insurance plans will cover any medical service that you may require while abroad.

By Boat

Local boat tours and excursions are available in coastal and riverside cities. There are also options for longer trips.

Amazon River boat trips last from a day up to a week or more. These range from luxury floating hotels to basic accommodations. Boat trips can be taken on the São Francisco River in the northeast and in the Pantanal marshlands of Mato Grosso, popular for wildlife safaris and for angling.

Nowadays, ships from all the world's top cruise lines sail in Brazilian waters. The high season for cruising is December through March and the main ports of call are Rio de Janeiro, Manaus, Recife, Salvador, and Búzios. It is possible to travel from the US and Europe to Brazil by ship at the start and end of the Brazilian cruise season when the ships are relocating.

By Rail

Except for crowded urban commuter railways, trains are not a major form of transportation in Brazil and rail links are minimal. There are a few train trips, which are tourist attractions in themselves, either because they are so scenic or because they run on antique steam-powered equipment.

In the southern state of Paraná, the Curitiba–Paranaguá railroad is famous for spectacular mountain scenery. A return trip can be done in a day. Bear in mind that you may not see much on a cloudy day.

In Minas Gerais, antique steam locomotives haul passengers between São João del Rei and Tiradentes on Friday, weekends and holidays. In the state of Rio de Janeiro, the Mountain Steam Train runs between Miguel Pereira and Conrado every Sunday.

By Taxi

Taxis are the best way for visitors to get around. Radio taxis are slightly more expensive, but safer and more comfortable. In major cities, there are two metered rates. Rate 2 is higher and charged after 9pm and on weekends. Make sure the driver puts the meter on and charges the right rate. Some drivers try to make money from tourists by refusing to put the meter on. If a driver tries to agree a fixed fare, he is probably overcharging you. Insist on the meter being used, or take another cab.

By Car

Car rental facilities are available in the larger cities. Both **Avis** (tel: 011-2155 2846, www.avis.com.br) and **Hertz** (tel: 0800-701 7300 toll-free, www.hertz.com.br) operate in Brazil. The largest Brazilian national chain is: **Localiza** (tel: 0800-979 2000, www.localiza.com.br). There are also good local companies. You can rent a car with your regular driver's license. For a relatively modest additional fee you can hire a driver with the car.

If you plan to drive a lot in Brazil, buy the excellent Quatro Rodas (Four Wheels) *Guia Brasil*, complete with road maps, city and regional itineraries, and hotel and restaurant listings (in Portuguese), available at most newsstands.

Speeding fines can be high (several hundred dollars).

Business Hours

Business hours for offices in most cities are Mon–Fri 9am–6pm.

Lunch-time closures may last hours.

Banks open Mon–Fri 10am–3pm. Currency exchange houses usually operate 9am–5.30pm.

Public Holidays

January 1 New Year's Day (national holiday); Good Lord Jesus of the Seafarers (four-day celebration in Salvador da Bahía).
January 6 Epiphany (regional, mostly in the northeast).
January (3rd Sunday) *Festa do Bonfim* (Salvador da Bahía).
February 2 Iemanjá Festival in Salvador.
February/March (movable) Carnival (national holiday; celebrated all over Brazil on the four days leading up to Ash Wednesday. Most spectacular in Rio, Salvador, and Recife/Olinda).
March/April (movable) Easter (Good Friday is a national holiday; Ouro Preto puts on a colorful procession; passion play staged at Nova Jerusalem in Pernambuco).
April 21 Tiradentes Day (national holiday in honor of the martyred hero of Brazil's independence – celebrations in his native Minas Gerais, especially Ouro Preto).
May 1 Labor Day (national holiday).
May/June Corpus Christi (national holiday).
June/July *Festas Juninas* (a series of street festivals in honor of saints John, Peter, and Anthony, featuring bonfires, dancing, and mock marriages).
June/July *Bumba-Meu-Boi* (processions and street dancing in Maranhao).
September 7 Independence Day (national holiday)
October *Oktoberfest* in Blumenau (put on by descendants of German immigrants).
October 12 *Nossa Senhora de Aparecida* (national holiday honoring Brazil's patron saint).
November 2 All Souls' Day (national holiday).
November 15 Day of the Republic (national holiday, also election day).
December 25 Christmas Day (national holiday).
December 31 New Year's Eve (on

Rio de Janeiro beaches, gifts are offered to the goddess Iemanjá).

Media

The *Miami Herald*, the Latin America edition of the *International Herald Tribune*, and the *Wall Street Journal* are available on many newsstands in the big cities, as are a selection of international weekly magazines. There is no nationwide newspaper, but the most respected newspapers include São Paolo's *Folha de São Paolo*, *Estado de São Paolo*, and *Gazeta Mercantil*, and Rio's *Jornal do Brasil* and *O Globo*.

Postal Services

Post offices generally open Mon–Fri 9am–5pm, Sat 9am–1pm. In large cities, some branch offices stay open until later. The post office in the Rio de Janeiro International Airport is open 7am–7pm.

Communications

Telephones

Pay phones in Brazil use phone cards (cartão de telefone), which are sold at newsstands, bars, or shops.

An orange sidewalk *telefone público* is for local or collect calls; blue is for direct-dial long-distance calls within Brazil.

The explosion in cellphones has led to a fall in the number of public pay phones. Several companies offer short-term rentals to visitors that can be picked up at the international airports or delivered to your hotel. Visitors will also be able to use their own cellphones in Brazil as long as their handset is at least tri-band or preferably quad-band.

Internet

Brazil is very well connected with internet services, and internet cafés are found throughout the country. Connections tend to be slower and more expensive away from major cities.

Useful Websites
Brazilian Government
www.brazil.gov.br/ingles

Brazilian Embassy in London
www.brazil.org.uk
Brazilian Embassy in Washington
www.brasilemb.org
In Portuguese only:
Estado de São Paulo
(newspaper/links)
www.estado.com.br
O Globo (newspaper/links)
http://oglobo.globo.com

Tourist Information

Embratur is the international arm of the Ministry of Tourism, but mainly deals the travel trade. Its only interface with the public is its website, www.braziltour.com. Each state and major city has its own tourism bureau. The principal offices are:
Manaus: Emamtur, Avda Sete de Setembro 1546. tel: 92-633 2850
Rio de Janeiro: Riotur, Rua da Assembleia 10, 9th floor, tel: 21-2542 8080, www.riodejaneiro-turismo.com.br/en. Information centers: international airport, bus terminal, Copacabana, Centro.
Recife: Empetur, Complexo Viario Vice Governador Barreto Guimarães, Olinda, tel: 81-3427 8000, www.empetur.com.br. Information centers: international airport, docks, Casa da Cultura, Recife Antigo.
Salvador: Bahiatursa, Loteamento Jardim Armação, Centro de Convenção da Bahia, tel: 71-3117 3000, www.bahia. com.br. Information centers: airport, bus station, Mercado Modelo, Pelourinho, Porto da Barra.
São Paulo: São Paulo Turismo, Avda Olavo Fontoura 1209, Parque Anhembi, tel: 11-6226 0400. www.spturis.com

Embassies/Consulates

Canada: Brasília: SES, Avda das Nações Unidas 16, Quadra 803, Lote 16, s1. 130, tel: 61 3424 5400. São Paulo: Avda das Nações Unidas 12901, 16th floor, Torre Norte, tel: 11 5509 4343. Rio de Janeiro: Avda Atlantica 1130, 5th floor, tel: 21-2543 3004.
UK: Brasília: SES, Sector de Embaixadas Sul, Quadra 801

Conjunto K, tel: 61 3329 2300. Rio de Janeiro: Praia do Flamengo 284, 2nd floor, tel: 21-2555 9600. São Paulo: Rua Ferreira de Araújo 741, 2nd floor, Pinheiros, tel: 11-3094 2700.
US: Brasília: Avda das Nações Unidas, Quadra 801, Lote 3, tel: 61-3312 7000. Rio de Janeiro: Avda Pres. Wilson, 147, tel: 21-2292 7117. São Paulo: Rua Henry Dunant 700, Chácara Santo Antônio, tel: 11 5186-7000, www.embaixada-americana.org.br

Where to Stay

Tourist offices can provide visitors with comprehensive lists of hotels in all price ranges. This listing features mainly upscale hotels.

Rio de Janeiro (City) (21)
Caesar Park, Avda Vieira Souto 460, Ipanema, tel: 2525 2525, fax: 2521 6000, www.caesar-park.com. Slick and well located in Ipanema. $$$
Copacabana Palace, Avda Atlântica 1702, Copacabana, tel: 2548 7070, fax: 2235 7330, www.copacabanapalace.com.br. Exquisite 1920s hotel; the best in town. $$$
Intercontinental Rio, Rua Perfeito Mendes de Morais, São Conrado, tel: 3323 2200, fax: 3323 2295, www.ichotelsgroup.com. Polished and up-market resort. $$$
Ipanema Plaza, Rua Farme de Amoedo 34, Ipanema, tel: 3687 2000, fax: 3687 2001, www.ipanemaplaza.com.br. Popular mid-range modern hotel in the heart of Ipanema. $$$
Iberostar Copacabana, Avda Atlântica 1020, Leme, tel: 3873 8888, fax: 3873 8777, www.iberostar.com. Smart, international hotel. $$$

São Paulo (City) (11)
Caesar Park, Rua das Olimpíadas 205, Faria Lima, tel: 3049 6622, fax: 3049 6699, www.caesar-park.com. Leading business hotel. $$$
Fasano, Rua Vittorio Fasano 88, Jardim Paulista, tel: 3896 4000,

Hotel Price Guide

Prices for a double room including continental breakfast:
$ = US$100 – inexpensive
$$ = US$100–200 – moderate
$$$ = US$200 plus – expensive

fax: 3896 4155, www.fasano.com.br. The city's top boutique hotel, with a fine restaurant. $$$
Grand Hyatt São Paulo, Avda das Nações Unidas 13301, Brooklin, tel: 6838 1234, fax: 6838 1235, www.saopaulo.hyatt.com. Magnificent modern and stylish world-class executive hotel. $$$
L'Hotel, Al Campinas 266, Bela Vista, tel: 2183 0500, fax: 2183 0505, www.lhotel.com.br. Traditional elegance. $$$
Normandie Design, Avda Ipiranga 1187, Sta Efigênia, tel: 3311 9855, www.normandiedesign.com.br. Recommended budget hotel. $

Brasília (61)
Blue Tree Park, Setor Hoteleiro Norte, Lago Norte, tel: 3424 7000, fax: 3424 7001, www.bluetree.com.br. The city's outstanding hotel, a mixture of resort and business. $$$
Kubitschek Plaza, Setor Hoteleiro Norte, Quadra 2, Bloco E, tel: 3319 3543, www.kubitschek.com.br. Modern, centrally located executive hotel. $$$

Belo Horizonte (31)
Belo Horizonte Othon Palace, Avda Afonso Pena, 1050, Centro, tel: 2126 0000, fax: 3212 2318, www.othon.com.br. Spacious rooms; overlooks the park in the center of town. $$$

Salvador da Bahia (71)
Convento do Carmo, Rua do Carmo, Pelourinho, tel: 3327 8400, fax: 3327 8401. www.pestana.com. Landmark hotel in a colonial cloistered convent. $$$
Pestana Bahia, Rua Fonte de Boi 216, Rio Vermelho, tel: 2103 8000, fax: 2103 8001, www.pestana.com. Modern hotel with stunning sea views. $$$

Pousada Redfish, Ladeira do Boqueirão 1, Santo Antonio, tel: 3243 8473, fax: 3326 2544. www.pousadaredfish.com. Cozy *pousada* in the historic center. **$$$**
Vila Galé, Rua Morro do Escarvao Miguel 320, Praia de Ondina, tel: 3263 8888, fax: 3233 8800, www.vilagale.pt. Modern beach-front hotel near city center. **$$$**

Olinda (81)
Pousada dos Quatro Cantos, Rua Prudente de Morais 441, tel: 3429 0220, fax: 3429 1845, www.pousada4cantos.com.br. Beautiful old building. **$$$**

Recife (81)
Blue Tree Tower, Avda Bernardo Vieira de Melo 550, Piedade, tel: 2123 4567, fax: 2123 4568, www.bluetree.com.br. Modern beach-front property. All rooms have sea views. **$$**
Recife Palace Hotel, Avda Boa Viagem 4070, tel: 4009 2500, fax: 4009 2525, www.lucsimhoteis. com.br. Stylish, exclusive hotel right on Recife's most famous beach. **$$$**

Manaus (92)
Monaco, Rua Silva Ramos 20, Centro, tel: 2121 5026, www.hotelmonaco.tur.br. Central hotel with great river views. **$$**
Novotel, Avda Mandil 4, Distrito Industrial, tel: 2123 1211, fax: 3613 1094, www.accorhotels. com.br. Modern executive hotel. **$$$**
Tropical Manaus, Praia de Ponta Negra, tel: 2123 5000, fax: 3658

Brazil's National Dish

Considered to be Brazil's national dish, *feijoada* consists of black beans simmered with a variety of dried, salted and smoked meats. Originally made out of odds and ends to feed slaves, nowadays the tail, ears, feet, etc. of a pig are thrown in. *Feijoada* for lunch on Saturday is an institution in Rio de Janeiro, where it is served with white rice, shredded *couve* (kale), *farofa* (manioc-root meal toasted with butter), and sliced oranges.

3034, www.tropicalhotel.com.br. Large resort hotel within its own park, and its own zoo and jungle tours; 12 km (7 miles) from city center. **$$$**

What to Eat

A country as diverse as Brazil naturally has regional specialties, a result of varying geography, climate, and immigration patterns. In parts of the south, the cuisine reflects the influence of a German community, while Italian and Japanese immigrants brought their skills to São Paulo. Some of the most traditional dishes are adapted from African or Portuguese foods.

The staples for many Brazilians, however, are rice, beans, and manioc. Although not a great variety of herbs is used, Brazilian food is tastily seasoned. Many Brazilians enjoy hot pepper *(pimenta)*, and the local *malagueta* chilis range from pleasantly nippy to infernally fiery.

The most unusual Brazilian food is found in Bahia, where a distinct African influence can be tasted in the *dendê* palm oil and coconut milk. The Bahianos are fond of pepper, and many dishes call for ground raw peanuts or cashew nuts and dried shrimp. Two of the most famous Bahian dishes are *vatapá* (fresh and dried shrimp, fish, ground raw peanuts, coconut milk, *dendê* oil, and seasonings thickened with bread into a creamy mush); and *moqueca* (seafood in a *dendê* oil and coconut milk sauce). Although delicious, the palm oil together with the coconut milk can be a rich mixture to digest.

Popular all over Brazil is the *churrasco* or barbecue. Most *churrascarias* offer a *rodizio* option: for a set price diners eat all they can of a variety of meats.

Dishes found in the Amazon include those prepared with *tucupi* (made from manioc leaves and having a slightly numbing effect on the tongue), especially *pato no tucupi* (duck) and *tacacá* broth. There are also many varieties of fruit that are found nowhere else. The rivers produce many fish, including piranha.

Coffee Stop

Café is roasted dark, ground fine, prepared strong, and taken with plenty of sugar. Coffee mixed with hot milk *(café com leite)* is the traditional breakfast beverage throughout Brazil. Other than at breakfast, it is served black in tiny *demitasse* cups.

Drinking Notes

Brazilians are great social drinkers and love to sit for hours talking and often singing with friends over drinks. Brazilian beers are really very good (note that *cerveja* usually refers to bottled beer; draft beer is *chope*).

Brazil's own unique brew is *cachaça*, a strong liquor distilled from sugar cane, a type of rum, but with its own distinct flavor. Each region has its locally produced *cachaça*, also called *pinga*, *cana*, or *aguardente*. Some delightful mixed drinks are concocted with *cachaça*. Tops is the popular *caipirinha* – a simple concoction of *cachaça*, crushed lime – peel included – and sugar topped with plenty of ice.

Where to Eat

Lunch time is usually noon–3pm, although some restaurants stay open all afternoon. For locals, this is the heaviest meal of the day. Dinner is 7pm–midnight (locals tend to eat late), but some restaurants stay open until 1 or 2am. Many restaurants in Brazil are closed Sunday evening and/or Monday. It is advisable to make reservations for the more expensive restaurants.

A portion is usually for two people. It is perfectly acceptable to ask for a doggy bag.

Comida a kilo restaurants (meaning food by weight) are great, cheap places to get a wide choice of good-quality dishes.

The following is a small selection of places to eat in the main cities.

Rio de Janeiro (21)
Cais do Oriente, Rua Visconde de Itaborai 8, Centro, tel: 2233 2531.

Popular bar/restaurant located in an old warehouse. **$$**.
Carlota, Rua Dias Ferreira 64, Leblon, tel: 2540 6821. Stylish and eclectic Brazilian bistro. **$$**
Casa da Feijoada, Rua Prudente de Morais 10, Loja B, Ipanema, tel: 2247 2776. Specializes in Brazil's favorite dish. **$$**
Confeitaria Colombo, Rua Goncalves Dias 32 (Center), tel: 2232 2300. Worth a visit for the fantastic Art Nouveau decor. Afternoon teas a specialty. **$**
Olympe, Rua Custódio Serrão 62, Jardim Botanico, tel: 2539 4542. Home to Claude Troisgros, Rio's most inventive chef. **$$$**
Porcão, Avda Infante Dom Henrique, Flamengo, tel: 3389 8989. Outstanding chain of barbecue houses; other branches in Ipanema and Barra. **$$**

São Paulo (11)
Arabia, Rua Haddock Lobo 1397, tel: 3061 2203. Wonderful Lebanese food. **$$**
Baby Beef Rubaiyat, Alameda Santos, 86, Paraíso, tel: 3141 1188, Avda Brigadeiro Faria Lima, 2954, Itaim Bibi, tel: 3078 9488. Rubaiyat are among the best of the city's barbecue houses. **$$**
Cheiro Verde, Rua Peixoto Gomide 1413, tel: 289 6853. Cheap and cheerful vegetarian restaurant. **$**
Koyama, Rua 13 de Maio 1050, Bela Vista, tel: 283 1833. Excellent Japanese food. **$$**

Brasília (61)
Porcão, SCES, trecho 2, conjunto 35, restaurante 3, tel: 3223 2002. Branch of Brazil's most popular up-market chain of *churrascaria rodízios*. **$$**
Vila Borghese, Comércio Local Sul, Quadra. 201, Bloco A, lj.33,

tel: 226 5650. Open daily for traditional Italian food. **$$**

Salvador (71)
Barbacoa, Avda Tancredo Neves 909, Pituba, tel: 342 4666. Open daily. One of the best barbecue houses in Salvador. **$**.
Trapiche Adelaide, Praça dos Tupinambas 2, Avda do Contorno, tel: 326 2211. International cuisine right on the bay. **$$$**
Yemanjá, Avda Otávio Mangabeira, 4655, Jardim Armação, tel: 3461 9010. If you visit Salvador you must try Bahian food, and Yemanjá is one of the city's best. **$$**

Recife/Olinda (81)
Bargaço, Avda Boa Viagem 670, tel: 3465 1847. On the sea front; seafood a specialty. **$$$**
Oficina do Sabor, Rua do Amparo 335, Olinda, tel: 3429 3331. One of the best restaurants in the region. **$$$**

Music and Dance

Brazil has exerted great influence on musical styles abroad, especially jazz. It is easy to buy Brazilian music abroad, but there is much more to discover on-the-spot.
 A huge variety of musical forms have developed in different parts of the country, many with accompanying forms of dance. Bossa nova, samba, *choro*, and *seresta* are popular in Rio and São Paulo, for example. And if you are visiting at Carnival, you'll see and hear plenty of music and dancing in the streets, mostly samba in Rio and frevo in the northeast. There are also shows all year long that give tourists a taste of Brazilian folk music and dance.
 The classical music and dance season runs from Carnival through mid-December. Major Brazilian cities (mainly Rio, São Paulo, and Brasília) are included in world concert tours by international performers. One of the most important classical music festivals in South America takes place in July each year in Campos do Jordão in the state of São Paulo.

Chile
A – Z

Getting Acquainted

Area 756,626 sq. km (292,134 sq. miles)
Capital Santiago de Chile
Population 16 million, 90 percent of whom are mestizo.
Language Spanish
Currency Peso
Weights & measures Metric
Electricity 220 volts
Time zone GMT -4hrs, EST +1hr
Dialing code 56 (Santiago +2)

Government & Economy

Chile had a military dictatorship with a horrendous human rights record until 1990, when a peaceful transfer of power to a civilian government took place. Michelle Bachelet became Chile's first woman president in 2006.
 Chile is a stable country with a free-market economy. Main exports are copper, fruit, forestry products, salmon, wine, and methanol.

Visas

Passports and tourist cards only are required by citizens of Australia, Canada, Ireland, New Zealand, South Africa, the UK, and the US. However, there is an entry tax for citizens of the US (US$100), Canada (US$132), Australia (US$56), and Mexico (US$15). Tourist cards valid for 90 days are issued upon arrival (Australian and North American nationals will be charged for this), and can be renewed for a further 90 days for a small fee at the immigration office on Calle Moneda in Santiago. To stay longer than 180 days, go to a

Embassies/Consulates

Australia: Isidora Goyenechea 3621, Santiago, tel: 550 3500, fax: 331 5960, www.chile.embassy.gov.au
Canada: Calle Nueva Tajamar 481, Torre Sur, 12th floor, Santiago, tel: 362 9660, fax: 362 9663, www.maeci.gc.ca
New Zealand: El Golf 99, Office 703, Santiago, tel: 290 9802, www.nzembassy.cl
South Africa: Avda 11 de Septiembre 2353, 17th floor, Santiago, tel: 231 2862, www.embajada-sudafrica.cl
UK: El Bosque Norte 0125, 3rd floor, Santiago, tel: 370 4100, fax: 370 4160, www.britemb.cl
US: Avda Andrés Bello 2800, Santiago, tel 232 2600, fax: 330 3710, www.usembassy.cl

border country and return – a quicker method than the bureaucratic application procedure.

Customs

Bags may be searched for agricultural products that may harbor disease, so food should be eaten or disposed of.

Clearance at border posts inland can be a bit more cumbersome: bags here are thoroughly searched for agricultural products, and contraband searches are more frequent. Still, delays are not that long.

Money

Changing money on the streets is not advisable anywhere.

ATMs, called *Redbanc*, are prolific, even in quite small towns. They accept most major credit cards and bank cards, although not in remote areas. Hotels, restaurants, and shops generally take most credit cards. Major banks, bureaux de change, and hotels will change dollar traveler's checks, and some shops and restaurants also accept them, albeit for a large fee.

US dollars are the most easily exchanged currency in Chile.

Getting Around

From the Airport
Santiago's main airport for international and domestic flights is **Arturo Merino Benítez Airport**, 26 km (16 miles) west of the city. It is relatively small and customs procedures are quick and easy. There are frequent buses from the airport for about US$1.30, and shuttle buses, which cost around US$12. If taking a taxi, it is advisable to use the official service, which has a desk close to the arrivals exit. A taxi to the center of town should cost around US$30.

There is an exit tax of about US$30 on international flights; on domestic flights it is around US$9.

By Air
Flying long distances in Chile is rather expensive, although cheap last-minute offers are available. Domestic flights are operated by LAN (tel: 600 526 2000) and two much smaller companies, **Sky Airline** (tel: 600 600 2828) and **Aerolíneas del Sur** (tel: 800 710 300). Tickets with LAN can also be purchased online at www.lan.com for pick-up at the airport.

By Bus
Chile's private intercity bus services are excellent and inexpensive. Roads are well maintained and buses are new, comfortable, and run on time. In Santiago, do check carefully which terminal your bus leaves from, as there are several, all on the main underground line: **Terminal Santiago**, Avda B O'Higgins 3848, tel: 376 1750; **Terminal Norte** (also known as Terminal San Borja), Borja 184, tel: 776 0645; **Terminal Los Héroes**, Tucapel Jiménez 21, tel: 672 4396; **Terminal Alameda**, Avda B O'Higgins 3750, tel: 776 0645. Buses to Valparaíso and Viña del Mar are best caught outside the **Pajaritos Station** of the Metro (Avda General Bonilla 5600), where they leave approximately every 15 minutes.

During off-peak times, you can bargain for a cheaper fare; always

ask before you pay full fare.

In 2007, all Santiago's bus routes changed in a bid to rationalize the previously chaotic situation. The new Transantiago system uses smaller buses on short "feeder" routes that connect with "trunk" routes along major arteries, served by larger articulated buses, and the metro. Fares are paid using a prepaid smartcard called BIP! which can be purchased at metro stations and many shops. One fare, currently around US$0.80, covers up to three connections (only one of which can be to the subway), within a 2-hour period.

By Train
Sadly, rail travel in Chile is a shadow of its past glories. The remaining services cover only destinations between Santiago and Chillán in the south. There are no services to the north or the coast. All trains leave from Santiago's Estación Central.

Train timetables can be obtained and bookings made by calling (600) 585 5000, or in person at Estación Central, Av. B. O'Higgins 3170, Mon–Sat 7am–11.45pm, Sun 8am–11.45pm, or at the railway office in the Universidad de Chile metro station (tel: 02-688 3297), Mon–Fri 9am–8pm and Saturday 9am–2pm.

Public Holidays

- **January 1** New Year's Day
- **March/April** Easter
- **May 1** Labor Day
- **May 21** Navy Day
- **June** Monday closest to St Peter and St Paul
- **July 16** Day of the Virgin of Carmen (Chile's patron saint)
- **August 15** Assumption
- **September 18** Independence Day
- **September 19** Army Day
- **October 12** Discovery of America
- **November 1** All Saints' Day
- **December 8** Immaculate Conception
- **December 25** Christmas Day

Hitchhiking

Hitchhiking in Chile is relatively safe, except for women on their own, and relatively easy. Truckers will pick you up sometimes, but motorists are reluctant to stop, so don't depend on it. Traffic is sparse in isolated regions.

By Metro (Subway)

Santiago's metro is comfortable and efficient. There are four lines: one runs east–west beneath Av. B. O'Higgins and on through Providencia, while the other three link residential suburbs in the south of the city to this line. Buy tickets at the various stations – currently US$0.80 per ticket – or use a prepaid BIP! smartcard *(see page 374)*.

By Taxi

Black taxis with yellow roofs can be found at taxi ranks or can be flagged down in the street, and all run on meters. However, women on their own at night are advised to call a radio taxi rather than to flag one down in the street. Tipping the driver is not customary.

Collective taxis *(colectivos)* have a fixed route similar to buses and may carry up to five passengers. The fare is displayed on the windshield. Tourist taxis are blue, but are more expensive and do not run on a meter. They can be found in front of hotels.

Emergencies

The police *(carabineros)* patrol regularly, and they are generally helpful and friendly.

Call **133** for police, **131** for ambulance, **132** for the fire brigade.

There are several good hospitals in Santiago, such as **Clínica Las Condes**, Calle Lo Fontecilla 441, emergency tel: 800 211 800/210 5150; **Clínica Santa María**, Avda Santa María 0500, tel: 461 2001; and **Clínica Aleman**, Avda Vitacura 5951, tel: 210 1111. Contact your embassy for a list of physicians.

Business Hours

Business hours change from city to city. In Santiago: they are as follows: Mon–Fri 9am–1.30pm, 2.30–6.30pm. Banks open Mon–Fri 9am–2pm. Exchange houses generally open Mon–Fri 9am–6pm, and Sat am.

Newspapers

There are several dailies such as *El Mercurio, La Tercera, La Nación,* and *La Segunda.* For business and finance read *El Diario Financiero* and *Estrategia.* International newspapers are available, with a delay of several days.

Postal Services

Most post offices open Mon–Fri 9am–6pm, and Sat until noon. The system is fairly reliable. Poste restante in Santiago is in the main post office on Plaza de Armas.

Telephones

Calls overseas can be made direct from public telephones and from call centers. You must prefix the code of the carrier you want to handle your call: there are over 30, but the largest – although not necessarily the cheapest – are Entel (its code is 123) and CTC (188). It is possible to call collect (reverse the charges), and the quality of the lines is excellent. Off-peak rates apply after 8pm on weekdays, after 2pm on Saturday, and all day on Sunday.

Where to Stay

There is a high standard of hotels in Chile, especially in the main cities. Recommended places in the major tourist areas include:

Santiago (02)

Hotel Foresta, Calle Victor Subercaseaux 353, tel: 639 6261, fax: 632 2996. A beautiful place overlooking Santa Lucía Park. **$$**
Hotel Four Points by Sheraton, Santa Magdalena 111, tel: 750 0300, fax: 750 0434. An excellent hotel at the lower end of the top price range. **$$$**
Hotel Los Españoles, Calle Los Españoles 2539, tel: 232 1824, fax: 233 1048. Classy, quiet establishment, near shopping and restaurant district. **$$**
Hotel Montecarlo, Victoria Subercaseaux 209, tel: 638 1176, fax: 633 5577, www. hotelmontecarlo.cl. Traditional hotel overlooking Santa Lucía Park. **$$**
Radisson Plaza Hotel, Avda Vitacura 2610, tel: 203 6000, fax: 203 6001. One of the best-located of the city's many 5-star hotels. **$$$**
Residencial Londres, Calle Londres 54, tel: 633 9192, fax: 638 2215. Good atmosphere. Single rooms available. **$**
Hostelling Santiago, Calle Cienfuegos 151, tel: 671 8532, fax: 672 8880, www.hostelling.cl. Near the Los Héroes subway station. **$**

Viña del Mar (032)

Cap Ducal, Avda Marina 51, tel: 262 6655, fax: 266 5478. The best sea-front view, with an excellent but expensive restaurant. **$$**
Hotel del Mar, Avda Perú, esq. Los Héroes, tel: 250 0800, fax: 250 0801, www.hoteldelmar.com. Modern luxury hotel adjoining the casino. **$$$**
Hotel Monterilla, Dos Norte 65, tel: 297 6950, fax: 269 8795. Pleasant and centrally located. **$$**
Hotel O'Higgins, Plaza Vergara s/n, tel: 288 2016, fax: 288 3537, www.panamericanahoteles.cl. Viña's famous grand hotel. **$$**
Residencial Victoria, Calle Valparaíso 40, tel: 297 7370. Large and characterful place, opposite the railway station. **$**

Valparaíso (032)

Puerto Natura, Hector Calvo 850, Cerro Bellavista, tel: 222 4405,

Hotel Price Guide

Prices for a double room including continental breakfast:
$ = US$50 – inexpensive
$$ = US$50–100 – moderate
$$$ = US$100 plus – expensive

www.puertonatura.cl (in Spanish). This lovely B&B, with spa and massage services, was the home of the architect who designed Neruda's house La Sebastiana. **$$$**

Arica (058)
Hotel Arica, Avda San Martín 599, tel: 254 540, fax: 231 133, www.panamericanahoteles.cl. Good access to the best beaches. **$$**
Hotel Azapa Inn, G. Sánchez 660, tel: 244 517, fax: 225 191, www.azapainn.cl (in Spanish). Located in pleasant grounds, but some distance from the beach. **$$**
Hostal Huanta Jaya, 21 de Mayo 660, tel: 314 605. In the center of town; cheap and basic, but clean. **$$**
Savona, Calle Yungay 380, tel: 232 319, fax: 231 606. Quiet and comfortable and it has a laundry. **$.**

Castro (065)
Hotel Unicornio Azul, Avda Pedro Montt 228, tel: 632 359, fax: 632 808. Don't miss this delightful hotel. A good base to see the best of Chiloé Island. **$$**

Easter Island (039)
Unfortunately, hotels on Easter Island are both expensive and mediocre. Two of the better options are:
Hotel Manutara, Hanga Roa s/n, tel: 210 0768. On edge of the main town, clean and comfortable. **$$$**
Hotel Iorana, Ana Magaro s/n, tel: 210 0312. Slightly more luxurious than Hotel Manutara, but a taxi ride from town. **$$$**
Many local families also rent out cabins or rooms; these are best chosen on arrival (and after inspection) from among the many offers touted at the airport.

What to Eat

Lunch is the main meal of the day in Chile, and restaurants have lunch menus for as little as US$4. It starts with a simple salad, followed by a hot bowl of *cazuela* (soup with meat, chicken or seafood) or *empanadas* (pastries stuffed with meat, onions, a boiled egg, and a couple of olives). In summer don't miss *humitas*, seasoned puréed corn wrapped in

Drinking Notes

Wine is by far the best alcoholic drink in Chile. *Concha y Toro, Carmen, Santa Rita,* and *San Pedro* are among the oldest names. They are all worth sampling and most are inexpensive *(see page 284 for more details).*

corn leaves, or *pastel de choclo*, a corn and meat pie. Seafood is a favorite in Chile. Try *jaiva* (crab) or *locos* (abalone). The main course usually consists of rice and chicken, meat or fried fish. Dessert is followed by a cup of instant coffee.

At night, sandwiches are popular fare: Chile is famous for its *churrasco* (steak sandwich with avocado), *chacarero* (steak with green beans), or *completos* (hot dogs with tomatoes, avocado, and mayonnaise).

Where to Eat

Santiago (02)
For good, inexpensive eating, try the Bellavista neighborhood, along Calles Pío Nono, Constitución, and Antonia López de Bello. Watch your belongings.
Aquí Está Coco, Calle La Concepción 236, tel: 235 8649. Not cheap, but by far the best place in Santiago to sample Chile's wonderful fish. **$$$**
Astrid y Gastón, Antonio Bellet 201, tel: 650 9125. Excellent Peruvian food in one of the city's most acclaimed restaurants; booking ahead recommended. **$$$**
Café Melba, Don Carlos 2898, tel: 232 4546. A good place for breakfast, lunch, or coffee. **$$**
Europeo, Alonso de Córdova 2417, tel: 208 3603. Perhaps Santiago's best restaurant and one of its most expensive. **$$$**
Frederick's, Alimirante Gotuzzo 102, tel: 696 1890. An oasis of good food in crowded downtown Santiago. Food is served from 7.30am to 9pm. **$$$**
Patio Bellavista, Pío Nono 55, tel: 777 4582. A new restaurant and

arts and crafts center located in the heart of Bellavista. The complex includes Italian, Peruvian, Mediterranean, and seafood restaurants. **$$**
If you are near the downtown Mercado Central at lunch time, go to **Donde Augusto** for fish and shellfish and lots of atmosphere. **$**

Valparaíso (032)
Pasta e Vino, Templeman 352, tel: 249 6187. An excellent restaurant but booking is essential. **$$$**
Café Vinílico, Almirante Montt 448, tel: 223 0665. Bar/restaurant serving simple meals. **$**

Viña del Mar (032)
For cheap meals, it is best to eat sandwiches and *platos del día* at Viña's innumerable cafés. **Cap Ducal**, the city's most famous waterfront restaurant, serves excellent seafood. For a reasonable lunch, try the daily menu at **Club de Viña** on the plaza. North of Viña, the coastal stretch is a happy

Restaurant Guide

Prices for a three-course meal for two, including house wine:
$ = US$15 – inexpensive
$$ = US$15–25 – moderate
$$$ = US$25–30 – expensive

hunting ground for small restaurants, serving local seafood.

Culture in Santiago

There are over 100 theaters in Santiago, putting on classical, modern, or avant-garde plays by Chilean and other playwrights. The best theaters are:
Centro Cultural Matucana 100, Avda Matucana 100, tel: 682 4502.
Teatro La Comedia, Calle Merced 349, tel: 639 1523. The home of one of Chile's best theater groups.
Teatro Antonio Varas, Calle Morandé 25, tel: 698 1200.
The best of the city's multi-screen cinema complexes, **Cinemark 12**, is in Alto Las Condes shopping mall, while **Showcase**

Cinemas Parque Arauco is in the shopping mall of the same name.

Nightlife

Santiago
Nightlife starts late in the capital – bars begin to fill up at about 10pm; and don't even think about going to a nightclub before midnight. For bars, try the area around the junction of Manuel Montt with Providencia and along nearby Santa Beatriz. On Manuel Montt itself, you'll find the famous **Liguria**, but there are plenty of other options.

Drinks are cheaper in bars around Plaza Ñuñoa, which attract a younger crowd. At Jorge Washington 52, you'll also find **Batuta**, one of the best places in Santiago to hear live music. Bars abound in the Bellavista neighborhood and many new bands play there. **La Casa en el Aire** (Antonia López de Bello 0125) also has live music most nights of the week and, for dancing, try **La Havana Salsa** (Dominica 142).

Where to Shop

Chile's most exclusive shopping street is **Alonso de Córdova**, off Adva Vitacura, but the **Alto Las Condes** and **Parque Arauco** malls (both on Avda Kennedy) also offer a wide range of local and imported goods.

Stores open Mon–Fri 10.30am–7.30pm, Sat 9.30am–1.30pm. Most, except for the malls, are closed on Sunday.

On Avda Apoquindo 9085, **Alba Pueblito de los Dominicos** is a collection of old-style buildings housing 200 shops where more than 300 craftsmen and women work and sell their goods.

Art in Santiago

There are several art galleries in the upmarket Vitacura neighborhood, including Galería Animal, Galería Art Espacio, and Galería Isabel Aninat on Alonso de Córdova, and AMS Marlborough on Nueva Costanera.

Colombia A – Z

Getting Acquainted

Area 1,140,000 sq. km (439,600 sq. miles), bordering Panama with coasts on the Caribbean Sea and the Pacific Ocean.
Capital Bogotá
Population 43 million, of European, African, and Amerindian descent. Nearly half a million belong to one of 60 tribes.
Language Spanish
Currency Colombian peso
Weights & measures Metric
Electricity 110 volts
Time zone GMT –5hrs, EST
Dialing code 57 (Bogotá +1)

Government & Economy

Colombia's "limited democracy" is based on the constitution of 1991. The president and members of the Senate and House of Representatives are directly elected. Indigenous and Afrocolombian peoples have the right to two Senate seats each. Right-wing Alvaro Uribe has been in power since 2002 (re-elected in 2006).

Colombia has one of South America's strongest economies and is self-sufficient in energy. Manufacturing and agriculture are the most important sources of revenue; Colombia is a major exporter of cut flowers and coffee, and produces 60 percent of the world's emeralds and 70 percent of the world's cocaine.

Money

There are some legal *casas de cambios* (exchange bureaux) but it is best to exchange cash and traveler's checks (in US dollars) at a bank. Since a photocopy of your passport is often required, you can speed up transactions by taking a supply of spare photocopies with you from home. Do not change money on the street and avoid carrying large amounts of cash.

Credit cards (Visa, MasterCard, American Express) are widely used, but often accepted only in high-priced establishments in bigger cities. Debit cards (Cirrus or Maestro) can be easily used at ATM machines in cities. Avoid withdrawing money after dark.

Visas

Visitors to Colombia need a passport but currently do not require a visa. Check, however, since regulations may change. Visitors are given a 60-or 90-day stay on arrival. Stiff fines are imposed if passports are not stamped on arrival and if stays exceeding 60 days are not authorized by the Colombian Immigration Agency (DAS, tel: 01-640 8997/408 8000).

Extensions of 15 days for a maximum six-month period may be applied for.

Exit stamps are necessary on departure. Foreigners pay US$37 departure tax when leaving Colombia by air. Make sure that your documentation is stamped on arrival, to avoid paying double the exit tax on departure.

Getting Around

From the Airport
Bogotá's international airport is at **El Dorado**, about 12 km (7 miles) from the city center. Registered yellow taxi services will take you to the city centre. The rate will be determined at the Taxi Registration Point and the address will be registered and handed to the taxi driver. Local buses run to and from the airport during the day but luggage space is very limited.

By Bus
Within Bogotá, the Transmilenio, a modern rapid-transit system, runs

on certain routes and is faster than other buses. Several countries' foreign ministries advise visitors to avoid overland routes, to travel by air and only to major cities. Bus transportation along the main routes is generally good, but deteriorates when heading into the more remote areas. The alternative on main routes is a *buseta* (minibus) or *colectivo* (a shared taxi that is more expensive but much quicker).

From Ecuador, buses go to and from the border at Tulcan/Ipiales. From Venezuela, you can choose between the coastal route from Maracaibo to Santa Marta, or the highland route from Caracas and Mérida to Cucuta via San Cristobál. From Brazil, the only way to enter is via Leticia in the Amazon basin and then fly to Bogotá.

By Taxi
In main cities, taxis are cheap and relatively reliable. Every taxi has to use a meter. It is advisable to order a taxi by phone (especially at night) on 01-3 111 111 or 01-4 111 111 (the operator will give you the car number and the key code). Always lock the door once inside the car.

Crime
Although most Colombians are honest and friendly, theft occurs in the larger cities, and visitors should look after valuables at all times. The Tourist Police Office is at Carrera 13 No. 26-62, Bogotá, tel: 01-337 4413, open daily 8am–5pm. In case of theft or loss of documents or valuables, call the number of the national police (112) or ask for the nearest police station.

Medical Services
Medical centres in Bogotá include: **Cruz Roja Colombiana**, Carrera/Avda 68 No. 68B-31, tel: 01-437 53 00. Emergency, tel: 01-437 6369 or 132.
Hospital San Ignacio, Carrera 7 No. 40-62, tel: 01-594 6161, Call Centre: 01-422 7722.

Clínica del Country, Carrera 16 No. 82-37, 01-530 1350 or 530 1340 Make sure you have valid health insurance before you travel.

Newspapers
National daily papers include the liberal *El Tiempo*, the evening *El Espacio*, the business paper *La República*, and the conservative *El Nuevo Siglo*. *El Espectador* is a weekly newspaper. International newspapers can be found at the Librería Nacional, Puente Aereo No. 93-30. *Plan B* and *Go* are monthly magazines that include an English-language listings section.

Postal Services
There are two national postal systems in Colombia. The more reliable and efficient one consists of private companies (e.g. Deprisa and Servientrega). They have many offices in most large cities. The other system, Adpostal, is state-run, cheaper but less reliable and used in small towns and rural areas as well as for international post.

Business Hours
Bogotá: generally Mon–Fri 8am–5pm. Banks are open Mon–Fri 9am–3pm; some branches open additionally 5pm–7pm and on Saturdays. Outside of Bogotá: usually Mon–Fri 8am–noon and 2pm–4pm, Sat 10am–4pm.

Telephone & Fax
Telephone systems are automated and phone cards can be used. People on the street offer cheap cellphone calls to local, national, or any other cellphone number in Colombia. Telecom offices in cities have international call facilities.

Parks & Reserves
Permits are sometimes required to visit Colombia's parks and nature reserves. For permits and

information contact the **Office of Ecotourism and Attention to Visitors**, Caja Agraria building, Carrera 10, 20–30, 4th floor, Bogotá; tel/fax: 243 3095, www.parquesnacionales.gov.co

Useful Addresses
Tourist Offices
There are several tourist information offices in Bogotá, including at Carrera 8 No. 9-83, tel: 01-327 4916 or Unicentro, Avenida 15 No. 123-30, 1st floor, Entrada 8, tel: 01-213 8800. Limited information is also available at the Edificio Centro de Comercio Internacional, Calle 28 No. 13A-15, Local 5. Additional information: www.bogotaturismo.gov.co or www.culturayturismo.gov.co

Tourist Agencies
Bogotá: Panamericana de Viajes, Carrera 11A No. 93A-80, Oficina 104, tel: 01-635 4000 or Fundación Colombiana de Caminantes Sal Si Puedes, Carrera 7 No. 17-01, Oficinas 640, tel: 01-283 37 65.
Santa Marta: Reales Tours, Carrera 1A, 20–09, tel: 054-214 418, can arrange trips to Ciudad Perdida, Parque Tayrona, Cabo de la Vela, and the Guajira Peninsula.
Cartagena: There are many tourist agencies in Bocagrande, the modern beach resort.

Embassies/Consulates
Canada: Carrera 7, 115–33 14th floor, A.A. 110069, Bogotá, tel: 01-657 9800, fax: 657 9912.
UK: Carrera 9 No. 76-49, 9th floor, tel: 01-317 6690, fax: 317 6265.
US: Calle 22D-bis, No. 47–51, tel: 01-315 0811, fax: 315 2197.

Hotel Price Guide
Prices for a double room including continental breakfast:
$ = US$20 – inexpensive
$$ = US$20–50 – moderate
$$$ = US$50 plus – expensive

Where to Stay

Bogotá (01)

Hosteria de la Candelaria, Calle 9, 3–11. tel: 342 1727. In a converted colonial mansion and furnished with beautiful antiques. **$**

La Fontana Estelar, Avda 127, 21–10, tel: 615 4400, fax: 216 0449. Recommended; good food, lovely gardens. **$$$**

Tequendama, Carrera 10, 26–21, tel: 382 0300, fax: 282 2860. Gym, sauna, and spa facilities. **$$$**

Budget hotels, often dismal, are located between calles 13 and 17, and Avda Caracas and Carrera 17. This area can be unsafe after dark.

Cartagena (05)

Cartagena-Hilton, Avda Almirante Brion, El Laguito, tel: 665 0666, fax: 665 0661, www.cartagena hilton.com. A luxury hotel with several restaurants. **$$$**

Hotel de Caribe, Carrera 1, 2–87, tel: 650 155, fax: 653 707, www.hotelcaribe.com. A palatial building, close to the sea and the historic town center. **$$–$$$**

What to Eat

A few Colombian specialties worth trying are:

ajico: a soup of chicken, potatoes, and other vegetables.

arepa: a maize pancake.

arroz con coco: rice cooked in coconut oil.

bandeja paisa: a dish of ground beef, sausages, beans, rice, plantain, and avocado.

carne asada: grilled meat.

cazuela de mariscos: seafood stew.

chocolate santafereño: hot chocolate accompanied by cheese and bread.

comidas corrientes: literally, ordinary meals; usually a fried piece of meat with beans and rice, found in many cheap restaurants.

puchero: broth of chicken, beef, and pork.

tamales: chopped pork with rice and vegetables wrapped in maize pastry.

Restaurant Guide

Prices for a three-course meal for two, including house wine:
$ = US$20 – inexpensive
$$ = US$20–50 – moderate
$$$ = US$50 plus – expensive

Where to Eat

Bogotá (01)

Carbón de Pal, Avda 19, 106–12, tel: 214 0450. The place to go for grilled meats. **$$**

Casa Vieja, Avda Jiménez 3–63; Carrera 10 No. 26-60, Carrera 13 No. 3-7 and Carrera 11 No. 89-08. The four branches of this restaurant offer excellent regional food. **$–$$**

La Tienda del Café, Carrera 5 No. 70A-05, tel: 542 4884. Colombian and international meals. **$$**

Nightlife

Bogotá

There are several good bars in the zona rosa, calles 81 and 84, carreras 11 and 14, or in the Parque de la 93, Calle 93, Carreras 11A and 13. Nothing gets moving until after 10pm on weekends.

Cartagena

A Caribbean trio plays on weekends at **Paco's** opposite Santo Domingo church – a good place to drink into the small hours. The bar attached to **La Quemada** has live salsa on Friday and Saturday. For discos, head for the **Bocagrande** district.

Where to Shop

For Colombian handicrafts, the best place in Bogotá is **Artesanías de Colombia**, Carrera 3 No. 18A-58 or Carrera 11 No. 84-12. Emeralds can be bought in the joyeías in La Candelaria Centro, plus **Palacio de la Esmeralda**, Calle 16 No. 5-24, tel: 01-283 3578 or **The Emerald Center**, Corner Avda Jimenez and Carrera 5. For an exclusive collection of Colombian jewelry visit **L.A. Cano**, Centro Andino, Carrera 11 No. 82-51, Local 210, tel: 01-610 1175.

Ecuador A – Z

Getting Acquainted

Area 270,700 sq. km (104,500 sq. miles), bordering Colombia in the north, Peru to the south and east and the Pacific Ocean in the west.

Capital Quito

Population 13 million, 40 percent of whom are native Quichua.

Language Spanish and Quechua

Currency US Dollar = 100 cents

Weights & measures Metric

Electricity 110 volts

Time zone GMT -5hrs (Galápagos Islands -6hrs)

Dialing code 593 (Quito +2)

Government & Economy

Democracy was established in Ecuador in 1979. Rafael Correa became president in 2006. The economy is based on oil, fishing, bananas, coffee, and cocoa. Tourism is also an important source of foreign revenue, in addition to the funds sent home by the large number of migrants who have moved to North America and Europe in search of better opportunities.

Visas

Visas are not required for a stay of up to 90 days. Permits (known as T3s) for a 30-day stay are issued at the border or point of arrival and can easily be extended. For visa extensions, go to Avda Amazonas 2639, opposite El Jardín shopping mall, open 8am–noon and 3–6pm. The immigration office in Quito is at Calle Independencia and Amazonas 3149, tel: 2454 122. The main police office dealing with tourist matters is on Calle Mantúfar. To enter the country, you will need a passport valid for six months, a return ticket, and proof of sufficient funds for your stay.

Money

Travelers' checks and credit cards are more widely accepted than debit cards and in rural areas it is best to travel with small denomination notes.

On Sundays and holidays, when banks and *casas de cambio* are shut, you can change money in the big hotels. Travelers' checks can be changed almost as easily as cash.

Major credit cards (particularly Visa and MasterCard) are accepted in the larger hotels, restaurants, and tourist-oriented shops.

ATMS are common throughout the country, but they can be unreliable.

Newspapers

The main daily newspapers are *El Comercio, Hoy, Tiempo*, and *Ultimas Noticias*. Foreign papers are on sale in Quito.

Getting Around

By Air

AeroGal, Icaro, and TAME connect the principal urban centers – Quito, Guayaquil, and Cuenca. Flying time Guayaquil–Quito is about 30 minutes. AeroGal and TAME run regular services to the Galápagos.

Ecuador has international airports at Quito and Guayaquil. From Quito's **Mariscal Sucre Airport** there are buses to the old and new city centers, and taxi fares are around US$5. Taxis from Guayaquil's **José Joaquin de Olmedo Airport** to the city cost US$4–5, and there are also buses. Ensure your carrier has arranged to get you to Quito if you are landing at Guayaquil. There is a departure tax of US$32 for international flights.

By Bus

Buses in Ecuador are cheap, plentiful, and the most convenient way to travel, even though many roads are unpaved, and landslides

are common in mountainous regions. Some air-conditioned, luxury buses *(autobús de lujo)* cover the most popular routes. Always carry your passport when traveling by bus.

Many travelers enter Ecuador from Peru at the Tumbes–Huaquillas border post, changing buses at the frontier. Buses are frequent both ways. To Colombia, almost everyone takes the Quito–Ibarra, Tulcán–Pasto road.

Postal Services

It is worth having your letters certified *(con certificado)* for about 10 cents – you get a receipt which won't do much practical good, but means that your letter's existence is recorded somewhere.

The main post office in Quito is at Calle Eloy Alfaro 354 and 9 de Octubre (New Quito). Poste restante *(lista de correos)* letters should be sent to Calle Espejo 935 and Guayaquil (Old Town).

Telecommunications

Ecuador's telephone network is run by Andinatel, Pacifitel, Etapa, and a couple of private companies, and one of the best places to make calls is at the telephone company's office in each town. Debit cards for public telephones are not interchangeable between networks.

Hotels add hefty surcharges, usually with discounts after 7pm.

There are numerous internet cafés in Quito, Guayaquil, and Cuenca, many of which also offer a cheap internet phone service.

River Transport

In the Oriente (Eastern lowlands), motorized dugout canoes are the chief form of public transport on Ecuador's main rivers. They can carry up to 30 passengers, as well as an unbelievable amount of cargo and livestock. Seating is on wooden boards, and bags are usually stashed up at the front end of the boat under a tarpaulin.

Embassies/Consulates

Canada: Avda 6 de Diciembre 2816 and Paul Rivet, Quito, tel: 02-223 2114, www.quito.gc.ca
UK: Edificio Citiplaza, Avda Naciones Unidas and República de El Salvador, Quito, tel: 02-297 0800/0801, fax: 297 0809, www.britembquito.org.ec
US: Avda 12 de Octubre and Patria, Quito, tel: 02-256 2890, www.usembassy.org.ec

Public Holidays

● **January 1** New Year's Day
● **January 6** Festival of the Three Kings
● **March/April** Carnival (date variable, precedes Lent)
● **April** Holy Week; festivities on Good Friday and Easter Sunday (date variable)
● **May 1** Labor Day
● **May 24** Commemoration of the Battle of Pinchincha.
● **July 24** Simon Bolívar's birthday
● **August 10** Independence Day
● **October 12** Columbus Day
● **November 1** All Saints' Day
● **November 2** All Souls' Day
● **December 25** Christmas Day

Tours

For a useful list of some of the many companies offering trips in Ecuador, check out www.lata.org, the website of the Latin American Travel Association in the UK.

The Oriente

Metropolitan Touring, República de El Savador 970, Quito, tel: 02-298

A much more comfortable (and expensive) alternative is the *Manatee Amazon Explorer*, which sails on the River Napo and offers a full program of excursions. Fully-inclusive packages can be booked through **Advantage Travel**, El Telégrafo E10-63 and Juan de Alcántara, Quito, tel: 02-246 2871, www.advantageecuador.com.

Excursions

Among Ecuador's snow-capped peaks, Chimborazo, Cotopaxi, El Altar, and Tungurahua are certainly the most challenging, and 20 km (12 miles) north of Quito is **Mitad del Mundo**, where a monument and museum mark the equator. On a clear day, a train or bus ride along the Avenue of the Volcanoes from Quito to Riobamba is recommended.

Pasachoa is a refuge for native birds and plants and has been declared a protected forest. It is run by the Fundación Natura, which is based in Quito. Ideal for a day trip from Quito.

A cable car operates from Quito to the summit of Cruz Loma, Pichincha, at an altitude of 4,050 meters (13,290 ft). The cloud forest around Mindo and the western slopes of Pichincha are excellent for bird-watching and walking.

Antisana volcano is possible to visit as a day trip from Quito. Overnight tours combine Antisana with Papallacta hot springs.

8200, fax: 02-246 4702, www.metropolitan-touring.com, offers luxury all-inclusive, 3–4-day tours staying in jungle lodges. This area is excellent for viewing wildlife. Cheaper and longer excursions can be organized in Misahualli. However, wildlife is very limited here, and trips can be disappointing. Dayuma Lodge is well established and reliable.

The Galápagos Islands

On arrival, all non-Ecuadorian travelers to the islands must pay a US$100 entrance fee in cash (no credit cards). Keep the receipt: you may have to show it again.

There are daily flights by local airlines. Flights are heavily booked so you should confirm and reconfirm your seat and check in early at the airport. Note that if you want to be on Puerto Ayora, it can be difficult to travel between the islands.

The Galápagos archipelago is almost entirely a national park, and no visitor is allowed to enter it without a qualified guide on an organized tour.

A trip on one of the largest cruisers is the most comfortable way to visit the islands. However, access to some islands is limited to smaller vessels.

The **Galápagos Explorer II**, operated by Canodros, is the most luxurious boat touring the islands. Contact any travel agency that specializes in Latin America or see www.canodros.com. The **Santa Cruz**, run by Metropolitan Touring, has all the comforts of a luxury liner. By traveling overnight, these cruisers can easily reach outer islands that smaller yachts struggle to get to. The going is smoother on a large ship too. Both boats are based in the Galápagos, taking around 100 passengers on three- or four-day cruises – one covering the northern islands, the other the southern. You can combine both trips to make a seven-day cruise. Passengers visit the islands in groups of 10 on motorboats (*pangas*) accompanied by English-speaking naturalist guides. The cost works out to US$200–300 per person per night on a twin-share basis (all inclusive, except for bar and airfare), depending on cabin and length of cruise.

Bookings for the *Santa Cruz* can be made at Metropolitan Touring (*see above*) in Quito or Guayaquil, or their US agents Adventure Associates (tel: 800-527 2500, www.adventure-associates.com).

The **Eclipse** is a luxurious, medium-size vessel, holding 48 passengers. It is operated by Ocean Adventures, tel: 02-322 8337, www.oceanadventures.com.ec

There are dozens of yachts operating cruises around the islands, most of which work out of Puerto Ayora, with a growing number based in Puerto Baquerizo Morena. They can take from 6–20 people.

Galápagos Sub-Aqua, Avda Charles Darwin, Puerto Ayora, Isla Santa Cruz, tel/fax: 05-526 350, www.galapagos-sub-aqua.com, offers scuba-diving tours and instruction.

In the UK, many operators feature Galápagos cruises, including **Select Latin America**, tel: 020 7407 1478, www.selectlatinamerica.co.uk

Where to Stay

Quito (02)

Café Cultura, Calle Reina Victoria and Robles, tel/fax: 222 4271, www.cafecultura.com. Unusual decor in individually designed rooms; good restaurant. $$$
Magic Bean, Calle Foch 681 and Juan León Mera, tel: 256 6181, www.ecuadorexplorer.com/magic. Attractive house with shared or private rooms. Good restaurant downstairs. Centrally located. $
Nü House, Plaza del Quinde, tel: 223 0567. A boutique hotel offering style and modern amenities for a reasonable price. $$$
Real Audiencia, Calle Bolívar 220 and Guayaquil, tel: 295 2711, fax: 258 0213, www.realaudiencia.com. In historical center. Well-furnished, spacious rooms. $$
Swissôtel, Avda 12 de Octobre, tel: 256 7600, fax: 256 8079, www.swissotel.com. A large, luxurious hotel with five restaurants, spa, and pool. $$$

Hotel Price Guide

Prices for a double room including continental breakfast:
$ = US$20 or less – inexpensive
$$ = US$20–50 – moderate
$$$ = US$50–100 – expensive

Guayaquil (04)

Hotel Palace, Chile 214, tel: 232 1080, www.hotelpalaceguayaquil.com.ec. Centrally located with a restaurant, laundry, and travel agency. $$$
Ramada, Malecón and Orellana, tel: 256 5555, fax: 256 3036. www.hotelramada.com. Lovely rooms with view of the river, good restaurant, indoor pool. $$–$$$
Tangara Guest House, Block F, House 1, Mañuela Sáenz and O'Leary, tel: 228 4445. $$

Restaurant Guide

Prices for a three-course meal for two, including house wine:
$ = US$10 or less – inexpensive
$$ = US$10–20 – moderate
$$$ = US$20 plus – expensive

Where to Eat

Quito (02)

The main meal of the day is lunch *(almuerzo)*, usually a soup followed by a main dish. The streets off Avenida Amazonas in the new town have many good restaurants.
Astrid y Gastón, Avda La Coruña N32–302 and González Suárez, tel: 250 6621. A clone of the enormously popular restaurant in Lima, Peru, which pairs South American dishes with a contemporary touch and a hip, elegant setting. **$$$**
La Choza, Calle 12 Octubre 1821 and Cordero, tel: 223 0839. Good traditional Ecuadorian food. **$$$**
Su Ceviche, Calle Juan León Mera 1232 and Calama, tel: 252 1843. Good place to try the local *ceviche* (marinated fish). **$**
Zócalo, Calle Calama 469 and Juan León Mera. Terrace restaurant/bar with international food. **$**
Mea Culpa, Plaza Independencia, tel: 295 1190. An elegant restaurant offering international and Mediterranean gourmet cuisine. **$$$**
Theatrum, on the 2nd floor of Teatro Sucre, Plaza del Teatro, tel: 228 9669. Good creative dishes in the city's main theater. **$$**
La Cueva del Oso, Chile and Venezuela, tel: 257 2786. A good place to try Ecuadorian specialties in attractive surroundings. **$$$**

Guayaquil (04)

In Guayaquil, the most pleasant place to eat is aboard one of the boats moored along the Malecón.
For cheaper and often more fiery seafood meals, the area just north of Parque del Centenario is good. Calle Escobedo has popular street cafés serving breakfast.
El Caracol Azul, Calle 9 de Octubre and Los Rios, tel: 228 0461. Said to be one of the best seafood restaurants in Guayaquil. **$$$**
Restaurant Nuvó, Avda Alzibar and Edificio Torrers del Norte Torre B, Local 7, tel: 268 7758. Modern, elegant restaurant with international fusion cuisine and a lengthy wine list. **$$**
Lo Nuestro, Calle Victor Emilio Estrada 903 and Higueras, tel: 238 6398. The most famous steakhouse in Guayaquil. **$$$**

Nightlife

Nightlife in Ecuador often involves bars with astonishingly loud music. In Quito, the new town has its share of clubs, as well as a reasonably authentic English pub, the **Reina Victoria**, on the street of the same name. The best *peña* (folk club) is the **Taberna Quiteña**, which has two venues – Avda Amazonas and Calle Manabí in the old city. **El Pobre Diablo**, La Católica and Galavis, is an authentic Ecuadorian café-bar with a friendly atmosphere.
In Guayaquil, many all-night clubs play the latest American and Latino tunes, and some good Colombian salsa. They are not places for the faint-hearted.
Otavalo has a couple of *peñas* which are lively at the weekend.

Where to Shop

There are dozens of artensanías stores and kiosks in Quito, especially in the Avenida Amazonas area. Several have outstanding selections of high-quality folk art and clothing.
Otavalo market (Wed and Sat; daily June–August) is well worth the 30-minute bus journey from Quito. It is famous for hand-knitted clothing, jewelry, woodcarvings, tapestries, leather goods, and textiles, and offers the best buys in Ecuador, but there are also stores in Quito, Guayaquil, Cuenca, and Baños where similar goods are sold at good prices.
Cuenca is the best place to buy gold and silver jewelry.
Ecuador (*not* Panama) is also the place for Panama hats, which are made by hand in Montecristi but sold all over the country *(see page 213)*.

French Guiana A – Z

Getting Acquainted

Area 91,000 sq. km (35,135 sq. miles)
Capital Cayenne.
Population 199,000; 65 percent of people are of Creole (African/Afro-European) descent.
Languages French (official language), French Guianese Creole and English
Currency Euro (€)
Weights & measures Metric
Electricity 220 volts
Time zone GMT -3hrs, EST +2hrs
International dialing code: 594

Climate

The best times to visit French Guiana are August through December and March through April; the rest of the year there is heavy rain. Even during the dry period it is still very humid.

Government & Economy

French Guiana is an overseas *département* of the French Government. The country receives large subsidies from the French Government and the EU, and the economy is closely bound to that of France. Major sources of income include shrimping, gold mining, and forest products. The European Space Agency operates a satellite launching facility at Kourou.

Visa & Customs

All visitors except EU nationals need a visa to enter the country. There are no restrictions on the amount of currency visitors can bring in to the country.

Money

French Guiana is expensive. It is easy to change US dollars or traveler's checks in Cayenne. Major credit cards are widely accepted, and visitors can get cash advances from ATMS at post offices.

Getting Around

From the Airport
Cayenne-Rochambeau airport is 16 km (10 miles) from Cayenne. There are no buses; taxis cost US$25 (more at night).

By Air
Air Guyane has regular services to Maripasoula and Saül from Cayenne.
Air Guyane: Rochambeau Airport, 97351 Matoury, tel: 293 630; fax: 293 631, www.airguyane.com
To rent a plane or book a charter flight contact: **Guyane Aero Services**, Zone d'aviation générale, 97351 Matoury, tel: 356 162, fax: 358 450. It is also possible to hire a helicopter. Contact **Heli Inter Guyane**, Rochambeau Airport, 97351 Matoury, tel: 356 231, fax: 358 256.

By Boat
Visitors can reach the interior of Guiana by boat. *Pirogues* (dugout canoes) are equipped with outboard motors. Wooden *pirogues* can carry up to 14 passengers. Tours can be arranged; the average journey time is five to six hours. Contact local tour agents in Cayenne or Kourou for details.

By Bus
Cayenne and its suburbs are served by a regular bus network. Buses do not run on Sunday. Routes and schedules are available from SMTC, 3 place des Palmistes, tel: 314 566.
Minibuses *(taxis colectifs)* run between Cayenne and all the coastal towns to St Laurent du Maroni. Departures set out from the bus station, opposite the

Laussat Canal in Cayenne. Information and bookings, tel: 307 305/305 225.

By Car
It is possible to hire cars in French Guiana but it is not advisable unless you are used to driving in developing countries. Driving along dirt tracks is dangerous in the rainy season.

Business Hours

As a general rule, shops open Mon–Fri 9am–12.30pm and 4–7pm; Sat 9am–12.30pm. Banks open Mon–Fri 7.45–11.30am and 3–5pm.

Tourist Information

French Guiana Tourist Board, 12 rue Lalouette, BP 801, 97338 Cayenne; tel: 296 500, fax: 296 501, www.tourisme-guyane.gf

Tourist Offices Overseas
In Paris, the French Guiana Tourist Board is located at 1 rue Clapeyron 75008, Paris, tel: 01 42 94 15 16, www.tourisme-guyane.com
Elsewhere, you should refer to the French tourist office:
Australia: French Govt Tourist Office, Level 20, 25 Bligh Street, 2000 NSW, Sydney, tel: 02 9231 5244, fax: 02 9221 8682, www.aufranceguide.com
Canada: French Govt Tourist Office, 1981 Avenue McGill Collège, Tour Esso, Suite 490, Montreal PQ, H3A 2W9, tel: 514 288 4264, fax: 514 845 4868, www.ca-ukfranceguide.com
UK: French Govt Tourist Office, 178 Piccadilly, London W1J 9AL, tel: 0906 824 4123 (premium-rate line), fax: 020 7493 6594, www.ukfranceguide.com
US: French Govt Tourist Office, 444 Madison Avenue, NY 10022, tel: 212 838 7800, fax: 212 838 7855, www.usfranceguide.com

Media & Communications

Daily newspapers include *France-Guyane* and *La Presse de Guyane*.

There are no English-language newspapers available.
The BBC World Service broadcasts on MHz 17.79, 15.19, and 5.970. The Voice of America can be heard on MHz 13.74, 9.775, 7.405, and 5.995.
The whole telephone system is completely interconnected with that of France. The internet is available in a few places in Cayenne, Kourou, and St Laurent du Maroni, but access can be difficult elsewhere.

Car Hire

Most car-hire agencies open 8am–noon and 2.30–5.30pm, and 8am–noon on Sat.
Avis, 58 Blvd Jubelin (Zone Industrielle), Cayenne, tel: 302 522; fax: 310 791; airport tel: 353 414, www.avis.com
Hertz, Zi Collery Building, Cayenne, tel: 296 930; fax: 244 910; airport tel: 356 069, www.hertz.com
Europcar, Zi Collery Ouest, Cayenne, tel: 351 827; fax: 351 557; airport tel: 356 269, www.europcar.com

Tour Operators

Espace Amazonie, 7 Centre Commercial, Simarouba, tel: 323 430, www.espace-amazonie.com. Highly recommended local operator, **Jal Voyages**, 26 Ave du Général de Gaulle, Cayenne, tel: 316 836 www.jal-voyages.com. Long-established operator.

Tipping

At hotels and restaurants the service charge is always included in the bill. Taxi drivers do not receive a tip.

Where to Stay

Cayenne
Bar Hotel La Bodega, 42 Ave du Général de Gaulle, tel: 302 513, fax: 294 284, www.labodega.fr. Intimate hotel, good value. **$$**

Hotel Price Guide

Prices for a double room
including continental breakfast:
$ = US$20–50 – inexpensive
$$ = US$50–100 – moderate
$$$ = US$100 plus – expensive

Best Western Hotel Amazonia,
28 Ave du Général de Gaulle, tel:
288 300, fax: 319 441,
www.amazonia-hotel.com. Some
rooms have kitchenettes. Air
conditioning, restaurant, and
swimming pool. **$$$**
Central, at the crossroads of rues
Molé and Mecker, tel: 256
565/311 296, fax: 311 296,
www.centralhotel-cayenne.fr **$$**
Hôtel Ajoupa, 160 Route de
Cabassou, tel: 303 308,
fax: 301 282, email:
hotel.ajoupa@wanadoo.fr.
Pool and garden. **$$**
Hotel Ket Tai, 72 Blvd Jubelin,
tel: 301 100, fax: 309 976.
Restaurant and meeting room. **$$**
Novotel, Route de Montabo,
Chemin St Hilaire, tel: 303 888,
fax: 306 356. On the beach with a
swimming pool and restaurant.
$$$

Kourou
Hôtel des Roches, Pointe des
Roches, tel: 320 066, fax: 328
315, www.hotelderoches.com.
Beach-side hotel, with pool, tennis
court, and restaurant. **$$$**
Hôtel Atlantis, Lac Bois Diable, tel:
321 300, fax: 324 012. Swimming
pool. **$$$**
Mercure Ariatel, Lac Bois Diable,
tel: 328 900, fax: 326 160. Luxury
bungalows, with pool. **$$$**

Remire Montjoly
Motel Beauregard, PK 9, 2
Route de Rémire, tel: 354 100,
fax: 354 405. Restaurant; bunga-
lows with kitchen, TV, refrigerator.
Recreation club on site. With pool,
horseback riding, mini golf, and
tennis. **$$**
Motel du Lac, Chemin Poupon,
tel: 380 800, fax: 381 034, email:
moteldulac@opensurf.net. Modern
motel in tranquil setting with

swimming pool and gardens. All
rooms are air-conditioned. **$$**

Matoury
La Chaumière, Chemin de la
Chaumière, tel: 255 701, fax: 352
503. Bar, banquet room, in-room
TV, minibar, and pool. **$$$**
Le Grillardin, PK 6, Route de
Matoury, tel: 356 390, fax: 358
605. **$$$**

St-Laurent du Maroni
Chez Julienne, Route des
Malgaches, tel: 341 153. Small
hotel with restaurant. **$**
Hôtel Star, 109 Rue Thiers,
tel: 341 084, fax: 342 519. Pool,
restaurant, 38 rooms. **$$**
La Tentiare, 12 Ave Franklin
Roosevelt, tel: 342 600, fax: 341
509. Swimming pool, restaurant, 20
rooms. **$$**

Roura
Hôtel Relais de Patawa, BP 98,
97351, Matoury, 40 km (25 miles)
from Roura, tel: 280 395. Owners
are keen entomologists. **$**
Auberge des Orpailleurs, 62 Route
de l'Est, tel: 376 297. Meals
available; hammock space. **$$$**
La Crique Gabrielle, Dacca
village, tel: 280 104, fax: 280 104.
Restaurant with rooms sometimes
available for rent. **$**

Sinnamary
Hôtel du Fleuve, 11 Rue Léon
Mine, BP 114, tel: 345 400, fax:
345 303, www.hoteldufleuve.com.
With 121 rooms, two seminar
rooms, swimming pool. **$$**

Accommodation Agencies

**Syndicat des Hôteliers,
Restaurateurs et Cafetiers de
Guyane** (Guiana Federation of Hotels,
Restaurants, and Cafés), PK 9, 2
Route de Rémire, 97354 Remire
Montjoly, tel: 354 100, fax: 354 405
**Relais Départemental des Gîtes de
France** (Guest Houses of France,
Departmental Office), Immeuble
CTG, 12 Rue Lallouette, 97338
Cayenne, French Guiana, tel: 296
501, fax: 296 516.

Tourist Lodges

The following places offer
traditional wooden lodges *(carbets)*
located in areas of natural beauty,
often deep in tropical forest:
Campement de Saut Sonnelle,
30 minutes by boat along the Inini
River from Maripasoula, tel: 344
945. Hammocks.
Degrad Cascades (La Marine),
Cascades River, one hour from
Tonnégrande by *pirogue*, tel: 399
365. Hammocks and beds.
Gîte Quimbe Kio, village of Cacao,
97352, Cacao, tel: 270 122.
Hammocks/beds.
Saut Athanase, on the Approuague
River, tel: 381 528.
Saut Mathias, on the Approuague
River, tel: 287 000.

What to Eat

As a *département* of France,
French Guiana has a high standard
of food, particularly in and around
Cayenne, Kourou, and St Laurent,
with added color and variety
provided by its rich racial mix.
There is a wide choice of
restaurants, mostly serving French
and Creole food, but Vietnamese,
Indonesian, and Chinese food can
also be found.
    Prices are relatively high at
good restaurants, but a decent,
cheap meal can be had at one of
the many Asian cafés or food
stalls. Ti' Punch is a traditional
aperitif made from lime, rum, and
sugar-cane syrup, often served
with cod rolls and blood sausage
(black pudding).

Where to Eat

Cayenne
By the Canal Laussant are many
Javanese and Creole cafés and

Restaurant Guide

Prices for a three-course meal for
two, including house wine:
$ = US$20–50 – inexpensive
$$ = US$50–70 – moderate
$$$ = US$70–120 – expensive

Carnival

Carnival usually starts in January. While it's not the extravaganza of Rio de Janeiro or the Caribbean, it is a vibrant affair with a cultural mix of Creole, Brazilian, and Haitian influences. Every weekend from Epiphany festivities are held until they reach a five-day non-stop climax before Ash Wednesday. In the colorful parades in central Cayenne, dancers dress in elaborate costumes, each day based on a different traditional theme.

food stalls, although some are not particularly clean and it is not a safe area at night.

Bar des Palmistes, Place des Palmistes. Simple French and Creole cuisine in good central location. **$$**

DeliFrance, corner of Rue Justin Cayatée/Ave du Général de Gaulle. Good snacks, pastries, and coffee. **$**

La Victoire, 40 Rue du 14 Juillet. Chinese and Creole cuisine served at outside tables; tasty and good-value meals, friendly atmosphere. **$**

La Kaz Kreol, 35 Ave d'Estrées. Creole cuisine served by waiters in traditional costume. **$$**

Les Pyramides, corner of Rue C. Colomb and Rue Malouet. Inexpensive Middle Eastern dishes, such as couscous and grills. **$**

Kourou

Ballahou, 1 Rue Armet Martial. Good fish and seafood. **$$**

Le Bistrot du Lac, Hôtel Mercure Ariatel. French Creole food and a good wine list. **$$$**

St-Laurent du Maroni

Chez Felicia, Ave du Général de Gaulle. Creole cuisine. **$$**

La Goélette, Balaré Plage, 2.5 km (1½ miles) from the town. Atmospheric converted boat; Brazilian and French dishes. **$$**

There are also several good-value Asian restaurants in the town.

Guyana A – Z

Getting Acquainted

Area 215,000 sq. km (83,000 sq. miles)
Capital Georgetown
Population 800,000
Language English (official language), Creole, Hindi, Urdu, and several Amerindian languages.
Currency Guyana dollar
Weights & measures Officially metric although imperial measures are widely used.
Electricity Some 220V in Georgetown; 110V is most common throughout the country.
Time Zone GMT –4hrs, EST +1hr
International dialing code 592

Climate

The temperature remains warm with equatorial humidity all year round, but not excessively hot; average temperatures are between 24°C (75°F) and 31°C (88°F). The best time to visit is July–November, between the two wet seasons, which are from May through June and from December through January. Average annual rainfall is 230 cm (91 inches).

Government & Economy

Guyana gained independence in 1966 and became a republic in 1970. The government is democratically elected and the president (Bharrat Jagdeo of the People's Progressive Party, in power since 1999), who is elected by the majority party in the National Assembly, is head of state.

The economy is based on five export products: bauxite, gold, sugar, timber, and rice. Gold production has increased in recent years. Guyana is one of the poorest countries in the Western Hemisphere.

Visas

Visas are not required by visitors from the US, Commonwealth, and most EU countries. Proof of onward travel is necessary.

Customs

No duty is charged on personal goods, but there are high charges on items brought in for commercial purposes.

Money

The currency is the Guyanese dollar, available in denominations of 1, 5, 10 (coins), 20, 100, 500, and 1,000 (notes). The value of the Guyanese dollar (G$) is revised weekly.

Most banks and *bureaux de change* buy only US or Canadian dollars and UK sterling. It is possible to change traveler's checks at the larger stores and travel agents in Georgetown.

Getting Around

From the Airport

Chedi Jagan International Airport is 40 km (25 miles) from Georgetown at Timehri. Minibuses (No. 42) to

Public Holidays

- **January 1** New Year's Day
- **February 23** Republic Day and Mashramani Festival
- **March/April:** Phagwah (Hindu Religious Holiday), Good Friday, Easter Monday, and Eid-ul-Azha (Muslim Holy Day)
- **May 1** Labor Day
- **May 26** Independence Day
- **July 1** Caricom Day
- **August 1** Freedom Day
- **December 25** Christmas Day
- **December 26** Boxing Day

the center cost US$1, and will take you to your hotel for a small fee; taxis cost US$20–25 (more at night; it is cheaper to book a seat on a minibus on arrival). Departure tax is G$4,000.

By Air

Internal flights are the best way to get around Guyana. **Trans Guyana Airways** has scheduled flights from Georgetown to Lethem. Charter companies include Trans Guyana Airways and **Air Services Ltd**. An airstrip at Ogle, about 20 minutes from the center of Georgetown by road, is used for domestic flights.

Emergency Numbers

Police: 911
Fire: 912
Ambulance service: 913

By Bus & Taxi

Minibuses and collective taxis run along the coast and to many destinations inland. This form of transport is cheap but slow. Taxis have an H in their number plates.

By River

Guyana has over 965 km (600 miles) of navigable waterways. There are frequent services but they tend to be erratic. *Ballahoos* are six-seater boats; *corials* are four-seater boats.

By Car

Most of the main roads are found in the coastal area. There is a highway between Lethem in Guyana and Boa Vista in Brazil.

Tourist Offices

Guyana Tourism Authority, National Exhibition Centre, Sophia, Georgetown, tel: 233 6351, www.guyana-tourism.com
Tourism Association of Guyana, 157 Waterloo Street, North Cummingsburg, Georgetown, tel: 225 0807, fax: 225 0817, www.exploreguyana.com

Specialist Tour Operators

Wilderness Explorers, Cara Suites, 176 Middle Street, Georgetown, tel: 227 7698, fax: 226 2085, www.wilderness-explorers.com

Media & Communications

International direct dialing is available in most main towns and cities. Faxes can be sent from the **Guyana Telephone and Telegraph Company**, the **Bank of Guyana Building** in Georgetown, and larger hotels. Postal services are very good and cheap. The main post office is on North Road in Georgetown.

The Guyana Chronicle is a state-owned daily newspaper. Other papers include *The Mirror*, *The Kaieteur News*, the liberal independent *Stabroek News*; and the respected and popular weekly *Catholic Standard*.

The BBC World Service (MHz 17.79, 15.19, 11.75, and 9.915), and the Voice of America (MHz 13.74, 9.775, 7.405, 5.995) are broadcast on radio. There are 14 TV channels, showing mainly US programs, but with increasing local productions.

Embassies/Consulates

Canadian High Commission corner of High St and Young St, Georgetown, tel: 227 2081.
UK (High Commission): 44 Main Steet, PO Box 10849, Georgetown, tel: 226 5881–4.

Security

Georgetown is a colorful and attractive city but you should take care in some areas (avoid Tiger Bay and Albouystown in particular) and do not walk around the streets at night. Violent crime on the streets and highways is common, and there are many beggars, although most are harmless.

Car Hire

Camex, 125 'D' Barrack Street, Kingston, Georgetown, tel: 276 976.
Trident Auto Rentals, 215 Camp Street, Georgetown, tel: 250 675; fax: 256 864.

US: 100 Young Street, Georgetown, PO Box 10507, tel: 225 4900.

Where to Stay

Most of the luxury and business hotels are in Georgetown; quality ranges from good to reasonable.

Georgetown

Cara Lodge, 293 Quamina Street, tel: 2255 301, fax: 2255 310, www.carahotels.com. Small and luxurious; converted 150-year-old mansion with good restaurant, bar, and service. **$$$**
Florentene's Hotel, 3 North Street, Lacytown, tel: 226 2283. Clean and economical; highly recommended. **$**
Le Meridien Pegasus, Seawall Road, tel: 225 2853–9, fax: 226 0532, www.lemeridien-pegasus. com. Pool, restaurants, tennis court, gym. **$$$**
Rima Guest House, 92 Middle Street, New Cummingsburg, tel: 225 7401. Safe and central budget hotel, with good-value restaurant. **$**
Tower Hotel , 74–75 Main Street, tel: 227 2011–5, fax: 225 6021, www.hoteltowerguyana.com. Swimming pool and very good restaurant. **$$$**

Lethem

Savannah Inn, General Store, tel: 772 2035. Good and clean. Organizes jungle tours. **$$**

New Amsterdam

Astor Hotel, 7 Strand, tel: 33578. Comfortable mid-range hotel; breakfast served; recommended.
Parkway Hotel, 4 Main Street, near the mosque, tel: 33134. Reasonable mid-range place; clean, friendly, and safe. **$$**

Hotel Price Guide

Prices for a double room
including continental breakfast.
$ = US$30 or less – inexpensive
$$ = US$30–50 – moderate
$$$ = US$50 plus – expensive

Jungle Lodges

There are many lodges and camps
in the tropical forest interior,
catering for the eco-tourism market.
These establishments, whose
facilities range from basic to
up-market, usually run their own
nature safaris. Recommended:
Timberhead Rainforest Resort, two
hours from Georgetown by air and
boat up the Kamuni River, tel: 223
5108, www.timberheadguyana.com.
Three lodges built on stilts. Jungle
walks, bird-watching, and creek
activities.
Dadanawa Ranch, 97 km (60
miles) south of Lethem, is a huge
establishment which runs
horseback riding and trekking
expeditions. Can be booked through
Wilderness Explorers *(See
Specialist Tour Operators, page
386).*
Rock View Lodge, Annai, a village
112 km (70 miles) from Lethem,
www.rockviewlodge.com (or book
through Wilderness Explorers, *see
Specialist Tour Operators, page
386*). Eight spotless rooms with
showers.
Karanambu Ranch, 2 hours south
of Annai by boat. Thatched clay-
brick huts. Exceptional wildlife
excursions to see giant anteaters.
www.taranambu.com

What to Eat

Guyanese cuisine is good and
varied, combining influences from
the Caribbean, Africa, Europe, North
America, and Asia, as well as
indigenous cooking. Seafood is
particularly tasty. Interesting Creole
dishes include the traditional
Christmas dish, pepperpot (meat
cooked with hot spices and cassava
juice); cow-heel soup, and saltfish.
There is a wide range of tropical
fruits (often served in some
excellent juice bars) and
vegetables. Locally produced rum is
the favored tipple, and the beer,
Banks, is quite palatable.

Where to Eat

Many restaurants close on public
holidays; cheaper places are often
open only for lunch. The most
formal restaurants are found within
the best hotels.

Georgetown

Browne's Café, Le Meridien
Pegasus, Seawall Road, tel: 225
2853–9. International and Creole
cuisine, good English breakfast. **$$**
Eldorado, Le Meridien Pegasus,
Seawall Road. International and
Creole cuisine. Up-market. **$$$**
Palm Court, Main Street, tel: 227
0008–9. Serves Chinese and
Creole food. **$$**
Sidewalk Café and Jazz Club, 176
Middle Street, tel: 227 0152. Local
and international cuisine. **$$**

New Amsterdam

Brown Derby, corner of Church and
Main streets. East Indian and
Chinese food. **$**
Circle C, Lot 7, Main and Charlotte
streets. Good Creole cuisine. **$**

Restaurant Guide

Prices for a three-course meal for
two, including house wine:
$ = US$25 or less – inexpensive
$$ = US$25–50 – moderate
$$$ = US$50 plus – expensive

Outdoor Activities

Guyana's most popular sport is
cricket. The Georgetown Cricket
Club at Bourda is one of the most
famous grounds in the Caribbean.
The Providence Stadium has been
built specifically for the World
Cricket Cup in 2007.
   The coastline is not ideal for
water sports, but there are some
good opportunities in the interior for
trekking and river-rafting, which can
be arranged by local tour operators.

Paraguay A – Z

Getting Acquainted

Area 406,800 sq. km (157,000 sq.
miles)
Capital Asunción
Population 6 million. Eighty percent
of Paraguayans are mestizo (mixed-
race Amerindian and European).
There has also been heavy
immigration from Korea, Japan, and
Taiwan.
Language Spanish and Guaraní
Currency: Guaraní = 100 centimos
Weights & measures Metric
Electricity 220 volts
Time zone GMT -3hrs in east, -4hrs
in the west (EST +3hrs, EST +1hr)
International dialing code 595
(Asunción +21)

Government & Economy

General Alfredo Stroessner was
overthrown in 1989 after 35 years
in office, yet both the Colorado
Party and the armed forces remain
highly influential in national politics.
   Political reforms since the
demise of Stroessner include the
adoption of a new constitution in
1992, and a process of
decentralization of power to local
departmental and municipal
government. Despite an attempted
coup in May 1996, democracy
seems assured. The ruling Colorado
Party won the presidency again in
April 2003, for Nicanor Duarte
Frutos, extending their run to over
half a century.
   Agricultural products such as
meat, soya, and cotton account
for the main bulk of exports,
although the economy still relies
strongly on contraband and drug
smuggling.

Visas

US and Canadian citizens need a visa, but visitors from the UK, Australasia, and most of Western Europe do not. Check with your local travel agent for the latest requirements.

Customs

Alcohol, tobacco, and electronic items for personal use are admitted to the country duty-free.

Money

It is not possible to exchange guaraní outside the country – so only change what you will need. *Casas de cambio* will accept traveler's checks. ATM dispensers are fairly widespread, and major credit cards are widely accepted.

Getting Around

From the Airport
Asunción's **Silvio Pettirosi Airport** is 16 km (10 miles) from the city center; taxis can be reserved at agencies' desks, and cost approximately US$15; buses to the center cost US30¢, but luggage space is limited.

There is an international departure tax of around US$23 (it is cheaper to pay in guaranís). Domestic departure tax is about US$2.50.

By Air
Líneas Aéreas de Transporte Nacional (LATN), **Aeronorte**, **Líneas Aéreas del Este** (LADESA), **Aerosur**, and **Transporte Aéros del Mercosur** (TAM) have flights to northern Paraguay and parts of the Chaco region.

By Bus
Buses are the main means of transport within Paraguay (there is no national rail network); the main bus terminal is a 20-minute cab ride from the center of Asunción at Avda Rep. Argentina and Fernando de la Mora, tel: 553 050/040. "Executive" buses vary according to company. There is a luxury international bus

service that serves Asunción and Ciudad del Este, Pedro Juan Caballero and Encarnación by way of Argentina, Uruguay and Brazil.

By River
There are several boats that sail up the Paraná River to Concepción every 2–3 weeks, a journey of 27–30 hours. An irregular passenger boat service shuttles downstream between Buenos Aires and Asunción. The journey takes five days and can be suspended during the dry winter months. *(For further details contact tourist information, see box above.)*

By Car
Petrol is cheap and car hire fairly inexpensive; contact **Touring y Automóvil Club Paraguayo**, 25 de Mayo and Calle Brasíl, tel: 210 550.

Taxis are inexpensive, averaging US$2 per journey in Asunción. Minimum charge is about US80¢; more by night. One main taxi stand is in front of the Hotel Guaraní on the Plaza de los Héroes; or call RadioTaxi: 550 116/311 080.

Emergencies

A satisfactory ambulance service is not available; it's best to transport the patient by private means or taxi. Have someone phone the hospital, stating the nature of the problem and asking that a doctor receive the patient in the emergency room. To

Public Holidays

- **January 1** New Year's Day
- **January 6** Three Kings' Day
- **March 1** Heroes' Day
- **Late March/April** Maundy Thursday, Good Friday, Easter
- **May 1** Labor Day
- **May 15** Independence Day
- **June 12** Chaco Armistice
- **August 15** Founding of Asunción
- **September 29** Commemoration of the Battle of Boquerón
- **December 8** Immaculate Conception
- **December 25** Christmas Day

Tourist Information

The *Dirección General de Turismo Paraguayo* is at Avda Palma 468, Asuncíon, tel: 491 230/441 530/441 620/494 110, www.senatur.gov.py. Information is available at the Touring & Automobile Club of Paraguay at Calle 25 de Mayo and Brasil.

contact the police in an emergency, dial **442 111**.

For emergencies, contact any of the Asunción emergency rooms: **Hospital de Clínicas**, Avda Dr Monterro and Lagerenza, Asuncíon, tel: 420 982/983. **Hospital Bautista**, Avda Rep. Argentina and Campos Cervera, Asuncíon tel: 600 171 or 607 944.

Business Hours

During the hot season (December through February), a long midday siesta is observed and many shops and offices open Mon–Sat 6.30am–noon and 3–7pm. Banks tend to be open Mon–Fri 7.30–11am, although some stay open for longer hours. Dinner is served somewhat earlier than in neighboring countries, that is, around 8.30–11pm.

Media

Radio is very popular, and one of the best-known stations is *Radio Ñandutí*. Three privately owned television networks operate in Paraguay; all TV drama programs are imported from neighboring countries or the United States.

The widest-circulating daily newspapers are: *ABC Color*, *Noticias*, *La Nación*, and *Ultima Hora* (an afternoon daily).

Telecoms

It is wise to send important letters by registered mail. All mail must be deposited at a post-office counter. Long-distance calls can be made from **ANTELCO** office on N.S. de Asunción and Presidente Franco.

Telex and fax services are also available. International calls are called either *ordinario* or *urgente*, urgent calls costing twice as much.

Embassies/Consulates

UK: Honorary Consul, Bogarin 4846, Asunción, tel: 210 405, fax 600 448. Nearest British Embassy: Dr Luis Agote 2412, Buenos Aires, Argentina, tel: (54 11) 4808 2200, www.britain.org.ar
US: Avda Mariscal López 1776, Asunción, tel: 213 715, fax: 213 728, http://asuncion.usembassy.gov

Religious Services

The state religion is Roman Catholicism. In Asunción, there is a Sunday Mass in English at Padres Oblatos de María Chapel, on Calle Gómez de Castro and Quesada. Other places of worship include the Anglican Church on Avda España 1261, the Mormon Church on Avda España and the Brasília Synagogue on Calle General Díaz 657.

Where to Stay

Asunción (21)
Cecilia Hotel, Calle Estados Unidos 341, tel: 210 033/034, fax: 497 111. Has a good restaurant. **$$**
Chaco Hotel, Calle Caballero and Mariscal Estigarribia, tel: 492 066/9, fax: 444 223. Has a rooftop pool. **$$**
Excelsior Hotel, Calle Chile 980, tel: 496 743, fax: 496 748, www.excelsior.com.py. The best in town. Modern, with conference rooms. **$$$**
Gran Hotel, De la Residenta and Padre Pucheau, tel. 200 051, www.granhotel.com.py. Pleasant colonial-style hotel in the city center. **$$$**
Guaraní Hotel, Calle Independencia Nacional and Oliva, tel: 491 131,

Hotel Price Guide

Prices for a double room including continental breakfast:
$ = US$50 – inexpensive
$$ = US$50–100 – moderate
$$$ = US$100 plus – expensive

fax: 443 647. Central; tried and tested. **$$**
Hotel de Yacht y Golf Club Paraguay, PO Box 1795, tel: 906 117, fax: 906 120, www.hotelyacht.com.py. Sporty with all the trimmings. **$$$**

What to Eat

Paraguayan specialties include *surubí*, a tasty fish dish; *sopa paraguaya*, a rich cornbread made of ground maize and cheese; *soyo*, a beef and vegetable soup; *empanadas*, and fresh tropical juices. Paraguayan beef is excellent. Also make sure you try *tereré*, a local ice-cold drink.
   There are also a number of excellent Brazilian restaurants with succulent barbecue-grilled meats and large self-service buffets.

Restaurant Guide

Prices for a three-course meal for two, including house wine:
$ = US$50 – inexpensive
$$ = US$50–100 – moderate
$$$ = US$100 plus – expensive

Where to Eat

Asunción (21)
Amstel, Avda Rep. Argentina 1384, tel: 600 923. Expensive; serves good traditional food. **$$$**
Bar San Roque, Calle Eligio Ayala corner of Tacuary, near Plaza Uruguaya. Old-style café-restarant with an excellent selection of different cuisines. Closed Sunday. **$**
Bolsi, Calle Estrella 399, tel: 491 841/494 720. Asunción institution that has been serving local and Mediterranean food for over 40 years. **$$**
Il Capo, Avda Perú 291 and Calle José Berges, tel: 213 022, fax: 204 401. Classy Italian and international cuisine. **$$**
La Preferida, Calle 25 de Mayo and Estados Unidos, tel: 491 126. Excellent international cuisine. **$$**
Piroschka, Sargento 1, Manuel Benítez 1575 and Avda Santísima Trinidad, tel: 280 533. Serves a

Drinking Tips

Paraguayan beer is made according to German methods and is excellent. The national wine is not recommended. The local sugar-cane liquor, *caña*, is popular and many liquors are imported at low prices.

variety of Paraguayan dishes cooked to perfection. **$$**
Sukiyaki, Avda Constitución 763 and Luis A. de Herrera, tel: 222 038. Japanese. **$$**
Talleyrand, Calle Mariscal Estigarribia 932, tel: 441 163/445 246. Highly respected local chain serving French cuisine. Reservations essential. **$$$**

Theater Restaurants

A typical evening's entertainment is a restaurant floor show, with Paraguayan harp and guitar music, and sometimes the (indescribable and unmissable) bottle dance. Prices vary according to the quality of the show, but are generally about US$10 per person. Recommended spots in Asunción include:
Hermitage, Calle 15 de Agosto 1870.
Ita Enramada Hotel & Casino, Calle Cacique Lambares and Ribero del Río Paraguay, tel: 332 044/333 041. Open 9pm–4am.

Tours

Check with recommended tourist agencies such as: **Inter Express**, Calle Luis A. de Herrera and Yegros, Asunción, tel: 490 111, fax: 449 156, e-mail: iexpress@interexpress.com.py or **Time Tours**, Calle 15 de Agosto and General Díaz, tel: 493 527, email: timetour@conexion.com.py.

Where to Shop

The **street market** in Calle Palma is pedestrianized on Saturday mornings and has a variety of goods; leather and lace goods are great value.

Peru
A – Z

Getting Acquainted

Area 1,285,000 sq. km (496,100 sq. miles)
Capital Lima
Population 28 million, of whom 45 percent are indigenous, 32 percent Amerindian and European (mestizo), 12 percent white (criollo), and 2 percent black and Asian. The cohesive black population live mainly in the southern coastal cities.
Language The official languages are Spanish and Quechua. Near Puno and Lake Titicaca, Aymara is spoken.
Currency Nuevo Sol
Weights & measures Metric
Electricity 220 volts
Time zone GMT -5hrs, EST
Dialing code 51 (Lima +1)

Government & Economy

Since 1979 Peru has been run by a democratic government under a constitution. The country is divided into 24 departments and the province of Callao, which is where the country's main port is located.

Fishing, mining, and tourism play important roles in the economy. Petroleum is extracted from the Amazon jungle area, providing half the domestic demand.

In June 2001, Alejandro Toledo, the first Peruvian president of Andean indigenous extraction, was elected. His election ended more than a decade of rule by Alberto Fujimori (1989–2000), who fled to Japan in disgrace amid allegations of corruption.

Toledo's presidency saw many strikes, and placed him at the center of several scandals. By the end of his presidency his popularity rating

had dropped to just 8 percent. In 2006, national elections returned Alán García of the left-wing APRA movement to the presidency with 52 percent of the vote, while Toledo and his wife, Elaine Karp, were being investigated for fraud.

Visas

Visas are not required by citizens of the EU, the United States, Canada, Australia, New Zealand, or South Africa. With a valid passport, citizens of these countries receive a tourism card which is usually good for 90 days.

A 30-day extension is available upon payment of US$20 and presentation of a return travel ticket. Contact the Dirección General de Migraciones in the Oficina de Migración, Avda España 730, cda 7, Breña, tel: 330 4114.

A US$30.25 exit tax on international flights, and US$6 on domestic flights, must be paid.

Customs

It is illegal to take archeological artifacts out of the country. Permits are no longer required for bringing camera equipment into Peru.

Money

On Plaza San Martín, in downtown Lima, hundreds of outdoor bankers run alongside the traffic exchanging US dollars – the rate is usually a little better than in the banks. It is legal to change with these *cambistas*, who generally wear a green jacket and carry a calculator, and usually quite safe. Banks will

Emergencies

Tourist police, Lima, Southern Districts, tel: 460 4525; Northern Districts, tel: 424 2053.
General police emergency number, tel: 105.
The tourist information service **iperú** can assist in contacting police to report a crime. 24-hour hotline, tel: 574 8000.

change your currency at a slightly inflated rate and good hotels have exchange services or will send a hotel courier to one of the *casas de cambio* for a better rate (remember to give him a tip). Travel agents accept payment in some foreign currencies and exchange small amounts. It is convenient to carry some US cash as well as travelers' checks, and credit and debit cards. It is not always possible to change checks, and cash dollars get a better rate. American Express will replace lost travelers' checks only in Lima.

Most international credit cards are accepted. Credit card loss can be reported on the following numbers. **Visa**: 108 001 410 581 9754/0120 (collect).
MasterCard: 108 001 636 722 7111 (collect).
American Express: 441 4744/441 4762 (Lima).
Diners Club: 422 6572 (Lima).

Getting Around

From the Airport
The most reliable bus service to and from **Jorge Chávez International Airport** is **Shuttle Bus Urbanito**, Calle Manoa 391, Breña, tel: 424 3650/425 1202. A fare to central Lima is US$6, and to Miraflores or San Isidro, US$8–10.

Reliable taxi services include: **Taxi Green**, tel: 484 4001, email: taxigreen@peru.com; CMV **Taxi Remisse Ejecutivo**, tel: 422 4838; **Mitsui Taxi Remisse Ejecutivo**, tel: 349 7722; and **Taxi Seguro** tel: 241 9292. A taxi fare to the center of Lima is US$10–15, and to Miraflores or San Isidro, about US$20. *Ejecutivo* taxis charge a little more.

You can also rent cars at the airport, where **Avis, Budget, Hertz**, and **National** have offices open 24 hours a day. An international driver's license is needed and is valid for 30 days. For additional days, you must obtain authorization from the **Touring y Automóvil Club del Perú (TACP)**, Calle César Vallejo 699, Lince, Lima, tel: 01-211 9977, www.touringperu. com.pe (in Spanish).

By Air

Domestic airlines LAN, Aero Condor, and TACA serve most cities in Peru. For domestic flights there is an airport tax of US$6 at all airports.

By Bus

Numerous transport companies operate morning and evening departures from Lima to most cities. Reliable companies include: **Cruz del Sur**, Jr Quilca 531, Lima, tel: 431 5125, www.cruzdelsur.com.pe (northbound, southbound, and eastbound buses, including excellent bus-cama, bus-bed, coaches with comfortable reclining seats). **Ormeño**, Paseo de la República 801, La Victoria, Lima, tel: 427 5679, www.grupo-ormeno.com.pe (in Spanish); (southbound buses). **Tepsa**, Jr Lampa 1237, Lima, tel: 427 5642/3 or 470 6666, www.tepsa.com.pe (in Spanish) (northbound and southbound). **Civa**, Avda 28 de Julio, corner of Paseo de la República, tel: 418 1111, www.civa.com.pe (in Spanish).

From Bolivia, efficient minibus services will take you from La Paz to Puno. **Crillon Tours**, Avda Camacho 1223, La Paz, Bolivia, tel: (591) 2 233 7533, fax: (591) 2 211 6482, www.titicaca.com, runs several hydrofoil services across Lake Titicaca. The journey from Ecuador is also straightforward: take a bus to the Huaquillas border and walk through to Tumbes. Other buses operate from there.

By Rail

PeruRail operates three daily services from Cusco to the ruins at Machu Picchu: the luxury *Hiram Bingham* train, the *Vistadome* service whose panoramic windows offer passengers spectacular views, and the no-frills *Backpacker* service. Tickets can be purchased at the PeruRail office in Cusco (Avda Pachacutec, tel: 084-238 722, fax: 084-222 114) or through their website: www.perurail.com

The Lima–Huancayo passenger service, the world's highest train journey, operated by **Ferrocarril Central Andino S.A.** (tel: 226 6363, www.ferrocarrilcentral.com.pe). See

also www.incasdelperu.org for up-to-date information on this service.

Medical Services

Most major hotels have a doctor on call. Three clinics in Lima and its suburbs have 24-hour emergency service and usually an English-speaking member of staff on duty: **Clínica Anglo-Americana**, Calle Alfredo Salazar 350, San Isidro, tel: 712 3000; **Clínica Internacional**, Jr Washington 1471, tel: 619 6161; and **Clínica San Borja**, Avda Guardia Civil 337, San Borja, tel: 475 4000. **Hospital de Emergencia José Casimiro Ulloa**, Avda República de Panamá 6355, San Antonio, Miraflores, tel: 445 5096. A recommended English-speaking dentist is **Victor Manuel Aste**, Calle Antero Aspillaga 415, Dpto 101, San Isidro, tel: 441 7502.

Business Hours

In Lima office hours are Mon–Fri 9am–5pm with a noon lunch break. Shops are open from 10 or 11am until 8 or 9pm. Banks are generally open Mon–Fri 9am–6pm. Outside Lima, both shops and banks usually close at lunchtime. Weekend banking hours depend on the bank, although most are open on Saturday. *Casas de cambio* open 9am–6pm, while money changers are on the streets nearly 24 hours a day.

Communications

Local, national, and international calls can be made from public phone boxes using coins or telephone cards, available from newsstands. Alternatively, calls can be made from a *locutorio* (call center), where you pay for the call after you have made it. *Cellulares* (mobile phones) are ubiquitous in Peru and relatively inexpensive, and signal coverage is good. Calls from hotel phones range from reasonable to expensive. Check before you call – phone cards can sometimes be used in conjunction with hotel phones.

Most of the country is serviced by internet booths and cafés.

Useful Addresses

Tourist Information Centers

Lima: Jorge Chávez International Airport (24 hours), tel/fax: 01-574 8000. Jorge Basadre 610, San Isidro, tel: 01-421 1627. Larcomar Entertainment Center, Module 14, Plaza Gourmet, Miraflores, tel/fax: 01-445 9400.
Cusco: Velasco Astete Airport, tel/fax: 084-237 364. Main office: Avda Sol 103, Oficina 102, Galérias Turísticas, tel: 084-234 498.
Also worth visiting is the **South American Explorers' Clubhouse**, Calle Piura 135, Miraflores, Lima, tel: 01-445 3306, www.saexplorers.org

Useful Websites

www.peru.info
Comprehensive travel information from Peru's national tourism body.
www.perulinks.com
Thousands of links to Peru-related sites in Spanish and English.
www.magicperu.net
Information on a wide range of Peru-related subjects.
www.peru-hotels.com
Hotel listings and bookings, and transport and flights information in English.
www.andeantravelweb.com/peru
Excellent travel site with many useful Peru links.

Embassies/Consulates

The following diplomatic representatives are based in Lima:
Australia, Victor A. Belaunde 147, Edificio Real 3, Of. 1301, San Isidro, tel: 01-222 8281.
Canada: Calle Libertad 130, Miraflores, tel: 01-444 4015.
South Africa: Victor A. Belaunde 147, Edificio Real 3, Of. 801, San Isidro, tel: 01-440 9996.
UK: Torre Parque-Mar, 22nd floor, Avda José Larco 1301, Miraflores, tel: 01-617 3000, www.britemb.org.pe
US: Avda La Encalada s/n, cuadro 17, Santiago de Surco,

Hotel Price Guide

Prices for a double room
including continental breakfast:
$ = US$50 – inexpensive
$$ = US$50–100 – moderate
$$$ = US$100 plus – expensive

tel: 01-434 3000,
http://lima.usembassy.gov

Where to Stay

Arequipa (054)
Hotel La Casa de mi Abuela, Calle
Jerusalén 606, tel: 241 206; fax:
242 761, www.lacasademiabuela.
com. Constantly receives rave
reviews. Large complex of
bungalow-style rooms in a garden
setting. **$**
Hotel Libertador, Plaza Bolívar,
Selva Alegre, tel: 215 110, fax: 241
933, www.libertador.com.pe.
Beautiful, colonial-style hotel in the
heart of old Arequipa. **$$$**
Hotel Posada del Puente, Avda
Bolognesi 101, tel: 253 132, fax:
253 576, www.posadadelpuente.
com. Interesting design on the
banks of the River Chili. **$$**

Cajamarca (076)
Hotel Laguna Seca, Avda Manco
Cápac 1098, Baños del Inca, tel:
584 300, fax: 584 311,
www.lagunaseca.com.pe. Situated
at the thermal baths, the waters of
which enter the bathrooms. **$$$**
Hotel Sierra Galana, Jr Comercio
773, tel/fax: 822 470. Comfortable
and central. **$$**
Posada del Puruay, Carretera Porcón
Hualgayoc, Km 4.5, tel: 367
928/367 028, Reservations in Lima:
tel: 01-336 7869, fax: 01-336 7835,
www.posadapuruay.com.pe.
Beautiful, small hotel in a country
setting just outside Cajamarca. **$$**
El Portal del Marques, Jr del
Comercio 644, tel: 368 464,
reservations in Lima: tel: 01-9880
5440, www.portaldelmarques.com.
Excellent views and rooftop pool. **$$**

Cusco (084)
Hostal Corihuasi, Calle Suecia 561,
tel: 232 233, www.corihuasi.com.

Colonial-style house with warm and
quiet rooms. Hot water. **$**
**Best Western Los Andes de
América**, Calle Garcilaso 236,
tel/fax: 606 060,
www.bestwestern.com. Rooms
arranged around an interior
courtyard. Helpful staff; excellent
buffet breakfast included. **$$**
Monasterio de Cusco, Calle
Palacios 136, Plazoleta
Nazarenas, tel: 241 777,
fax: 246 983,
www.monasterio.orient-
express.com. Elegant converted
monastery. **$$$**

Iquitos (065)
Explorama Lodge. In virgin
rainforest. To make reservations in
Iquitos, go to Avda de la Marina
340, tel: 252 530, fax: 252 533.
Reservations in Lima, tel: 01-244
764, fax: 01-234 968,
www.explorama.com. **$$$**
Hostal La Pascana, Calle Pevas
133, tel: 231 418. Basic but
comfortable budget hotel, with
garden. **$**

Lima (01)
Gran Hotel Bolívar, Jr de la Unión
958, Plaza San Martín, tel: 619
7171, fax: 619 7170,
www.granhotelbolivarperu.com. The
doyen of Lima's historic hotels. **$$$**
Country Club Lima Hotel, Los
Eucaliptos 590, San Isidro, tel:
611 9000, fax: 611 9002,
www.hotelcountry.com. Perhaps
Lima's smartest hotel, in a lovely
setting. **$$$**
Hotel Residencial Europa, Jr
Ancash 376, Plaza San Francisco,
tel: 427 3351. Very cheap and
lively hotel in downtown Lima. **$**
Hotel España, Jr Azángaro 105,
tel/fax: 428 5546,
www.hotelespanaperu.com. Central
budget hotel; shared bathrooms. **$**
Hostal El Patio, Calle Diez Canseco
341A, tel: 444 4884, fax: 444
1663, www.hostalelpatio.net.
Colonial-style hotel in the heart of
Miraflores. **$$**
Miraflores Park Hotel, Avda
Malecón de la Reserva 1035,
Miraflores, tel: 242 3000, fax: 242
3393, www.mira-park.com. Luxury

Drinking Tips

Peru has several **beers**, including
Cristal, Pilsen, Arequipeña, and
Cusqueña, all of which are light
lagers. Its best **wines** are
Tacama, Ocucaje, Tabernero, and
Vista Alegre. The national **cocktail**
is *pisco sour* – made from *pisco*,
a kind of brandy, lemon juice,
and egg white with a dash of
cinnamon (the Hotel Grand
Bolívar in Lima serves the
Catedral pisco sour, claimed to
be the best in Peru).
   Travelers should drink only
bottled water (and specify
sin hielo – no ice – in other
cold drinks).
   The soft drink *chicha morada*,
made with purple maize, is
popular. It's different from the
chicha de jora, the traditional
home-made alcoholic brew known
throughout the Andes. The bright
yellow *Inka Kola* is more popular
than its northern namesake.
   Jugos (juices) are a delightful
alternative to sodas and there are
many choices available. Instant
Nescafé is often served up even in
good restaurants, although real
coffee can be found. Tea drinkers
would be advised to order their
beverage without milk, to avoid
receiving some odd concoctions.

business hotel; part of the Orient
Express Group. **$$$**

Nazca (056)
Hostal de la Borda, Carretera
Panamericana Sur, Km 452, tel/fax:
522 750. Reservations must be
made in Lima, tel: 442 6391, email:
turmajoro@yahoo.com. Near the
airfield, hacienda with garden,
swimming pools, hot showers, and
friendly service. **$$**
Nazca Hotel, Jr Bolognesi 147,
tel: 522 293, fax: 522 112.
Comfortable and clean, with a
swimming pool. **$$**
Casa Andina Nazca Hotel, Jr
Bolognesi 367, tel: 523 563, fax:
521 067, www.casa-andina.com.
Smart, modern hotel, just 5
minutes from the Nazca airstrip **$$**

Puno (Lake Titicaca) (051)
Hotel Libertador Puno, Isla Esteves, tel: 367 780, fax: 367 879, www.libertador.com.pe. Large modern building with excellent view of Lake Titicaca. **$$$**

Trujillo (044)
Libertador Trujillo, Jr Independencia 485, Plaza de Armas, tel: 232 741, fax: 235 641, www.libertador.com.pe. Beautiful historic building in the very heart of Trujillo; good value. **$$$**
Los Conquistadores, Calle Diego de Almagro 586, tel: 203 350, fax: 235 917, www.losconquistadoreshotel.com. Comfortable. **$$**
Hostal Trujillo, Calle Grau 581, tel: 258 271. Budget hotel, clean rooms with private bathrooms. **$**

What to Eat

Peru's cuisine ranges from scrumptious seafood to potatoes – the staple in a variety of highland dishes – to tropical fruits from the Amazon jungle. Recommended dishes include ceviche, raw fish and/or shellfish marinated in lemon juice and onions. A typical chicken entrée is ají de gallina served in a lightly spiced creamed sauce. Also with a spicy sauce, but this one cheese-based, is papa a la Huancaina. For the adventurous, cuy or guinea pig is available stewed or fried. Hot peppers (ají or rocoto) are used liberally in many typical dishes.

The Peruvians have a variety of wonderful fruits including chirimoya (custard apple), a large green fruit with creamy flesh; lúcuma, a small, tangy, nut-like fruit; and tuna, the sweet crisp fruit of the cactus. Mazamorra morada, a fruity pudding dating from colonial days, is a favorite.

Restaurant Guide

Prices for a three-course meal for two, including house wine:
$ = US$25 – inexpensive
$$ = US$25–40 – moderate
$$$ = US$40 plus – expensive

Where to Eat

Arequipa (054)
Wayrana, Calle Santa Catalina 210, tel: 285 641. Stylish restaurant with a pleasant outdoor courtyard. Specializes in cuy (guinea pig). **$$**

Lima (01)
Astrid y Gastón, Calle Cantaurias 175, Miraflores, tel: 242 5387. Arguably Lima's best restaurant. Serves contemporary Peruvian cuisine. **$$$**
La Costa Verde, Playa Barranquito, tel: 477 5228. One of the best restaurants in Lima, for great seafood and atmosphere. **$$$**.
La Gloria, Calle Atahualpa 201–205, Miraflores, tel: 445 5705. Serves delicious Mediterranean-style food. **$$$**
Huaca Pucllana, Calle General Borgoño, cdra 8 s/n, Miraflores, tel: 445 4042. Contemporary Peruvian food, overlooking a 2,000-year-old archeological site. **$$**
Junius, Jr Independencia 125, at junction of cdra 4 de Avda José Pardo, Miraflores, tel: 617 1000. Buffet of Peruvian specialties and daily folklore shows. **$$$**
La Rosa Nautica, Calle Espigón 4, Costa Verda, Miraflores, tel: 447 0057. Lima's best seafood restaurant, set on an ocean boardwalk. **$$$**

Cusco (084)
El Truco, Plaza Regocijo 261, tel: 232 441. Nightly dinner and show; very good value. **$$**
Inka Grill, Portal de Panes 115, Plaza de Armas, tel: 262 992. Great atmosphere and good food; there are folklore shows most nights. **$$**
Kusikuy, Calle Suecia 339, tel: 262 870. Typical local food. **$**
Pachapapa, Plazoleta San Blas 120, tel: 241 318. Highly recommended, serving traditional Peruvian food. **$**
Pizzeria Chez Maggy, Calle Plateros 348, tel 234 861. Excellent place for good pizza; there's another branch on Avda Pachakutesi 156, tel: 211 006. **$**

Trekking

The Peruvian dry season, May through September, offers the best views and finest weather. For safety reasons and for greater enjoyment, parties of three or more should hike together. Groups are easily formed in Cusco, and the tourist office on the Plaza de Armas provides a noticeboard for this purpose. In Huáraz, contact the Casa de Guías, Parque Ginebra 28 G, Huaraz-Ancash, tel: 721 333.

Supplies should include a backpack, hiking boots, warm clothes, sleeping bags, insulated pad, tent, and stove. This equipment can be hired in Huaraz and Cusco but, although the cost is minimal, the quality often suffers. Inspect hired equipment carefully before departure. It can get extremely cold at night, and by day the Andean sun burns quickly. Have a hat handy.

In the Cordillera Blanca, arrieros, or mule-drivers, are quite inexpensive and readily available.

It is not possible to hike the Inca Trail independently; you must pre-book with a tour operator. It is wise to arrange this well in advance of your arrival in Cusco.

Where to Shop

Each region has its own distinctive crafts, but if your time is limited, you will find most of them in Lima. **Las Pallas**, Calle Cajamarca 212, Barranco, tel: 01-477 4629, sells selected crafts and collectors' pieces. **Inkaplaza**, Avda Petit Thouars 5330, Miraflores, is bazaar-style market with stalls containing a great variety of traditional crafts. **Peru Artcrafts**, Larcomar Mall, Miraflores, have top-quality arts, crafts, and clothing, while **Alpaca 859**, Avda Larco 859, Miraflores, tel: 01-447 7163 is best for Alpaca and Pima cotton garments. **Kunturwasi**, Calle Ocharán 182, Miraflores, tel: 01-447 7173, has a good selection of Peruvian crafts.

Most organized treks provide all the food and camping equipment for the 3–4-day trip, as well as porters to carry it, but make sure you understand what you will need to bring yourself. If you feel the cold more than the average person, bring along extra warm layers or blankets.

All food should be brought from a major town; very little is available in the smaller villages. A variety of dried fruit, cheese, package soups, and tinned fish can easily be acquired. Drinking water should be treated with iodine. Add instant drink mixes like Tang to offset the unpleasant taste.

The unpleasant symptoms of altitude sickness (soroche) – nausea, exhaustion, headaches – can be significantly diminished by avoiding alcohol and physical exertion and not overeating for the first day or two, or longer if you need it. Drinking ample liquids helps the system adjust quickly. The sugar in hard candy stimulates the metabolism, and aspirin eases headaches. Mate de coca, tea brewed from coca leaves, is said to relieve the symptoms.

Nightlife

Lima is full of colorful peñas where there is non-stop folk music and dancing into the early hours. Aim to arrive about 9pm to get a good seat. Barranco is the neighborhood where there is most going on.
Brisas del Titicaca, Calle Walkuski 168, tel: 332 1901. An authentic peña with Peruvian dance shows. Popular with the locals and cheap.
Manos Morenas, Calle Pedro de Osma 409, Barranco, tel: 467 0421. Good Peruvian food. Afro–Peruvian dance group Wed and Thur; general Peruvian music Fri and Sat. Shows start 10.30pm.
La Noche, Avda Bolognesi 307, Barranco, tel: 247 2186. A good, lively bar for a beer.
La Candelaria, Avda Bolognesi 292, Barranco, tel: 247 1314. A fun peña with boisterous music and traditional dancing, Friday and Saturday nights from about 10pm.

Suriname
A – Z

Getting Acquainted

Area 163,265 sq. km (63,037 sq. miles)
Capital Paramaribo
Population 480,000
Language Dutch (official language) Sranan Tongo, Hindi, Javanese, English, Chinese, French, and Spanish are also spoken
Currency Suriname Dollar (SRD)
Weights & measures Metric
Electricity 110/220v AC, 60Hz
Time zone GMT –3hrs; EST +1hr
International dialing code 597

Government & Economy

Suriname has a democratically elected government, with one legislative house, the National Assembly. The president – currently Runaldo Ronald Venetiaan of the New Front – is head of state and head of government.

Major industries in Suriname include the export of bauxite and aluminum, shrimp, fish, bananas, and rice. The US is a major trading partner.

Visas

Visas are required by almost all visitors. Two good passport photographs, an application form in duplicate, and a fee are necessary for the visa, which can be obtained upon arrival.

Visitors from the UK can contact the Honorary Consulate of Suriname, 33 Pier House, 31 Cheyne Walk, London SW3 5HN, e-mail: ajethu@honoraryconsul.info.

Visitors from the US can contact the Surinamese Embassy at 4301

Connecticut Avenue NW, Suite 460, Washington DC 20008, tel: 202 244 7488/7590–2, fax: 202 244 5878.

Customs

There is no limit on the amount of local or foreign currency that can be imported, but any amounts over US$10,000 should be declared on entry. The export of local currency is limited to SRD1,000.

Money

Most transactions should be made in cash; checks are not accepted. It is difficult to buy Suriname dollars abroad, so most travelers take US dollars into the country. The best place to change money is at banks or cambios.

MasterCard and American Express are accepted in most large hotels and tourist restaurants and shops, but Visa and Diners Club are not widely used.

Public Holidays

January 1 New Year's Day
March/April Good Friday, Easter Monday
May 1 Labor Day
July 1 National Unity Day
November 25 Independence Day
December 25 Christmas Day
December 26 Boxing Day
Hindu and Muslim holidays are also taken, dates varying, according to the lunar calendar: **Holi Phagwah** (March or April, Hindu New Year); **Id ul Fitr** (end of Ramadan); **Id Ul**

Consulates/Embassies

Canadian Consulate, Wagenwegstraat, 50 Boven, Paramaribo, tel: 424 527, fax: 425 962.
UK: (Honorary Consulate), c/o VSH United Buildings, PO Box 1300, Van't Hogerhuysstraat 9–11, Paramaribo, tel: 402 558, fax: 403 515.
US: PO Box 1821, Dr Sophie Redmondstraat 129, Paramaribo, tel: 472 900, fax: 425 690.

Azah; **Youm un Nabi**; and **Deepavali** (usually November).

Getting Around

From the Airport

All international flights land at **Johan Adolf Pengel Airport** which is about 50 km (32 miles) south of Paramaribo. There are several minibus companies, which charge about US$5 to the city center, or taxis which cost around US$35.

The airport at **Zorg en Hoop** in Paramaribo is used for domestic flights.

By Boat

There is a daily four-hour journey up the Commewijne River. A ferry travels between Paramaribo and Meerzorg on opposite sides of the Suriname River, and smaller boats travel between Leonsberg (5 km/ 3 miles north of Paramaribo) and New Amsterdam. Or you can explore the rivers in *korjaals* navigated by highly skilled Maroons.

By Road

In Paramaribo, public transport consists of taxis or buses. It is possible to rent a car; driving is on the left-hand side of the road.

There are no major roads in the interior except for the east–west highway which runs from Albina in the east to Nieuw Nickerie in the west. Buses operate on the coastal highway but they are a very uncomfortable way to travel. It is also possible to use taxis around the coastal regions. There are road links from Guyana and French Guiana.

Rainforest and Coastal Tours

Much of Suriname's countryside is tropical forest, and many visitors take guided tours into its rainforest and coastal reserves. As the road system is minimal, the most practical form of transport is by small plane, or by boat up one of the many rivers.

Among the highlights for scenic and cultural interest are: the **Galibi Nature Reserve** on Marowijne River near the village of Albina (turtle-nesting site in July and August);

Marienburg, the last remaining sugar estate in the country, in the Commewijne district; **Jodensavanne**, south of Paramaribo on the opposite bank of the Suriname River, where an old synagogue has been restored; and the **Natuurpark Brownsberg** in montane rainforest, two hours from Paramaribo.

Suriname has an impressive national park system. Contact Stinasu (the Nature Preservation Foundation of Suriname) for more information and details of their inexpensive guided tours, Cornelis Jongbawstraat 14, P.O. Box 12252, Paramaribo, Suriname, www.stinasu.com

Business Hours

Banking hours are Mon–Fri 9am–2pm. Shops and businesses are open Mon–Fri 9am–4.30pm, Sat 9am–1pm.

Communications & Media

International direct dialing is available. There are no area telephone codes. Offices of **Telesur**, the national phone company, throughout the country can be used to send telegrams.

De West and *De Ware Tijd* are Dutch-language daily newspapers. The BBC World Service (MHz 17.79, 15.19, 9.915, and 5.970) and Voice of America (MHz 17.71, 13.74, 9.455, and 5.995) are easy to receive.

Useful Websites

www.surinametourism.com
An on-line tourist guide in English.
www.parbo.com
Site dedicated to Paramaribo.

Tourist Organisations

Suriname Tourism Foundation, PO Box 656, Dr JF Nassylaan 2, Paramaribo, tel: 410 357, fax: 477 786, www.suriname-tourism.org
Suriname Tourism Department, Communication and Tourism, Prins

Hendrikstraat 26–8, Paramaribo, tel: 420 422, fax: 420 425.

Specialist Agencies

METS **Travel and Tours**, Dr J.F.Nassylaan 2, Paramaribo, tel: 477 088, fax: 422 332, www.surinamevacations.com
Oetsi Tours, Parijsstraat 40, Munder, Paramaribo, tel: 441 488, fax: 442 307, www.oetsitours.com
Sun & Forest Tours, Kleine Waterstraat 1b, Paramaribo, tel/fax: 478 383, www.surinamesunforest.net

Where to Stay

Paramaribo

Ambassador Hotel, Dr Sophie Redmonstraat 66, P.O. Box: 2632, tel: 477 555, fax: 477 903. Very good budget hotel, with restaurant. **$**
Guesthouse Flair, Kleine Waterstraat 7, tel: 422 455/ 474 794. Clean, reasonable, and recommended. **$$**
Residence Inn Paramaribo, Anton Dragtenweg 7, tel: 472 387, fax: 424 811, www.resinn.com. Comfortable hotel with restaurant and pool. **$$**
Torarica Hotel and Casino, Mr Rietbergplein 1, P.O. Box 1514, tel: 471 500, fax: 411 618, www.torarica.com The best hotel in the city, with pool, restaurants, and all facilities. **$$$**

Nieuw Nickerie

Hotel Ameerali, Maynardstraat 32, P.O. Box 6049, tel: 231 212, fax: 231 066. Clean, if small, rooms; comfortable. **$**
Hotel Luxor, St Jozefstraat 22, tel: 231 365. Old-fashioned and friendly place; clean rooms with private baths. **$$**

Hotel Price Guide

Prices for a double room including continental breakfast:
$ = US$50 – inexpensive
$$ = US$50–100 – moderate
$$$ = US$100 plus – expensive

Residence Inn Nickerie, RP
Bharosstraat 84, tel: 210 950, fax:
210 954, www.resinn.com. One of
the best in town; spacious rooms
and pool. **$$**

What to Eat & Drink

The standard of food in Suriname
is high but so are the prices as
most produce is imported. The
local cuisine matches the rich
ethnic mix of the Surinamese
people, and can be very good.
Indonesian dishes, such as *bami*
(fried noodles) and *nasi goreng*
(fried rice) are spicy and served in
cheap and cheerful food stalls.
Manioc (cassava), sweet potato,
planta..., chicken, shrimp, and fish
feature prominently in Creole
cuisine; while Hindustani
specialties include *roti* (mixed
curried vegetables and chicken
wrapped up in a fried pancake)
and *phulawri* (fried chickpeas).
Chinese cuisine is also plentiful
and good value. The locally
produced beer, **parbo**, is quite
drinkable and cheaper than
imported brands. The most
popular spirit is rum.

Where to Eat

Paramaribo
Chalet Swiss, Lim-a-Po Straat.
Good, cheap sandwiches (more
Dutch than Swiss-style). **$**
Chi Min, Cornelis Jongbawstraat 83.
Recommended for Chinese cuisine. **$**
Sarinah, Verlengde
Gemenelandsveg 187, tel: 430
661/492 045. Far from downtown
but excellent Indonesian cuisine. **$**

Nieuw Nickerie
Spice Quest, Nassylaan 107, tel:
520 747. Atmospheric and
romantic Asian restaurant. **$**

Restaurant Guide

Prices for a three-course meal for
two, including house wine:
$ = US$50 – inexpensive
$$ = US$50–100 – moderate
$$$ = US$100 plus – expensive

Uruguay
A – Z

Getting Acquainted

Area 176,200 sq. km
(68,000 sq. miles)
Capital Montevideo
Population 3.4 million
Language Spanish
Currency 1 Uruguayan peso = 100
centesimos
Weights & measures Metric
Electricity 220 volts
Time zone GMT –3hrs, EST +2hrs
International dialing code 598
(Montevideo +2)

Government & Economy

With the exception of the 1973–85
military dictatorship, Uruguay has
enjoyed a liberal democratic system
for the past century. Presidents are
elected for five years, and cannot
run for consecutive terms. The
constitution has traditionally
provided for a wide array of social
services, and the gap between rich
and poor is less extreme than in
neighboring countries. In 2005,
Tabaré Vázquez, representing the
Broad Front coalition, became the
country's first left-wing president.
    The economic crises in Argentina
and Brazil led to a recession in
Uruguay in 2002, but a fragile
recovery is underway.
    Chief exports are beef, rice,
leather products, automobiles,
dairy products, wool, and electricity.

Visas

Tourists traveling to Uruguay from the
UK, Western Europe, US, Canada, or
Australasia do not require a visa. A
tourist card must be filled out on
arrival, and surrendered on

Public Holidays

Uruguay has a strong secular
tradition: Christmas is known as
Family Day; Holy Week is Tourism
Week, celebrated with horse
shows, etc. During Tourism Week,
hotels must be booked in
advance. Carnival features lively
parades of minstrels *(murgas)*,
and businesses close on Monday
and Tuesday of that week.
    Other holidays are:
● January 1 and 6
● April 19
● May 1 and 18
● June 19
● July 18
● August 25
● October 12
● November 2
● December 8

departure. The stamp on passports
is usually good for 90 days and can
be extended for a small fee at the
Oficina de Migraciones, Calle
Misiones 1513, Montevideo, tel. 02-
916 0471. Alternatively, those
wanting to stay longer can cross the
border into Argentina and get a fresh
stamp on their return to Uruguay.
This usually works, but is frowned
upon if done regularly, and the
provision of a stamp is at the
discretion of the border guards.

Customs

There are no special restrictions on
liquor, tobacco, or electronic goods
brought in for personal use.

Getting Around

From the Airport
Montevideo's airport is at
Carrasco, 30 km (19 miles) away.
It's 30 minutes by taxi, and costs
about US$30, but arrange the price
beforehand; you can pay in dollars as
well as pesos. Various bus services
to the city center charge between
US$1 and US$4. The trip takes up
to 55 minutes, and the bus
terminates at either the Río Branco
or Tres Cruces bus terminal.
    International departure tax is

US$26 (except for flights to Buenos Aires, for which US$8 is charged).

By Boat
The most enjoyable way to travel from Buenos Aires to Montevideo is by night ferry, which leaves at 9pm, arriving at 8am the following morning. The cost is around a third of the air fare, and includes a sleeping berth. A catamaran *(buquebus)* from Buenos Aires takes 2½ hours and sails several times a day each way. Fares and schedules are available from www.buquebus.com.

Also from Buenos Aires, there are daily ferries and hydrofoils to Colonia (about 160 km/100 miles to the west of Montevideo). The journey can be rough. There is a connecting bus service to Monte-video, which takes about 3 hours.

By Road
As there are no internal flights or national rail network in Uruguay, buses are the main means of long-distance transportation. The nation's bus system is good, with a number of competing companies whose rates can vary. All long-distance buses depart from the Tres Cruces terminal in Montevideo.

In Montevideo, taxis are cheap though not always plentiful. The city bus system is a mixture of old British Leyland buses and ancient electric trolleys, but the service is fairly efficient. Bus No. 104 (catch it on Calle 18 de Julio) makes a slow but scenic tour of the beaches as far as Carrasco.

There is a daily bus service from Buenos Aires to Montevideo. The trip takes 10 hours. Buses also run on the Pan-American Highway from Rio de Janeiro to Montevideo and on to Colonia.

For information on driving in Uruguay, contact the Automovil Club de Uruguay, Avda Libertador 1532, tel: 1707, www.acu.com.uy (in Spanish only).

Business Hours

Most shops open Mon–Fri 9am–noon and 2–7pm, Sat

9.30am–12.30pm. In Montevideo, banks are open Mon–Fri 1–5pm.

Money

Most banks and exchange offices *(casas de cambio)* make a small charge for cashing US traveler's checks into dollars (rather than pesos). Credit cards and traveler's checks are widely accepted in Montevideo, but not elsewhere. ATMS on the Cirrus network are widely available in Montevideo and Punta del Este. If you travel outside these cities, you will need pesos.

Media

There are four television stations in Uruguay, one of which is state-run. A large percentage of programs come from Argentina. Uruguayans are avid newspaper readers; dailies include *El Observador* and *El País* as well as the left-leaning *República* (good for film, theater, and other social events). There are also a number of interesting weeklies – *Busqueda* is considered foremost.

Postal Services

Letters for overseas *(extranjeros)* should be sent by airmail *(por avión)*. There are post offices *(correos)* throughout the country.

Telephones & Telexes

Antel, the national telephone company, operates *telecentros* in most towns; these are the most efficient places to make international calls. Internet and fax services are also available. Payphones require tokens *(fichas)* which can be bought at Antel or at newsstands. International calls are expensive, but rates are discounted Mon–Fri 10pm–7am, Sat 1pm–midnight, and all day Sunday.

Check with your home cellular service provider to establish compatibility if you want to use your cellphone in Uruguay.

Tourist Information

The main tourist office is on Plaza Fabini (Entrevero). It offers free maps, hotel information, etc. The tourist office at the Tres Cruces bus terminal is open 7am–11pm.

The **Ministerio de Turismo** is at Avda Libertador 1409, 2nd floor, tel: 900 4148, fax: 902 1624, www.turismo.gub.uy.

An online hotel information and reservation system, in English, is www.visit-uruguay.com. The site also provides useful general information on the country.

Embassies/Consulates

Australia: Cerro Largo 1000, Montevideo, tel: 901 0743.
Canada: Plaza Independencia 749, Montevideo, tel: 902 2030.
UK: Calle Marco Bruto 1073, Montevideo, tel: 622 3630, www.britishembassy.gov.uk
US: Calle Lauro Muller 1776, Montevideo 11200, tel: 418 7777, fax: 418 8611, http://uruguay.usembassy.gov.

Where to Stay

Montevideo (02)
Belmont House Hotel, Avda Rivera 6512, tel: 600 0430, fax: 600 8609, www.belmonthouse.com.uy. Near Carrasco Airport. Surrounded by gardens and near the beach. **$$$**
Ermitage Hotel, Calle Juan B. Blanco 783, tel: 710 4021, fax: 710 4312. Good-value hotel opposite Pocitos beach. **$**
Hotel Lafayette, Calle Soriano 1170, tel: 902 4646, fax: 927 367. First choice for top business people. **$$**
Hotel La Rochelle, Calle Fernández Crespo 1714, tel: 409 7176, fax: 401 9367. Centrally located hotel, close to Tres Cruces **$$**
Oxford House Hotel, Calle Paraguay 1286, tel: 902 0046, fax: 902 3792, www.oxford.com.uy. Classic English atmosphere. **$$**
Hotel Mediterraneo, Calle Paraguay 1486, tel: 900 5090, www.hotelmediterraneo.com.uy. Modern hotel; no credit cards. **$**

Near Atlantida
Fortín De Santa Rosa, Ruta Interbalnearia, Km 42, tel: 376 7376. Charming converted fortress, with a quiet beach a few meters away and an excellent restaurant. **$$**

Punta del Este (042)
Hotels are invariably expensive, especially in high season. Those recommended include:
Conrad Resort and Casino, Calle Biarritz and Avda Artigas, Parada 4, La Mansa, tel: 491 111, fax: 489 999, www.conradhotels.com. Enormous, centrally located, with spa and several restaurants. **$$$**
L'Auberge, Barrio Parque del Golf, tel: 482 601, fax: 483 408, www.laubergehotel.com.uy. Sophisticated boutique hotel in 18th-century tower. **$$$**
Clarion, Avda Pedragosa Sierra and Avda Las Delicias, tel: 491 515, fax: 491 530. Modern hotel with three pools and a spa. **$$$**
Hotel Palace, Avda Gorlero and Calle 11, tel (toll-free): 1-877 987 8482, fax: 424 4695. Traditional, with colonial garden. **$$**

Colonia (052)
El Mirador, Avda Roosevelt 381, tel: 22004. A luxury hotel and casino, located just outside the city with a decent restaurant and sizable swimming pool. **$$$**
Posada Plaza Mayor, Calle del Comercio 111, tel: 23193, www.hotelplazamayor.com.uy. Hotel converted from stunning colonial house, with a beautiful central patio. **$$**
Sheraton Colonia Golf y Spa Resort, continuación Rambla de las Américas, tel: 29000. The enormous pool and great golf facilities will keep you busy in this luxurious hotel. **$$$**

Hotel Price Guide

Prices for a double room including continental breakfast:
$ = US$50 – inexpensive
$$ = US$50–100 – moderate
$$$ = US$100 plus – expensive

What to Eat

Breakfast consists of coffee and croissants; lunch is the main meal and is served from 1–3pm. Dinner tends to be quite late. On weekends, restaurants are jammed at midnight. Portions are often enormous; it's quite all right to order one dish for two people.

Uruguayan food consists of two staples: beef and pasta. Uruguayans also like seafood. Try *calamares a la plancha* (griddled squid), *cazuela de mariscos* (seafood stew), and *lenguado* (sole) *a la provenzal*. Ice cream and pizza are excellent snacks, as is *chivito*, a steak and salad sandwich.

Where to Eat

Montevideo (02)
El Abasto, Bacacay 1309, corner of Buenos Aires, tel: 916 9025. Serves a good, fresh selection of fish and pasta. **$$**
El Aguila, Calle Buenos Aires 694, next to Teatro Solis. Elegant service with a continental menu. **$$**
Arcadia, Plaza Independencia 759, tel: 902 0111. One of the best in town. Classic surroundings and food. **$$$**
Doña Flor, Calle Artigas and Avda España, tel: 708 5751. Classy French cuisine. **$$$**
El Palenque, Pérez Castellano 1579, in the Mercado del Puerto, tel: 915 4701, closed on Sunday evenings. Situated in the historic market port, this is a beautiful place specializing in fish. **$$$**
Parrillada Venítez, Libertad 2536, tel: 708 6855. Rumored to be the best *parilla* in Montevideo. **$**

Punta del Este (042)
La Bourgogne, Avda Pedragosa Sierra, tel: 482 007. Memorable French restaurant. Elegant surroundings and one of the best chefs in South America. **$$$**
Los Caracoles, Avda Gorlero 20, tel: 440 912. Steak and salad house with lively atmosphere. **$**
Lo de Tere, Rambla del Puerto and Calle 21, tel: 440 492. Harbour-side views and excellent fresh fish. **$$**

Restaurant Guide

Prices for a three-course meal for two, including house wine:
$ = US$50 – inexpensive
$$ = US$50–100 – moderate
$$$ = US$100 plus – expensive

Colonia (052)
Posada Gondwana, Tula Suarez de Cutinela. A friendly family-run establishment. **$$**
Pulpería de los Faroles, Misiones de los Tapes 101, tel: 523 0271. In Colonia's historic center, this quaint choice offers Uruguayan dishes at reasonable prices. **$**
Viejo Barrio, Vasconcellos 169, tel: 522 5399. Great service and good food in the historic district. **$$**

Drinking Notes

For coffee or snacks in Montevideo, try the **Café La Pasiva** in Plaza Matriz Sarandi 600 or **El Lusitano** at Calle 18 de Julio across from the Plaza Cagancha. **Cakes** on the pedestrianized Rambla has superb cakes, coffee, and beer. **Sokos**, on Calle 18 de Julio, has good sandwiches and more substantial meals. Uruguayan wine is drinkable but nothing special. Beer is made with spring water and is very good, especially *Norteña*.

Bars & Nightclubs

Montevideo has a very vibrant nightlife, with plenty of live music. You can hear Brazilian music at **Clave de Fu**, 26 de Marzo 1125. For tango, try **Living de Tango**, Edil Hugo Prato. The most popular nightclubs are **Makao**, on Mar Artico 1227, which serves good food and plays 1970s and 80s music, and **Luna Gaucho**, on Motivos de Proteo and Rambla. You can gamble at **Casino Parque Hotel**, Gonzalo Ramírez 2067, the **Hotel Casino Carrasco**, Rambla, República de México, and the **Radisson Casino**, Plaza Independencia 759.

Venezuela
A – Z

Getting Acquainted

Area 916,442 sq. km (352,143 sq. miles), with a 2,700-km (1,700-mile) Caribbean coast, and 72 islands.
Capital Caracas
Population 24 million. There is a mix of African and European descendants. The native population is fewer than 200,000. More than 80 percent live in urban areas, the largest of which are concentrated on or near the northern coast.
Language Spanish
Currency Bolívar (Bs)
Weights & measures Metric
Electricity 110 volts
Time zone GMT -4hrs, EST +1hr
International dialing code 58 (Caracas +212)

Public Holidays

- **January 1** New Year's Day
- **February**, on the Monday and Tuesday before Ash Wednesday Carnival
- **Late March/April** Thursday to Saturday Holy Week
- **April 19** Anniversary of the National Declaration of Independence
- **May 1** Labor Day
- **June 24** The feast day of St John the Baptist
- **July 5** Anniversary of the signing of Venezuelan National Independence Act
- **July 24** Anniversary of the birth of the Liberator, Simón Bolívar
- **October 12** Columbus Day (Anniversary of the Discovery of America)
- **December 25** Christmas Day

Government & Economy

Venezuela is a democratic republic. The election of former coup leader Hugo Chávez Frías in 1998 as president brought with it major changes in the country's political structure, and raised concerns over the growing concentration of power in central government.

Venezuela is the world's fifth biggest oil exporter, and the economy relies heavily on the petroleum industry. Since 2000, the government has spent much of its vast oil revenues on social programs for the poorest sectors of society and on major infrastructure projects. Political unrest, however, has been severe, with a nine-week strike in 2002 that encouraged capital flight and a downturn in foreign investment. There was continued strife following a referendum on Chávez's rule in 2004, which divided the nation. However, he was re-elected in a landslide victory in December 2006, and has declared his long-term goal to be the transformation of Venezuela into a socialist state.

Emergencies

The nationwide emergency telephone number, **171**, is for police, fire, and ambulance.

Visas

Entry is by passport and visa or passport and tourist card. If arriving by air, tourist cards (valid for 90 days) can be issued to citizens of the UK, the USA, Canada, and Australia. If arriving by land, a visa must be obtained from a consulate before arrival – requiring a letter of reference, for which there is a charge. However, regulations sometimes change overnight, so double-check in advance with your nearest Venezuelan Consulate.

It is a good idea to carry your passport with you at all times (be sure to have photocopies of all

Tourist Information

Inatur www.inatur.gov.ve (in Spanish) is the national tourism body for Venezuela. There are no tourist information kiosks in Caracas; there is a booth at Maiquetía airport but the opening hours are irregular.

documents in a separate location in case of loss) as the police mount spot checks and anyone without ID may be detained.

Money

US dollars, in cash and travelers' checks, can be exchanged for bolívars upon arrival at the airport and at *casas de cambio* in major cities. Some banks, such as Banco Mercantil, will buy US dollars for bolívars, however it is advisable to obtain bolívars before travelling to Venezuela, where possible. The artificial (official) exchange rate is fixed, but there is a rampant black market operating with a fluctuating rate. It is illegal and can be dangerous to exchange on the black market. ATMS are widely available for withdrawing bolívars. Credit-card fraud is rife, even at large, well-known establishments.

Emergency Money

Western Union is represented by **Grupo Zoom**, which has more than 40 offices in Caracas alone. For information, see www.western union.com. **Intercambio** offer a service called Moneygram and also have a national network. Details on www.italcambio.com (in Spanish).

Getting Around

From the Airport

The **Simón Bolívar International Airport** is in Maiquetía, 28 km (17 miles) from Caracas. The international and domestic terminals are very close to each other and there are shuttle buses every 10 minutes between the two. Shuttle buses also run to Caracas with stops by the Gato Negro Metro station (use this stop only during daylight hours) and at their terminal two blocks west of the Bellas Artes Metro station and Caracas Hilton (Calle Sur 17). It costs less than US$2 and usually takes just under an hour.

The black Anfitriónes de Venezuela taxis charge fixed prices (around US$25 to the center of town); tickets can be bought in the domestic or international terminals. Otherwise, the **taxis** which park near the departure area have a monopoly and charge nearly double the going rate. To avoid paying over the odds, call Tele-taxi on 753 4155/9122 (pre-paid phone cards are sold in dispensers next to the banks of phones in the terminal). Do not get into unlicensed taxis, as foreign visitors are sometimes mugged by these drivers.

Every state has at least one airport for commercial flights, except for Delta Amacuro. Travelers wishing to reach this state by air will have to fly in to Monagas' Maturín airport, then use public transportation or rent a car to reach the delta.

Aeroportal, **Avior**, **Santa Barbara**, **Lasca** and **ConVIASA** dominate the domestic market. However, a number of regional or specialized airlines offer

The Subway

The Metro has three lines providing stops all along the main corridors for business, shopping, and cultural attractions. A complementary system of Metrobuses combines Metro travel with buses which cover extensive routes from each stop. Tickets can be purchased singly for the Metro alone or *combinado*, good for a Metro ride and service on a Metrobus. Much more economical are the *multi-abono* tickets, valid for 10 rides for a flat fee. Tickets are available at many newsstands (those identified with a large M).

The Metro runs from 5am–11pm and is very clean, with excellent security.

alternatives, as well as scores of charter services.

Airport departure tax for international flights is US$60 and liable to change; for national flights it is roughly US$2.

By Bus

Cheap public transportation is found virtually everywhere. From Caracas, long-distance eastbound bus lines operate from the Terminal del Oriente, Avda General Antonio José de Sucre, on the eastern outskirts of the capital. Westbound buses leave from La Bandera, at the junction of Avda Nueva Granada and the El Valle *autopista*, near Los Próceres, with the La Bandera Metro stop nearby.

Arrangements for inter-urban bus travel must be made at the *Terminal de Pasajeros* (passenger terminal), found in all towns and cities.

By Ferry

Conferry in Caracas, tel: 709 0000, www.conferry.com, offers a service between Puerto La Cruz and Cumaná, and Margarita Island. **Gran Cacique Express** (Puerto La Cruz, tel: 281 263 0935; Margarita, tel: 295 239 8339) has a passenger service from Cumaná to Margarita. **Naviarca** (tel: 293 433 0909) also runs from Cumaná to Araya and Cumaná to Margarita. Neither of these routes has set schedules: the ferries simply depart when full.

There is a very inexpensive passenger-only service between Chacopata (on the Araya peninsula, Sucre state) and Coche Island, continuing to Margarita (landing in Porlamar, by the shopping area).

By Car

Driving in Caracas is an exercise in self-preservation, so proceed with extreme caution. However, driving in the interior is pleasant, and the roads are of good quality, apart from the potholes. In many areas, driving is the *only* way to appreciate landscapes, explore villages, and mingle with local people. A little Spanish will go a long way.

Driving at night is not advisable since lighting, lane markings, and warnings of obstacles are poor to non-existent, and there are frequently animals in the road.

Health Matters

No inoculations are needed, but a yellow fever certificate is recommended if you intend traveling in the jungle: Venezuela is an endemic area for yellow fever, although this applies mainly to the upper Orinoco near La Esmeralda and Parima in Amazonas.

The incidence of cases of dengue fever is on the increase, primarily in poor urban areas. Malaria can also be a problem in some areas. It is essential to obtain proper advice and suitable medication before you leave your home country and also to take protective clothing with you. In the UK, contact the **Medical Advisory Service for Travellers Abroad** (MASTA), tel: 0906 8224100, www.masta.org

For minor medical problems, the better hotels have physicians on call. Every town has a system to ensure a pharmacy is open 24 hours; these are marked with a *turno* sign.

In an emergency, contact the national emergency number **171**: **ambulances** can also be called on tel: 545 4545/577 9209.

The **Centro Móvil de Medicina Permanente** in Caracas is an emergency service with doctors who can make 24-hour house calls, tel: 483 7021/6092.

Two useful addresses are: **Hospital Universitario** (UCV), south from the Plaza Venezuela freeway exit, tel: 606 7111; and **Clínica de Emergencia Infantil** (Children's Emergency Clinic), Edificio Topacio, 4th floor, Avda Avila, between Avdas Caracas and Gamboa, tel: 577 6136/7381.

Business Hours

Generally Mon–Fri 8am–noon and 2–6pm. Most shops open Mon–Sat 9am–1pm and 3–7pm; but in high season, Mon–Sat 9am–7pm, Sun 9am–1pm.

Newspapers

The *Daily Journal* is the country's only English-language paper. Its "Week in Review" supplement, printed on Monday, provides a useful summary. *El Nacional* and *El Universal* are the two most important national papers.

Postal Services

The Venezuelan postal system (IPOSTEL) is extremely inefficient, but much better for international than domestic mail. For Europe or the US, mail takes 10 days to three weeks. For a small extra charge, you can have your letter certified *(certificado)* or ask for a return receipt *(con aviso de recibo)*.

Communications

Telephone
Most numbers are seven digits. To make national calls, add a zero before the area code. **CANTV** is the national telephone company. Dial 122 for the long-distance operator.

Internet
In most places frequented by tourists, you will find internet cafés. Useful websites: www.think-venezuela.net offers comprehensive information in English, Spanish, and German. www.venezuelatuya.com has a useful search facility for finding accommodations and www.venezuelavoyage.com features recommendations for places to visit and links to other useful websites.

Embassies/Consulates

The following diplomatic missions are located in Caracas:
Australia: Quinta Yolanda, Avda Luis Roche, between 6th and 7th transversals, Altamira, tel: 261 4632, fax: 261 3448.
Canada: Edificio Omni, Avda 6 between 3rd and 5th transversals, Altamira, tel: 264 0833.
UK: Torre Las Mercedes, Avda La Estancia, 3rd floor, Urb. Chuao, tel: 993 4111/5280, fax: 993

9989, www.britishembassy.gov.uk
US: Calle F and Calle Suapure, Colinas de Valle Arriba, tel: 975 6411, fax: 975 8971, http://caracas.usembassy.gov

Where to Stay

El Litoral is the area of the Caribbean coast nearest Caracas and Simón Bolívar National and International Airport in Maiquetía which serves Caracas, but due to the natural disaster which devastated this area in 1999, there are still few lodging options due to lack of infrastructure. Virtually all beaches were destroyed by mudslides, and vast areas are still in a state of ruin. The best option is **Best Western Puerto Viejo**, tel: 0212-352 4044, www.bestwestern.com

Hotels

Caracas (212)
Avila, Avda George Washington, San Bernardino, tel: 555 3000, fax: 552 8367. Traditional flavor in quiet residential neighborhood. **$$**
El Cid, Avda San Felipe, between 1st and 2nd transversals, La Castellana. tel: 263 2611, fax: 263 5578. Modest, fully equipped suites with kitchens, in quiet side street in heart of La Castellana–Altamira district. **$$**
El Condor, Avda de Las Delicias 3, Sabana Grande, tel: 762 9911–15/762 7621, fax: 762 8621. An old favorite, near the main shopping centers. **$$**
Tamanaco Inter-Continental, Avda Principal las Mercedes, tel: 909 7111, fax: 909 7116, www.interconti.com. The best hotel in Caracas.**$$$**

Ciudad Guyana (286)
Hotel Inter-Continental Guayana, Avda Guayana, Parque Punta Vista, tel: 713 1000, fax: 713 1001, www.interconti.com. Great location overlooking the river and Cachamay Falls, connected by jogging path to Cachamay Park. Private dock and boats for river tours. **$$$**

Hotel Price Guide

Prices for a double room including continental breakfast:
$ = US$50 – inexpensive
$$ = US$50–100 – moderate
$$$ = US$100 plus – expensive

Mérida (274)
Posada de Luz Caraballo, Avda 2, 13–80, tel: 252 5441, fax: 252 0177, www.andes.net/luzcaraballo. Reliable, comfortable, economical, and in the town center. **$$**
Posada Los Bucares de Mérida, Avda 4, 15–5, at Calle 15, tel/fax: 252 2841/0566. Typical vintage house with central patio and spotless comfortable rooms. Very friendly owners. **$$**
Posada Papá Miguel, Calle Piñango 1, La Mesa de Los Indios (5 km/3 miles north of Ejido), tel/fax: 252 2529. Delightful house; restaurant has delicious home cooking. **$$**

Puerto la Cruz (281)
Hotel Caribe Mar, Calle Ricaurte 12, tel: 267 5722, fax: 267 2096. Good option for tight budgets. Near ferry terminal and Paseo Colón. **$$**
Gaeta Hotels, Beach hotel – tel: 65 1822/65 0411, fax: 65 0065; City hotel – tel: 65 0536. These two hotels have plain but comfortable rooms, and good locations, Continental breakfast included. **$$–$$$**

What to Eat

Pabellón, the national dish, combines rice, black beans, shredded beef, and *tajadas* (fried ripe plantains). The Andes is known for *pisca* (a rich broth with eggs and bread), trout, and smoked cheese. Coro is famous for *tarkari de chivo* (curried or roasted goat) and goat's milk cheese. Zulia state has delicious coconut-based specialties like *conejo en coco* (rabbit cooked in coconut milk). The coastal region is known for *consomé de guacucos* (clams) and *empanadas de cazón* (shark-meat pies), lobster, and fish such as grouper.

At Christmas, *hallaca* (a stew of chicken, pork, beef, spices, olives, raisins, and capers wrapped in banana leaves and steamed) is the most traditional dish.

A typical and very popular Venezuelan dish is *mondongo* (tripe stew with chickpeas). *Arepa* is traditional flat round bread made from corn meal or wheat flour.

The beef is excellent throughout the country.

Where to Eat

Outside the capital, head for the following area to find the greatest concentration of restaurants: **Barquisimeto**, along Avda Lara between Paseo Los Leones and the Barquisimeto Country Club; **Maracaibo**, along Calle 5 de Julio and Avda 4 Bella Vista; in **Maracay**, along Avda Las Delicias; in the city of **Mérida**, on Avda Chorro de Milla or Calle 24 facing Plaza Los Heroínas; **Puerto La Cruz**, along Paseo Colón and in **Valencia**, along Avda Bolívar Norte.

Most of the economical spots offer a daily *menú ejecutivo*, usually with soup, a main dish, dessert, and a drink for a low, fixed price.

Food in bars may cost 50 percent more and there is no need to feel reticent about asking for prices before you order. You save the 10 percent service charge if you eat at the bar, not at a table.

Caracas (212)

Las Mercedes and the **Altamira–Los Palos Grandes** zone offer a huge variety of restaurants and trendy, more upscale dining spots; **Avda Francisco Solano**, between Chacaíto and Avda Las Acacias, has a large concentration of Italian restaurants; **Candelaria** (recommended only for daytime

Restaurant Guide

Prices for *a* three-course meal for two, including house wine:
$ = US$50 – inexpensive
$$ = US$50–100 – moderate
$$$ = US$100 plus – expensive

visits) is popular for Spanish food and *tascas*.

An excellent source of information is **Miro Popic's *Guía Gastronómica de Caracas***, updated annually, in English/Spanish, available in bookstores and hotels.

Ara, Centro Lido, 8th floor, Avda Francisco de Miranda, El Rosal, tel: 953 3270. Bistro-style menu in rooftop setting. Chic clientele. Live music and comedy. Closed Sun. **$$$**
Arábica Coffee Bar, Avda Andrés Bello at Los Palos Grandes, tel: 285 6748. Estate-grown, single-variety coffees roasted daily. Also a great choice of pastries. **$**
Aventio, Avda San Felipe and Calle José Angel Lamas, La Castellana, tel: 267 5422. Traditional, high-class French restaurant. **$$$**
Bar Basque, Alcabala a Peligro, La Candelaria, tel: 576 5955. Considered one of the best restaurants in Caracas. Tiny, with Basque home cooking. Closed Sun and Aug. Booking recommended. Zone best visited only by day. **$$**
El Buffet Vegetariano, Avda Los Jardines 4, La Florida, tel: 730 7490/7512. Healthy, generously served vegetarian fare. Fixed-price menu. No smoking or alcohol. Open 11.30am–2.30pm weekdays. **$**
El Portón, Avda Pinchincha and Calle Guaicaipuro, El Rosal, tel: 952 0027/0302. Traditional Venezuelan-style specialties, particularly beef; usually with live *música criolla*. **$$**
Le Petit Bistrot de Jacques, Avda San Felipe, La Castellana, tel: 263 8595. Authentic, intimate French bistro serving classic offerings such as *cassoulet*, *choucroute*, and *steak frites*. Closed Sat lunch and Sun. **$$$**
Maute Grill, Avda Rio de Janeiro, Las Mercedes, tel: 991 0892. The restaurant surrounds a traditional tree-filled patio. Excellent beef. **$$**

Mérida (274)

Date con Rolando, Avda Urdanea and Calle 49. Snack bar on wheels serving high-quality fast food. **$**
La Gruta, Prolongación Avda 2,

Where to Shop

In the Caracas area, **Hannsi** in El Hatillo has the widest selection of Venezuelan arts and crafts in the country, with items for every budget. The most exquisite objects are found in **Casa Caruba**, Avda Andrés Bello between 1st and 2nd transversals, Los Palos Grandes.

The **Sabana Grande Boulevard** is an excellent commercial artery with numerous boutiques and assorted stores.

tel: 634 828. Offers a great regional menu. **$$**
Restaurante Bimbo, Calle 23 (between avdas 4 and 5), tel: 528 950. Traditional Italian with international dishes. **$$**

Puerto la Cruz (281)

Brasero Grill/La Boite del Brasero, Paseo Colón (east end), tel: 67 4850/266 0923. Beef and seafood. Upscale crowd. **$$$**
El Parador del Puerto, Paseo Colón, tel: 265 0391/3950. Seafood specialties, elegant-looking dark interior. **$$–$$$**
Fuentemar, Paseo Colón, tel: 68 7623. Long-established place on the beach, with inside and outside seating. At the latter, a distinct soda-fountain-style menu; the formal interior has seafood. **$$**

Nightlife

Caracas is a swinging city by night and there are many and varied nightclubs. *Caraqueños* usually eat at home at 8pm and between 9pm and 11pm when they go out to restaurants; the partying goes on until well into the early hours of the morning. There are many small clubs, restaurants, and bars on **Plaza Altamira Sur** and along the **Sabana Grande Boulevard**.

Language

Making Contact

Whether you need to know what time the next bus leaves or how to book a hotel room, making yourself understood in the local language will really help you get the most out of your stay in South America. The good news is that you can get by in the whole continent with just two languages: Spanish and Portuguese (with the obvious exceptions of the Guianas).

While people in many tourist establishments will speak English, once you are off the beaten track, hardly anyone will, and just making the effort to speak a few words will gain you a lot of appreciation. There are idiomatic differences from one country to the next, but you will soon pick these up as you go.

It would be impossible for us to give a complete language guide here, but the following are some useful words, phrases, and tips that will hopefully ease understanding.

Spanish

There is a colorful variety of local idioms throughout Spanish South America. In Argentina, the Spanish "ll", as in "*llanos*", comes out like something between a **j** and **zh**; while the familiar "*tu*" is replaced by the archaic sounding "*vos*." In Chile and to a lesser extent Peru, they are notorious for dropping the ends off their words, particularly those that end in "–ado", which become "ao" instead. It may come as a relief to know that Colombians pride themselves on speaking the clearest and purest Spanish in South America.

In the Andes, *indígenas* all speak Spanish but you will hear Quechua (also spelt Quichua) words that have crept into the language: *wambras* translates as "guys," and *cheveré* means "cool."

Berlitz publishes an excellent *Latin American Spanish Phrase Book and Dictionary*, containing vocabulary and phrases for every situation.

Pronunciation

Vowels
a as in cat
e as in bed
i as in police
o as in hot
u as in rude
Consonants are approximately like those in English, the main exceptions being:
c is hard before **a**, **o**, or **u** (as in English), and is soft before **e** or **i**, when it sounds like **s** (as opposed to the Castilian pronunciation of **th** as in think). Thus, *censo* (census) sounds like senso.
g is hard before **a**, **o**, or **u** (as in English), but where English **g** sounds like **j** – before **e** or **i** – Spanish **g** sounds like a guttural **h**. **G** before **ua** is often soft or silent, so that *agua* sounds more like *awa*, and Guadalajara like Wadalajara.
h is silent.
j sounds like a guttural h.
ll sounds like y.
ñ sounds like ny, as in the familiar Spanish word *señor*.
q sounds like **k**. *¿Qué quiere Usted?* is pronounced: Keh kee-ehr-eh oostehd?
r is often rolled.
x between vowels sounds like a guttural **h**, eg México.
y alone, as the word meaning "and", is pronounced **ee**.
Note that **ch**, **ll**, and **ñ** are separate letters of the Spanish alphabet; if looking in a phone book or dictionary for a word beginning with **ch**, you will find it after the final **c** entry; **ll** will be listed after the **l** entry, and **ñ** after **n**.

Greetings
Hello! *¡Hola!*
Hello (Good day) *Buenos días*

Good afternoon/night *Buenas tardes/noches*
Goodbye *Ciao/¡Adios!*
My name is... *Me llamo...*
What is your name? (formal) *¿Cómo se llama usted?*
Mr/Miss/Mrs *Señor/Señorita/Señora*
Pleased to meet you *¡Encantado(a)!*
Do you speak English? *¿Habla inglés?*
How are you? (formal/informal) *¿Cómo está? ¿Qué tal?*
Fine, thanks *Muy bien, gracias*
See you later *Hasta luego*

Getting Around
Where is...? *¿Dónde está...?*
Which way is it to...? *¿Cómo se va a...?*
Yes *Sí*
No *No*
Thank you *Gracias*
You're welcome *No hay de que/De nada/ Por nada*
Alright/Okay/That's fine *Está bien*
Please *Por favor*
Excuse me (to get attention) *¡Permiso!/¡Por favor!*
Excuse me (to get through a crowd) *¡Permiso!*
Excuse me (sorry) *Perdóneme, Discúlpeme*
I need... *Necesito....*
I'm lost *Estoy perdido(a)*
I'm sorry *Lo siento*
I don't know *No sé*
I don't understand *No entiendo*
Slowly *despacio/lentamente*
What? *¿Qué?/¿Cómo?*
When? *¿Cuándo?*
Why? *¿Por qué?*
Who? *¿Quién(es)?*
How? *¿Cómo?*
Which? *¿Cuál?*
How much/how many? *¿Cuánto?/ ¿Cuántos?*
How long? *¿Cuánto tiempo?*
Big, bigger *Grande, más grande*
Small, smaller *Pequeño, mas pequeño/chico, más chico*
I want.../I would like.../I need... *Quiero.../Quisiera.../Necesito...*
Where is the lavatory? *¿Dónde se encuentra el baño?*

Shopping
What time do you open/close? *¿A qué hora abren/cierran?*

Open/closed *Abierto/cerrado*
I'd like... *Quisiera...*
Do you have...? *¿Hay...?*
How much does it cost?
¿Cuánto cuesta?
smaller/larger *más pequeño/*
más grande
It's too expensive *Es demasiado*
caro
Do you have something less
expensive? *¿Tiene algo más*
económico?
Anything else? *¿Quiere algo más?*
a little more/less *un poco más/*
menos
That's enough/no more
Está bien/no más

At the Hotel
Do you have a vacant room?
¿Tiene una habitación disponible?
I have a reservation *Tengo una*
reservación
I'd like... *Quisiera...*
a single/double (with double bed)/
a room with twin beds *una*
habitación individual/
una habitación matrimonial/una
habitación doble
for one night/two nights *por una*
noche/dos noches
Could you show me another room,
please? *¿Puede mostrarme otra*
habitación, por favor?
I would like to change rooms
Quisiera cambiar de habitación
How much is it? *¿Cuánto*
cuesta?

At the Restaurant
Waiter *Garzón/mozo*
I'd like to book a table *Quisiera*
reservar una mesa, por favor
Do you have a table for...? *¿Tiene*
una mesa para...?
I have a reservation *Tengo una*
reservación
breakfast/lunch/dinner
desayuno/almuerzo/cena
I'm a vegetarian *Soy*
vegetariano(a)
menu *la carta (or el menú)*
wine list *la carta de vinos*
fixed-price menu *menú fijo*
special of the day *plato del día*
mineral water still/carbonated
agua mineral sin gas/con gas
  with/without ice *con/sin hielo*
coffee *un café*

tea *té*
beer *cerveza*
soft drink *bebida/refresco*
a glass of red/white wine *una*
copa de vino tinto/blanco
pollo **chicken**
cerdo/chancho **pork**
pescado **fish**
arróz **rice**
azúcar **sugar**
huevos **eggs**
mantequilla **butter**
pan (tostado) **bread (toast)**
queso **cheese**
sal **salt**
arróz **rice**
azúcar **sugar**
mantequilla **butter**

Time
morning *la mañana*
afternoon *la tarde*
evening *la noche*
last night *anoche*
yesterday *ayer*
today *hoy*
tomorrow *mañana*
now *ahora*
early *temprano*
late *tarde*
a minute *un minuto*
an hour *una hora*
half an hour *media hora*
a day *un día*
a week *una semana*
a year *un año*

Days of the Week
Monday *lunes*
Tuesday *martes*
Wednesday *miércoles*
Thursday *jueves*
Friday *viernes*
Saturday *sábado*
Sunday *domingo*

Months of the Year
January *enero*
February *febrero*
March *marzo*
April *abril*
May *mayo*
June *junio*
July *julio*
August *agosto*
September *septiembre*
October *octubre*
November *noviembre*
December *diciembre*

Numbers

1	uno
2	dos
3	tres
4	cuatro
5	cinco
6	seis
7	siete
8	ocho
9	nueve
10	diez
11	once
12	doce
13	trece
14	catorce
15	quince
16	dieciséis
17	diecisiete
18	dieciocho
19	diecinueve
20	veinte
21	veintiuno
25	veinticinco
30	treinta
40	cuarenta
50	cincuenta
60	sesenta
70	setenta
80	ochenta
90	noventa
100	cien
101	ciento uno
200	doscientos
300	trescientos
400	cuatrocientos
500	quinientos
600	seiscientos
700	setecientos
800	ochocientos
900	novecientos
1,000	mil
2,000	dos mil
10,000	diez mil
100,000	cien mil
1,000,000	un millón

Portuguese

Although Portuguese, and not
Spanish, is the language of Brazil, a
knowledge of Spanish will certainly
prove useful: you will recognize
many similar words, and most
Brazilians will understand you if you
speak in Spanish. The Berlitz
*Portuguese Phrase Book and
Dictionary* is an excellent guide to
the language, with a comprehensive
guide to the rather complex

pronunciation rules, and includes Brazilian variants.

First names are used a great deal in Brazil. In many situations in which English-speakers would use a title and surname, Brazilians often use a first name with the title of respect: *Senhor* for men (written *Sr* and usually shortened to *Seu* in spoken Portuguese) and *Senhora* (written *Sra*) or *Dona* (used only with first name) for women. If *João Oliveira* or *Maria da Silva* calls you Sr John, rather than Mr Jones, then you should correspondingly address them as *Sr João* and *Dona Maria*.

There are three second-person pronoun forms in Portuguese. Stick to *você*, equivalent to "you," and you will be all right. *O senhor* (for men) or *a senhora* (for women) is used to show respect for someone of a different age group or social class or to be polite to a stranger. As a foreigner, you won't offend anyone if you use the wrong form of address. But if you want to learn when to use the more formal or informal style, observe and go by how others address you. In some parts of Brazil, mainly the northeast and the south, *tu* is used a great deal. Originally, in Portugal, *tu* was used among intimate friends and close relatives, but in Brazil, it's equivalent to *você*.

If you are staying longer and are serious about learning the language, there are Portuguese courses for non-native speakers. Meanwhile, here are some of the most essential words and phrases:

Greetings

Tudo Bem, meaning "all's well," is one of the most common forms of greeting: one person asks, "*Tudo bem?*" and the other replies, "*Tudo bem.*" This is also used to mean "OK," "all right," "will do," or as a response when someone apologizes, meaning, "that's all right, no worries." Other forms of greetings are:

Good morning (good afternoon) *Bom dia (boa tarde)*
Good evening (good night) *Boa noite*
How are you? *Como vai?*
Well, thank you *Bem, obrigado*
Hello (to answer the telephone) *Alô*
Hello (common forms of greeting)

Bom dia, boa tarde etc.
Hi, hey! (informal greeting also used to get someone's attention) *Oi*
Goodbye (very informal and most used) *Tchau*
Goodbye (literally "until soon") *Até logo*
My name is (I am) *Meu nome é (Eu sou)*
What is your name? *Como é seu nome?*
It's a pleasure *É um prazer*
Pleased to meet you *Prazer*
Yes *Sim*
No *Não*
Good! Great! *Que bom!*
Cheers! *Saúde*
Do you speak English? *Você fala inglês?*
I don't understand (I didn't understand) *Não entendo (Não entendi)*
Do you understand? *Você entende?*
Please *Por favor*
Thank you (very much) *(Muito) Obrigado* (or *Obrigada*, for a woman speaking)
You're welcome (literally "it's nothing") *De nada*
Excuse me (to apologize) *Desculpe*
Excuse me (taking leave or to get past someone) *Com licença*

Getting Around

Where is the...? *Onde é...?*
beach *a praia*
bathroom *o banheiro*
bus station *a rodoviária*
airport *o aeroporto*
train station *a estação de trem*
post office *o correio*
police station *a delegacia de polícia*
marketplace *o mercado*
embassy (consulate) *a embaixada (o consulado)*
currency exchange *uma casa de câmbio*
bank *um banco*
pharmacy *uma farmácia*
(good) hotel *um (bom) hotel*
(good) restaurant *um (bom) restaurante*
bar *um bar*
snack bar *uma lanchonete*
bus stop *um ponto de ônibus*
taxi stand *um ponto de taxi*
subway station *uma estação de metrô*

service station *um posto de gasolina*
newsstand *um jornaleiro*
public telephone *um telefone público*
hospital *um hospital*
taxi *taxi*
bus *onibus*
car *carro*
airplane *avião*
train *trem*
boat *barco*
A ticket to... *Uma passagem para...*
I want to go to... *Quero ir para...*
How can I get to...? *Como posso ir para...?*
Please take me to... *Por favor, me leve para...*
Please call a taxi for me *Por favor, chame um taxi para mim*
I want to rent a car *Quero alugar um carro*
Where are we? *Onde estamos?*
How long will it take to get there? *Leva quanto tempo para chegar lá?*
Please stop here (Stop!) *Por favor, pare aqui. (Pare!)*
Please wait *Por favor, espere*
What time does the bus (plane, boat) leave? *A que horas sai o ônibus (avião, barco)?*
Where does this bus go? *Este ônibus vai para onde?*
Airport (or bus station) tax *Taxa de embarque*

Shopping

Do you have...? *Tem...?*
I want... please *Eu quero... por favor*
I don't want... *Eu não quero...*
I want to buy... *Eu quero comprar...*
Where can I buy... *Onde posso comprar...?*
film *filme*
a ticket for... *uma entrada para...*
this (that) *isto (aquilo)*
something less expensive *algo mais barato*
shampoo *xampu or shampoo*
soap *sabonete*
toothpaste *pasta de dente*
sunscreen *filtro solar*
aspirin *aspirina*
I need... *Eu preciso de...*
a doctor *um médico*
a mechanic *um mecânico*

transportation *transporte*
help *ajuda*
How much? *Quanto?*
How many? *Quantos?*
How much does it cost? *Quanto custa? Quanto é?*
That's very expensive *É muito caro*
money/cash *dinheiro*
Do you accept credit cards? *Aceita cartão de crédito?*

At the Hotel
I have a reservation *Tenho uma reserva*
I want to make a reservation *Quero fazer uma reserva*
a single room (a double room) *um quarto de solteiro (um quarto de casal)*
with air conditioning *com ar condicionado*
I want to see the room *Quero ver o quarto*
suitcase *mala*
bag or purse *bolsa*
key *chave*
the manager *o gerente*

At the Restaurant
Waiter! *Se faz favor!*
I didn't order this *Eu não pedi isto*
The bill, please *A conta, por favor*
Is service included? *Está incluido o serviço?*
I want my change, please *Eu quero meu troco, por favor*

cardápio menu
carta de vinhos wine list
café da manhã breakfast
almoço lunch
jantar supper
especialidade da casa house specialty
água mineral com gás carbonated mineral water
água mineral sem gás still mineral water
café coffee
chá tea
cerveja beer
vinho branco/tinto white/red wine
um refresco (suco) soft drink (juice)
gelo ice
sal salt
pimenta pepper
açucar sugar
um tira-gosto an appetizer

um lanche a snack
porco pork
frango chicken
peixe fish
camarão shrimp
carne beef
bem passado well done
ao ponto medium rare
mal passado rare
verduras vegetables
salada salad
fruta fruit
pão bread
manteiga butter
torradas toast
ovos eggs
arroz rice
batatas (fritas) (fried) potatoes
feijão beans
sobremesa dessert

Days of the week, etc.
Monday *Segunda-feira*
Tuesday *Terça-feira*
Wednesday *Quarta-feira*
Thursday *Quinta-feira*
Friday *Sexta-feira*
(Monday to Friday are often written as *2a, 3a, 4a, 5a*)
Saturday *Sábado*
Sunday *Domingo*
hour *a hora*
day *o dia*
week *a semana*
month *o mês*
When? *Quando?*
What time is it? *Que horas são?*
Just a moment please *Um momento, por favor*
What is the schedule? (bus, tour, show, etc.) *Qual é o horário?*
How long does it take? *Leva quanto tempo?*
At what time? *A que horas?*
At one-o-clock *A uma hora*
(two-, three-...) *(duas, três...)*
An hour from now *Daqui a uma hora*
Which day? *Que dia?*
yesterday *ontem*
today *hoje*
tomorrow *amanhã*
next week *a semana que vem*

Months
January *Janeiro*
February *Fevereiro*
March *Março*
April *Abril*

May *Maio*
June *Junho*
July *Julho*
August *Agosto*
September *Setembro*
October *Outubro*
November *Novembro*
December *Dezembro*

Numbers

1	*um*
2	*dois*
3	*três*
4	*quatro*
5	*cinco*
6	*seis*
half a dozen	*meia*
7	*sete*
8	*oito*
9	*nove*
10	*dez*
11	*onze*
12	*doze*
13	*treze*
14	*quatorze*
15	*quinze*
16	*dezesseis*
17	*dezessete*
18	*dezoito*
19	*dezenove*
20	*vinte*
21	*vinte e um*
30	*trinta*
40	*quarenta*
50	*cinqüenta*
60	*sessenta*
70	*setenta*
80	*oitenta*
90	*noventa*
100	*cem*
101	*cento e um*
200	*duzentos*
300	*trezentos*
400	*quatrocentos*
500	*quinhentos*
600	*seiscentos*
700	*setecentos*
800	*oitocentos*
900	*novecentos*
1,000	*mil*
2,000	*dois mil*
10,000	*dez mil*
100,000	*cem mil*
1,000,000	*um milhão*

Further Reading

Argentina
In Patagonia, by Bruce Chatwin, (Penguin USA, 2003). Chatwin's classic journey.
Natural Patagonia: Argentina & Chile by Marcelo D. Beccaceci, Victoria Lichtschein (Pangaea, 1998). Mostly photographic Spanish-English edition.
Buenos Aires: A Cultural and Literary Companion by Jason Wilson (Signal Books, 2000). Explores the history of the city.
Motorcycle Diaries: A Journey Around South America, Ernesto "Che" Guevara (Verso Books, 2003). The entertaining story of 23-year-old Che Guevara's road trip.
Bad Times in Buenos Aires by Miranda France (Orion, 1999). A young British woman's experience of living in Buenos Aires in the 1990s.
The History of Argentina by Daniel K. Lewis (Palgrave Macmillan, 2003). Covers entire history from pre-Columbian times to 2001.

Bolivia
Marching Powder by Rusty Young (Sidgwick & Jackson, 2003). Bizarre world of Bolivian prison portrayed by English drug smuggler.
Bolivian Diary by Ernesto "Che" Guevara (Pimlico, 2000). Weighty narrative of last, doomed, 11 months of the revolutionary.
Bolivia in Focus: A Guide to the People, Politics, and Culture by Paul Van Lindert (Interlink, 2004).
The Incredible Voyage: A Personal Odyssey by Tristan Jones (Adlard Coles, 1996). Author sailed small craft from Dead Sea to Lake Titicaca.
We Eat the Mines and the Mines Eat Us: Dependency and Exploitation in Bolivian Tin Mines by June Nash (Columbia University Press, 1993). On life and death in the Bolivian tin mines.

Brazil
Futebol: The Brazilian Way of Life by Alex Bellos (Bloomsbury, 2002). Wonderful combination of history and anecdote.
Pelé (Simon & Schuster, 2006). Autobiography of the world's greatest and most famous soccer player.
A Concise History of Brazil by Boris Fausto (Cambridge Concise Histories, 1999). 500 years of Brazilian history.
Dona Flor and Her Two Husbands by Jorge Amado (Serpent's Tail, 1999). Colorful novel by Brazil's favorite author.
Tropical Truth by Caetano Veloso (Bloomsbury). The John Lennon of Brazil tells how Tropicalismo revolutionized the country's culture and politics.
Eat Smart in Brazil by Joan and David Peterson (Ginkgo Press, 1995). Recipes and vocabulary from *abacaxi* (pineapple) to *patinho de carangueijo ao vinagrete* (marinated crab claws).
Brazil-Amazon and Pantanal by David Pearson (Academic Press, 2001). Written by professional biologists, but accessible.

Chile
My Invented Country: A Memoir by Isabel Allende (Flamingo, 2003). Autobiographical account from Chile's acclaimed novelist.
Between Extremes: A Journey Beyond Imagination by Brian Keenan and John McCarthy (Black Swan, 2000). Travels along South America's backbone by the former Beirut captives.
Travels in a Thin Country: Journey Through Chile by Sara Wheeler (Abacus, 1995). Lone woman's travels along longest mountain range on earth.

Colombia
The Making of Modern Colombia: A Nation in Spite of Itself by David Bushnell (University of California Press, 1993). Remarkable examination of a country that is so much more diverse than its stereotype.
My Cocaine Museum by Michael T.

Taussig (University of Chicago Press, 2004). Imaginative look at south Colombia's poor communities.
Colombia: Fragmented Land, Divided Society by Frank Safford, Marco Palacios (Oxford University Press, 2001). Most comprehensive single-source on Colombia's history.
More Terrible than Death: Massacres, Drugs, and America's War in Colombia by Robin Kirk (Public Affairs, 2004). Compelling narrative by human-rights investigator into effect of US role in drug war on Colombian lives.
One Hundred Years of Solitude by Gabriel García Márquez (Perennial, 2004). Classic work of magical realism by Nobel Prize-winning author.
News of a Kidnapping by Gabriel García Márquez (Penguin USA, 1998). Chilling, journalistic account of kidnapping of prominent journalists.

Ecuador
Galápagos: A Natural History Market by Michael Jackson, 1987 (Univ of Calgary Press, 1994).
The Voyage of the Beagle by Charles Darwin, 1835–1836 (Penguin USA, 1989). Darwin's epic voyage around the coasts of South America which led, 20 years later, to his theory of evolution by natural selection.
Eight Feet in the Andes: Travels with a Donkey from Ecuador to Cusco by Dervla Murphy (John Murray, 1983). An Andean adventure.
Ecuador: A Climbing Guide by Yossi Brain (Mountaineers Books, 2000).

The Guianas
Mad White Giant by Benedict Allen (Macmillan, 1994). Account of his 2,400-km (1,500-mile) journey from the mouth of the Orinoco to the mouth of the Amazon in 1983 and his time with the Wai-Wais.
Papillon by Henri Charrière (Harper Collins, 1973). Classic story of Henri Charrière's daring escape from penal colony in French Guiana to Colombia, Guyana, and eventually to Venezuela.

Peru

Lost City of the Incas by Hiram Bingham (Triune Books, 2000). Bingham's enthusiastic account of discovery of Machu Picchu – a treasure.

The Conquest of the Incas by John Hemming (Harvest Books, 2003). Authoritative look at 16th-century Spaniards and Indians in Peru.

The Bridge of San Luís Rey by Thornton Wilder (Perennial, 2003). An acclaimed, sombre tale, by Pulitzer Prize-winner, about a bridge that collapses in 18th-century Peru.

Go and Come Back by Joan Abelove (Puffin, 2000). Tale of Peruvian jungle village for people of 12 years of age and older.

Aunt Julia and the Scriptwriter by Mario Vargas Llosa (Penguin 1995). Entertaining novel set in Lima about a young writer's affair with his aunt, and an enigmatic radio scriptwriter.

Venezuela

Hugo Chávez: The Bolivarian Revolution in Venezuela by Richard Gott (Verso, 2005). Excellent account of the Bolivarian revolution.

The Hacienda by Lisa St Aubin de Terán (Virago, 1998). Lively and often tragic account of the author's time in 1970s Venezuela.

In Trouble Again by Redmond O'Hanlon (Vintage, 1990). Erudition and hilarity as O'Hanlon travels up the Orinoco.

Personal Narrative of Travels in the Equinoctial Regions of America 1799–1801 by Alexander von Humboldt. Pick up Vol. II for Humboldt's marvelous descriptions of Venezuela.

Hungry Lightning: Notes of a Woman Anthropologist in Venezuela by Pei-Lin Yu (University of New Mexico Press, 1997). Journal of the Pum way of life.

South America

The Argentina Reader: History, Culture, Politics by Gabriela Nouzeilles and Graciela R. Montaldo (Duke University Press, 2003; also Peru, 1995, and Brazil, 1999). Comprehensive introduction to history, culture, and society.

Wines of South America by Jason Lowe and Monty Waldin (Mitchell Beazley, 2003). Comprehensive look at emerging wine-producing regions.

Around South America: By Ship by Charles R Dillon (Writers' Club Press, 2001). A journey through Panama Canal to every major city on coastal South America.

Where to Watch Birds in South America by Nigel Wheatley (Princeton Univ. Press, 2000). Excellent reference guide for birders.

The South American Table: The Flavor and Soul of Authentic Home Cooking from Patagonia to Rio De Janeiro by Maria Baez (Kijac Harvard Common Press, 2003). Comprehensive cookbook that also touches on culture and geography.

The Explorers of South America by Edward J. Goodman (Univ of Oklahoma Press, 1992). Colorful look at nearly 500 years of exploration, with personal accounts.

Other Insight Guides

In the *Insight Guide* series, South America is covered by books on *Argentina, Brazil, Rio de Janeiro, Amazon Wildlife, Chile, Ecuador, Peru,* and *Venezuela.*

Feedback

We do our best to ensure the information in our books is as accurate and up-to-date as possible. The books are updated on a regular basis, using local contacts, who painstakingly add, amend and correct as required. However, some mistakes and omissions are inevitable and we are ultimately reliant on our readers to put us in the picture.

We would welcome your feedback on any details related to your experiences using the book "on the road". Maybe we recommended a hotel that you liked (or another that you didn't), as well as interesting new attractions, or facts and figures you have found out about the country itself. The more details you can give us (particularly with regard to addresses, e-mails, and telephone numbers), the better.

We will acknowledge all contributions, and we'll offer an Insight Guide to the best letters received.

Please write to us at:
**Insight Guides
PO Box 7910
London SE1 1WE
United Kingdom**
Or send e-mail to:
insight@apaguide.co.uk

ART & PHOTO CREDITS

Danny Aeberhard 189T, 289T, 290T
Adorama 331
Andes Press Agency 280, 289
Fiora Bemporad 35, 315, 324, 325
Nair Benedicto 42/43
Jevan Berrange/SAP 124/125,
126, 128T, 161
Biografia de la Pampa 322
Daniel Bruhin 6/7, 297, 298L,
299T, 300, 300T, 301
Roberto Bunge 318, 319
Camera Três Fotografic 246, 248,
253
Carlos Carrio 323
James Carmichael/NHPA back
cover bottom
Roberto Cinti 275
Marcel Ryes-Cortez 289
Country of New York Library 26,
29, 30, 230, 266, 298L, 317
Courtesy of the University of
Chile 34
Sue Cunningham 149, 152T, 236,
239, 239T, 293
Thomas Daskam 299
Vautier de Nanxe 64, 242L&R,
247, 250
Peter Dixon/SAP 132
Tui de Roy 1
Donna Elmendorf 197, 352
Ray Escobar 54
Robert Fried 62, 72, 201, 203T,
204T, 234T, 252, 324T, 340, 340T,
343T
Glyn Genin 74/75
Robert Gibbs/Impact 182
Eduardo Gil back cover right, 3B,
10/11, 16/17, 23, 28, 29, 32, 36,
37, 39, 45, 46, 48, 49L&R, 53,
54, 55, 56, 58, 59, 61, 63, 64,
65, 66, 67, 68, 69R, 70, 71,
78/79, 82/83, 84, 86/87, 88, 92,
93, 95, 96, 97L, 97R, 98T, 102,
103, 104, 105, 106/107, 108,
138, 140/141, 142, 143, 145,
147, 148, 150, 152, 152T, 159,
160, 161, 162, 164, 165,
170/171, 172/173, 175, 181,
185, 188, 189, 192, 196, 203,
204, 205, 206, 207, 208, 211,
212, 213, 213T, 214, 220/221,
229, 242L, 243, 251R, 256/257,
267, 268, 269, 270, 275,
276/277, 278, 279, 280T, 281L,
282, 282T, 283, 284, 285T, 288,
292, 294, 295, 295T, 296L, 297,

298R, 302, 303, 304, 305,
307/308, 310, 311, 313, 314T,
316, 317T, 320, 321, 323, 326,
327, 328, 328, 330, 334, 338,
342, 343, 344, 345, 346, 347;
*Eduardo Gil/courtesy of Gold
Museum, Lima* back cover center
Andreas M Gross 61, 164T, 179, 203
Emily Hatchwell 168L, 266T, 272,
273
J. Henderson/Hutchison Library
127, 129, 129T
Huw Hennessy 57, 122, 122T,
123, 123T, 131T, 145T, 154T,
160T, 161T, 175T, 177T, 241T,
242T, 250T, 251T, 252T, 253T,
290, 297T
Jeremy Horner/Hutchison 98, 99
Richard House 251L
Helen Hughes 285R,
Hutchison Library 348/349
Marcos Joly/Focus 14, 258
Elizabeth Kline 113L, 113R, 114,
114T, 115, 117, 118, 118T, 119,
120, 120T, 121, 293
Eric Lawrie back cover left, spine
4/5, 93T, 100, 101, 101T, 104T,
185T, 190, 193, 194/195, 196,
200T, 207T
John Maier 8/9, 12/13, 38, 69L,
185T, 222, 224/225, 228, 231,
232, 233, 234, 237, 240, 241,
244L
Luiz Claudio Marigo 337T
Natalie Minnis 156T, 167, 187
Jornal Do Brasil 36
Tony Morrison/SAP 23R, 133,
133T, 307
Kal Muller 134/135, 262/263
Alex Ocampo 333T
Tony Perrottet 153, 183, 184,

210, 245, 258, 315
Heinz Plenge 118T
Jennifer Ross/Latinphoto.org 285L
Steven Rubin 306
Christopher Sainsbury 291
Jorge Schuttle 329T
David Simson front flap bottom,
265, 274, 335, 336
Nigel Sitwell/Hutchison 350, 351
South American Pictures 130,
131, 131T, 133T
Selio Villon 236, 46
Mireille Vautier 1, 27L&R, 109,
112, 116, 136/137, 151, 157,
158, 173, 208T, 209, 210T, 231T,
244T, 286, 286T
Bill Wassman 40/41
David Welna 55, 329
Werner Forman Archive 23L

Picture Spreads

Pages 18/19 All by Werner Forman
Archive, except bottom row, right:
Sue Cunningham/SCP
Pages 24/25 Top and middle rows:
A M Gross; bottom row left to right:
Mireille Vautier, D Bernstein, Werner
Forman Archive, British Museum
London.
Pages 50/51 All Mary Evans
Picture Library except: top left:
Mireille Vautier; bottom row left to
right: Robert Fried, Mireille Vautier.
Pages 168/169 Top row left to
right: Natalie Minnis, Eric Lawrie,
Mireille Vautier, Emily Hatchwell;
middle row left to right: Eric Lawrie,
Lisa Payne/Andes Press Agency;
bottom row left to right: Eric Lawrie,
Mireille Vautier, Eric Lawrie.
Pages 218/219: Top row left to
right: A M Gross, A M Gross,
Natural History Museum; middle
row left to right: Stephen Trimble, A
M Gross; bottom row: Robert Fried,
A M Gross, A M Gross.
Pages 254/255 Top and middle
rows: A. M. Gross; bottom row left
to right: M. Vautier, D. Bernstein,
British Museum London.

Map Production: Berndtson &
Berndtson Productions
© 2008 Apa Publications GmbH & Co.
Verlag KG (Singapore branch)

INSIGHT GUIDE
SOUTH
AMERICA

Cartographic Editor
Zoë Goodwin
Art Director Klaus Geisler
Picture Research Hilary Genin

Index